New England
TO
Gold Rush California

ALFRED AND CHASTINA WALBRIDGE RIX,
VERMONT, JULY 1850

Print from daguerreotype made in Danville, Vermont, on their first anniversary. In this photograph Alfred wears the standard dark suit of the period. His shirt has a standing collar, which was on its way out of fashion; he wears a stiff silk stock around his neck. Chastina wears a late 1840s–style dress with a pointed waist accented by a ribbon and buckle and a gathered bodice with the fullness fanning out to the shoulders. The sleeves are slightly full, extending from under epaulette caps at the shoulders. She wears a ribbon at her neck around the collar of her chemisette. In her hair she wears a carved tortoiseshell comb tucked into a bun at the back of her head. Her hair is fashionably pulled back, with little wings over her ears. Her undersleeves extend from under the sleeves of her dress, keeping that area of the dress clean. The skirt of her dress is gathered very full and would have been bell shaped, worn over numerous petticoats, possibly along with a stiff horsehair or corded petticoat. *California Historical Society, FN-31393.*

New England
TO
Gold Rush California

THE JOURNAL OF
ALFRED AND CHASTINA W. RIX
1849–1854

Edited with Commentary by
Lynn A. Bonfield

THE ARTHUR H. CLARK COMPANY
An imprint of the University of Oklahoma Press
Norman, Oklahoma
2011

Library of Congress Cataloging-in-Publication Data
Rix, Alfred, 1822–1904.
   New England to Gold Rush California : the journal of Alfred and Chastina W. Rix, 1849–1854 / edited with commentary by Lynn A. Bonfield.
      p. cm.
   Includes bibliographical references and index.
   ISBN 978-0-87062-392-9 (hardcover : alk. paper)
   1. Rix, Alfred, 1822–1904—Diaries. 2. Rix, Chastina W. (Chastina Walbridge), 1824–1857—Diaries. 3. Vermont—Social life and customs—19th century—Sources. 4. Vermont—Biography. 5. San Francisco (Calif.)—Social life and customs—19th century—Sources. 6. San Francisco (Calif.)—Biography. 7. California—Gold discoveries—Sources. I. Rix, Chastina W. (Chastina Walbridge), 1824–1857. II. Bonfield, Lynn A., 1939– III. Title.
   CT275.R627A3 2011
   979.4´61030922—dc22
   [B]
                           2010030401

The paper in this book meets the guidelines for permanence and durability of the Committee on Production Guidelines for Book Longevity of the Council on Library Resources, Inc. ∞

Copyright © 2011 by Lynn A. Bonfield.

Published by the University of Oklahoma Press, Norman, Publishing Division of the University. Manufactured in the U.S.A.

All rights reserved. No part of this publication may be reproduced, stored in a retrieval system, or transmitted, in any form or by any means, electronic, mechanical, photocopying, recording, or otherwise—except as permitted under Section 107 or 108 of the United States Copyright Act—without the prior written permission of the University of Oklahoma Press.

1 2 3 4 5 6 7 8 9 10

Contents

List of Illustrations 7
Preface 9
Acknowledgments 15
Editor's Note 19
1 Biographies and Wedding Trip: July 29–August 16, 1849 . 23
2 Village Life in Vermont at Peacham Corner:
  August 17–December 31, 1849 45
3 Married Life, Teaching, and Politics:
  January 1–May 14, 1850 95
4 "Boarding Ourselves" and Ending Alfred's Principalship:
  May 15–August 14, 1850 123
5 Studying Law, Preparing for Baby, and Catching
  Gold Fever: August 15–December 31, 1850 . . 149
6 Practicing Law and Caring for Baby and Home:
  January 1–September 14, 1851 181
7 Alfred Prepares for California:
  September 15–October 4, 1851 217
8 Chastina in Vermont and Alfred in California:
  October 5, 1851–August 22, 1852 225
9 Chastina Prepares for California:
  August 22–November 16, 1852 281

10 Travels to California: Recounting Events of
   October 1851 to February 1853 295
11 The San Francisco Years: May 12, 1853–April 23, 1854 . 307
12 Alfred's Afterword: May 21, 1857 355
Epilogue 357

Appendices

1 Alfred's Rix Family Noted in the Rix Journal . . 365
2 Chastina's Walbridge/Watts Family Noted
   in the Rix Journal 367
3 The 25 Men Who Left for California with Alfred Rix,
   October 1851 371
Bibliography 373
Index 381

Illustrations

Alfred and Chastina Walbridge Rix, Vermont, July 1850 *frontispiece*
First Page of Journal 26
Watts Farmhouse, Peacham, ca. 1890 . . . 31
Stevens Farm, Peacham, ca. 1900 38
Peacham Corner Tavern and Livery Stable, ca. 1880 . . 47
Peacham Corner, ca. 1900 48–49
Peacham Corner Store, ca. 1867 50
Peacham Academy, ca. 1870 51
John S. and Sarah Walbridge Way, Vermont, 1849 . . 68
Rev. David Merrill, Vermont, ca. 1845 . . . 125
Roxana Brown Walbridge Watts, Vermont, ca. 1850 . . 155
Chastina Walbridge Rix and her son Julian, Vermont, 1852 . 280
Clara Walbridge, San Francisco, 1854 . . . 312
Dustan Walbridge and Ira Rix, San Francisco, ca. 1854 . 313
The Rix Family Home, Market Street, San Francisco,
   August 1855 354
Brothers Julian and Edward Rix, San Francisco, August 1855 356
Hale and Alice Locke Rix, San Francisco, ca. 1855 . . 363

Preface

Alfred S. Rix and Chastina Walbridge Rix started a shared journal in Peacham, Vermont, on their wedding day in July 1849. For almost five years they alternated entries, writing about everything from their roles within the marriage, to the birth and raising of their first child, to their differences when it came to deciding whether they should go to California along with the many other Americans who were being drawn west by "gold fever." The journal is informative in its detail and scope and engaging in its tone. Through their interaction on its pages, Alfred and Chastina have provided a unique perspective on life in the mid-nineteenth century, both on the home front and on the local and national political and social scene. Their individual entries reflect differing views as well as differing writing styles: Alfred put his keen analytic skills, intellect, and wit to good use in his entries, while Chastina chronicled the day-to-day events in a more straightforward way. Together they produced a faithful joint documentation of their lives.

Alfred and Chastina were well educated for the time. Alfred was born in Stanstead, Canada, in 1822, the second of eleven children. When he was a young boy, his family moved to a farm in Dalton, New Hampshire, where he lived until 1841, when he decided to be "fitted" for college. He moved to Peacham to live with his great aunt Sarah Morrill Stevens while attending the Peacham Academy. From there he went to Burlington to enroll at the University of Vermont, where he paid his bills in part with money loaned from Aunt Sarah's son, the noted U.S. congressman and anti-slavery leader Thaddeus Stevens. After graduating from the university in 1848, Alfred returned to Peacham to serve as the principal of the Academy.

Chastina, born in 1824, was also the second of eleven children. She spent her early years on a farm in Wolcott, Vermont, but after the death of her father when she was eleven, her mother remarried, and the family moved to her new husband's farm in the East Part of Peacham, near the Stevens farm. Chastina attended the district school and the Peacham Academy. After passing the school superintendent's examination for teaching in 1844, she taught in towns in the Peacham area, often "boarding around," the term used for living with the families of her students.

Alfred and Chastina were first introduced at a quilting hosted by Sarah Stevens in 1841. Thus began an eight-year courtship that led to their marriage. The first entry in the journal is dated July 29, 1849—their wedding day. They began by relating their individual life stories, but in the months and years to come, they would note even daily details of their life together. The main purpose of the journal was to document their achievements, and from their biographies at the start of the journal and their frequent references to "future generations," it is clear that they expected their words to be read. They seem to have felt that their shared natural intelligence and good education would make them superior chroniclers, examples for their children and others.

They were dedicated to their shared endeavor. When one of them had been away, the returned journalist caught up by writing a summary of the missed days, often on lines left blank for that purpose by the one who had remained at home. They read each other's entries, often commenting on something the other had written. Sometimes they wrote things they might not have said aloud to the other, or that they later wished they had not written. But the tone of the entries makes it obvious that they enjoyed a warm and close relationship.

New England village life is the central theme of the first years, with Alfred teaching at the Peacham Academy and studying law, and Chastina working in the home, teaching part-time at the Academy, and in the second year of marriage preparing for the birth of their first child. Reflections on married life are prominent, with Alfred writing in oblique language about their sexual relations, Chastina's menstrual cycle, and their desire for children. There are interesting comments on the nation's political struggles over slavery. Alfred and Chastina both supported California's admittance to the Union as a free state, a stance consistent with the political sentiments of Alfred's cousin Thaddeus Stevens, who kept them apprised of the conflict brewing in Washington. In addition, Alfred was a strong supporter of the need for reform in Peacham, and he sought to bring others around to his way of thinking. Those views put him at odds with the local leaders in Peacham, however, and he soon began to write more frequently about the problems that resulted.

Since the discovery of gold at Sutter's Mill in 1848, people had been traveling to California from all across the country, and even from abroad, in the hope of striking it rich. Local men were not immune to the dream. Groups of them had been leaving Peacham for the Golden State, including Chastina's brother-in-law John S. Way, who returned home in August 1850 with enough earnings to buy a farm. Alfred, who had become increasingly frustrated with the "old blue partisans" of Peacham and the rigid limitations of "the established notions and customs," began making plans to try his own luck at mining. In early October 1851 he led a group of twenty-five men from Peacham and surrounding towns to California, leaving behind Chastina and their nine-month-old son. His entries in the journal capture his first thoughts of going to California, his ultimate decision to go, and his preparations for the long and potentially dangerous trip. Chastina's entries express her concerns about his plans and her reaction to the idea of being left at home with the responsibilities of their young child. After Alfred's departure, she continued the journal on her own, describing her anxieties and her loneliness and summarizing his frequent letters home.

Alfred's quest for gold was not a success, and he spent only a short time mining before returning to San Francisco. He saw the advantages of settling in California, however, and instead of making plans to go back to Peacham, he took a job as a teacher and "invited" his wife to join him there. Chastina struggled for months with the decision, concerned about having to travel so far with their child without her husband to protect them, but she finally agreed to the trip. In February 1853, sixteen months after Alfred had left Peacham, they were reunited in San Francisco to begin a new life together. And once again they started writing in the journal. Their first new entries recounted the stories of their individual trips to California. They then returned to their pattern of writing alternating entries, describing their daily activities in the developing city.

This joint narrative is unusual, and possibly unique, in connecting the personal story of a young married couple to the epic story of the California Gold Rush. No other "double gender" journal on the subject has been found in American diary literature. In documenting their lives and offering their individual perspectives on their shared experiences, the Rixes have opened a window onto both the excitement of "gold fever" and the stresses created by the resulting absence of husbands and fathers from the home. Chastina's struggle with the decision to make the trip to California to rejoin her husband offers rare insight into what it was like to be a woman leaving family and community to embark on a long and potentially dangerous journey, unaccompanied by a husband, to a strange land and an unknown future.

Chastina was not the only Walbridge sister whose life was changed by the California Gold Rush. Sarah, three years younger than Chastina, married a man just as he was leaving Vermont for the gold fields. Pregnant with his child, she gave birth to a girl while he was away. The father did not see his daughter until he returned, when she was three months old. Clara, six years younger than Chastina, left Peacham for California after her dreams of marrying a Peacham man, recently graduated from Dartmouth, vanished when he announced his plans for going west to teach. With no prospect of marriage, Clara decided that a new life in a land that held a promise of opportunity would be best. She agreed to accompany Chastina to California, where she hoped to find a better future, as San Francisco was an ideal location for a hard-working single young woman who wanted to forget her past.

The journal evokes a number of more general themes as well, including large-scale migration out of New England; the increased role of professionals and merchants in village life; the growing interest in temperance and abolition; the rise of consumerism and reliance on ready-made goods; changing ideas on child rearing; the value of education for both men and women; the decreased influence of religion in community and family life; and improved transportation for both goods and people. The entries written in California tell of the development and skyrocketing population of San Francisco; personal relations between Anglos and the Spanish-speaking community; the establishment of a public school system; setting up a law practice; women's work in sewing, washing, and taking in boarders; and the cultural and social events of the bustling western city.

By the spring of 1854, the couple had settled into a busy routine in San Francisco, with one day much like the last. Alfred, a busy lawyer, no longer had much time or inclination to record their activities. The couple who in July 1849 were newlyweds celebrating their commitment to each other, excited by the challenges and opportunities that lay ahead, by April 1854 had accepted the bittersweet compromises of adulthood. In their new life in California, they followed separate schedules, with Alfred out of the house dealing with people Chastina did not know, and Chastina at home taking care of their son and performing domestic duties. The purpose of their journal as a record of their accomplishments detailed "for later generations," as Alfred once noted, had been achieved. They were comfortably settled in a place where they were well respected—Alfred having been elected a justice of the peace in the fall of 1853. Chastina wrote the last journal entry on April 23, 1854. Three years later, Alfred picked up the journal one last time and added a single-page summary of recent events, some of them tragic.

At Alfred's death in 1904, the journal passed to their youngest son, Edward, who was born in San Francisco in 1855. A graduate of the University of California and a successful civil engineer, Edward was living with his family on Russian Hill in San Francisco at the time of the 1906 earthquake and fire. According to family history, he buried the journal and some family heirlooms in a rug-lined pit dug in the front garden before fleeing down the peninsula. Three months later, when the family returned to the house, they found "our treasures safe." This story was related by Edward's oldest child, Genevieve Rix Burrows, who inherited the journal at her father's death in 1930. In 1949 she donated "the cherished record of early Vermont and San Francisco days written by my pioneer grandparents" to the California Historical Society, and it was there that I found the journal on the library shelves in the 1970s. I have lived with the Rixes for all the years since, and now, through this book, I introduce them, their dreams, and their times to the rest of the world.

Acknowledgments

IN 1972 MY LIFE CHANGED COURSE WHEN, AS CURATOR OF manuscripts for the California Historical Society, I first held the Rix journal in my hands. My early fascination with this story of a New England husband and wife who wrote alternating entries in a copy book grew into a research project that has lasted more than a quarter of a century.

I am indebted to the California Historical Society for preserving this journal and making it available to researchers. The journal was originally transcribed for me in the early 1970s by Annette Glabe, using a manual Underwood typewriter. Later it was keyboarded for the computer by Lisa Rivers, with revisions through the years made by Suzanne Forsyth Doran, Joanne McClintock, and Carma Muir Berglund Zisman, the last of whom also transcribed many Rix and Walbridge/Watts family letters. Other letter transcribers were Tanja Anguitar, Halle Gayle Lewis, and Janet B. Smith. Many friends helped with proofreading, including Jean Pauline, Dorothy Shaw, and Sue Wheeler. Susan Parker Sherwood provided computer expertise, as did Conor M. Casey, who also gave reference help. Deborah Duncan Hudson, an excellent writer, contributed her editing skills. Lynne Z. Bassett, costume and textile historian and consultant, advised on the fashions pictured in the photographs that add to the story.

In spring 1978 I made my first trip to Peacham, where the town clerk, Louis Lamoureaux, and the president of the Peacham Historical Association, Edmund A. Brown, assured me that there were ample records to use in identifying the many people who were mentioned in the journal. In 1980 I began spending several months a year in Peacham, sifting through historical material and talking to old-timers. I wish especially to thank Nancy Bundgus, Jim and Clara Craig, Phyllis Craig Graves, Verna Rowe Kinsey, Carolyn Martin Long, Francis and Erlene Moore, Lorna Field Quimby, Frank Bailey Randall, Helen Clark Severinghouse, James and

Verna Varnum, Margaret Walbridge, and Thelma and Charles White. To them and many others in Vermont's Northeast Kingdom, I express my gratitude and affection.

The descendants of Chastina and Alfred Rix have provided support for this project, sharing many family materials. In particular, I thank Mildred Maurer Brown, Charles and Mary Jane Choate, Jonathan Choate, Paul and Elvira Choate, Chris Choate-Raible, Allura Cockley, Jennie Smith Donaldson, Elizabeth Rix deWolf Fairfax, Roberta Choate Gaudette, Janice Rogers Manjoras, Hazel E. Mills, June Sterling Park, Helen Watts Richter, Jeri Fuller Surad, Roberta Garry Trunzo, Elsie B. Watts, and Christopher K. Way. The descendant I came to rely on most was the late Mary C. Morrison, my co-author on *Roxana's Children: The Biography of a Nineteenth-Century Vermont Family* (1995). For more than a dozen summers, Mary and I spent every Thursday morning together, trying to make nineteenth-century Peacham village life come alive.

I am grateful to the following people who helped with research and encouragement: David E. L. Brown, Thomas Cary, Allen F. Davis, William M. Ferraro, Gary L. Holloway, Wilbur R. Jacobs, Beth Kanell, Lucy Kendall, Wilbur Leeds, Maxine Martin Long, Philip P. Mason, Hazel E. Mills, and John W. Turner. My thanks especially to Gary F. Kurutz, who pointed out to me the importance of this journal in relation to the California Gold Rush and never stopped encouraging me to publish it.

I am also grateful to the archivists, librarians, court clerks, and town clerks who helped me, too many to list other than by institution: the California Historical Society; Special Collections and University Archives of the University of Vermont; the Vermont Historical Society; the Vermont State Archives; the St. Johnsbury Athenaeum; the Peacham Historical Association; the St. Johnsbury Academy Archives; the New Hampshire Historical Society; Special Collections and College Archives of Dartmouth College; the Bancroft Library of the University of California; the Society of California Pioneers; the History Center at the San Francisco Public Library; the Sutro Library and the California Section of the California State Library; the Oakland Museum of California; the town clerks of Barnet, Danville, Peacham, and Wolcott, Vermont; and the probate clerks of Caledonia County and Lamoille County. On almost a daily basis, I am thankful for the helpful people at San Francisco State University, especially those at the Labor Archives and Research Center, the J. Paul Leonard Library, and the University Mail Department.

Acknowledgments

I want to express my appreciation to Beverly Wilson Palmer and "Camp Edit 1989," the outstanding NHPRC program of the National Archives where I learned the standards for documentary editing.

Also, I want to acknowledge the late Edward Dyba for reproducing many of the photographic prints used in this book, including those from daguerreotypes.

The publication process was made easier by the helpful and professional work of the University of Oklahoma Press staff, especially publisher Robert A. Clark of the Arthur H. Clark imprint, readers Gary F. Kurutz and Marlene Smith-Baranzini, and copyeditor and outstanding Internet detective Jane Lyle. The Rix journal seemed to delight each of them, as it has me.

To Karen R. Lewis, who has lived with the Rixes almost as long as I have, I am especially grateful for archival, editing, and research help, and above all for her common sense, her humor, and the distractions she provided when I was ready to give up on this project.

LYNN A. BONFIELD
Peacham and San Francisco, October 2008

Editor's Note

THE RIX JOURNAL IS A LEATHER-BOUND VOLUME MEASURING 8½ × 14" with blue-lined paper. Alfred called it the "old Copy Book." The entries were handwritten in black iron gall ink, often made by Alfred, that has browned with age. The pages were numbered by the journalists, 1 to 254, and then with no explanation the numbering restarted from 155 to 227, which should have been 255 to 327. There is no indication of who wrote a particular entry—Alfred or Chastina—other than the handwriting or the context, and the latter is not always clear, for sometimes the writer used the third person. In addition, it can be hard to identify the author when, for example, an entry was written in haste or when illness, stress, or a factor such as the quality of pen or the brightness of candlelight changed the writing style. In editing the journal, I have, to the best of my ability, identified the author of each entry by placing the writer's initials, ASR or CWR, in brackets at the beginning. (Alfred's middle name is always given simply with the initial "S"; it probably was Stevens, but I did not find it recorded anyplace.) Additionally, the initials of the author continuing from the preceeding page are added at the outer shoulder of the following page to aid the reader.

In the journal, each entry date was handwritten flush to the left-hand margin of the page, with the entry most often beginning on the next line. I have standardized the date line to day, month, and date, given in brackets. The year has been added for the first day of each new year. Errors in dates have been silently corrected except in one case where Chastina corrected it in the text. The entry follows on the same line as the date.

Punctuation was inconsistently used throughout the journal and has been retained with few exceptions. Dashes were used within sentences, sometimes at the end of a sentence, often to carry the reader to the end of the line, but also often at random, maybe reflecting a pause to let the journalist think. Most dashes have been retained except when they were inserted at the end of a line at the end of an entry; those dashes have been changed to periods. When no period ends a sentence or an idea, the words run on. Some commas and periods were removed when upon careful examination they seemed to be a resting point for the pen rather than a punctuation mark. Brackets enclose quotation marks or commas that I have added.

Capitalization was also inconsistent but has been retained as written in most cases. In some places, nouns clearly were capitalized for emphasis. Distinguishing between capital and lowercase letters has been challenging, especially for "c," "e," "k," "s," and "w." If the letter is larger than the other letters in the word, a capital has been retained. Many times the writer did not close the top of the letter "a," making it look more like a "u." This has been transcribed as an "a." Spelling errors often were intentional, especially when Alfred was trying to be clever and humorous, as with his use of "colledge" for "college" and "sodgers" for "soldiers." These were retained.

Most abbreviations have been spelled out in brackets for clarity. However, "C" for Chastina and "A" for Alfred have not been changed. The ampersand has been retained except when it was used to mean "at" rather than "and." In those cases, "at" has been spelled out. When a name was given with initials, the full name, if known, has been added in brackets and the period after the initial has been removed.

Some idiosyncrasies have been retained: words such as "today," "tomorrow," and "anything" appear as two words, contractions usually have the apostrophe before rather than after the "n" (e.g., "do'nt"), possessives often lack an apostrophe, and dollar signs are often missing in reference to sums of money or follow the sum. Words are often written without a final "e," as with "hous" for "house." Some words have been shortened, such as "wout" for "without" and "awy" for "away." Misspellings have not been corrected, although where confusion might result, the correct word or letters have been added in brackets. Speculative words have been put in brackets with a question mark. Ellipsis points indicate the omission of words, but only in a quoted letter, never in the journal entries. Some names, such as Dustan, Leverett, and McLeran, have been spelled inconsistently throughout and have been retained as written. (It is no wonder that Dustan's name is given on his gravestone as "D. S. Walbridge." Even his sister Chastina did not spell it consistently!) When a word is illegible because either the handwriting is impossible to read or the ink has been smudged, the word "illegible" has been placed in brackets at the spot. In most cases, the journalists' applied paragraphing has been ignored.

Editor's Note

After the journal was written, someone went through and underlined all references to Alfred's brother Hale Rix and Hale's wife, Alice Locke. These penciled underlines have not been retained.

There are no divisions in the journal save those of the dated entries. I have created chapters for the sake of a storyline. Chapter introductions include quotes from family correspondence to help fill in the story. For the most part these letters are in private family collections, although a few are preserved at the California Historical Society, the Bancroft Library at the University of California at Berkeley, the Peacham Historical Association, and Special Collections at the University of Vermont. My own large collection will eventually be donated to the latter to join the Isaac N. Watts Family Papers donated by Mary C. Morrison.

Throughout the journal, Alfred made drawings, some realistic and some comical. Not all of them have been included in this book.

Sometimes an entry was written at the end of a day or under circumstances of emotion and stress, so errors and inconsistencies are not surprising. They reveal the author's state of mind. I have presented the entries as they were written, with only the minor emendations described above. A few words have been silently corrected, especially if they were spelled right in other places.

Biographical information and vital dates found in the notes were taken silently for the most part from Jennie Chamberlain Watts and Elsie A. Choate, comps., *People of Peacham*; Guy Rix, comp., *History and Genealogy of the Rix Family of America*; and William Gedney Wallbridge, comp., *Descendants of Henry Wallbridge Who Married Anna Amos*. The names of Peacham Academy students have been taken from the Peacham Academy Catalogues, 1839–53. Graduates and faculty of the University of Vermont have been identified by Sylvia J. Bugbee of Special Collections, and those from Dartmouth College by Sarah Hartwell of Rauner Special Collections. Full names and vital dates of family members are not given in the notes but appear in the family charts in appendixes 1 and 2.

CHAPTER ONE

Biographies and Wedding Trip
July 29–August 16, 1849

We should pause a moment after having given, as novelists are accustomed to do, the introduction to the 2d chapter, and give the first.
ALFRED

ON A RAINY DAY IN AUGUST 1849, ALFRED AND CHASTINA RIX turned to the blank pages they had left at the front of their new journal and penned their biographies—not fiction as "novelists" might write it, but the real story of two young people who were just starting off in married life. They began by announcing their marriage, then told how they met and courted, and followed with details about their families and education. Alfred wrote about Chastina at length, emphasizing her attractive appearance and outstanding qualities. He described her talents and her work ethic, presenting a glowing picture of his bride. Only a few blank pages remained for his own biography, an indication that, as he admitted, he was keeping the journal primarily for Chastina. He was writing at the request of, and for the amusement of, the woman he loved.

Like many young people of their generation who were educated in the district schools of New England, Chastina and Alfred had purposely decided to leave farming and become part of the professional world. They wanted something different for themselves from the hard life their farmer parents had, one where they could work with their minds rather than their hands. They were fortunate in being able to strike out on their own, because it would not have been possible in every rural family; children's labor was essential to the operation of a farm. But Alfred and Chastina each had an older sibling who had already left home, preparing the parents, and each had younger siblings who could take their place at the plow or the washboard when they left.

Alfred had left his father's farm in Dalton, New Hampshire, at age nineteen to be "fitted" for college. He went to stay with his maternal great-aunt Sarah Morrill Stevens, who lived in Peacham, Vermont, a town with a noted academy, as high schools in New England were called at the time. It was at Aunt Sarah's house that he and Chastina were introduced in 1841. "The mutual impression was favorable," and thus began the courtship that would lead to their marriage eight years later. During those years, Chastina studied to become a teacher, which was one of the only roles in the public sphere in rural New England available to educated women in the mid-nineteenth century. She was the first of the six girls in her family to earn money at a job outside the home. Alfred attended the University of Vermont from 1844 to 1848 before returning to Peacham to assume the principalship of the Peacham Academy.

Alfred and Chastina were married on July 29, 1849, after the Sunday meeting at the Peacham Congregational Church, two miles from the farm in the East Part of Peacham where Chastina had lived since 1840, when her widowed mother married a local farmer named Lyman Watts. That morning Alfred borrowed a carriage for the trip to the Watts farm, where he picked up Chastina along with her sister Sarah and her brother Dustan, who would be standing up as witnesses for the pair. The appointed place was unusual; New England weddings were most often held at the home of the bride's father, but because Alfred was the popular principal of the local academy, a ceremony open to the public seemed appropriate. The wedding supper, held at the Watts farm, included a select group of relatives, mainly from Chastina's large family, and close neighbors. Alfred's side of the family was represented only by his maternal great-aunt Sarah, her grandson Alanson Stevens, and Alfred's younger brother Hale, who had traveled from New Hampshire for the occasion.

The couple left on their wedding trip the following morning. They made a stop in St. Johnsbury at the office of the local newspaper, the *Caledonian*, to drop off their wedding announcement, along with a piece of wedding cake for the editor. From there they traveled northwest to New Hampshire to spend two weeks with Alfred's family. After a stay at the home of his parents and siblings in Dalton, they moved on to neighboring relatives.

After retiring for the night during a visit at the home of his uncle and aunt in Haverhill, New Hampshire, Alfred returned unexpectedly to the kitchen and was surprised to hear a baby crying. The family's unmarried granddaughter had recently arrived and given birth to a baby girl. The father of the baby had "left for California under rather suspicious circumstances" without marrying the mother—presumably to join the thousands of other "forty-niners" who were making their way there in a quest for gold. The family had tried to conceal the baby from the Rixes, but her cries had announced her presence. Was the mother abandoned, or did the father rush off in hopes of making a fortune to provide for his family? That answer has been lost to history. But this first brief mention of California was only a foreshadowing of what was to come.

Daily Journal.
of
Alfred & Chastina W. Rix

July 1849.   Sunday. 29th.

1½ O'clock P.M. We, that is to say, Alfred Rix & Chastina Walbridge, are married — Therefore, according to custom & law the said Alfred Rix will retain his name and gain a wife, while the said Chastina Walbridge will lose hers and gain a husband — time and trial will determine whether one or both have got "shaved" in this exchange. The World at large is solemnly "warned and notified" from this day forth to address us as Mr. & Mrs. and also, especially, to kick every dog that barks at us.

Here it seemeth proper if not profitable that we should pause a moment after having given, as novelists are accustomed to do, the introduction to the 2nd Chapter, and give the First.

We mean to be pretty faithful Biographers — Yet we shall make no solemn engagements that we shall not finally give over in our good resolutions and flat out — nor can we promise but there will be a flat out even should we write true things faithfully.

Our text is in Hosea —
"Ephraim is a cake not turned."

Daily Journal of Alfred and Chastina W. Rix

[*ASR*] [Sunday, July 29, 1849]¹ 1½ o'clock P.M. We, that is to say, Alfred Rix & Chastina Walbridge, <u>are married</u>— Therefore, according to custom & law the said Alfred Rix will retain his name and gain a wife, while the said Chastina Walbridge will lose hers and gain a husband—time and trial will determine whether one or both have got "shaved" in this exchange. The World at large is Solemnly "warned and notified" from this day forth to address us as Mr. & Mrs. and also, especially, to kick every dog that barks at us.

Here it seemeth proper if not profitable that we should pause a moment after having given, as novelists are accustomed to do, the introduction to the 2d chapter, and give the first.

We mean to be pretty faithful Biographers— Yet we shall make no solemn engagements that we shall not finally give over in our good resolutions and flat out—nor can we promise but there will be <u>a flat</u> out even should we write true things faithfully.

Our text is in Hosea—²

"Ephraim is a cake not turned."

Therefore let us proceed to turn him—

1st. Inside out,

2d. Backside before,

3d. Tother end up.

---

¹The biographical section here was written on August 23, 1849, on pages left blank at the beginning of the journal for that purpose.

²Alfred introduced their biographies with Hosea 7:8, a biblical text that refers to a major change in life.

ASR Miss Chastina Walbridge was born in Wolcott, Lamoille county, State of Vermont, Nov. 6 A.D. 1824. Her father's name was Daniel—he died when Chastina was but 11 years old, leaving six children of which Chastina was the second. Mr. Walbridge was a farmer of moderate pretensions and moderate circumstances: Therefore his daughters not only wanted the means of elegant life and the facilities for a good education, but found imposed upon them very many tasks and hardships even in their youth. The death of the father caused these to be increased. The course of our heroine's life till she reached her thirteenth year was the same as that of most girls in the country—the daughters of farmers—That is, labor six days in the week—attend church on Sunday—at home, mostly, summers and at school—the district school—winters.

We can now see, in the eye of imagination and memory, the little fair faced Chastina at the wheel—while scarcely tall enough to reach the spindle—drawing out the thread from morning till night and humming to herself some favorite ditty. Sometimes the thread would break. On such an occasion it was possible to mark the difference of disposition in the two girls Martha [Walbridge] & Chastina, the former would bite her lip, seize hold of her wheel and give it a hearty shaking, while the latter would half say and half sing as she was mending the break, "Fush-fiddle-dum!" Again we behold her—the quiet & gentle thing—trudging away to school but not to a school-house, but to a barn used for one. Here we can imagine her seated upon an ox-yoke or a hen-coop trying her utmost to learn the task assigned her by her stern mistress. We can behold the child's very face and from the working of her open features can almost determine the thoughts she thinks, the joys and sorrows she feels as the various duties and incidents of the day take place and wear it away. What a mingling of childish glee and prudential perplexion must she have experienced when some young hen, proud of the egg she had laid, quitted her nest and whirred up to the mistress herself and began such a cackle as a hen of good habits and firm constitution is capable of—or when some ancient cock, glorying in his tail & spurs, mounted the beam over their heads and crowed as if to crow the dead to life and bring the day of judgement—after "clapping his glad wings" louder than Miller's metamorphosed saints.³ *ASR*

[CWR] Such was C's childhood until the death of her father, when she was often from home striving to help herself & mother as much as was in her power. At the age of thirteen she went with an uncle—Mr [Chauncey] Clement—to reside in Dunham C[anada] E[ast]. This being the first time that she was ever far from home—a long journey it seemed to her. From W[olcott] by way of Stanstead about seventy five miles— She had scarcely ever seen her relatives there, so that it was among strangers that she was going to reside. Her aunt was very kind to her, taught her in many useful branches of home industry, especially in taking care of children. A little cousin nine months of age was committed almost entirely to her care—its mother being an invalid was unable to wait on herself—so it was Chastines business to wait on her aunt—take care of the little Ellen [Clement] & sew the rest of the time. She did not attend school at all while there—upon the whole it was rather a tedious year to her—a year that is termed in Dunham the "rebellion." C's uncle Brown was imprisoned about six durin[g] her residence in Canada because he was not on the <u>right side</u>.⁴ After a stay of one year our little girl returned to W[olcott] glad enough once more to see mother & sisters &c.

---

³William Miller (1782–1849) was a Baptist preacher who led the "Millerite Movement" in New England. He claimed to have found evidence in Scripture of an imminent Second Coming, predicting that it would happen "on or before 1843." Miller attracted a strong following in Vermont. Chastina's mother sympathized with the Millerites in wanting Christ in her life, but she could not accept the teaching to neglect daily needs or the idea that "sinful weak minded man" could know the date when Jesus would return. Roxana Walbridge Watts, Peacham, to Martha Walbridge Gregory, Jackson, Mich., September 27, 1844, Walbridge-Gregory Family Papers. On the assigned day, Miller's followers climbed to the highest places they could find, awaiting their ascension to heaven; in Rutland, a resident even constructed wings, climbed to the top of his barn, and leapt off, resulting in a broken leg. Sherman, Sessions, and Potash, *Freedom and Unity*, 203–205.

⁴Chastina's aunt Sarah Brown Clement lived in Dunham, Canada East, or what became known as Quebec. Chastina mistakenly calls Chauncey Clement, her aunt's husband, "Uncle Brown." His role in a rebellion against the British government that was defeated in late 1838 is unclear, but rebel leaders were executed or exiled. Bernard, "Vermonters and the Lower Canadian Rebellions," 250, 261.

[ASR] After remaining another year in Wolcott she came with her mother & family to Peacham Co[unty] of Caledonia—being the month of Nov. A.D. 1839. In Dec. of the following year the widow [Roxana Brown] Walbridge married Mr. Lyman Watts, a farmer of the "East Part" of Peacham. Mr Watts was appointed guardian for his wife's children and took them all to his own home and from that time to the present has uniformly treated them and cared for them as if they had been his own and we cannot forbear recording here our earnest thanks to him for all his kindness.[5] During the winter following her mother's marriage Chastina attended school partly in the East Part but mostly at Ewell's District where Stillman Moulton taught. The previous winter she studied arithmetic at the same place, for the first time, under Mr. Moody Boyington. Ebenz Smith taught school at the E[ast] Part in the winter of 1840–1.[6] In the spring of the year 1841 the usual quiet of our maiden's life and heart was slightly disturbed by the arrival in her neighborhood of a young man by the name of Alf. Rix—who was just commencing his studies preparatory to entering college. For some days before she had seen Mr Rix she found herself considerably interested with regard to him from neighborhood talk and especially after a bold young stripling declared to her that after Alvah Watts & young Rix had been through college the former would be minister and marry the latter, who was to be a lawyer, to Miss Chastina Walbridge.[7] On the very important and ominous occasion of a quilting, at Mrs [Sarah] Stevens where Alfred resided the two were introduced to each other.[8] The mutual impression was favorable and from that hour until the present each has not ceased to be of more importance in the eyes of the other than any other individual.

[CWR] The summer of the year 1841 Chastine worked at Mr

---

[5]Guardianship papers signed by Lyman Watts in 1848 for Dustan, Daniel Augustus, Chastina, Sarah, and Clarissa Walbridge, Caledonia County Probate Records, Peacham, 1790s–ca. 1910, Box 10, W–Y, Walbridge, Daniel.

[6]In 1840 Peacham had twelve school districts, including Ewell's and the East Part. Bogart, *Peacham*, 143. Moody Boynton (1815–1902) is misnamed in the journal.

[7]Alvah Watts, Chastina's stepfather's nephew, attended the University of Vermont, class of 1849.

[8]Sarah Morrill Stevens was a maternal great-aunt to Alfred, who lived on her farm west of the Watts farm. Her son Thaddeus Stevens, a prominent anti-slavery congressman, had purchased the farm for his mother in 1821. "Quilting" was the New England term for what later became known as a quilting bee. Bonfield, "Four Generations of Quilters," 39.

WATTS FARMHOUSE, PEACHAM, CA. 1890

The farm in Peacham's East Part where Chastina moved in 1840 when her widowed mother married Lyman Watts. This cape-style cottage, twenty-eight by thirty-six feet, had an unfinished chamber on the second floor most likely used as sleeping quarters for the children. In 1845 Lyman Watts built a barn. Two years later he added "a shed" to the house and finished off the kitchen and milk room. This architectural style was common in northeastern New England in the midnineteenth century, when farmers reorganized their detached house, back house, and barn into connected buildings. *Private collection.*

D[avid] Curriers part of the time; the remaining part at home, occasionally seeing the said Alf. who on the whole was extremely shy of the girls.[9] One Amanda Morrill, who was aunt to Alfred, & resided

---

[9]David Currier (1795–1872) and his family lived on a farm east of the Watts farm. It was common for young women to help their neighbors, not quite serving as "hired girls" but rather learning domestic chores. Cott, *Bonds of Womanhood*, 28–30; Bassett, *Growing Edge*, 42.

CWR at Mrs S[tevens] seemed to be his guardian. That is she took especial pains to inform the girls in the "East Part" that Alf's heart was impregnable—"and the girls need not try to catch him for he cared nothing about any of them." Amanda & Chastine were on pretty good terms, so that she above all the others had the advantage. In the fall of 1841, there was a writing school at the school house in the "East Part," and Mr. R[ix] was the teacher. For some reason he took especial pains to have C. attend. And moreover, when the school closed, the usual fee handed to him by her was rejected![10] What did this all mean! "Quiltings," "Paring-bees," &c. brought them more or less together that autumn, & the next winter, C. attended school to Mr R[ix] in their district. He was young, but taught an excellent school, where all the scholars made rapid improvement, & C. among the rest began that winter to learn. She had scarcely been through the four first rules in arithmetic until then. Then she had her eyes open to a love of learning—not because there was any peculiar charm about the "master," but she saw a need of study. In the spring C. attended school six weeks in the "old academy" on the hill, Mr [Charles C.] Chase, the preceptor.[11] The next summer of 1842, C was at home most of the time, during which time, the intimacy between the above mentioned two was growing more strongly.

[ASR] During the next winter Young Rix again taught at the East Part and again Chastina was his pupil. Her progress was rapid and as satisfactory as it had been the previous winter. The slight courting skirmishes begun the year before were continued this winter at intervals somewhat shortened. It was rather a queer business for both as well as new and was of course entered upon with no very definite ideas of what would be the result. Careful & easy! Spring came—and with it came

---

[10] The tuition for attending school at this time was usually paid by each pupil directly to the teacher. In 1844 the cost was ten cents a month per scholar. Bogart, *Peacham*, 152–53. This writing school may have been an extra class. At this time, Chastina was twenty years old, Alfred twenty-two.

[11] The Peacham Academy was founded in 1795 as the Caledonia County Grammar School. It served students not just from the area but from more distant parts as well. Quimby, *Peacham Academy*, 2. From 1839 to 1845, Charles C. Chase (1818–1900), a graduate of Dartmouth, served as principal. Bogart, *Peacham*, 472. The academy movement in New England by 1850 included approximately 140 academies in Vermont towns, with Peacham being the oldest in Caledonia County. Beck, *Proud Tradition*, 5–6.

a severe bilious fever upon Chastina—by which she was reduced to a   *ASR*
state bordering on death, but finally after suffering a great deal, and
eating the whole list of Dr [Gardner] Cobb's calomels she recovered
or rather <u>partially</u> recovered her health—for it was more than a year
afterwards before the immediate effects of this illness disappeared—
and to this day the more remote effects remain.[12] During this summer,
1843, she commenced her school-teaching in her own district at $1.40
per week & boarded herself—and a sorry time it proved to be.

[*CWR*] (Owing to some freak of Chastina's, the connection between
the two parties of which we are speaking, was broken off. She behaving very foolishly about it, all the while regreting what she had done,
still refusing the opportunity to make herself happy, in the choice of
the only one she loved. Things went on pretty much in this way until
the 27th of Aug. 1843, when, after many doubts & fears, C. confessed
her faults, and asked for that which she once refused. The generosety
as well as the love of young Rix was here put to the test. All was settled, and Chastina still blesses the time in which they plighted their
vows to each other. Perhaps, what is written above would lead one to
think Chastine was a coquette, or something of the kind. This would
be rather an erroneous idea, because she had never had any attention
paid her by the other sex, except that of the ordinary kind.)

Chastina was at home some of the time this fall. The remaining
part she lived with her Grandfather & Grandmother [Brown] at
Peacham Hollow. Alfred was, during this time, attending school at
St. Johnsbury. C. attended school at Peacham Hollow during the
winter.[13] Brock Darling of Barnet taught. Chastine better have been
at home, for it seemed like spending time for nothing to go to a poor
school. C. boarded at Mr. I[saac] Watts;[14] she goes to a temperance
meeting at Danville with Mr Rix.[15] The spring of 1844 Chastina

---

[12]Dr. Gardner W. Cobb (1816–47), an 1840 graduate of the medical school at Dartmouth College, practiced in Peacham. Bogart, *Peacham*, 235.

[13]David and Olive Lamb Brown, the parents of Chastina's mother, Roxana, lived in Peacham Hollow at this time.

[14]Isaac Watts, a brother to Alvah (noted above), owned a store in Peacham Hollow. Bogart, *Peacham*, 273. He was listed as a merchant in *Walton's Vermont Register* from 1845 through 1857.

[15]The temperance movement gained popularity during the mid-nineteenth century. The Peacham Temperance Society was formed in 1842 and continued for more than forty years. Bogart, *Peacham*, 215–16; *Caledonian*, especially April 1, 1844, and February 12, 1853.

CWR   attended school at the academy. Mr [Charles C.] Chase the teacher. She boards at Mr [Trustram] Sanborns.[16] Alfred goes to school at the same time. The summer of '44 C. teaches school again in their own district for 5.s[hillings] per week and boards in the district.

    In the fall she attends school again at the academy and boards at her uncle Browns in the Hollow.[17] Mr [Charles C.] Chase & Miss Sarah Baley of Hopkinton were the teachers.[18] This season was noted as that in which Alfred first went to College. Chastine goes in November to Wheelock to teach a winter school, her school was small, but rather a pleasant school had it not been for a certain <u>scratching disorder</u> prevalent among the scholars.[19] Alfred went <u>after</u> her once during the winter— He this season was teaching at Peacham Corner—and as a matter of course, would carry her back. They had rather a rainy time going to Wheelock, but were partly compensated by calling at a house during one shower, and receiving an <u>orange plant</u> which Alfred <u>did</u> up in an <u>old shoe</u> very carefully, and when a convenient place upon the road appeared, they transplanted it to a snow bank. They went to C.'s boarding place to a Mr Morgans, where they kept them in the <u>kitchen</u> until A. asked for a room for a short time. How many Hearty laughs they have had about their adventure at Wheelock, which is "way up north." C. made out to stay her time out, but she had rather a <u>hard</u> time.

[ASR] This was the beginning of the year 1845. In the spring she boarded at Mrs [Lucinda] Sanborn's and attended Mr [Charles C.] Chase's school again. She spent the summer teaching in Wheelock village. In the fall Alfred attended her to Newbury—found her a boarding place and left her alone and rather sad hearted. She spends

---

[16]Students who traveled from a distance to attend the Peacham Academy paid a weekly fee to board in private homes at Peacham Corner. Girls from Peacham farms usually returned home on weekends; boys walked back and forth every day so that they could perform their daily morning and evening farm chores. Bonfield and Morrison, *Roxana's Children*, 159, 180. Trustram Sanborn (1815–65), a shoemaker, and his wife, Lucinda Clark Sanborn (1818–51), lived at Peacham Corner and boarded students.

[17]Chastina's uncle Simeon Brown, her mother's brother, lived at Peacham Hollow, so she had only a mile's walk to the Academy rather than the two miles from the Watts farm.

[18]Sarah T. Bailey was preceptress at the Peacham Academy. *Caledonian*, December 16, 1844.

[19]Alfred entered the University of Vermont in the fall of 1844. Chastina's first teaching job was at Wheelock, Vt., about twenty miles from Peacham. Fleas were a common problem at this time.

a very profitable time and returns and spends the winter at home. *ASR* The summer of 1846 she taught school at Peacham Hollow at 1.00 per week & "boarded round."[20] Sometime during this summer (July) Chastina's oldest sister the wife of Hubbel S. Gregory died at Jackson, Michigan. The Autumn and Winter of this year was spent at St Johnsbury Academy—studying French, Arithmetic[,] Algebra, Intellectual Philosophy, &c.[21] In the spring at home (1847) and very much out of health. Taught school in the Summer at Topsham where she formed some new and valuable acquaintants. In the Fall she began to attend school at Peacham Academy under Mr [John] Paul, but ill health prevented and she was compelled to spend an unhappy time at home—[22] In the winter taught at the East Part. In the spring of 1848 at home & unwell. The following summer & winter teaching again at home.

[*CWR*] The spring & summer of 1849 Chastine spent in "fixing."[23] And a hard time it was for her. Girls usually work themselves beyond what they are able in such times. It was so with C. her health was poor most of the time during the summer: and by the time she was ready to be married—as the saying is—"She was poor as a crow."

[*ASR*] It seems proper to say something of the character and person of our heroine. She was of the ordinary hight—well proportioned—skin fair and clear save an inclination to moles. Her head was larger than the usual size— high forehead—thin, dark hair— arching eyebrows—dark hazle eyes, clear and of a mild expression. Her hands and feet were rather small & neatly fashioned. In all her

---

[20]"Boarded around" refers to the practice of having teachers in the district schools board with the families of their students. Sometimes the length of stay related to the number of students from a family, but often the family who charged the lowest amount to the district provided the board. Bonfield and Morrison, *Roxana's Children*, 80–81; Nelson, "Vermont Female Schoolteachers," 8–9. In a letter to her sister Sarah Walbridge, Chastina related that she had "changed my boarding place six times since I came here, found all good boarding places too." Chastina, Topsham, Vt., to Sarah Walbridge, Lowell, Mass., July 1, 1847, private collection.

[21]Chastina Rix was listed as a student in the 1845–46 and 1846–47 St. Johnsbury Academy Catalogue, both times residing at "Mr. Fuller's," the home of Elizabeth A. Fuller, a classmate. Joanne Bertrand, Archivist, St. Johnsbury Academy, e-mail message to editor, December 16, 2008.

[22]John Paul, Jr. (1821–1903), Dartmouth College, class of 1847, served as principal of the Peacham Academy in 1847–48. Bogart, *Peacham*, 472.

[23]Chastina is referring to her preparation for marriage, particularly preparing household linens and clothing. Rothman, *Hands and Hearts*, 166.

ASR habits she was fastidiously neat and all with which she had to do was done in season, in order, and with remarkable taste and elegance. She was of a mild and gentle disposition. Her heart was full of kindness and good will. Extremely indulgent and forgiving—ready, perhaps too ready to bear an injury and suffer wrong and altogether incapable of doing one to another. She was one bound to make her way in the world by her patience & sweetness of temper and not by opposing and overcoming. Withal she was singularly prudent, both in counsel and action. Of all young ladies the least offensive in speech or behavior—trustworthy in all her intercourse with her friends and faithful in every relation of life. Her intellect was above the ordinary standard. Though laboring under the triple disadvantage of a neglected youth, poverty and almost constant ill-health, she yet, by her own efforts alone—clothed herself appropriately and even elegantly, and attained a good knowledge of the English Sciences and made considerable advancement in the study of the French language. Her modesty, being excessive, greatly retarded her in her dearest plans. She never, or at least very seldom, claimed her due—she never assumed even what was her own. She had a strong power of forecast—she saw a thing from its beginning to its end—was rather slow, quite cautious and hence, scarce a plan of her laying or a work of her undertaking disappointed her in its application or result. In addition to her natural prudence her circumstances have contributed greatly to make her economical—a thing too often wanting in the young wives of this day. Such was the character, or some of the more prominent features in the character of Chastina Walbridge at the time of her marriage and it is hoped and believed that these qualities will not grow dim in her new relation or prove to be wanting, but rather to grow brighter and more beautiful as her life passes and her personal charms fade—and prove to be in Eternity more than they have seemed to be in Time.

 Alfred Rix was born Apr. 7, 1822 at Stanstead Lower Canada where he vegetated till his 5th year when his parents removed to Littleton N.H. U.S.A. His father was a poor man who began married life before he had got a farm and raised babies faster than money and so <u>took</u> farms at halves. Alf. was the second child and went to work as soon as he could lift a hatchet and continued to do so till his 19th year when he took it into his noddle to go to colledge and so he did. He spent 3 years in fitting—boarding at Mrs [Sarah] Stevens and then spent 4 years at College graduating Aug. 2, 1848.[24] During the year 1849 he was Principal of Peacham Academy and did a pretty fair business in teaching Greek and courting. For particulars we recommend a perusal of the Journals of the several years.[25] The marriage affair between the said Alfred Rix & Chastina Walbridge took place after the following fashion—namely—On the Saturday a week previous Alf. slipped a half eagle into the hand of the Rev. David Merrill[26] and sloped & finished his school in a week from that day and then made ready with Horse Carriage and so forth and on the morrow, the 29th of July, at 9 A.M. appeared at the bride's residence—a neat white cottage on the East Part hill. At 12 o'clock the bride, aided by her kind sister Sarah [Walbridge], was arrayed and beautifully and tastily arrayed too.

ASR

[*CWR*] Her dress was of white muslin, plain, with the exception of some blonde about the neck & lace sleeves. She had about her waist a white satin sash. This, with a white crape shawl & bonnet, completed the outside attire of the bride. As we have described the dress of the bride it is no more than fair to serve the bridegroom after the same fashion. Of the looks of this person we need say but little, for those who have seen him will remember him. He is about six feet in height, well proportioned, light complexion, brown hair, & blue or rather greyish eyes, on the whole a good looking young man. Upon this occasion his usually neat appearance was somewhat improved upon.

---

[24] Alfred Rix was a student at the Peacham Academy in 1841, 1842, and 1844. Peacham Historical Association [hereafter PHA], Peacham Academy Card File, created from catalogues. He was listed as a student in the 1843 St. Johnsbury Academy Catalogue. During these years, he taught several terms in the Peacham School District No. 1. According to the Peacham School Records in the town office, he earned $42 "for keeping School 3 months" in a year identified only as "1840s"; an entry from March 4, 1846, reads: "Paid Alfred Rix for keeping school 3 months $48.00."

[25] Separate journals have not been located.

[26] David Merrill (1798–1850), a native of Peacham and a graduate of Dartmouth, served the Peacham Congregational Church from 1841 to 1850; he was only the second minister of the church, which was founded in 1794. Comstock, *Congregational Churches of Vermont*, 101, 205. The Half Eagle was a U.S. coin produced from 1792 to 1929; composed almost entirely of gold, it had a face value of $5.

STEVENS FARM, PEACHAM, CA. 1900
Home of Sarah Morrill Stevens purchased in 1821 by her son Thaddeus Stevens. Alfred lived here while attending the Peacham Academy before going to college. *Peacham Historical Association.*

His dress was very plain but neat & rich, composed of black with the exception of his cravat, vest of black satin, and the remaining garment of the materials used for gentlemens apparel, viz—Doeskin. At the time for the commencement of the afternoon services, the bridegroom & bride—accompanied by her brother & sister—Dustan [Walbridge] & Sarah [Walbridge]—started for the church about two miles distant from her fathers. They arrived at the church in good time & quietly took their seats in her fathers pew. A more than usual number had assembled, for a wedding in a country church is a rare thing in these days, so there was considerable of a commotion among the good people of P[eacham] to get a peep at this wonderful pair.[27] This no doubt was extremely annoying to them during divine service to be gazed at so. Well at the close of a discourse by the Rev. Mr.

---

[27] More common at that time was a wedding at the home of the bride with only family in attendance. Rothman, *Hands and Hearts*, 169–70.

Blanchard, Mr. [David] Merrill arose & published & then called on the parties to attend to the ceremony.[28] The bridegroom took his lady quietly by the hand & led her to the altar (or the place for one)[29] & there amid this assembled congregation, they ratified the vows long before pledged to each other. After closing the service as usual, Mr. & <u>Mrs.</u> Rix returned to her father's, where they met some of their friends invited to take supper with them. They had tables spread and a good wedding feast was neatly laid upon the cloth, by mother, sister & Cousin Chastina Brown. Those who were present were as follows: Mrs. [Sarah] Stevens, Mr. Sargeant & Lady, Mary Elisa Sargeant, Mr. James Morse & Miss Margaret Blanchard, Brother Hale Rix & Miss Alice Lock, Cousins Chastina & Cynthia Brown, Moses & Alma Currier, John Way, Alanson Stevens.[30] These with father[,] mother[,] brothers & Sisters (Clara [Walbridge] was not there) made up the company. They stayed a short time, then went to their homes. Mr and Mrs Rix Stayed at home until Monday morning when they started for N.H. on a visit to friends.[31]

[ASR] [Monday, July 30] "After life's fitful fever they slept well!"[32] and on the morrow arose and with Mr [Samuel] Bruce's horse and Aunt [Sarah] Stevens' bran-new carriage away they started—why say they?—away we started for N.H.[33] We called at St. Johnsbury

---

[28] Amos Blanchard (1800–69), a native of Peacham and a graduate of Andover Theological Seminary, "supplied pulpit in Peacham and surrounding towns." Watts and Choate, *People of Peacham*, 37; Comstock, *Congregational Churches of Vermont*, 165.

[29] The church building had been moved in 1844 from the hill across from the town common to a location closer to the center of town. The altar and other church fixtures had not yet been built. Peacham Congregational Church, *Anniversary Exercises*, 15; Bogart, *Peacham*, 165.

[30] The guests at the wedding feast included family members, neighbors, and former classmates. For names and vital dates of relatives, see appendix 1, "Alfred's Rix Family Noted in the Rix Journal," and appendix 2, "Chastina's Walbridge/Watts Family Noted in the Rix Journal." Both Alanson Stevens and Hale Rix had been students under Alfred's principalship at the Peacham Academy. Their names appear in the Peacham Academy Catalogue [hereafter PAC] in 1849.

[31] It was common for newlyweds to take a wedding trip, which at that time was not called a honeymoon. Rothman, *Hands and Hearts*, 81, 175. Alfred decided that he and Chastina would visit his parents in Dalton, N.H., as only his brother Hale had attended the wedding. The term "friends" was commonly used in reference to relatives.

[32] Alfred was making a play on words from Shakespeare's *Macbeth*, III, ii, 11: "Duncan is in his grave. After life's fitful fever he sleeps well."

[33] Samuel Bruce (1810–89) ran a tavern and livery stable in Peacham. Watts and Choate, *People of Peacham*, 53; Bogart, *Peacham*, 276.

ASR   Plain & left the printer a loaf of the wedding cake & subscribed for the Caledonian[34] and put up at East St. Johnsbury where we remained in fine spirits till

[Tuesday, July 31] When we gathered up our duds and were off 'Sblood and rain & galled horse which we righted at Hill's and then drove to Higgins' in North Littleton and waited for Hale [Rix] & Miss [Alice] Locke a couple of hours when we dined and drove home to Dalton.[35] Our Father's house is situated on the high lands between the Connecticut and John's rivers about 2 miles from Summers Mills.

[CWR] We found father's family well, and a goodly number of them there are. Four boys & one girl at home, & six absent, besides, two daughters that have been added to the family, by the marriages of Oscar [Rix] & Alfred, the two eldest sons. This being C.'s first visit at her new father's, as a matter of course, she felt very strange at first, to be calling father & mother Rix. She enjoyed herself first-rate. Alfred was so highly elated to get home, that he really behaved like a school boy, out of school. The first week—or from Tuesday Eve. until Saturday—we spent at home. Alfred in "cutting all the shines" possible, besides eating green peas to such an extensive amount that it is probable, the crop will be rather light this year. As for C. she was not far behind her illustrious spouse in anything except the eating of green peas Although she had some work to do, but to no great amount. The raspberries were ripe, & we had a good time eating them. We went once, out upon a hill side, picked enough so we had some "short cake" for breakfast. It is a grand place to live over there. If one is of a romantic disposition he could easily spend his time in rambling among the hills & in the forests. The place where father R[ix] is very pleasantly situated. The land is rather new, or is

---

[34]The editor, Albert G. Chadwick, printed the marriage announcement, in which he gave "thanks for a whole wedding loaf, and his best wishes for the happiness of his kind friends." *Caledonian*, August 4, 1849. Chadwick served as the newspaper's editor from its beginning in 1837 until 1855. Fairbanks, *Town of St. Johnsbury*, 219–20. Alfred knew how to cultivate a relationship with the local newspaper editor, as he often reported announcements about the Peacham Academy.

[35]Alice Locke was the daughter of David and Florinda Locke of Lyman, N.H., where Hale worked and boarded in 1849. I thank Mary Locke Eysenbach for information on the Locke family.

so in comparison to the first settled towns of the State. The house is yet unfinished, but will be finished soon. Father has been unfortunate in loosing his property, or most of it, but he has now bought a farm, half of which Alfred holds a deed of, so should they again be as unfortunate, they can have a home in their old age. Mother [Rix] works very hard, she has only one girl to assist her, and she is but fourteen years of age. She has fifty pounds of wool to work this summer. Well we staid at home until Aug. 4. When we visited at Mr [David] Lock's, the place where Hale [Rix] boards. We had a very pleasant time. Visited the saw-mill where H[ale Rix] works, had a ride on the mill pond, a long way up the Connecticut. The river very low, so it was difficult to get along for the rocks & sand. We saw Mrs [Florinda] Lock, the mother of Alice, at her sons. Took tea at Mr Lock's when we proceeded to a Temperance meeting, but there was no speaker, so we came away. Called at Mr [Thomas] Cranes. Mrs [Margaret Rix] C[rane] an aunt of Alfreds.

[CWR at Dalton, N.H.] [Sunday, August 5] Found us again at home. We did not attend church. The meetings in Dalton are very thin & uninteresting, because they have no regular preaching. We spent our time in reading writing &c. Saw Ira [Rix] first time.

[Monday, August 6] Mother [Rix] is unwell. C. washed for herself. Somewhat rainy. Alfred reading law and other things.

[ASR] [Tuesday, August 7] Mowed & spread hay—talked, loafed & laughed & eat till our stomachs & visibilities were rather lame and overdone.

[Wednesday, August 8] Went over the ridge to visit Cousin Clark Rix. Clark is very well off—he has got 1 wife and 2 fine babies—a boy and girl. His farm is the rockiest & roughest of all the Devil's pasture. But he has one advantage—he goes clear of taxes—the constable cant find him & if he could there's nothing to tax. Go it Clark & Becky!

[Thursday, August 9] Waked up at Moses Rix's. After leaving Clark [Rix]'s yesterday we mounted the "ridge" once more & looked over our shoulders for a scene and we got it—The whole chain of the White Mountains stretching north and south as far as we could see and the narrow & dark valley between over which villages and farms were scattered here and there amidst the huge timbers. Found Moses

ASR & Louisa [Rix] at home, jolly and good natured as ever— They have just built a new barn—a first rate one. Moses is the representative this year from Dalton to the N.H. Legislature. Took dinner at Murray Brooks—the P[ost] M[aster] of Dalton & storekeeper. Took tea at Mr Tenning's after making Mr. Oliver Brooks a call & seeing Augusta go the John Herrick mode of "sticking the mouth." Saw Philetta & Julia &c. Went home at Dusk.

[Friday, August 10] Mother [Rix] is very sick. The fires which have for some time past been raging all over Whitefield and its neighborhood have to day been greatly checked by a heavy and constant fall of rain.

[Saturday, August 11] Our intention was to leave to day for Franconia—but the rain prevents. Chastina bakes bread & cleans 'taters while Alf. looks on and laughs and bothers. Dr. Winch of Whitefield calls to see mother [Rix] & on a statement of the case says that Chastina's disease is one of a nervous kind—probably of the sympathetic nerve—can be cured by carbonate of iron & galvanic shocks.

[Sunday, August 12] Went to church and found it and nothing else—Old Glines of Lunenburg a superannuated Pastor—and a goose pasture at that tried to preach & we thought he made out to do it but it all most destroyed him and his audience too—poor old fellow—the Lord dont do him justice to "call him to preach" or "woe be to him if he do it not" while it is "woe" to the whole congregation that sit under the infliction of his ministration. It is our humble opinion that christianity is one of the good causes that suffer very much through the zealous folly of weak advocates.

[Monday, August 13] Started from Dalton on our way home—called at Whitefield & Bethlehem & arrived at Dr Colby's in Franconia about noon. Saw brother Austin [Rix], whose knee is now and has been for 3 or 4 months very lame with white swelling or scrofula. Visited the Iron Works and received presents from Miss Martha Colby. Chastina is tired all out and falls abed and asleep quite naturally. Austin [Rix] talks over his case and concludes some other employment would suit him better than farming.

[Tuesday, August 14] Chastina feels this morning somewhat refreshed but not so well as she should be for the journey before her. Bade the Dr's folks good morning and rode 5 miles up into the mountains and refreshed our eyes with a sight of Mt. Lafayette and the "old man of the mountain." This is a wonderful and interesting freak of nature.[36]

[Alfred drew a picture of the Old Man in the Mountain here.]

A very correct copy of the Old Man is here shown. There is no flattery in this picture—it is as true a likeness as we could take—and one would no more mistake the profile of the Mountain than this one on paper. This looks to the south east—and is high above all the hills and forests. At the base of the mountain is a beautiful little pond out of which Chastina would have a handfull of pebles for a keep-sake.

After spending an hour here we turned our course directly back— and after having our horse bitten by a dog at the Lafayette House where we saw Mr Bowman—& driving about two miles we again turned southward on our road to East Haverhill. We were obliged to call twice on our way once on 'Tina's account, for her nervous pain began to come on very seriously early in the day, & once for the rain & dinner. We dined at Mr Edwards' of Landaff and then in a kind of half shower & half mist we drove to Haverhill where we arrived about 6 p.m. where we met Uncle [Joel Eastman], Aunt Lucretia [Rix Eastman], Alfred Eastman, Susan E. Rix & her father & a small baby or so all by itself. Eliza Rix, Wilder's eldest daughter is at uncles and is a pretty girl.

[CWR] The baby belongs to Mr —— Somebody of Lowell Mass. & <u>Miss</u> Melvina Gile, daughter of Persis, daughter of Uncle. This Mr. courted Melvina and got her with child and then left for California under rather suspicious circumstances—such as lead many to believe he means to desert Melvina.[37] She came from her mother's, in Lowell, to be delivered at her Grandfather's and in order to keep the case a secret. She was delivered of a fine little girl last Sunday night.

Before we retired for the night we heard the squall of the child and

---

[36] The "Old Man of the Mountain," a stone formation that resembled a face in profile, was carved by glaciers into the rocks at the top of Cannon Mountain. Long New Hampshire's most recognizable symbol, it attracted tourists such as Alfred and Chastina to Franconia Notch. The formation crumbed in May 2003.

[37] It is rare to find a diary or letter reporting a man going off to California, leaving behind an unmarried and pregnant woman.

CWR wondered a little what babies could be here. Our bed-room was next adjoining that of the young mother and to save a further pulmonary exhibition the infant was upon our entrance into our room suddenly transferred into the kitchen—just at that moment Alf. recollecting his long beard, dodged into the kitchen entry for his razor and Aunt supposing he was coming into the room dropped the baby into her lap & covered it with her apron & loose garments and so all of a sudden found herself in one of the most awkward & ticklish of all positions. Oh, that Alf. had gone in and looked on while the "young'un" squalled like <u>natur</u>.

[ASR] But the next morning they were forced by this by itself to let us into the secret. And we enjoyed a hearty laugh at the narrow escape on the previous evening. Poor Susan [Rix] was afraid we should think the infant hurt and like to have suffered the pains of travail at the thought. Uncle [Eastman] was as merry as a sailor—telling over his old stories &c. We laid our bodies down at night pretty well fitted to sleep soundly

[Wednesday, August 15] Went to day (Alf.) up to the tip top of Sugar Loaf mountain in company with Mr Eastman & little Alf. The wind blew cold and some rain fell and scared us down in pretty good season but not before we had one of the grandest of views—the valley of the Connecticut for thirty miles above and below was before us full of villages and farms. Half Vermont & and the Green Mountains lay over opposite to us— I picked a quart of blueberries, fell & spilt them and went home thankful that I'd not spilt my bowels. Uncle [Eastman] discourses on Physic & old times—gives an account of our ancestry and then we go to bed again after making Melvina [Gile] a short call—she seems to take it rather hard—we cheered her as much as we were able. Alas for the unfortunate.

[CWR] [Thursday, August 16] Bade Uncle [Eastman]'s folks farewell and started for home. We had a very pleasant day for our last ride, & we enjoyed it highly. We dined at McIndo's Falls, about eight miles from home. Stayed there and rested us for a time—and arrived at father [Lyman] Watts about four o'clock P.M. Found our people all well, and the little girls very much pleased to see Tina, that "married girl," as little Alice [Watts] says.

CHAPTER TWO

Village Life in Vermont at Peacham Corner
August 17–December 31, 1849

We each day attend to our respective business. Alfred teaching his school & studying law. And Chastine doing her work, that is taking the care of her rooms and mending <u>the boys</u> clothes . . . Chastina enters upon her duties as teacher of Geography & Arithmetic.
ALFRED

THE EARLY WHITE INHABITANTS OF PEACHAM HAD COME FROM southern New England in the 1770s, traveling north along the valley of the Connecticut River. By 1792 it was the largest town in the newly formed Caledonia County and could have claimed the right to be named the county seat and the site of the county courthouse. Instead, at the recommendation of General William Chamberlain, a Revolutionary soldier and one of the town's earliest settlers and officeholders, at a meeting in 1795 the town voted in favor of becoming the site of the county grammar school.[1] Soon known as the Peacham Academy, the school ranked high in academic excellence throughout the area.

In the mid-nineteenth century, Peacham had four village centers: Peacham Corner, the main center, where the Academy was located; Water Street, later called South Peacham; Peacham Hollow, later called East Peacham; and Ewell's at Ewell's Pond. The 1850 census showed that there were 1,377 people living in Peacham, down a few dozen since 1840, when the town had reached its peak population. The decline was due to families

---
[1] Bogart, *Peacham*, 108–17.

moving west in search of better economic opportunity, especially cheaper and more fertile land.

The Rixes settled into married life, boarding at the home of David and Aurilla Choate at Peacham Corner. According to a letter from Chastina to her sister Clara, written two weeks before their wedding, they had originally planned to live with Alfred's great-aunt Sarah Stevens on her farm on the road to the East Part. But when Aunt Sarah's son Thaddeus arrived for a visit from Washington, D.C., where he was serving as a U.S. congressman from Pennsylvania, he advised them to live at the Corner so that Alfred could use his spare time to study for a law career instead of doing farm chores for his great-aunt.[2]

In addition to the Peacham Academy building, there were two churches at Peacham Corner, along with a district school, a tavern and livery stable, a tannery, a blacksmith shop, and three stores, one of which served as the post office. According to the town's 1850 grand list, the Corner was home to two ministers, an attorney, a physician, a blacksmith, a carpenter, a cooper, a carriage maker, a tanner, a shoemaker, a dressmaker, a tailor, a hatter, and a milliner.[3] Residents at the Corner supplemented their incomes by boarding Academy students and staff, as the Academy had no dormitory. There were no farms at the Corner, but most of the residents kept a pig, a cow or two, chickens, and sometimes a horse, and most had a small garden for vegetables.

In anticipation of moving into their living quarters, Chastina cut out and sewed rugs; Alfred readied the rooms and arranged the furniture. Then they packed their clothes and linens and moved in. Although Chastina was sad to be leaving her old home, Alfred pronounced her "much pleased with her new apartments." At the Choates', the couple lived in a private area consisting of two rooms connected by a short hallway on the second floor of the house. Mrs. Choate provided meals, which they ate with the family's four young children, ages three to fifteen. Chastina was responsible for cleaning their rooms and doing their personal laundry, and she busied herself with sewing and other tasks. She enjoyed socializing in the afternoons, and in the evenings she made time to study, in preparation

---

[2] Chastina, Peacham, to Clara Walbridge, Oakfield, N.Y., July 13, 1849, private collection.

[3] Throughout the nineteenth century, Vermont towns were required to prepare a listing, called the grand list, of the names of taxpayers, mainly men, with the valuation of their property including land and buildings, animals, and personal wealth such as clocks, carriages, bank accounts, and stocks. These records were prepared by the town listers, who were elected at a town meeting in the fall. The grand lists are available in the town clerk's office.

PEACHAM CORNER TAVERN AND LIVERY STABLE, CA. 1880
Before going to California in 1852, Dan Foster ran the tavern and livery stable where Alfred rented a horse and buggy for excursions from Peacham. The buildings at the right side of the photograph burned in 1959. *Peacham Historical Association.*

for the two classes that Alfred had asked her to start teaching at the Academy. She was, as Alfred noted, "an excellent wife."

Alfred had been named the twenty-seventh principal of the Peacham Academy in 1848, an appointment that usually lasted only a few years, as men moved on to larger schools. He was the first graduate of the University of Vermont to hold the position; most of the former principals had been graduates of Dartmouth, with some from Yale and Middlebury and one from Harvard.[4] According to the Academy catalogue published in October 1849, there were 163 scholars, as the students were called, enrolled for that term—93 males and 70 females. The principal taught most of the

---

[4]Bogart, *Peacham*, 472.

classes, with a lecturer brought in to teach anatomy and physiology. The 1849 catalogue listed three women teachers, including the preceptress, a teacher in drawing and painting, and Mrs. Chastina Rix. Three students, all males, were listed as "Assistants." The fall term began early in September and ended in the middle of November. It usually had the largest attendance of the four terms, as it fell during the time of year with the fewest farm work demands.[5] The students came mainly from Peacham and neighboring towns, and some from as far away as Wolcott, but there were also students listed from Maine, New Hampshire, and New York, and even one from Wisconsin.

In 1849, only six scholars were listed in the catalogue as being "Fitted for College," meaning that they had chosen the course of study called "Higher English Studies and Languages." The majority chose "Common English Studies," consisting of arithmetic, grammar, geography, bookkeeping, physiology, reading, and spelling, classes that would prepare them for "the common business of life." Forty-four scholars signed up for Latin, thirteen

---

[5]Quimby, *Peacham Academy*, 63.

PEACHAM CORNER, CA. 1900
A view of Peacham Corner, the most populated area of Peacham, surrounding the Congregational Church, often referred to as the Bell-House because of its Revere bell in the steeple. Across the road is the Methodist Church, called the Chapel. In the background is the Peacham Academy. Houses at the crossroads include the one owned by Abigail Chamberlain where Julian Walbridge Rix was born in 1850 and the home of David and Aurilla Choate, where the Rixes first boarded after marrying in 1849. *Private collection.*

for French or Greek. The Academy was governed by a board of trustees consisting of nine men: three ministers, two doctors, three lawyers, and one farmer, the latter from one of the well-respected families who had settled early in Peacham.

The tuition per eleven-week quarter was $2.00 for "Common English Studies," $3.00 for "Higher English Studies and Languages," with additional charges for drawing and painting ($1.75) and use of the library ($.12). Board for the students ranged from $11.00 to $16.50, with the additional option of "boarding one's self" at $1.75, meaning that those students had a room in a local home but brought food from home and did their own washing.

The 1849 catalogue includes a listing of "Text-Books" used at the Academy, ranging from "Russell's American School Reader" to "Weld's Latin Lessons." A paragraph describes the facilities:

> A pleasant location—a convenient and elegant building—a Library for general reading—a Table Library of Dictionaries and Encyclopedias for school-room reference—full sets of Mitchell's Outline Maps and Cutter's Anatomical Plates—a Debating Society—Lectures weekly during most

PEACHAM CORNER STORE, CA. 1867
Ambrotype of store run by merchant John M. Martin in the 1850s. At the crossroads, it served as a gathering place. This photograph was probably taken after a church meeting, as the men appear to be dressed in their Sunday best. *Peacham Historical Association.*

of the year—classes in English Composition and Declamation—Teachers' classes—Reviews, thorough and impartial, monthly—special efforts for substantial attainments in the *elementary*, and high character in the *practical*.

A chart on the last page of the catalogue lists the classes offered: Geography, Geography of the Heavens, History, English Grammar, Natural Philosophy, Chemistry, Physiology, Intellectual Philosophy, Rhetoric, Arithmetic, Algebra, Geometry, Surveying, Astronomy, French, Latin Lessons, Latin Reader, Virgil, Sallust, Cicero, Livy, Greek Lessons, Greek Reader, Xenophon's Anabasis, Herodotus, and Composition and Declamation.

In addition to teaching, Alfred ordered textbooks, prepared the catalogue, reviewed the teachers, informed the trustees about activities, and responded to inquiries from prospective students. He was responsible for monitoring his teachers, fixing equipment, and cleaning the building. The

PEACHAM ACADEMY, CA. 1870
This second building for the school, which was founded in 1795, was constructed in 1843. Its classical appearance is marked by a central gable-front pavilion flanked by matching wings. The building was expanded and remodeled in 1886. The Peacham Academy closed in 1971, and the building burned in 1976. *Private collection.*

principalship was a demanding position beyond the classroom as well.[6] On Sundays when the minister was not available and no deacon was present, Alfred was expected to read a printed sermon. Principals could be called upon to perform almost any duty in town.

Alfred was ably assisted in his many tasks by his wife, who knew the community well and was respected as a teacher. By agreeing to teach arithmetic and geography at the Academy, Chastina saved him from having to pay for another instructor and gave him a break from the classroom so that he had more time for his law studies. Unlike some states, Vermont had no law prohibiting married women from teaching, and Chastina, a well-respected scholar and district schoolteacher, was well qualified for this position.[7] She also joined Alfred in receiving scholars at their rooms in the Choate home. There was rarely an evening when a teacher, student, neighbor, or friend did not call on the couple. Some of these were social

[6]Ibid., 30.
[7]Gregory Sanford, Vermont State Archivist, telephone conversation with editor, summer 2007.

visits, but many were work-related, especially near the end of the term, when the students needed help in preparing their "dialogues." These were public presentations to be delivered at the final exhibition, showcasing the scholars' achievements during the term and providing a venue for the community to evaluate the teachers as well as the students.

As the Academy principal, Alfred also served as one of Peacham's superintendents of schools, along with the two ministers in town and the county superintendent. One of their responsibilities was to administer the licensing examination to older students who had applied for a certificate to teach in the common schools. This was a new state requirement that had been mandated by the Vermont legislature in 1846. An announcement by the county superintendent of schools published in the *Caledonian* on October 27, 1849, summarized the process:

> None should apply for licensure who are not prepared to realize, in some good degree, the expectations of the community in regard to them. It is better to chop wood well than to teach school poorly. Increased stress will be laid on a knowledge of the elementary branches; and in cases where individuals are not known to the superintendents, testimonials in respect to character will be required.

Chastina was as busy as Alfred. Besides teaching at the Academy and helping her husband with his professional responsibilities, she maintained their living quarters, sustained friendly relations with the landlord's family, made and mended clothes, and worked on finishing some rugs and her marriage quilt. She wrote letters to distant friends and family and also stayed in contact with nearby relatives. The couple noted their health concerns in the journal, including the first of many references to the severe headaches that Chastina was prone to, and they worried about getting enough sleep. They were also trying to live up to the expectations of the town's influential families. Such adjustments almost certainly created stress for both of them.

In the midst of this full schedule came the marriage on October 16 of Chastina's sister Sarah to John S. Way. The wedding had been hastily arranged to take place before the groom left for the California gold fields. It had only been a year since news of the discovery of gold at Sutter's Mill had reached the East Coast, and men young and old were being drawn by its siren call. Despite the difficulties of the long journey and the risks of failure, "gold fever" was infecting men not only in North America but in South America, Europe, and Asia as well. In Vermont, a young man such as John Way could not afford the price of land, and in fact, there was little land for sale. Vermont farms were often heavily mortgaged, and their owners were looking at a lifetime of debt. The dream of striking it rich in the California mines offered hope for the future. Marriage would not deter John S. Way from seeking a share of that fortune. Nor would other men from Peacham be able to resist the call. Alfred and Chastina, wrapped up in their new life, watched these exciting developments from front-row seats, but did not seem to hear the call.

[CWR at Watts Farm] [Friday, August 17, 1849] After brushing & washing Mrs [Sarah] Stevens wagon for the purpose of making it shine—Alfred takes his team home, & Chastina washes a good large wash she has too. A. brings a letter from sister Clara [Walbridge] & Miss [Sarah] Baley. In the afternoon we cut out our carpet & commenced sewing it. This kept us busy until night. A. sews pretty well for a beginner.

[Saturday, August 18] Finished our carpet in the A.M. and a pretty one it is too. Had a visit from Alva[h] Watts and C. irons. This completed the day.

[Sunday, August 19] Sunday 19 We did not attend church, <u>partly</u> because we wanted to rest & the <u>remainder</u> because we had no way to go. And we did rest—picking & eating green beans & corn at a great rate. It seemed like <u>old times</u> to have <u>A</u>. there at our house <u>sunday night</u> after <u>supper</u>.

[ASR at Peacham Corner] [Monday, August 20] Packed up and waited for

[Tuesday, August 21] Looked rainy— Mr [Lyman] Watts got in his wheat & moved our furniture to Mr. D[avid] W. Choate's at Peacham Corner—where A had gone and made ready.[8] Got Furniture from Bennetts.[9] A sets up the rooms & lays down the carpet &c &c and remains overnight at Mr Choate's. Chastina spins stocking yarn with

---

[8]David W. Choate (1806–94) owned a house at Peacham Corner with rooms for rent on the second floor. The Rixes boarded there, with meals provided by Aurilla Ingraham Choate (1806–89). The Choate children were Mary (b. 1834), Charles (b. 1838), Elsie (b. 1842), and Schuyler (b. 1846).

[9]Humphrey Bennett (1822–1905) was a furniture maker in town. Bogart, *Peacham*, 266; obituary, *Caledonian*, March 22, 1905.

ASR all her might—because her mother [Watts] gave her all she could spin before she left. Trouble arises between Miss Cotes & her beau.

[Wednesday, August 22] Mrs Rix leaves her old and comes to her new home—tired out and rather sad at heart—but not discouraged—she does not feel as if she had fallen into bad hands and trusts that it will prove so—she is much pleased with her new apartments.

[Thursday, August 23] Rainy— We wrote on Chastina's life as found in the first of this volume. C. trims her quilt & A. tinkers & laughs.

[Friday, August 24] Got [Chester] Guy to wash the Academy.[10] Helpt him. C makes her curtains.

[Saturday, August 25] C. works on her curtains. A washes Academy & looks up boarding places for his scholars.[11]

[Sunday, August 26] Attended church. Mother [Watts] dined with us. Heard Hale [Rix] had got his arm torn off—wrote to him also to J. P. Lee, Beattie, Mrs [Louisa] Balch & Emilyne. Miss Cotes' confession read at the chapel.[12]

[Monday, August 27] Chastina washed. A. studied. Calls from some 9 neighbors among others the Bradlee family— Johnson & [James M.] Dickson leave for college in Ohio.[13]

[Tuesday, August 28] Received to day 12 calls. Watts & Smith who remains over night. Call from Dr. [Josiah] Shedd.[14] 'S Blood! Whole length—in the business of calls.

[Wednesday, August 29] Saw Miss [Laura] Freeman at Dr [Josiah] Shedd's.[15] Opened our school with 51 pupils. Miss F. to board at

---

[10]Chester Guy (1805–73) seems to have served as the Peacham Academy handyman.

[11]Another duty for the Academy principal was finding private homes where the students and teachers could board.

[12]A confession was a profession of belief. The Methodist church at Peacham built a chapel in 1832 and was itself often referred to as the Chapel. Bogart, *Peacham*, 187.

[13]Nehemiah Bradlee (ca. 1779–1854) and his wife, Elizabeth Chamberlin Bradlee (1784–1860), were both from families who had settled early in Peacham. He was a longtime storekeeper. Bogart, *Peacham*, 271–72. Their name is sometimes spelled "Bradley." Their oldest daughter, Louisa (1811–70), taught in the Sabbath School at the Congregational church. James M. Dickson of Ryegate is listed as a student in the 1846–47 and 1848 PAC.

[14]Dr. Josiah Shedd (1781–1851), a local physician, was president of the board of trustees of the Peacham Academy from 1845 to 1851. [Caledonia County Grammar School], *100th Anniversary*, listing of officers through the years.

[15]Laura H. Freeman was listed as a teacher of drawing and painting in the 1849 PAC; newspaper announcement, *Caledonian*, August 11, 1849.

T[imothy] Cowles at 10 shillings a week.[16] William Mattocks nominated by the Free Democrats as Rep. to St. Legislature.[17] He'll get it. Chastina calls on Mrs [Abigail] Blake.[18]

[CWR] [Thursday, August 30] Received a call from Mrs. [Lucinda Johnson] Button, the methodist ministers wife, also calls from Margaret & Betsy Blanchard.[19] Chastine commenced studying some, with the intention of prepareing herself to teach if necessary. Whigs nominate Mr L[yman] Watts.[20]

[Friday, August 31] Rained. We went home. Our people all well. Father gone to Barton to look of a farm he talks of buying.[21]

[ASR] [Saturday, September 1] C. spinning & twisting. A. writing & playing. P.M. Visited Mrs [Sarah] Stevens—Alanson [Stevens] brought us home. C. hurt her knee. Letters from Hale [Rix] & Smith.

[Sunday, September 2] Went to church at Cong. A.M. at Methodist's P.M. Heard Mr [A. G.] Button for the first time. Wearing her wedding dress, poor Tina! Wrote to Boston for Books.[22]

[Monday, September 3] Tina always washes on monday so we need not repeat this important item. Called on Miss [Laura] Freeman.

---

[16] Timothy Cowles (1777–1859), a hatter, owned a house at Peacham Corner and boarded students and teachers. Bogart, *Peacham*, 264.

[17] At this time, each Vermont town elected a representative to the state legislature. William Mattocks (1818–59), a lawyer like his father, former governor John Mattocks (1777–1847), had agreed to run for election.

[18] Abigail Blake (ca. 1797–1858) of Peacham was the mother of Ira Green Blake, listed as a student in the 1846–47, 1849, 1851, and 1852 PAC. In 1852 he was also a teacher of vocal music.

[19] Rev. Amasa G. Button (1814–84), whose name usually appears as A. G., was the minister at the Methodist church from 1849 to 1851. He lived with his wife, Lucinda Johnson Button (1809–94), and family at Peacham Corner. Bogart, *Peacham*, 474. When Button died, the *Official Minutes of the Vermont Annual Conference of the Methodist Episcopal Church* reported that he had "transferred to the conference above." His funeral address, delivered by Rev. F. D. Hemenway, was published in 1884 by John A. Childs in Evanston, Illinois, where the Buttons had been living. Sisters Margaret Blanchard (1824–1900) and Betsy Blanchard (b. 1829) of the East Part were close friends of Chastina's, and one or both were listed as students in the 1846–47, 1849, 1851, and 1852 PAC.

[20] The Whig choice for state representative from Peacham was Lyman Watts, Chastina's stepfather and a farmer in the East Part. He was to run against Alfred's candidate, William Mattocks. *Caledonian*, August 25, 1849.

[21] Lyman Watts, like other farmers with no mortgage, was known to look at farms outside of Peacham, always trying to better his lot but also probably evaluating his own property.

[22] Vermont teachers ordered most of their books from publishing houses in Boston. The PAC listed the textbooks used at the school.

ASR Mrs A. A. & J. D. Wheeler called.[23] [James M.] Dickson leaves for the West after taking from us his certificate.

[Tuesday, September 4] Election Day in Vermont—Great times—Wm Mattocks—Free Dem. 57 majority—State ticket 84 Maj.[24] Hurrah! Hurra! Call from Mr Currier & Lyman [S. Watts] who takes Lat. Reader, gives Int. Phil. & gets us apples.[25]

[Wednesday, September 5] Ironing. A. lectured— Called at Dr [Asahel] Farr's.[26] Recd Books from Boston. Mrs [Lydia Chamberlain] Shedd & [Elisabeth Clark] Strobridge called in our absence.[27] About this time the Rug Fever attacks Chastina & she is <u>taken down</u> with it.

[CWR] [Thursday, September 6] We each day attend to our respective business. Alfred teaching his school & studying law. And Chastine doing her work, that is takeing the care of her rooms and mending <u>the boys</u> clothes, & at present engaged in making rugs, & studying some. The extra performances we record, as will be noticed. Mr. & Mrs. [David] Merrill made us a call.[28] Took a walk & was caught in a shower—came home & went to our evening's work, when Messrs. Brainards called with books.[29]

---

[23] The callers were Catherine Blanchard Wheeler (b. 1816), wife of Alexander A. Wheeler, and Dorcas Wheeler (b. ca. 1820), wife of Judah D. Wheeler (b. ca. 1818).

[24] The *Caledonian* reported the election results on September 8 and 15, 1849, with William Mattocks winning the race for state representative from Peacham for the term 1849–50. Bogart, *Peacham*, 466.

[25] Chastina's stepbrother Lyman S. Watts, an outstanding student at the Academy, was probably accompanied by one of the Currier boys, who were neighbors in the East Part. The Watts farm was known for its fine apple orchards.

[26] Asahel Farr (1820–87), who attended the St. Johnsbury Academy with Alfred, practiced medicine in Peacham from 1849 to April 1854. He then sold his house at Peacham Corner and moved to Kenosha, Wisconsin. Bogart, *Peacham*, 235, incorrectly reports that Farr practiced in Peacham until 1857. Peacham Historical Association, Manuscripts [hereafter PHA-MS], Farr, Asahel. Elisabeth Clark Strobridge, Peacham, to Ephraim Clark, California, January 1854, PHA-MS, Clark, Ephraim Wesson.

[27] The callers were Lydia Chamberlain Shedd (1790–1862), wife of Dr. Josiah Shedd, and Elisabeth Clark Strobridge (1826–99), wife of Lafayette Strobridge (1824–1908). The latter had been raised by the Shedds after her mother died in 1832. "Memorial of Elisabeth Clark Strobridge, 1899," PHA-MS, Clark, Clarissa Johnson.

[28] The callers were David Merrill, the Congregational minister, and his wife, Mary Hunt Merrill (1806–61). David Merrill was listed as secretary of the board of trustees of the Peacham Academy in the 1846–47, 1848, and 1849 PAC.

[29] There were a number of Brainerd and Brainard families in the area at the time, and there is no way to know who brought the books to Alfred.

[Friday, September 7] After tea, we called at Mr Bradlee's. Saw   CWR
Louisa, Mrs Lee & Fowler. Called on Mrs. [Sarah] Marsh—who
is <u>so</u> glad to see us.[30] Called also at Dr. [Josiah] Shedd's. The Dr. &
Alfred talk politics. Saw Mrs. [Elisabeth Clark] Strobridge & Miss
[Laura] Freeman at Dr. This is the ultimatum of our calls this day.

[Saturday, September 8] Alfred attends to his Saturday exercises.
Got Chitty of Mattocks. Walked round the "Pan cake"[31] Wrote in
Journal. Finished Phillips on Evidence.[32]

[Sunday, September 9] Attended church in A.M. & P.M. Saw Sarah
[Walbridge]. She told me father was going again to look at the farm
in Barton. After meeting read &c. C. attends Sabbath school. Miss
Louisa Bradlee teacher. We are now studying Character in the old
testament.[33] Wrote to Oscar [Rix].

[Monday, September 10] Had calls from Mrs. E[phraim] C. Brown
& Mary J. Weeks. We fairly get to studying when Miss [Laura] Freeman & Ann Cameron call.[34] Stayed almost all the evening. Miss F.
is a strange mixture of old maidism & <u>under twentyism</u>. Let the
case be as it may, she is a real old maid. Alfred writes a letter to Dr.
F. B. Brewer, & sends money for the table library at the academy.[35]

[*ASR*] [Tuesday, September 11] Recd a letter from J[ames] K. Colby

---

[30] Sarah K. Marsh (1798–1871) was the widow of Jonathan Marsh (1798–1849) and the mother of two sons, Newell (1832–52) and Benjamin (1836–99), and two daughters, Jane (b. ca. 1834) and Priscilla (b. ca. 1840). Either Newell or Jane was listed as a student in the 1846–47, 1848, 1849, 1850, 1851, and 1852 PAC.

[31] To walk the "pan cake," they went south toward Water Street (later called South Peacham) by Elkins Tavern and returned north up the Bailey-Hazen road, a little more than a mile.

[32] Alfred was studying law and borrowed books from William Mattocks, among them Joseph Chitty (1729–95), *Chitty on Contracts* (1826), and S. M. Phillips (1780–1862), *Famous Cases of Circumstantial Evidence* (2nd ed., 1857).

[33] Nineteenth-century churchgoers read the Old Testament closely and saw it as a guide to "the good life." Character development was important to them. David E. L. Brown, e-mail message to editor, November 20, 2008.

[34] Betsey Weeks Brown (1818–79) was the wife of local merchant Ephraim C. Brown (b. 1815). Her sister Mary Jane Weeks (b. 1829), a classmate of Chastina's, was living with the Browns when she was listed as a student from Lyndon in the 1846–47 PAC. Both she and Ann Cameron were listed as students in 1849 and 1850. Ann, from Peacham, was also listed as an assistant in 1852. The 1850 census has Mary J. Weeks living with Betsey and Ephraim, so she may have moved to Peacham permanently.

[35] Dr. Francis B. Brewer (1820–92), a Peacham Academy trustee and listed in the 1849 PAC as "Lecturer on Anatomy and Physiology," practiced in Barnet from 1846 to 1850. Wells, *History of Barnet*, 349.

ASR on Uniformity of Books.³⁶ Jones left. Rug-making. A call from Sarah [Walbridge] and Lyman [S. Watts] who bring us a cut of striped-blanket-timber. Walked round the "Pankake" again—let him who readeth understand by "Pankake" a certain portion of Real estate situated island fashion between two roads or parts of the same road between the Corner & Water street. The said land is hereby Christened Pancake Island or the Isle of Pankake. So no more! Wrote to Mr Colby. Sent Mr. [F. B.] Brewer $30.00. Something is required to fill out this page [of the journal] the opposite sketch has been suggested as being quite appropriate.

THE JOURNALIST.

[Wednesday, September 12] A fair day. Lectured at 5½ P.M. on Law. Calls from Misses Mariam & Lucy Eastman, also from Margaret Calder & M. P. Merrill.³⁷ The wife mends pants & stockings and always in the afternoon puts away her work—puts on her toggery & white dresses & either walks out or receives walkouters—Evenings she makes herself very busy with Algebra. The conclusion of the whole matter is that she is a very industrious & glorious young woman—and I know of but one reason for wishing I had not married with her, and that is, that <u>I cannot do it again</u>. This is warm weather and we are pretty well wearied out when we are done. GUESS.³⁸

[*CWR*] [Thursday, September 13] "The journalist" spent the most of the forenoon in writing to Miss E[lizabeth] A. Fuller of St. Johnsbury,

---

³⁶James K. Colby (1812–66) was the first principal of the St. Johnsbury Academy, which was founded in 1842. Beck, *Proud Tradition*, 14–22.

³⁷Miriam (1816–95) and Lucy Eastman (1826–72) were sisters to John Eastman (1832–59), who was listed as a student in the 1846–47, 1848, 1849, 1850, 1851, and 1852 PAC. Also listed in some years were Margaret Calder and Mary P. Merrill (b. 1832). All were from Peacham.

³⁸In the first years of their marriage, Alfred often made reference to their sexual activity, as he does here, usually noting that they were weary or slow to get up in the morning. Two nights after this entry, he wrote "GOOD NIGHT! GOOD NIGHT!!" probably implying that he was looking forward to having sex.

an acquaintance of mine, of course.³⁹ Alfred is as merry as a cricket these days, and it is more than I want to do to manage him. But as women are in the habit of doing so, I shall endeavor to do the best in my power. Miss Mary Calder made us a call this afternoon.⁴⁰ And in the evening a call from Miss [Laura] Freeman.

    [ASR] [Friday, September 14] A lucky day, for we have had no calls! Lawsuit on a horse by Mr. Evans v. Groton man. Walked round the fields a mile or two! C. made rug & sat in sack-cloth & ashes. She is rather down in the mouth and up in opposition! [Alfred wrote three Greek words here]⁴¹ C. into Algebra & parsneps. GOOD NIGHT! GOOD NIGHT!!

    [CWR] [Saturday, September 15] This morning we got up in good season and walked around what Alfred calls "pan-cake island" before breakfast. Alfred attends to his school exercises of about an hour, & reads law and bothers me the rest of the time. He weighs about 167.

    [ASR] [Sunday, September 16] Went to church—inclining to rain—listened to Mr. [David] Merrill on a text found in Titus 2. 11 & 12. The heads of his discourse are the following—

    1 "Denying ungodliness & worldly lusts"—that this is essential—must be denied at once and totally—perhaps all men mean to do so at last—the sensualist means not to indulge to his ruin—nor the drunkard to his death—but these are yet the almost enevitable consequences of indulgence.

    2 Youth ought to be aware, as too frequently they are not, that it is easier to avoid than to break off indulgence, for they do not mean to have it with all its consequences.

    3 But when once temptation has been yeilded to, and ungodliness & lusts have been indulged it is hard to break from them—they form a chain that is mighty to bind its followers forever to its worship.

---

³⁹Elizabeth A. Fuller was a classmate of Chastina's at the St. Johnsbury Academy. Chastina usually called her Lizzie.

⁴⁰According to Ernest L. Bogart, Mary Calder had a "millinery business" at the Choate home. Bogart, *Peacham*, 269. Later in the journal, it became clear that while Mary lived at Peacham Corner in 1849, she was not at the Choate house.

⁴¹Greek words loosely meaning "love" or "the heart covers all." Chastina, not feeling well, was overwhelmed with all of her duties and may have been resisting sex. I thank Leonidas Petrakis for the translation.

ASR 4 Reform cannot be gradual—the result of gradual reform in everything is the same; that is a return to the old way—the denial must be total and complete—there must be no clogs to draw back him who would ascend.

5 "Live Soberly"—That is reflectingly—that this world and all within it is but short—the good things and the evil things of it are so mingled that soberness alone can distinguish them—folly & lightness belong not here—the short space allotted us ought not to be triffled away.

6 "Sober"—as to ourselves—we should beware not to value ourselves too highly—but soberly—nothing perhaps lays the foundation for so much of evil as self-esteem. It is at the bottom of almost all the jars & strifes and envyings and jealousies & complainings of life.

7 "Soberly" as to others—give them their due—do them justice, perform all duties toward them faithfully.

8 "Righteously"—another injunction to do unto others as we would they should do unto us.

9 "And Godly"—All should be done with an eye to the honor & glory of God—he will dispise every act that is performed from any other motive.

10 "In this present world." All must be done in this world—What avails this world to us if we neglect these duties—for the performance of which the world was given us as a means—In this world or never.

11 "The Grace of God hath appeared to all men teaching" these things—The bible is given—no one can add or take away—these are its doctrines.

12 The Grace of God does not teach indulgence in any form—but denial— Some suppose it to be a garment of white wherewith to cover all manner of rottenness and sin—that if there is delinquency and transgresson the grace of God can & will cleanse & make pure again. But its direct teachings are soberness, righteousness & godliness in this present world.

13 And now do our consciences bear _us_ witness that we have followed the teachings of the Grace of God—by which alone there is salvation? Amen.

Remained at Sabbath school A. discussed in his class whether we ought ever to deceive—C. in hers, whether Solomon was a wise man in all points—which question is supposed to have been decidedly decided. *ASR*

[Monday, September 17] The following version of Jack & Gill is not bad, it comes from a correspondent of the Boston Post.

> Jack et Gilla
>> Ascendent montin
> Aquam parare
>> Ad centem fontem;
> Procidit Jack
> Et praeter hac,
>> Frangit ejus summum;
> Et de Gilla
> Etiam illa
>> Lepsa est Secundum!

[*CWR*] Alfred sends a letter to S. J. McIndoe respecting Catalogues. I have been washing as usual, only I am almost sick with a cold. The Misses Fowlers, Phebe Brock & Laura Ayer—young ladies belonging to the school—called on us this evening.[42] Alfred has just been at 7½ o'clock to the Store to get me some cough-candy—Candy is good.

[*ASR*] [Tuesday, September 18] Call from Mr. [Robert] Samuel & [Reuben] Harlow.[43] Answered Hemmis Argument as found in Int. Philosophy. Chastina greatly afflicted with a cough. The number of scholars is now about 75. Got 'Tina's shoe mended!

[Wednesday, September 19] Calls from Laura Harvey, Sarah Johnson, A[lvah] Watts, Cynthia & Sophia Merrill.[44] 3 Weeks and All's well!

---

[42] Anne and Sarah Fowler of New York City were listed as students in the 1846–47 and 1849 PAC, and Anne also in 1848. Phebe S. Brock (1834–1926) of Barnet was listed in 1846–47, 1849, 1850, and 1852. Wells, *History of Barnet*, 362. Laura W. Ayer of Haverhill, N.H., was listed in 1848, 1849, 1850, and 1851.

[43] Robert Samuel of Barnet and Reuben W. Harlow of St. Johnsbury were listed as students in the 1849 and 1850 PAC.

[44] Of these, only Cynthia Merrill (b. 1830) of Peacham was listed as a student in the 1849 PAC. Laura Harvey (d. 1853) was a former classmate of Chastina's.

ASR [Thursday, September 20] Mr [David] Choate killed his pig—⁴⁵ C. fitted a dress for mary [Choate] notwithstanding her cough & cold. Pleasant. Letter 2d from Mr McIndoe on the catalogues. A. reading Chitty on Contracts.

[Friday, September 21] Put off our Review— Received our Table Library by Mr [William] Mattocks from Dr [Francis B.] Brewer & 9.00 as balance— Got Lempriere's Dictionary of Mrs Chandler.[46] Chastina went to her old home—. Good luck to her—& bad luck to her cough & head ache— I think one can appreciate a wife pretty fairly if he will let her stay away a few days now and then.

[Saturday, September 22] I woke this morning and found <u>myself</u> all out of order—my head, for instance, <u>were</u> hanging out under the foot-board while my feet lay very composedly upon the pillows. Again, when I attempted to put on my shirt I was surprised to find it slipping on so tightly & still more astonished not to find a bosom in it—and then extremely <u>short</u> sleeves and an extremely <u>long</u> skirt— the truth at last forced itself upon me—the shirt was my wife's—I fainted, but came to in season for school. A Mr Bennett visited Mr. [David] Choates folks. Covered the Table Library— Bade farewell to Anne Eugenia, got my hair cut, dined and stuck myself down for work. Visit from Moses A. Burbank of Haverhill, N.H. who enters our school.[47]

[CWR] I returned, that is "my wife"—about six o'clock & found Alfred just ready to go after me—poor man! he had a dreadful time of it, from the account I find recorded in this journal. Had a good visit at home. Helped Sarah [Walbridge] quilt, on her pink & white quilt like mine.[48] Also assisted Charles [Watts] & Augustus [Walbridge] in their Algebra. My cold instead of growing better grows

---

[45]Most households, even at the Corner, kept a pig, which usually was slaughtered in the fall and butchered, with the meat then stored in barrels with salt brine and some saltpeter for the winter. Bogart, *Peacham*, 237. D. W. Choate is noted in the 1849 Peacham Grant List as having two horses worth $100, one cow worth $20, and one pig worth $5.

[46]John Lempriere (ca. 1765–1824) was an English classical scholar and noted dictionary compiler.

[47]Moses A. Burbank of Haverhill, N.H., was listed as a student in the 1849 PAC.

[48]Sisters Chastina and Sarah made similar pink and white quilts while fixing for marriage. Bonfield, "Four Generations of Quilters," 39.

worse, and I am comforted this day with a bad cough & an extreme head ache. Took some medicine. It is customary when women leave their children at home to bring them something. I brought <u>my boy</u> a large water-melon & some apples.

[Sunday, September 23] This Sabbath I do not feel able to attend church although I feel some better then yesterday. So we have read [illegible] &c. Mother [Watts] was down here to day noon. I have written a letter [to] Clara [Walbridge]. We have had a feast of watermelon.

[*ASR*] [Monday, September 24] Mr [David] Choate visits the crazy man, Lewis Ferrington. Mr [A. G.] Button dined with us. C. So Sick as not to wash. Had a visitor a certain nameless old lady—a friend of Chastina's and I think some way related to her—Heigh ho! Heave oh! Who cares!⁴⁹ The weather about this time is fine and cool.

[Tuesday, September 25] Mr [David] Choate started for Brattleboro with Mr. [Lewis] Ferrington.⁵⁰ Poor fellow, his insanity has driven him to the very extreme of politeness—he bows to all! Sent by [Ephraim C.] Brown for 12 Lat. Lessons & ½ Ream English letter paper.⁵¹ Chastina took a <u>shocking gal-vanic</u> trial and succeeded most admirably.

[Wednesday, September 26] Dr [Asahel] Farr took the Galvanic Battery. Recd a letter from Oscar [Rix]—he seems to be rather soberly funny. Got 5 vols. of Paly last night. We made calls this afternoon on Mrs A. A. Wheeler, Mrs F[ayette] Strobridge, Miss [Laura] Freeman & Mrs. Brown E[phraim] C. Delivered myself of a lecture on "Right and wrong" as I look at it. We finally came home, built a fire & eat 2 huge apples and laughed ourselves to sleep.

---

⁴⁹"A certain nameless old lady—a friend of Chastina's" was Alfred's way of noting that Chastina's menstrual period had begun. Victorian women used euphemisms for their monthly periods, a favorite seen in diaries being "unwell." Chastina later employed "had company." Brumberg, *Body Project*, xxvii; Delaney, Lupton, and Toth, *The Curse*, 116. Alfred's comment indicated a lack of concern that Chastina was not pregnant.

⁵⁰As Peacham's overseer of the poor, David W. Choate may have been responsible for the mentally ill and their removal to the Brattleboro Retreat, a hospital that opened in 1836. Bogart, *Peacham*, 273; Swift and Beach, *Brattleboro Retreat*, 13.

⁵¹Ephraim C. Brown was listed as a Peacham storekeeper in *Walton's Vermont Register* from 1845 through 1851. Bogart, *Peacham*, 274.

Heads of the Lecture!

[*CWR*] [Thursday, September 27] Mother [Watts] visited us to day—brought Alice [Watts] & Ella [Watts] with her. We went to the store. Mother [Watts] bought some things for Sarah [Walbridge] & for the children. Laura Harvey visited here this afternoon & will spend the night with us. We had a fine view of the moon through the telescope.

[*ASR*] [Friday, September 29][52] To day came our Review—passed off quite pleasantly, save that Mr Samuel could not exactly see into the Arithmetic. Mrs [Martha] Martin visits Mrs [Aurilla] Choate—[53] Brought Chastina another Rug. We reckoned up our standing and found ourselves clear of debt and starting in life with $300.00 at Interest. We think Chastine is rather the greatest pecuniary schemer of the two, though it is not certainly known as yet how it will prove. Received letters from J. P. Lee who is now in Stanstead, Mrs. Louisa C. S. Balch & a circular from Mr Hildreth of Bradford on catalogues. All's well!

[*CWR*] [Saturday, September 30] This morning I lined & finished our last rug, & I am very thankful that they are finished for I have been fussing & fixing these three weeks, & Alfred has been laughing at me all the while because I have had such a fever. It has been rather cloudy & somewhat rainy to day. Alfred brought me a letter from W[eltha] A. Cory.[54] Yesterday I carried Sarah [Walbridge]'s & my bonnet to Miss [Mary] Calder to have them dressed over. She was

---

[52] The dating gets briefly off track here. Friday was September 28, not 29. The misdating continues until Monday, October 1, when Chastina points out their error.
[53] Martha Sprague Martin (1808–52) was the wife of storekeeper John M. Martin (1804–77).
[54] Weltha Ann Cory, a longtime friend of Chastina's and possibly a cousin of Alfred's, was a student from Wenlock, listed in the 1850 PAC.

not at home, so I found her at Mr A. A. Wheeler's. Alfred attends to his Saturday exercises & reads "Coopers Treaties on Libel" which he is very much interested in.⁵⁵ This is a great country & great people live therein if we may judge by the specimen's on the opposite page. [Chastina is referring to Alfred's drawing "Tête a Tête" of September 26.]

CWR

[Sunday, October 1] It is a beautiful Sabbath morning. This first day of October brings with it a sunny day, although autumn is fast bringing decay upon our forests & meadows. The forests truly are not less beautiful in its varigated hues than its luxuriant green. We have been to church. We had a sermon this forenoon from the Rev. Mr. Parker of Canada, from 2 Cor. 5.21. After his sermon he gave an account of the condition of the congregational churches in C[anada] E[ast] in whose behalf he is soliciting aid from the churches in the United States. Attended Sabbath school for my lesson gave the cause of the separation of the twelve tribes of Israel & the life of Jeroboam, the first king of the ten tribes. Saw mother [Watts] at noon. Afternoon Mr [David] Merrill preached from a chapter & verse somewhere in Luke. [ASR] Very Definite, Sis!

[Monday, October 1] It will be seen that a mistake has been made by one of the family in dating the 28 of last month, the 29 & so on. 4 new scholars to day— Recd from Boston ¼ Ream English letter paper. Cold weather. C. Washes & A. has a sore throat. Trouble with the French Minister.⁵⁶ This is the house that Jack built. This is a great country especially California.

[CWR] [Tuesday, October 2] This is a very pleasant day, but extremely cold for the season. This afternoon I have been down to see Mrs. Morse. Saw Ellen [Morse], she returned from her journey to Boston last Friday.⁵⁷ Called on Miss [Mary] Calder found her at home with visitors, Mrs. [Martha] Farr & Miss A. McLary.

---

⁵⁵Alfred was reading *A Treatise on the Law of Libel and the Liberty of the Press* (1830) by Thomas Cooper (1759–1839).

⁵⁶On September 29, 1849, the *Caledonian* reported that the French ambassador had been sent home. This event allowed Alfred to take pride in President Zachary Taylor's leadership. Since Alfred read the local newspaper, he would have seen many articles about California, a topic of great interest to him.

⁵⁷Ellen M. Morse of Peacham was listed as a student in the 1846–47, 1850, 1851, and 1852 PAC.

CWR   A Mr Robinson called here with books—an Algebra, Astronomy, & Philosophy, of which he is author. He wishes to introduce them into school. Alfred buys <u>another</u> ¼ Ream of paper. The scholars are dissatisfied with Miss [Laura] Freeman on account of her marking them so low in Examination.

[*ASR*] [Wednesday, October 3] Concluded a contract with Mr. Robinson as to his books. Recd a catalogue of Dartmouth from H. Chamberlain. Sold My new harness for $20.00 to Mr Brown. 2 more scholars. Calls from Misses [Laura] Freeman, [Jane] McClary & [Elizabeth] Hopkins.[58] Distressing news of another flare-up between Mr Geo. Chandler & Miss Janette Craig. The weather is rather cold, but the affairs of the <u>family</u> move on very smoothly. Chastina makes an excellent wife. Tim Cowles & his wife have got a last-Sunday-born-baby-boy.[59] Mr [David] Choate is strayed or stolen.

[Thursday, October 4] Rainy & cold. [Thomas B.] Dow enters.[60] C. back. Got bonnets of Miss [Mary] Calder.

[Friday, October 5] Dunned the Students. Chastina trimmed her bonnet A.M. & P.M. Sarah [Walbridge]'s who made us a visit and brought us some fine apples. Visit from [Reuben] Harlow & [Alexander] Johnston, who went last night to a kick-up in Barnet & like to have died by congestion in the face.[61] Call from Mr. [John G.] Orcutt.[62] Attended The Lyceum on "Conscience."[63] Called on Miss [Mary] Calder & came home.

[*CWR*] [Saturday, October 6] Went into school this morning to hear the exercises in declamation & composition. Alfred received

---

[58] Jane McClary (1836–71) of Peacham was listed as a student in the 1846–47, 1848, 1849, 1850, 1851, and 1852 PAC. Elizabeth H. Hopkins of Peacham was listed in 1848, 1849, and 1850.

[59] Timothy Cowles, Jr. (1814–1910), and Cynthia Shaw Cowles (1827–84) became the parents of a son named Horace. Timothy Cowles first went to the California gold mines in 1851. He subsequently returned to Vermont and took his family back to San Francisco. Bogart, *Peacham*, 227; Bonfield, "Ho for California," 19. Wells, *History of Barnet*, 598, incorrectly reported that he "went to California in 1849 and sent for his family."

[60] Thomas B. Dow of Barnet was listed as a student in the 1849 PAC.

[61] Alexander J. Johnston of Barnet was listed as a student in the 1848, 1849, and 1850 PAC.

[62] John G. Orcutt of Marshfield was listed as a student in the 1849 PAC.

[63] Lyceums in New England were presentations given in educational and public halls. The Peacham Academy at this time held them on Friday afternoons; students and citizens gathered, and "essays were read, speeches declaimed, and a debate was held," often on literary and scientific subjects. Bogart, *Peacham*, 402.

$34.70 tuition this morning. After school I called at the P[ost] O[ffice]   *CWR* and also at [Ephraim] Browns store. Looked at the silks & satins and so on; but purchased nothing, excepting a pair of gloves. Called at Miss [Mary] Calders, & left her umbrella which we borrowed the evening previous. Saw her Boston bonnet, which she wishes me to purchase. Alfred makes out his accounts for tuition, & we prepare names for the Catalogue.

[Sunday, October 7] This is a real cold stormy day. And it has snowed almost all day. Rather an early commencement for winter. We have not been to church on account of the badness of the weather. Alfred has been writing a good part of the day; and I have written a part of two letters, one to Mother Rix & the other to Mrs Susan Rix. Thus we have spent the day—in reading, writing, eating apples, &c, &c.

[Monday, October 8] Have washed this day. Alfred makes arrangements for me to go into school— Receives eleven dollars & a half more tuition— We called to see Miss [Laura] Freeman to arrange school matters. Saw Mrs. S[amuel] A. Chandler & Susan—[64] Came home & look over our several studies. Laura Ayer took tea with us. Weather fair but cold.

[*ASR*] [Tuesday, October 9] This day has been one of some interest.

1 Chastina for the first time is slightly vexed at her husband because he pulled her great toe till she said "Crupper."

2 C's head aches very severely.

3 A. makes new arrangements in the classes.

4 Mrs. S[amuel] A. Chandler makes a call.

5 Chastina enters upon her duties as teacher of Geography & Arithmetic. She was rather frighted but came off shiningly.[65]

6 Visit from Mother Watts, and learned from her that Sarah [Walbridge] & John Way are to be married next Monday & that John is

---

[64] Sophia Wilkins Chandler (1824–69) was the second wife of Samuel A. Chandler (1805–55), a lawyer who served as treasurer of the Peacham Academy trustees and a director of the Bank of Caledonia. His daughters, Susan E. (b. 1834) and Laura (b. 1836), were listed as students in the 1846–47, 1848, 1849, 1850, and 1852 PAC, and Laura also in 1851.

[65] See Nelson, "Vermont Female Schoolteachers," 16, on nineteenth-century Vermont women teachers. Chastina was listed among the teachers as "Mrs. C. W. Rix" in the 1849 PAC.

JOHN S. AND SARAH WALBRIDGE WAY, VERMONT, 1849

These photographs, taken in the fall of 1849, weeks after their wedding in Peacham, show John on the eve of leaving for California, sporting a fashionable beard along the jaw line, called a "saucer" or "trencher" beard. His bride wears a dark silk cape or shawl—possibly to hide her pregnancy. Sarah has a fashionable hairstyle for the 1850s, with the hair puffed wider over the ears. Her photograph probably accompanied John to California, while his remained in Peacham, where Sarah sobbed over it the night before her baby girl was born in May 1850. *Private collection.*

to leave for California.[66] Our counsel having been asked we say— Put off marriage till Clarissa [Walbridge] comes & gold hunting forever. If they will marry—do it at Mr [David] Merrills and clear out for Canada!

[*CWR*] [Wednesday, October 10] Mrs. [Sarah] Stevens visited us to day— She came in the forenoon and caught me in the midst of my ironing; which of course I was oblige to finish— She brought us a bag of apples—good! Mrs. Stevens & myself called on Mrs. [Sarah]

---

[66]John S. Way, well known to the family as he had once been a hired hand at the Watts farm, had been expected to marry Sarah Walbridge when he returned from California. Bonfield and Morrison, *Roxana's Children*, 44.

Marsh a few moments. At 2½ o'clock, I start for my task. I think it will be quite pleasant for me after getting acquainted. My classes number seventeen scholars each. Alfred has a lecture this evening on "Parliamentary Practice." He is all tired out with this day's labor. His old complaint in his throat troubles him, when he works too hard. A letter from Smith.

[ASR] [Thursday, October 11] Had a letter from Smith yesterday. Answered it to day and wrote also to Watts and to the Dartmouth Press, all chiefly on the subject of catalogue printing. Our little wife, Mrs Chastina, feels rather sober for fear she shall not succeed to her entire satisfaction in hearing her classes, which, it must be acknowledged <u>are</u> large and somewhat loose. Nevertheless we entertain good hopes of a flourishing growth & a rich harvest of gumption in the premises. "It rained and rained" but there was no "bear's den" to go into. Alfred's weight this evening is 173 lbs. Gross!

[CWR] [Friday, October 12] Pleasant day. Alf. troubled with sore throat. Both went over to father's. Picked over the rasins for Sarah [Walbridge]'s wedding cake.

[Saturday, October 13] Waked up this morning by a loud call from mother [Watts] for breakfast before daylight. A. made Aunt [Sarah] Stevens a call & then paid Ike Watts 5.00 for Stevens & some for razor & strap &c. [ASR] Had a very interesting time in Rhetorical Exs. Wrote to C. S. Smith, Watts & Dartmouth Press.[67] Trying to make out a catalogue. Chastina comes home & purchases for Sarah [Walbridge] a satchel &c—brings John [S. Way]'s pants &c &c.

[CWR] [Sunday, October 14] We attended church—heard Mr. Carpenter of Cabot—a very moderate man—from Lamentations 1–5. Sarah B. Walbridge & J. S. Way were published.[68]

[ASR] Saw Alvah [Watts] at church & at home. Clear weather & a fine breeze. Hurra!

---

[67]Charles Strong Smith (1824–98), a native of Hardwick, attended the Peacham Academy. He graduated with Alfred from the University of Vermont, class of 1848, and taught one year at the Craftsbury Academy before studying theology. Comstock, *Congregational Churches of Vermont*, 221. The Smith who is noted on October 10 and 11 as having written to Alfred was probably Charles.

[68]"Published" here refers to a reading in church of the names of those intending to marry, sometimes called banns, a practice that ended in Vermont in 1868. Gregory Sanford, Vermont State Archivist, telephone conversation with editor, summer 2003.

ASR Chastina is rather worldly—Wilmot Proviso.[69]

[*CWR*] [Monday, October 15] Have washed—heard my classes & made a cap that I am going to send to my Grandmother [Olive Brown] in Dunham. We have had calls from Louisa and Elizabeth Martin[70]—also from [Reuben] Harlow & [Alexander] Johnson.

[Tuesday, October 16] This morning I made myself ready to go home whenever they came after me. But after waiting a long while, I heard by way of Alfred from school they were not comeing. So after putting my things in order I started on foot. And in one hour after starting got home tired enough. Everything at home showed that something more than common was going to happen; & sure enough, there was to be a fearful catastrophe! Such as a wedding for instance. At six o'clock the appointed time; the guests began to arrive. When what a flutter we are in! The brides dress is not fixed yet, because the boys have but just come home from school, and were to bring fixings for the dress, & hat from Cowls shop for the <u>man</u>. So, I had to apply my fingers to the work & found they could work pretty nimble. Well the dress is done! And the bride is dressed. She looks neatly dressed in white muslin, with blonde lace in the neck & about the sleeves. A white satin sash about her waist— But what of <u>poor me</u>. Here I have been fussing & fixing others, but myself I cannot fix, because Alfred has not come with my clothes. Well after waiting untill almost all arrived, my clothes came, & <u>my man</u> too. It took me but a short time to don my wedding suit— So we were dressed alike in almost everything— Alfred & I stood up with them. Everything as it should be except that Alfred could'nt find his "standing up gloves." Poor man! he did'nt ask his wife or she would have told him they <u>were</u> in his pocket. The pair did not seem much frightened, & did first-rate. Our refreshments consisted of tea, biscuit & butter, dough nuts, cookies,

---

[69]Proposed by anti-slavery leaders in Congress, the Wilmot Proviso, first introduced in 1846, sought to exclude slavery from any new states to be carved out of the territories acquired from Mexico. Although the act failed to pass in 1846 or when it was later reintroduced, it set the stage for subsequent action, such as the Compromise of 1850, and eventually led to secession and the Civil War.

[70]The Martin sisters, Louisa (1822–96) and Elizabeth (1828–1903), were former students at the Academy, well known to the Rixes. Elizabeth Martin was one of the first Peacham girls to go to college, attending Mount Holyoke Seminary in 1851–52. Patricia J. Albright, Mount Holyoke College Archivist, letter to editor, January 22, 1988.

tarts & two sorts of cake as usual. As near as I can remember, there were 33 there besides our family—which consisted of fourteen members after adding one new one. The only thing I regret is that Clara [Walbridge] was not there. I think she must be greatly disappointed & I should not blame her if she should be provoked— We got home about 9 o'clock. On the whole we had a very good time indeed.

[Wednesday, October 17] I have been ironing—just as I finished mother [Watts] & Mrs. [Ruth Watts] Parker called. Stayed untill after dinner— Mr. [John S.] Way & his wife started for Dunham C[anada] E[ast] this morning. Alfred is making out his Catalogue. Enos Stevens called this evening to explain some astronomical illustration which he has been preparing for schools—[71] It is quite warm to day, but cloudy.

[Thursday, October 18] It is a beautiful morning quite warm— Clear & pleasant. How *we* should delight to take a ride this morning—instead of the confinement which is attendant on school-keeping, how exhilarating would be a ramble free & unconfined. For myself—I should love it. But for Alfred it would be doubly refreshing—when he is constantly engaged in his school duties. I hope he may be free from school soon. Wrote a letter to Smith. Alfred completes his catalogue. We called at Mr [David] Merrills. Had a pleasant visit. [Reuben] Harlow calls here to see about Algebra Class. Not satisfied with Miss [Laura] Freeman's teaching.

[Friday, October 19] Alfred sends off his Catalogue this morning. I called with him to [John M.] Martins store & got the outside for a cloak which cost $4.50.[72] To day is the second review in school. Alfred is just about sick with a cold; his throat troubles him very much— [*ASR*] but Chastina is in pretty good health and spirits— rather wee now and then. Called to day to let Miss [Laura] Freeman Know that some of her scholars are dissatisfied with her instructions. Poor woman. Concluded to have Mr. [S. D.] Wheeler write &c.[73] Made a call on Miss F's room and found it at home.

CWR

---

[71]Enos Stevens (1816–77) graduated from the Peacham Academy and attended Middlebury College from 1817 to 1819. He published *Rudiments of Astronomy* in 1849. Wells, *History of Barnet*, 624; *Catalogue of the Officers and Students of Middlebury College*, 242.

[72]John M. Martin was a storekeeper at Peacham Corner from 1845 into the 1860s, often advertising in the *Caledonian*. Bogart, *Peacham*, 174; *Walton's Vermont Register*, 1845 through 1860.

[73]S. D. Wheeler was listed as teacher of writing in the 1848 PAC.

ASR [Saturday, October 20] Read results of examination. Students met & chose Mr A. Rix President of a meeting had on the subject of Exhibition. Chose 1st Committee of Prudence & <u>foresight</u>. Voted to have an ex[hibition] partly old fashioned & partly original. Call from Miss [Laura] Freeman. New York Sun.

[Sunday, October 21] Went to church. Listened to Mr. Brown that is John Mattocks A.M. but P.M. staid at home and did'nt hear Mr. Brown after all.[74] Was introduced to Mrs Whitelaw. Chastina's old friend called again to day & I met her at the door & bid her welcome—at this time we should be sorry to miss her visits—though we both hope we may soon come to that state of family independence when we can not not only dispense with the presence of this old lady but even violently exclude her from our intercourse—meanwhile we shall take care that her visits are regular & of service and that she be not prematurely offended.[75] Ch & Alf.

[*CWR*] [Monday, October 22] Mr Leonard Lee of N.Y. called here last evening to take his leave as he is going to take his family [illegible due to ink spill] this week.[76] A Rainy day we have to day. I have been washing as usual—went into school as usual. Alfred is looking over pieces for the boys to speak at their exhibition. Had letters from Alvah Watts & Emeline Chapin, my Topsham friend—Received a present (from her) of a book, sent in a packet by mail. Heard by Emeline of the death of Daphne Tabor—one of my scholars when I taught school at Topsham. She was a lovely girl then, though young—kind & gentle & good.

[*ASR*] [Tuesday, October 23] Rather dry—produced nothing but wind and a night-gown. Gave the boys their subjects. Writ a parody on "chained in the market place."

---

[74] John Mattocks (1814–75) was the first son of Governor John Mattocks. He went into the ministry and moved to St. Paul, Minnesota although he must have visited his family in Peacham.

[75] It was not common for husbands to document their wife's monthly periods, but Alfred did so regularly, even adding words this month implying that he and Chastina were having intercourse when her menstrual blood flowed. Alfred seemed happy that she was not pregnant at this time, because of their precarious financial situation, but he clearly looked forward to a time when Chastina would not have her period, and thus the "old lady" would be excluded and they would welcome a baby. The entry ends with their names as if they were signing a declaration.

[76] Leonard Lee was probably the father of Leonard H. Lee, who was listed as a student in the 1845–46 and 1846–47 PAC; Edward E. Lee, who was listed as a student in the 1846–47, 1848, 1849, and 1850 PAC; and Helen Irene Lee, who was listed as a student in the 1846–47 and 1849 PAC. No reason was given for their departure.

August 17–December 31, 1849 73

[*CWR*] [Wednesday, October 24] Mr & Mrs [David] Choate made us a visit in the evening— Reading writing &c. As for myself, I do not seem to accomplish much, though I do a little of several things.

[Thursday, October 25] Alfred has enough to do to get his scholars started for their exhibition— Miss [Laura] Freeman Called & also Susan Chandler to see about her exhibition piece— My Geography class numbers 23. A huge black spot will be noticeable on this page & others. Accidents will happen, so I spilt the ink bottle on this, the table, carpet, & sundry other articles were somewhat defaced by its contents— As I have not much to do, of course, I here found some work for a while.

[Friday, October 26] Have been ironing this forenoon. [*ASR*] Chastina is rather discouraged about her class in Arithmetic—they don't learn fast enough.

[Saturday, October 27] Scholars met and made further regulations in anticipation of their coming Exhibition. An excellent spirit seems to be prevalent. [Reuben] Harlow passed in his piece last evening and left for home. [Charles] Bowker also left. [James] Merrill handed in his original.[77] Calls from Miss [Laura] Freeman, Miss [Mary] Calder & Miss Laura Blanchard.[78] We made a call in co[mpany] with Miss F[reeman] at Mr. Eastmans. Finished the "First Locomotive." Called also on Mrs. Baker, she who was Permelia Blanchard.

[*CWR*] [Sunday, October 28] Attended church. Heard Mr [David] Merrill preach in A.M. In the afternoon we listened to a sermon from the Rev. Mr. Kidder, from Math. 6.27, and a very interesting discourse he had too. We did not attend in evening. Alfred wrote most of the time.

[*ASR*] [Monday, October 29] Wrote to Oscar [Rix]. Very windy & began to rain. [*CWR*] Washing day. Had my Arithmetic class divided to day. Alfred hears part of it in the laboratory. Mrs. William Mattocks made us a call.[79] I have been fussing all the evening, so my labor has amounted to once looking over my Geography lesson & Arithmetic.

---

[77] Charles A. Bowker of St. Johnsbury was listed as a student in the 1849 PAC. James Merrill (1831–66) of Peacham was listed in 1846–47, 1848, 1849, 1850, and 1851.

[78] Laura M. Blanchard (1825–86) of Peacham, a classmate of Chastina's, was listed as a student in the 1846–47 PAC. She was soon to marry Humphrey Bennett.

[79] Eliza Brock Mattocks (1820–98) of Barnet married William Mattocks on October 3, 1839.

CWR [Tuesday, October 30] A dreadful wind last night. Could'nt sleep on account of it. This morning Charles [Watts] called & told us Sarah [Walbridge Way] & John [S. Way] had got home, & that Clarissa [Walbridge] was up to Wolcott. This forenoon I commenced copying some pieces for the "Oracle."[80] Called on Mrs. [Lucinda] Button. She is very unwell. Alfred has enough to do & more than he ought. Mrs. Blake Johnson & Clark—a fortieth cousin of Alfred's— from Groton.

[Wednesday, October 31] I have been copying all day—and we shall no doubt have something of interest to read at the Exhibition. Alfred still has pieces to correct & it is quite a work. We called during this evening at Messrs. Guy's, Sanborns, Martin's, Mrs. Dana's, Mr Chandlers, Browns & McLarry's. Had very pleasant calls. Saw quite a number of the scholars. Alfred fixes, or trys to fix the Magic Lantern—it is a rickety old thing.[81] The scholars not satisfied with Miss [Laura] Freeman. She <u>is</u> an <u>old maid</u> & I don't blame them for not liking her if she does as they represent the case. Teachers should take an interest in the affars of scholars—and instead of <u>discourageing</u>, encourage them in any of their efforts, especially those from the <u>pen</u>.

[Thursday, November 1] The month is ushered in with extremely cold weather. The girls have sent in part of their dialogue it is very good indeed. Alfred was so much pleased with it that he started for dinner with his hat on— Miss [Laura] Freeman called. [Owen] McLeran also called with his dialogue.[82] Alfred spent some time in correcting suggested corrections to him. The boys informed me that Clarissa [Walbridge] was coming home to day. I want to see her very much— Alfred is getting all tired out. I fear he will get sick before the term closes.

[Friday, November 2] Clara [Walbridge] got home. Isaac [N.

---

[80] "The Oracle" was a literary paper put out by the St. Johnsbury Academy Union Club. Established in 1844, the club was made up of young men and women from St. Johnsbury as well as students at the Peacham Academy. Fairbanks, *Town of St. Johnsbury*, 237.

[81] The magic lantern was the first piece of equipment used widely for showing images on a screen for an audience. It was later replaced by the slide projector.

[82] Owen McLeran (1829–92) of Barnet was listed as a student in the PAC in 1848 and 1849. He also served as an assistant in 1849. His name is frequently misspelled in the journal.

Watts] came over to see me. I have been ironing this forenoon. I don't pretend to do much these days except what is necessary—and attending to school business. Alfred received the Catalogues this evening—and a most splendid lot of them too. I think they are the prettyest that ever I saw. Miss [Laura] Freeman, Phebe Brock, [Owen] McLeran & Harvey were all in this evening.

[Saturday, November 3] This morning the boys found out that the Catalogues had come—so Alfred had to go up to the Academy & distribute among them. Mary Choate went & carried me home this forenoon. Clar [Walbridge] is well.[83] I do not see as one year has altered her much, she is just as she used to be—Only perhaps she appears somewhat better than she did. The friends all well when she left N.Y. Sarah [Walbridge Way] has also returned from Dunham. The Aunts Uncles & cousins all quite well there. At Wolcot & Elmore they are also yet alive. Aunt [Hannah Walbridge] Davis (my fathers sister) has lately married a widower with five children. She poor woman has had a hard time. Uncle died eleven or twelve years ago, since which time she has buried her eldest son & her only daughter.[84] John [S. Way] is fixing up a room at home, for Sarah.[85] We had a "roast turkey" & some wedding cake for supper at home to night. Alfred came over after me. Well after we arrived at our room, young Clark called with a piece for correction— The young ladies sent in their piece—& [Owen] McLeran & [James] Merrill called with theirs, so Alfred has two long dialogues & one other piece on his hands for correction. We have heard to day that Miss [Sarah] Baley's husband is dead—poor girl I pity her, she was only married <u>three weeks</u>. Miss B. or Mrs. is a fine young lady. She has met with a loss that can never be made up to her. It is now after midnight, and still <u>we</u>, that is Alfred—while I am looking on—is at work on the young ladies dialogue.

CWR

---

[83] Clara Walbridge had been teaching and studying in upstate New York, living with relatives of her late father. Bonfield and Morrison, *Roxana's Children*, 81.

[84] Sarah Walbridge Way had returned from her wedding trip and was reporting on relatives of their mother's who were now living in Canada. The Wolcott relatives whom Chastina noted were from their late father's side.

[85] With the addition of Sarah Walbridge Way, there were ten people living in the small cape-style house in the East Part. Lyman Watts must have agreed to have his stepdaughter continue to live there while her husband went to California.

CWR [Sunday, November 4] We have not been to church to day. Alfred has worked so hard that he thinks it his duty to stay at home & rest. Mother [Watts] called at noon. Brought a letter from Hubbell S. Gregory's wife saying that he had left her or she was afraid he had, not having seen him since last spring. She expects that he is here in Vermont. We have heard nothing of him, though we rather conjecture he is at Montpelier taking Daguereotypes. We hope it will prove true if we may be permitted <u>by this means to see little Augusta, sister Martha's child</u>.[86] The following was written some weeks ago—it is a copy exactly as it was first penned without the least correction.

> [ASR] It is night abroad and night within
>   And the rain is pouring down;
> And we see as we look from our window out
>   A light or two from the town.
>
> O the lonely soul on a night like this—
>   In a room shut up alone;
> Or the lonely soul in a foreign clime,
>   In a heated or frozen zone.
>
> I pity his lot and I feel his woe,
>   The more because I am here
> In my pleasant room, with a pleasant wife;
>   For myself not a doubt or fear;
>
> So my thoughts and my heart may wander away
>   And think and feel for those,
> Who are sinking in want & blight & pain
>   Beneath a world of woes.
>
> Oh my gentle wife—my own—my dear,
>   Let us think how much happier we,
> Than thousands who waste in a distant land
>   Or sink in the stormy sea.

---

[86] Chastina's older sister, Martha Walbridge Gregory, had died in 1846, leaving a daughter, Augusta, and her husband, Hubbell Seth Gregory, who later remarried. Bonfield and Morrison, *Roxana's Children*, 29–38.

    And be content—and the closer cling
      To the joys we may call our own
    For the time may come when one shall be
      With the world and its woes alone.

                            Alfred Rix to his wife.

[*CWR*] [Monday, November 5] Cloudy & somewhat rainy— Mrs. Phenton Hutchins was presented with a son last night. The mother is not yet eighteen years of age. I have washed— Went into school in p.m. Did not hear my Geography class because the girls were copying their dialogue to learn— They are so pleased with the corrections & additions that Alfred made, that it seems as though they would <u>eat him up</u>. And the scholars all love him so well. I dont know but I shall have to give him up to them. We called at Miss [Laura] Freeman's room to see about examination— The scholars are not at all pleased with Miss F. and it is not altogether w[ith]out reason—she is rather hard hearted and has no compassion for her scholars.

[Tuesday, November 6] This day is my birth day and I am twenty five years old—quite an old lady to be sure; but I do'nt know as I have any of the "old maid" traits which begin to develop themselves about this time. To be sure I always had to bear the <u>name</u> of "old maid" because they say I am <u>particular</u> but there they are mistaken for once. I mean to dun Alfred for a bit of poetry on this my birthday. I have nothing worthy of rememberance on this most important day. I have been to hear the girls rehearse their dialogue—it goes first rate. The boys are also rehearsing & Alfred has not come home yet, & its after <u>nine</u>. Alfred has about concluded not to keep Miss F[reeman] another term.

[*ASR*]   To Chastina
      This is thy birth-day, dearest wife,
      The twenty-fifth one of thy life.
      And now, as we are wont to do
      At school, let's take a short review.
      Thy baby-hood is long gone by,
      Thy girl-hood, with its dreamy eye,
      Is passed, and womanhood is now

Writing its wrinkles on thy brow.
These stages of thy being gone,
Though longed for, never can return.
The joyous sports—the thoughtless glee
Of childhood is no more for thee.
The gay young girl of lightsome heart,
Free from all evil and all art,
Sporting with sunshine bird & flower
The angel of an Eden bower,
Thou'lt be no more.—No more the maid,
That lingers in the moonlight shade,
Waiting for tones of love—most dear
That fall upon a mortal's ear.
These days have gone, and down the past
They sink too fleeting and too fast.
The sun may rise—the sun may set,
And Time dash onward, Dear, but yet,
The rolling seasons shall restore
Thy childhood and thy youth no more.
Since thy last birth-day there has been
Another and a solemn scene,
One that foretells, as mortals see,
Much of what all the rest shall be.
According to thy maiden vow
To him thou art united now,
Whose heart and hope for many a year,
Has rested on they bosom dear.
And now once more, as there comes round
The signals of this yearly bound,
I sing my song—and tell the[e] true
Of changes both the old and new;
And tell thee of my soul's deep sense
Of joy and of full recompense
For all my toil and pain & care
To wed thee my Chastina fair;
I tell thee this, that if there come

> A storm that takes me from our home
> And sends me o'er the deep sea's wave
> Or sinks me to an early grave,
> Thou wilt have this—though slight it be,
> As record of my heart and me.
>
> A. Rix

[CWR] [Wednesday, November 7] Dr [Josiah] Shedd called to see about Miss [Laura] Freeman. Susan Chandler called to get help for her piece. Mary Jane Weeks also called about her piece. [Stephen] Morrill & [Moses] Burbank called to see about their piece. James Merrill & Harvey called to see about the programe. [Reuben] Harlow called to see about sending to Boston for copies.[87] All the above have called at our room to day for assistance from Alfred. He is about tired out and I expect he will be sick—before this term is through—last evening he had to make out the programe for the exhibition—& there is some such work all the time for him.

[Thursday, November 8] Boys called this morning for a certificate to carry in to examination of teachers by Mr [Austin O.] Hubbard.[88] Alfred has gone to school without a bit of breakfast—his throat very sore— This afternoon he stayed only part of the time, came home and had a nap, for which he feels better for. This evening he rewrites the programe & writes two letters, one for the boys to send to Boston for writing copies, and the other to the printer. We also sent away sixteen catalogues to various persons. Harvey, [James] Merrill & [Robert] Samuel & [Edgar] Richardson made calls to day[89]

[Friday, November 9] Rainy & bad going— Began to iron, when little Eunice Martin called for me to assist her in her Arithmetic—so according I attended to her for some time.[90] In the afternoon went into school; did not hear my Arithmetic because the girls rehearsed

---

[87] Students listed in the 1849 PAC included Susan Chandler of Peacham, Mary Jane Weeks of Peacham, Stephen S. Morrill of North Danville, Moses A. Burbank of Haverhill, N.H., and James Merrill of Peacham. Three Harvey men were listed.

[88] Rev. Austin O. Hubbard (1800–58) was a minister in Barnet from 1845 to 1850, and served as superintendent of common schools in Caledonia County. *Caledonian*, January 13, 1849; Comstock, *Congregational Churches of Vermont*, 194; Wells, *History of Barnet*, 164.

[89] Edgar Richardson of Lyndon was listed as a student in the 1849 PAC.

[90] Eunice Martin (1838–60) was the daughter of John M. and Martha Sprague Martin.

CWR their piece at that hour. Alfred is better very much, or he could not do what he is obliged to. This evening he has had eight pieces to correct, for the young ladies to read at Exhibition. Laur Ayer & Katy Chamberlain called for their pieces.[91]

[Saturday, November 10] The young gentlemen are making considerable of a stir about the teachers examination—because some of the <u>very best</u> scholars got no certificate, while others who did not deserve them, got one.[92] This seems on the whole rather unfair. We had three classes examined this forenoon, & in afternoon the gentlemen & ladies rehearsed their pieces together— I feel rather bad <u>to night</u> on account of some things which have been said against their pieces—but hope they will come off with honor. Dr [Josiah] Shedd called. Alfred has settled with Miss F[reeman] & told her she need not stay longer—she feels somewhat disturbed about it.

[Sunday, November 11] We were about preparing to go to meeting when it was noised abroad that a boy was lost in the woods. So, Mr. [David] Choate & Alfred started—& so also did a hundred or more other people & went to the ground. They were about starting into the woods when lo the lost one appeared in sight. Young Carter had lain in the woods all night, but in the morning found his way out & came home. I attended church all day. Alfred in the P.M.

[Monday, November 12] This day is examination, so we arose very early for us. I did my washing up in good season. Clara [Walbridge] & Lyman [S. Watts] came over so we went to school. The examination passed off quite well—better they say than last year—quite a number were in & the number was two or three college students, who have before attended this school— In Evening boys rehearsed again, so Alfred has been to work from eight A.M. to 9 P.M. Clara & I called at Mr A. A. Wheelers. Clara stayed all night. Had a very pleasant call.

---

[91]Catherine Mellen Chamberlain, called Katy, was the daughter of William Chamberlain (1797–1830) and Sarah Little Gilman (1800–48) of Hanover, N.H., where her father had taught at Dartmouth. Katy was probably under the guardianship of her uncle Ezra Carter Chamberlain, whose daughters Jane and Sarah attended the Academy. She was listed as a student in the 1846–47, 1849, 1850, and 1851 PAC.

[92]An examination for those seeking a teaching certificate by the county superintendent and a local committee was held in Peacham on Thursday, November 8. *Caledonian*, October 17 and November 3, 1849. The superintendent of Caledonia County, Austin O. Hubbard, was known to be severe and stern. Wells, *History of Barnet*, 175.

[*ASR*] [Tuesday, November 13] This morning the Girls rehearse their Dialogue and prepare for P.M. We made out the Standing of the Students. P.M. 2 o'clock, All ready and at it we went and exhibited in fine style for 2 hours—did ourselves honor in all points. Evening—Clarissa [Walbridge], John [S. Way] & Sally [Walbridge Way] present—proceed to business—See "Order of Exercises." The House crowded to excess—from 600 to 700. All went off in good style— And on the whole we reckon on some real improvement and a little honor from our Exhibition. Recd a roll of slips from Boston.

[Wednesday, November 14] Woke up all tired out— So we rested a minute or two and got up, strange to say! and found visitors waiting. Cleared up at the Academy. Ironed. Settled off with a lot o'folks. Sent Mr. E[phraim] C. Brown & Weeks a hundred dollars.[93] Visited Dr [Josiah] Shedd & played possum.

[Thursday, November 15] After picking up our duds we removed our quarters from the Corner to the East Part. Played—shot rifles—sewed on small garments &c.

[Friday, November 16] Cutting cloaks & Hunting.

[Saturday, November 17] A visit. At work on cloaks & out hunting. Rambled all over the Red House swamps and finally dined on one of Tom Clark's toughest roosters in company with Geo Currier, H[arvey] Blanchard & John Way, the two last of whom first drove out the fowl & shot him while Geo. & I made a fire in the midst of the woods—where he was duly coocked & devoured with the proper fun and fixins.[94] So mote it be.

[Sunday, November 18] At home— Reading & Eating. Another visit from the old Lady, Yesterday![95]

[Monday, November 19] Washed and sewed in the P.M. Read & played. Wrote to Miss [Sarah] Bailey

[Tuesday, November 20] Recd Catalogues from I[ra] O. Miller,

---

[93] Alfred was paying his and Chastina's bill at Peacham merchants Brown and Weeks, who are listed in *Walton's Vermont Register*, 1849, 1850, and 1851.

[94] At least two in the hunting party, Harvey Blanchard (b. 1823) and John S. Way, had signed a company contract before going to California. Bonfield, "Ho for California," 10–11. George Currier (b. ca. 1827) was the oldest son of the Currier family, who were neighbors of the Wattses in the East Part.

[95] Chastina's menstruation, "the old Lady," once again indicated that she was not pregnant.

ASR A[lvah] Watts & J[ames] K. Colby.[96] Rained and snowed a little on the highlands. Began to work on Chastina's cloak. Recd from Lizzie [Fuller], Jas. M. Dickson, & Otis Ballou of Boston inclosing 1.00 for catalogues—now his due 60 cts to be paid to S. H. Rowell of Littleton, N.H. Belle Center, Logan Co. Ohio is the address of J. M. D[ickson]. Clarissa [Walbridge] had two rotten teeth pulled last week and now she is more than ever troubled with two more achers.

[Wednesday, November 21] Got Mr. [David] Currier's Wagon and horse and C. & A went to Danville where Isaac Watts and Lady met them at Evans tavern, whence altogether they went to Alvah [Watts]'s school and listened to a few exercises till noon when they dined at the Hotel and went again to the Academy where they listened too long to speeches and papers—a very good but excessively long performance.[97] Introduced to Miss [Clara B.] Clark &c—[98] Purchased a cricket and came home.[99]

[Thursday, November 22] John Way & Lady went to Uncle [Thomas] Parker's at Danville—bag and baggage. Got a bottle of Ink. Some body wrote the following line and challenged the world to produce another that would read both ways alike. <u>Lewd I did live & evil did I dwel</u>. Chastina and I claim the stakes on this—<u>God dam a ton pin tub but nip not a mad dog</u>. The first will ease you but the next will turn you to a frog.

> The Loss of Palinurus, the Pilot
> Translation from the Aeneid.
> Now on the sea swells briskly up the wind,
> And pleasing thoughts thrill through Aeneas mind.
> Quick he commands to raise aloft each mast,
> The yards run up, and sails, to catch the blast;
> And all at once the hawser work, and free,

---

[96]These men were principals of local schools: Ira O. Miller (1823–1909) at the Hinesburgh Academy, Alvah Watts at the Phillips Academy in Danville, and James K. Colby at the St. Johnsbury Academy.

[97]Alfred and Chastina attended an exhibition at the Phillips Academy with Alvah's older brother Isaac and others.

[98]Clara B. Clark was the preceptress at the Phillips Academy. *Caledonian*, August 11, 1849.

[99]A cricket is a type of footstool.

To right and left, the canvas o'er the sea:　　　　ASR
Then to and fro the spreading pinions play,
And flies the squadron on its watery way.
Bold Palinurus joys the lead to take—
The rest close crowding follow in his wake.
The damp night pass'd to near its middle bound;
The sailors lay in quiet slumber sound
On bench and oar—their limbs relaxed in rest;
Sweet quiet reigning thro' each brain & breast;
When Somnus, gliding softly from the stars,
Brought down the shadows & dispersed the airs.
Bringing to thee, O Palinurus brave,
The dreams that plunged thee to thy Ocean-grave.
In form of Phorbas from the stern he sung
These tempting accents, from his drowsy tongue.
"O Palinurus, Iasus' strong son,
Behold the ships, all safe, are moving on.
Soft blow the gales— An hour for rest, O spare!
Lay down thy head and steal thine eyes from care:
I, for a little while, thy post will take."
To whom the Pilot answered, scarce awake,
"Dost thou, O Somnus, bid me to repose
Because the waves are low and fair wind blows?
How dare I trust e'en our Aeneas' eye,
So often cheated by a cloudless sky?"
He said and to the helm clung closer while afar
His eyes were gazing on his guiding star:
When lo, the god shook o'er his head anew
Dark foliage dripping with Sethean dew;
That dew, made sleepy by the Stygian stream,
Roll'd his dull eyeballs in an airy dream.
Somnus stood o'er him till his hold grew weak,
When down he plunged him from the lofty deck;
Still holding to the helm, torn off amain,
And calling on his friends for aid in vain.

The fleet dashed on—too swiftly on, while he
Sunk down forever in the deep cold sea.
End.

See Poe's last poem on <u>Annabel Lee</u>.

[Friday, November 23] Yesterday visited Aunt [Sarah] Stevens and remained with her over night. To day went home to Mr. [Lyman] Watts. By the way last evening we received a call from Alvah [Watts] who is set agoing by us for the first time on the higher wages Strike— and leaving Danville to go with us of Peacham. Another visit from Alvah. News from Canada and Mother [Watts] goes to Cabot. Clarissa [Walbridge] in Distress all day from bad teeth. Chastina finished her cloak.

[Saturday, November 24] Went to Corner—i.e. C & Mother [Watts]—to get materials for bonnets. Letters from Chas. Brown & C. Harvey Jr. & Susan E. Rix from which last we learn that the young man who left Miss Malvina Gile in so disagreeable a predicament has twice reported himself from California by letter.[100] The sky is now fair. Another call from Alvah [Watts] with whom we had a very conscientious discussion.

[Sunday, November 25] Bad weather so we dont go to church. Read & leaned up.

[Monday, November 26] Got up by star-light. Mr [Lyman] Watts went to Wells River. Went to the Corner. Sent Cloud Harvey Jr. 2 sets of copy slips & left the Cabot School with H. Chamberlain. Paid up the P[ost] O[ffice] Bill. Recd back 8 copies of Caesar from Mr [John M.] Martin.[101] Did some dunning and came to the Hollow where I gave up two small notes to I[saac] Watts or rather to Geo. Gill his clerk, and took, by paying 4.82 cts extra, one note for $150.00 & came home without finding Aunt [Sarah] Stevens' old brass watch. Read 100 pages in "Chitty on Contracts" and went to

---

[100] The name of the man who left Malvina Gile pregnant and unmarried is not known. According to family genealogy, she married Stephen H. Sanford on June 12, 1851. Rix, *History and Genealogy of the Rix Family*, 79, where her name is spelled Melvina.

[101] John M. Martin was the Peacham Corner postmaster from 1849 to 1853. The post office was in his store. Bogart, *Peacham*, 471. On the same trip, Alfred paid his bill and picked up copies of Shakespeare's tragedy *Julius Caesar* for the Academy students.

bed—but was called up by Mr A. J. Shaw Esq of Barnet to furnish him a set of copy slips.[102] After which we rested. C. Washed & got on to the frames her quilt.

[Tuesday, November 27] Chastina got out her quilt, and Alf. read 100 pages in Chitty & played.

[Wednesday, November 28] Reading and Sewing—Ironing & head-ache.

[Thursday, November 29] Thanksgiving Day— Recd a letter from Mrs [Louisa] Balch. Report of State Sup. In. Com. Sch. & Report of Vt. Bible Soc.[103] Wrote to Dustan [Walbridge]. Went to church & listened to Mr. [A. G.] Button on "Natur" & "No man lives to himself" i.e. "By himself" (Except bachelors, happy souls!) Visited the Exhibition of our Lord's Last Supper in Statuary at the Cong. Vestry. Worth seeing—though only a few of the people of Peacham seem to think so.[104]

---

[102] Albert John Shaw (b. 1830) of Barnet was listed as a student in the 1849 and 1850 PAC. Wells, *History of Barnet*, 598. Copy slips were used for teaching young students how to write.

[103] The "Report of the State Superintendent for Common Schools, 1849" ended with an aspiration for Vermont schools to be "cheap enough for the poorest, good enough for the wealthiest." *Caledonian*, December 29, 1849.

[104] This statuary exhibition came to Peacham from St. Johnsbury. *Caledonian*, November 17, 1849. It is unclear where it originated.

By turning to the 51st page [the page with Alfred's drawings] it will be seen that we have been to "Tea." There's some substance in Thanksgiving. Fasting was to us <u>always</u> a dry and profitless exercise, but Thanksgiving [w]as uniformly refreshing and acceptable a season. The World will not come to an end so long as its people continue to eat & give thanks—this is an India-rubber bellied world and it will hold a great deal without either losing its equilibrium or "busting its biler"— But let it only fast & starve itself and it will be likely to bring on the Millenium right off—a time when men's gravity has become so far diminished that they fly away into the air on a

broomstic or any thing else. This has been one of <u>the</u> Thanksgivings. *ASR*
A call from Misses Currier & Spencer.[105]

Thanksgiving-Song

Of all the days that natur made,
    Thanks-giving day for me,
Is rather most the cutest one,
    For reasons two or three.

The first is this—that on this day
    All work is put aside,
And if you've any fun on hand,
    You're bound to let'er slide.

Your Sunday, everlasting, long
    And sober seeming look
Dont mount your face; but with a grin
    It opens like a book.

Your heart and soul and gizzard and
    Your verry belly feels
Chock full of mirth; and first you know
    You're kicking up your heels.

The next one of my reasons is,
    That everybody sees,
At home or somewhere else, a friend
    To quiz and kiss and squeeze.

The Mother and the daughters meet,
    The father and his sons;
The younger kiss the older kin
    The old the younger ones.

A thousand ties about to break
    Are strengthened by this day;

---

[105] Like the Curriers, the Spencers were neighbors in the East Part. Alma Currier (b. 1835) was probably the visitor from the Currier family. The Spencers could have been represented by any one of the five girls born between 1832 and 1841.

ASR

And many a saddened soul is sent
    Rejoicing on his way.

The last and largest reason is,
    The Turkies, plums and pie
That fill my maw and stuff me out
    Until I almost die.

Then Hail to thee, thou good old day,
    Thou pet of all men living;
And luck and mirth & joy to thee
    Thou glorious Thanksgiving.

                    Chastina & Alfred Rix
          Peacham, Nov. 29, 1849, East Part Home.
              Sic transit gloria thanksgiving dei!

[Friday, November 30] Wrote to Mrs Louisa C. Balch. Read Law. Commenced making Lyonese dress. Visit from I[saac] Watts, Mr Aldrich & Mr. George & ladies.

[Saturday, December 1] Last evening, we were also visited by Eb[enezer] and & his two sisters, Betsey and Abigail, but it has appeared to us proper that the event should be placed among the chronicles of this day because <u>one</u> of the trio left too late to admit of being recorded yesterday.[106] Went to the Corner—got Clara [Walbridge]'s bonnet, letter from Carleton. Settled with Aunt [Sarah] Stevens &c. Snow for the first time of any amount. J[ohn S.] Way & Sarah [Walbridge Way] & Mrs [Ruth Watts] Parker arrive. Tina quit work & went to play with the "Stomach Ache" as of old—this evil has not showed itself for some 12 weeks. Hard labor has now, as formerly, brought it on.

[Sunday, December 2] Both at home. Tine quite sick with "that same old coon."

[Monday, December 3] Washed—Snowed—Calls from Messrs

---

[106] The Blanchards were neighbors in the East Part. Betsey was listed as a student in the 1846–47 and 1849 PAC; her sister, Abigail (1831–62), was listed in 1849, and their brother, Ebenezer Blanchard (1827–73), in 1846–47.

Burnham, Hatch & A[lvah] Watts, who left an abundance of books for examination.

[Tuesday, December 4] Letter from Mrs [Louisa] Balch—answered it. Miss [Sophia] Leavitt is to come—[107] Looked for a boarding for Miss L. Moved to the Corner. Visited with [Trustram and Lucinda] Sanborns.

[Wednesday, December 5] Opened school with 40 scholars all alone. Began to snow. Trimmed bonnets.

[Thursday, December 6] Spent the day at school—C. at home on her dress. Weltha Ann Cory & her Sister Sophia came from Canada or thereabouts, took dinner & tea with them or they with us, & at night moved to Miss [Mary] Calders.

[Friday, December 7] Oh the Miss Phippses have come! C. took her classes for the term, viz. Arithmetic, Geography & French. A call from John Balch Esq. of Littleton, N.H. accompanied by Miss Stevens of Barnet, Miss Sophia Leverett & Sister. They left Miss Sophia who is to aid in our school. Went to Mr [Nehemiah] Bradlee's to get her boarded, &c.

[Saturday, December 8] Played & laughed all day. Both! Call from Thos. S. Knight.[108]

[Sunday, December 9] Went to church & behaved decently—and did'nt fall asleep but once. Tine went to show her new cloak and bonnet and Alf. to hear what the folks had to say. Some go to hear the preaching—such are some green. On the next page will be found a quantity of doggrel—the first: "the right whereof Chastina claims as author," to wit.
>
> Dear Coz,
>   I take my pen in hand
>   To scribble you a letter,
>   To let you know my health is good
>   And hope your own is better;

---

[107]Sophia A. Leverett of Littleton, N.H., was listed as a student in the 1850 PAC. She agreed to help in the school, although she does not seem to have been called a preceptress. Her name was often misspelled as Leverette or Leavitt.

[108]Thomas S. Knight of Ryegate was listed as a student in the 1846–47, 1849, and 1850 PAC.

ASR

And tell you that our dog is dead;
   Poor Rover is no more!
He died as nobly as a dog
   Has ever died before.

He started out one sunny day
   To feast his canine eyes
On Nature's beauties and to take
   Some little exercise:

He wandered on until he came
   To where the high-ways met,
And there beside a large grey stone,
   Down on his tail he set.

A cruel neighbor passing by,
   Found Rover there alone
He seized him and the poor dog's head
   He pounded on the stone.

Thus Rover died, our faithful dog,
   The truest of his kind;
And we do mourn for him & think
   His like no more to find.

Our other folks are all as well
   As usual, 'cepting Granny
She's got the fits. And so no more!
               Your loving
                  Cousin, Annie

[Monday, December 10] Mr. [Olando] Carter buried.[109] Miss [Sophia] Leverett began her labors. Mrs [Aurilla] Choate overwhelmed with cousins. A pretty fair day's work in school to-day.

[Tuesday, December 11] Cold and blowing from the North & so blew along Miss [Laura] Freeman, as they say. School rather unruly—we are a little cross. Call from Ann Cameron. Pleasant evening in doors. TomTit.[110]

---

[109] Olando Carter died at age eighty-five. *Caledonian*, January 19, 1850.

[110] "TomTit" might be a reference to the English fairytale about a small magical creature who helps a young woman with her impossible sewing requirements.

[CWR] [Wednesday, December 12] Pleasant but cold. Miss [Laura] Freeman left town and we did'nt see her. Dustin [Walbridge] called this evening. I go into school these days but do nothing else of consequence, & this not a great deal. Pair of shoes sent from Danville?

[ASR] [Thursday, December 13] Nothing new. We find no owner of the shoes. Snowed a little. On the whole we are having a fine time & expect to do a pretty fair business in fun and frolic this winter. Chastina's Old <u>Acquaintance</u> came to day without giving notice— She was not expected these two days.[111]

[Friday, December 14] Harvey Clark called for the Academy. Mr & Mrs [David] Choate went visiting. And the children had what they called a great time.

[Saturday, December 15] Subscribed for the New Y[ork] Tribune. Dr [Luther] Parker bargains for Dr [Francis] Brewer's place.[112] First Saturday's exercises this term. Made writing books.

[CWR] [Sunday, December 16] We attended church both in the A.M. & P.M. Laura & Mary Blanchard were published to Humphry Bennett & George Dana. A notice was also given out that the ladies of Peacham are to meet & plan about raising funds to carpet & get blinds for the Meeting house. Gave the history of Queen Esther as a sabbath school lesson. Wrote letters to Oscar [Rix] & H[ubbell] S. Gregory. Read in evening in "Homer's Odessy"—translation.

[Monday, December 17] Warm & thawing this morning. <u>Washed of course</u>. In evening Mrs. Fenton Hutchins visited here with her new baby six weeks old—& herself eighteen to day. Quite motherly she is too. I must say here in regard to Alfred's health, that he is very poorly off these days as he has out grown almost all of his clothes—and poor boy! he is so fat he can hardly wag. Then too he is so good natured that we have a great deal of fun in our leisure hours. I believe good nature will make peopl in "good order."

[Tuesday, December 18] I am somewhat perplexed this afternoon on account of my classes, one of which troubles me greatly because of their "greenness." We this evening had an uncommon amount of

---

[111] Chastina must have been keeping close track of her periods and had not expected the early appearance of this one.

[112] Dr. Luther Fletcher Parker (1821–98), a classmate of Alfred's at the Peacham Academy and the University of Vermont, had set up his medical practice in Barnet and hoped to be appointed the lecturer on anatomy and physiology at the Academy. According to the 1850 PAC, that place went instead to Dr. Asahel Farr.

CWR work to do—making writing books for school— To help us a little first came an invitation to visit with Mr & Mrs Blake who were at Mr [David] Choate's—next a call from Weltha & Sophia Cory. Then Mrs [Betsey] Brown & Mary Jane Weeks who stayed part of the evening—& last came Louisa Bradlee & Miss [Sophia] Leverette who stayed the remaining part of the evening. We had a good visit indeed—but had to sit up until midnight to pay for it.

[*ASR*] [Wednesday, December 19] This has been a day of bad luck to the male portion of our family, for 1st. he let fall the drawer containing some 20 ink-bottles & 40 writing books & as many pens and of course broke the bottles & blacked & spoiled the books— So the evening was spent making new ones. 2d Simply leaned back in his chair, a joint slyly opened & took in a fold of his new 20 dollar broadcloth coat and when he got up suddenly (as he <u>always</u> does, you know) a large patch was torn clean out of the back forever & ever, amen.

[Thursday, December 20] Mr [David] Choate started with his butter for Wells River—[113] Thaws & Rains a little. Mary Choate preparing for her party. Chastina writes her billets for her in this form, viz, "Miss Mary B. Choate will be happy to see Mr &c. at her father's this evening at 6 o'clock. (Dated) Dec. 21." This is the Wedding evening for Humphrey H. Bennett & Laura Blanchard, also for Geo. Dana & Mary Blanchard.[114] It rains pretty briskly. Good luck to em.

[Friday, December 21] Scholars dont behave very well, scold em some. Chastina helps Mrs [Aurilla] Choate prepare for the party. Letter from Chas. S. Smith. Evening. Some 40 young folks of the place congregate and wear out carpets, daub mop-boards and eat all before them—behave as cunning as possible and go home at 9½ o'clock. First introduced the play of chasing with hands behind the back.

[Saturday, December 22] Heard Saturday's usual school exercise & went with Mr. [Samuel] Chandler to see about hiring Mrs. Dana's

---

[113] By November 1848, a railroad had been built as far as Wells River, allowing local farmers to send perishable products to Boston. Wells, *History of Barnet*, 235; Sherman, Sessions, and Potash, *Freedom and Unity*, 234. On November 26, Lyman Watts was also noted as having gone to Wells River, probably on the same errand.

[114] Rev. David Merrrill officiated at the Peacham weddings of Laura Blanchard to Humphrey Bennett and Mary S. Blanchard (1829–59) to George Dana (1824–95). *Caledonian*, January 19, 1850.

house. Saw Mr. Kidder & Mr Wm Dana & their wives.[115] P.M. C. & *ASR* A. both revisit Mrs. Dana's and also Weltha Ann [Cory]. Play & tell Riddles till supper—and then sit down in a warm room and hear the sleet rattle against the windows—it makes us feel very comfortable and also causes a thought or so for such as are in the same weather and out of the same comforts. I am greatly distressed about what to put into my wife's Christmas Stocking. I expect she will hang it out and it has got to be such a monstrous long and large thing that my hopes are rather slim for filling it. <u>nous verrons</u>.

[Sunday, December 23] Stormy day—At home. Read News & Pope's Odissey.[116]

[*CWR*] [Monday, December 24] Warm & snowy, very bad walking—as I am obliged to try it every day, I am a pretty good judge. The first number of New York Tribune came to day. Received a letter from a Miss Smith of Craftsbury, a former scholar of the academy here— She wants some dozzen examples wrought out in the Arithmetic. Alfred sent them this evening.

[Tuesday, December 25] I wish you a merry Christmas![117] I did hope the little fat old man would make us a call—& so with feverish anxiety I awaited the arrival of morning—when to my astonishment the old man in miniature stood upon the table with out stretched <u>hand</u> pointing to a well filled stocking which contained the following articles. Hair comb, thimble, dumb-watch, jews-harps, India rubber, steel ring, glass pen holder, spruce gum, shawl pin, thread & cambric for covering books &c. I think the old fellow did well only he rather made a mistake in bestowing children's playthings. Thanks, thanks for the gentle hint—& the playthings. This evening we were invited to spend the evening at Dr. [Josiah] Shedd's. They had a party select, that is only a few some dozen or so. We had a very pleasant time— Though were obliged to sit up until almost midnight.

---

[115]William Varnum Dana (1816–92) was married to Ann Eliza Muncey (d. 1850).

[116]On December 16, Alfred wrote that he was reading Homer's *Odyssey* in translation, and a week later he identified the translator as the English poet Alexander Pope (1688–1744).

[117]Chastina's mention of Christmas is the first time in the family sources that the holiday is noted and celebrated with gift giving, although the gifts appear to have been only from Alfred to Chastina. See Nissenbaum, *Battle for Christmas*, for the history of New England Christmas celebrations.

CWR [Wednesday, December 26] It has been extremely cold, but pleasant. Received a letter from Oscar [Rix]. We were glad to hear from him, as it has been a long time since we have heard. We have commenced making out cards for examinations. Covered the Journal.

[Thursday, December 27] Went to a donation visit to Mr [A. G.] Button's the methodist minister we had a very pleasant time, all young people, & no married ones excepting us, & I suppose we ought to be reckoned among the old ones.[118] We always obliged to sit up late after we have been out in the evening so there is not so much pleasure in it after all. Gave the minister $1.00.

[ASR] [Friday, December 28] Call from Miss [Sophia] Leverett. Chastina sheds tears because she thinks her education not equal to her position—Alfred comforts her as much as possible. She is naturally modest and wants self-confidence. Hope she will soon feel better.

[Saturday, December 29] We have now been married 5 months and if so long a time was ever spent happily by a new married couple it has been by us. We hope every succeeding 5 months may be as joyous as these. Visited Aunt [Sarah] Stevens, where I saw Mrs. [Laura] Bennett, & Father Watts' folks in company with Mrs & Mr [David] Choate. Mr. & Mrs. [David] Currier present. Carried J[ohn] S. Way & vol. of Am. Encyclopedia. Came home at nine. Wrote Oscar [Rix].

[Sunday, December 30] Went to church and listened to Mr. [David] Merrill. He advises all to settle up at the year's end. Cloud Harvey Jr. came home from his school.[119] Rather snowy under-foot.

[Monday, December 31] Disappointed in looking for a message from Oscar [Rix]. Called [Andrew J.] Brown & O[scar] Guy to an account.[120] Spent the evening with Mr. Steele & Lady & Mr. [David] Choate & Lady. Thus ends the year. On the whole as eventful an one as we can often expect.

---

[118]A donation party, usually held annually, supplemented the minister's meager salary, with church and community members contributing produce, wood, clothing, furniture, cash, and other articles. Bogart, *Peacham*, 423.

[119]Cloud Harvey, Jr. (b. 1829), of Barnet was listed as a student in the 1846–47 and 1848 PAC. Wells, *History of Barnet*, 478.

[120]Andrew J. Brown and Oscar Guy (b. ca. 1835), both of Peacham, were listed as students in the 1848, 1849, and 1850 PAC.

CHAPTER THREE

Married Life, Teaching, and Politics
January 1–May 14, 1850

> *We have about concluded to quit teaching and
> go into the Law Study so long neglected.*
> — ALFRED

> *Alfred went to the Hollow with me to get me [cloth for] a new dress...
> Have'nt had many sleigh rides this year, so a short one even, seems good.*
> — CHASTINA

ON NEW YEAR'S DAY OF 1850, ALFRED TOOK UP THE JOURNAL, having decided that it was "proper at this time . . . to state our case a little more at large." He then wrote an assessment of where he and Chastina stood in the town of Peacham and proclaimed his satisfaction with their position. They were doing fine financially: they earned a clear annual salary of $500 and had saved enough to lend money at interest. They were healthy and happy. They had an active social life, and their work at the Academy was rated highly. Alfred seemed to feel that their goal of recognition and status in Peacham had been achieved.

Chastina's brother-in-law John S. Way left for California the following week along with seventeen other men from the area. Twelve of the prospective miners had signed a "company contract," a two-page document common among New Englanders in the early years of the gold rush. They felt that greater success would be possible in an unknown place if they worked with men they knew and trusted. The signers agreed that each would pay his own passage and contribute an equal proportion for the purchase of mining tools. Also, each would "render all necessary aid and assistance" should one of their number become sick. They "further agreed that the proceeds of our labor shall belong to the whole of us jointly." Most company contracts were rescinded almost immediately after the group landed in California, as the men became familiar with the mining scene; and as the gold rush became familiar, the use of company contracts ceased.[1] Although the local newspapers from Danville and St. Johnsbury had been full of California news, this may have been the first time that someone the Rixes knew personally had packed his carpetbag and left town for the mines. The men had little concrete information to guide them on their impending adventure, but they were full of hope and high expectations. Alfred and Chastina bade them goodbye and wished them success, even as they feared for their safety "on their long & toilsome journey."

In addition to California gold, the themes of temperance and abolition were prominent in New England culture at the time. The 1820 Peacham grand list reported eight distilleries; many others went unreported. Hard cider, malt liquors, and home-brewed wine were part of everyday life in Peacham. Slowly, however, temperance sentiment grew as some families suffered from the husbands' drinking. Led by the church, and especially by Rev. David Merrill, the Peacham Temperance Society was organized in 1842. A law prohibiting the sale of "ardent spirits" passed in Peacham in 1845, requiring a license to sell medicinal liquor, but the majority was not decisive, and the law came up again in 1850. Neither Alfred nor Chastina expressed strong feelings toward the subject, although they attended temperance meetings, and Alfred expressed disgust when a local merchant was fined for selling liquor.[2]

Even more soul-stirring was the movement against slavery. Vermont's first constitution, that of 1777, outlawed slavery, and the "Declaration of Rights of the Inhabitants of the State of Vermont" proclaimed that "all men are born equally free and independent." Anti-slavery societies sprang up, with Peacham organizing the third in the state in August 1833. Peacham historian Ernest Bogart wrote that "humanitarian, religious, political, and economic factors all conspired to promote the movement against slavery." Alfred and Chastina were among those opposed to slavery, following the strong sentiments of Thaddeus Stevens, Alfred's cousin. Born in neighboring Danville, his mother, whose husband had deserted the family, moved to Peacham so that her four sons could be educated at the Academy. After graduating from Dartmouth, Thaddeus settled in Pennsylvania, where he

---
[1] Bonfield, "Ho for California," 10–11.
[2] Bogart, *Peacham*, 208–16.

soon was elected a member of the House of Representatives and became the most outspoken anti-slavery advocate in Congress. His support of education, libraries, and especially abolition made him famous throughout the North. His annual visits to his mother in Peacham were widely reported in the local newspapers, as were his speeches against slavery. The Rixes' interest in national politics just now was focused on California being admitted to the union as a state free of slavery, although the reason for this interest is never given.[3]

Alfred was involved with a new project, to which he was devoting a lot of time and energy. Some of the townsmen of Peacham were preparing to open a New England Protective Union cooperative store, and Alfred was one of the primary backers of the plan. He and Chastina had even decided to invest some of their own money in the venture. The 1840s had seen the rise of the consumer cooperative movement, which eliminated the middleman—the country store—and thus reduced the cost of products to workers and farmers. On January 16, 1840, a group of Peacham townsmen founded the Farmers and Mechanics Mercantile Company of Peacham, a stockholding store financed by about fifty shareholders, including Hazen Merrill, Simon Blanchard, Alanson Stevens, Lyman Watts, David Choate, Thomas Watts, and especially Isaac Watts, who bought twenty shares, by far the most. Isaac Watts was hired to run the business for $500 per year, board included. The minutes of this group do not describe why it was not profitable, but on March 16, 1841, the executive board agreed "to sell out their interest in the store" to Isaac Watts.[4]

With this experience behind them, some of the same men decided to join the New England Protective Union, which had a central agency in Boston, purchasing goods—from hardware and crockery, to lamp oil and boots, to farm products—directly from the manufacturers and farmers at a distinct price advantage over the country store, which handled everything on credit. The greatest number of these Union stores were in Massachusetts; Vermont was next, with fourteen stores opened in 1849 alone. The first Vermont store was in Winooski Falls, followed by Montpelier and five others in the state. Peacham's store was number 107 in New England, opening in David Choate's home. Alfred joined the organizers, and because of his involvement he became the target of the local merchants, who feared competition from the new store. Ephraim Brown, in particular, tried to

---

[3]Ibid., 216–21.
[4]Farmers and Mechanics Mercantile Company of Peacham, Minutes and Records, Vermont Historical Society, AC 840116.

do "injury" to him and the Academy by criticizing his work as Academy principal. Alfred met with him with no satisfaction. "They are going to drive us out of town," Alfred wrote, but he knew he had the upper hand and would pursue the matter later.[5]

Changes were taking place in domestic duties, too. While making a rug for their rooms after also mending Alfred's "darned pair of breeches," Chastina expressed her frustration with all of her work, and the two agreed to purchase a rug "from the store." Whether this was a case in which store-bought rugs were seen as more attractive or prestigious, this small gesture records a transition from home industry to ready-made retail purchasing. Even so, Chastina continued to make her own clothes from purchased cloth, and mending still took up much of her time.

Even before the problems with Ephraim Brown, Alfred had been looking beyond his tenure at the Academy. Since leaving his father's farm, he had been working toward the day he could enter the legal profession. From the beginning of his student days at the University of Vermont, he had described his "leisure time" as being "devoted to the study of Law."[6] The university curriculum did not include law as a separate discipline, but Alfred had attended some occasional classes on "Laws of Nature and Nations" taught by a philosophy professor, Joseph Torrey.[7] Back in Peacham, even as he chafed under the yoke of his duties as Academy principal, he still managed to study law on the side. But with the addition of his activities related to the Union store, he was beginning to feel the strain. It was time, he now decided, to focus on his legal studies.

In early February, Alfred asked the president of the Academy trustees, Dr. Josiah Shedd, whether it would be possible for him to step down as principal but continue as a part-time teacher. Dr. Shedd, with whom Alfred had enjoyed an easy exchange of ideas, eventually consented. Alfred then approached his University of Vermont classmate Ira O. Miller, a teacher in Chittenton County, to see whether he would be interested in assuming the principalship. Ira agreed to move to Peacham and serve as principal for the spring term, with Alfred teaching only two classes, Latin and mathematics.

---

[5]Rozwenc, *Cooperatives Come to America*, 8–9, 12–15, 57–62, 71–73, 125–27. Bogart reports incorrectly that the NEPU began in Peacham in 1854; *Peacham*, 274.

[6]Alfred, Burlington, Vt., to Hubbell and Martha Walbridge Gregory, Jackson, Mich., October 31, 1844, private collection.

[7]Sylvia J. Bugbee, Reference Specialist, Special Collections, Bailey-Howe Library, University of Vermont, e-mail message to editor, January 9, 2009. The lecturer for these occasional classes on the law was Joseph Torrey (1789–1867), professor of intellectual and moral philosophy from 1842 to 1867.

February also brought John S. Way's first letters to Sarah since he had left for California. They were circulated among others who were eager to hear the news, including Alfred. In the first letter, dated February 1 and written while they were crossing the Isthmus of Panama, John reported that most of the men in the company had been seasick on the Atlantic, and in his opinion the food they were eating "was not half as good as New England Hog's have." He said that the weather on the isthmus was "hot enough to cook eggs if we could get them to rost," but the company was "all in good health and Spirits." In fact, he reported, "they have been fiddleing and dancing while I am writing this letter." John and company arrived in San Francisco on February 21, thirty-four days after departing New York. According to a second letter, dated February 27, he had "rented a small Cottage for the Small Sum of 30 dollars for one week and the house would not of cost in the states more than $25 at the Most But we are getting used to California Prices very fast." After working a day and a half in San Francisco, John was debating whether to charge $15 or $20 for his work before heading to the mines.[8]

Alfred's own thoughts continued "in search of location for us" to settle. It was obvious that he was growing restless with his situation in Peacham. Chastina, too, now realized that their future lay elsewhere. When she was asked in January to make a donation toward carpeting for the church, she gave grudgingly, noting that she should not have been approached, for it was clear that they did not intend to stay in Peacham and thus "shall probably never have any benefit of it."

Chastina remained firm in her dedication to maintaining the journal, but by the time the entries in this chapter were written, Alfred had seemingly lost his initial enthusiasm for their joint undertaking, especially as he felt that there was little to record these days. In order to keep the discipline going, the couple devised a punishment for neglecting to write. They agreed that the person who missed a turn would have to "write from the time the Journal stops to the present moment." Alfred was the first to have to write two days in a row, and his entries show that he was tiring of this duty, summing up a day's activities with "Nothing!" and "Nothing at all."

If entry writing had turned into a chore for Alfred, he at least could take some pleasure in the ink he was using. Ever the inventor, he had been experimenting with making his own ink—and "Superior Rix Ink" it was, he wrote. He noted its "beautiful dark clear & deep blue" color, "fearing

---

[8]John S. Way, Panama, to Sarah Walbridge Way, Peacham, February 1, 1850; and John S. Way, San Francisco, to Sarah Walbridge Way, Peacham, February 27, 1850, both private collection.

lest it may change its complexion & so bring our good taste in question with after generations." He may have had the first of those "after generations" on his mind: Chastina was finally pregnant.

[*ASR*] [Tuesday, January 1, 1850] New Year's Day. Happy New Year! We awoke this morning after sunrise—shame on us—and, strange to say, got up—shook ourselves and dressed as usual. We think it proper at this time—it being the commencement of a new year—to state our case a little more at large. We are boarding out. D[avid] W. Choate, Esq. is our Keeper. We furnish our own rooms, do our own washing and pay 3.00 a week. We are employed in teaching in the Peacham Academy. Our salary is $300.00 [$800.00] a year with all the tuition. From this there must be subtracted about 300. for wood, repairs and extra instructors leaving about 500$ for us to live upon. We mean to manage to lay by about 300 of this yearly.[9] We have at interest at present $400. $100 with E[phraim] C. Brown & $300 with Isaac Watts.[10] We mean to teach we know not how long and eventually study Law. Personally we are pretty well to do. Chastina weighs 124, while Alf. goes quick at 184. Our health is excellent. The people seem to be well suited with us as teachers. These are some of our chief concernments. Today we have spent in making out cards for Review. A Ball, Jubilee or Oyster & Fish party was off this evening at our Hotel.[11]

[Wednesday, January 2] At work as usual. Chastina called at Mrs. [Betsey] Brown's. Weltha [Cory] & Sister call. C. making shirt. The curiosity box from Oscar [Rix] has not come.

[Thursday, January 3] All things as usual till about evening, when Alf. called on Mrs. Dana— Bought nuts & raisins for cousins &

---

[9] In total Alfred collected $800 in tuition and paid out $300 in expenses, leaving him a salary of $500.

[10] Local merchants Brown and Watts needed to borrow funds to invest in their store merchandise. The Peacham Grand List recorded the real estate and personal property of each resident. The 1850 listing shows Alfred S. Rix with a $1 poll tax, but with no bank savings or stock. When Alfred and Chastina had money that was not needed for daily expenses, they loaned it at interest; thus their "interest at present $400." Had he put this in a bank, the institution would have been required to report to the town the sum on account.

[11] The hotel at Peacham Corner, the White House Hotel, was located on the west side, north of the stores. Built about 1802, it burned in 1851. Scott, *Pictorial History*, 52–53.

about 7 o'clock as we were peeping out at the window we saw them driving like Jehu down along the street till they came to the fork in the roads when the horses took the wrong & John [S. Way] drew them into the right road so as to upset the whole sleigh load into the snow.[12] We helpt pick them up and found them to our great joy all whole. When they were in we found them to consist of the following named individuals, viz. J[ohn] S. Way, Esq., Lyman S. Watts, Earl Guyer, Harriet Guyer, Elizabeth Taylor of New York and Clarissa Walbridge, to say nothing of Mrs. Sarah W[albridge] Way & Tonker! Dustan [Walbridge] came also.[13] Therefore we had a fine visit. Mr [David] Choate & wife aided & Mary [Choate]. We gave Elizabeth a dollar to go in to make up for her lost trunk. It will be inferred no doubt, that we eat the nuts & raisins spoken of above, but that no one may fall into a mistake on the point we here make a full statement to that effect. This must be considered our New Year bust. We want to full-fill this [journal] page. We therefore say that this will be likely to effect our object especially if we put in this one additional line. Amen.

[Friday, January 4] To day came off our first review for this term. All went off well. Nihil Plus.[14]

[*CWR*] [Saturday, January 5] Stayed at home all day & sewed, my time for sewing is somewhat limited as I go into school in the afternoon; then studying & reading must be attended to some. We have been reading the Biography of the Rev. Wilbur Fisk, & find it quite interesting.[15] As it is proper to mention the marriage of our acquaintances, I will say that Thursday eve this week, F. B. Weeks & Mary Goodenough, residing in our village—were joined in the holy bonds of matrimony.[16] Thus making seven couples which have been married in our town in less than six months, our humble selves being first—

ASR

---

[12]In 2 Kings 9:20, Jehu drove his chariot "furiously."
[13]Children of the siblings of Chastina's deceased father, Daniel A. Walbridge, who hailed from Wolcott and upstate New York, accompanied Chastina's sisters and brothers.
[14]Translation: "nothing much."
[15]Wilbur Fisk (1792–1839), a graduate of the Peacham Academy, became a prominent Methodist minister, educator, and theologian. The Rixes were reading *The Life of Willbur Fisk, D.D., First President of the Wesleyan University* (1842) by Joseph Holdich (1804–93).
[16]Rev. David Merrill married Benjamin F. Weeks (d. 1907) and Mary C. Goodenough on January 3; both were from Peacham. *Caledonian*, January 19, 1850.

[*ASR*] [Sunday, January 6] Attended church A.M. P.M. we came home with little Alice [Watts] & Elly [Watts]. After Service went over to the East Part, took tea with our folks and bade John S. Way, Goodbye.[17] Charles [Watts] came home with us.

[Monday, January 7] Blew up the students for ill-behavior. Gave Dr. [Josiah] Shedd $1.00 for the Bible Society.[18] Chastina washed as usual. The California Company started to day on their long & toilsome journey & labor. We have no hope that they will all, 18 in number, ever come back alive. But still we say, "Success to ye! Bet you'll find more yellow things than gold—more blue one than the sky." We have <u>looked</u>, according to direction, for Oscar [Rix]'s curiosity box, each night for a week.

[Tuesday, January 8] To day to our utter astonishment nothing of importance has taken place. Chastina first suggests the plan of going to Littleton &c. Warm & Pleasant. Busy!

[Wednesday, January 9] All's well. P.M. <u>The Old lady arrived</u>.[19] Called up E. G. Kavanaugh & E. C. G. Martin. Mr & Mrs. [David] Choate start for Barre.

[*CWR*] [Thursday, January 10] Had a great time. "Father & Mother [Choate] gone," so the <u>children</u> have real good times. Ironed in the forenoon, & helped Mary [Choate]. Alfred went to the Hollow with me to get me a new dress. Had a good ride. Have'nt had many sleigh rides this year, so a short one even, seems good. Received a letter from A. B. Hadsdor of Granville, GA.

[*ASR*] [Friday, January 11] Mr. [David] Choate & Wife arrived. Rainy & Snowy. Heard of an invention for making oxygen & hydrogen from water without cost. Recd. the President's Message from T[haddeus] Stevens Esq.[20] Chastina took cold in wading through the slosh to school.

---

[17] John left the next day for California. Bonfield, "Ho for California," 10–18. The *Caledonian* was the first local newspaper to list men from the area who were going to California; an article on January 19, 1850, named eighteen men along with their home towns.

[18] Dr. Josiah Shedd and his wife, Lydia Chamberlain Shedd, were supporters, both through their lives and through their estates, of the American Bible Society, founded in 1816 in New York. PHA-MS, Shedd, Josiah; ibid., Account Book, Lydia Shedd.

[19] Chastina's menstruation indicated that she was not pregnant.

[20] Thaddeus Stevens, serving in Congress as a representative from Lancaster, Pennsylvania, sent copies of speeches from Washington to his cousin Alfred, including President Zachary Taylor's message to Congress in which he approved of the admittance of California as a free state. *Caledonian*, January 5, 1850.

[Saturday, January 12] Reading Newspapers & making Tina's new dress. We have about concluded to quit teaching and go into the Law-Study so long neglected. Mr. Wheeler's little girl died.[21]

[Sunday, January 13] Attended church A.M. at Bell-House and listened to the Rev. Mr. Delano of North Haverhill N.H.[22] He is very pecoolar. P.M. Attended the funeral at the Chapel. Wrote to Oscar [Rix] & the Sisters. That's all.

[Monday, January 14] Nothing of importance.

[Tuesday, January 15] Went to Cabot to the Temperance Meeting. In company with Geo. Clarke Jr. & some others in his big carriage.[23] Pleasant day. Put up at Bliss' Hotel & met many of our old friends there. P.M. Listened to an Address from Mr. Rev. [W. W.] Thayer of Lyndon, &c.[24] Soon after our arrival home Chastina was taken with a violent headache & chilliness. Called in the Dr & she took a sweat & felt better.

[Wednesday, January 16] Raked down my scholars most sweetly. Chastina gets better. Another call from the Dr. & Physic. Getting better. Letter from Oscar [Rix].

[Thursday, January 17] Chastina quite well. Call from Mother [Watts] and Daniel Lee & Aunt [Sarah] Stevens. Attended the Donation visit at Mr. [David] Merrill's. Gave a dollar. Saw Watts & every body else.

[Friday, January 18] Got our chess men & board & played for the First time with Chastina. First meeting of the Citizens of this town in regard to Protective Union. Listened to the exposition of the thing by Mr. Bickford of Montpelier. The result was that 19 were ready to put down their names for it at once among which <u>am we</u>! Mr. [David] Choate quite excited. Go it!

[Saturday, January 19] Discussed Protective Union & Played chess

ASR

---

[21]Sarah Wheeler was the eight-year-old daughter of Judah D. Wheeler, a farmer, and his wife, Dorcas. *Caledonian*, January 26, 1850.

[22]"Bell-House" is a reference to the Peacham Congregational Church, which has a Revere bell in the steeple. Bogart, *Peacham*, 422. Samuel Delano (1795–1877), a graduate of Dartmouth, was secretary of the Vermont Domestic Missionary Society. Comstock, *Congregational Churches of Vermont*, 177.

[23]George W. Clarke, Jr., of Peacham was listed as a student in the 1849 PAC.

[24]Temperance meeting, *Caledonian*, January 12, 1850. William Withington Thayer (1809–81) attended Bangor Seminary in Maine and later performed pastoral services in Lyndon. Comstock, *Congregational Churches of Vermont*, 225.

ASR with Chastina & got Checkmated. Great excitement in Congress on The Wilmot Proviso.[25]

[Sunday, January 20] Both of us at home—reading and busling &c. We cant find much for record.

[Monday, January 21] Chastina making her dress & washed. She is almost dead with a cough. Beat me in a game of chess. A.

[*CWR*] [Tuesday, January 22] A very fine snowy day. Snow since last night has fallen about fourteen inches. But has not drifted much— Another "Protective Union" meeting this Evening— Alfred has got into office. That is, he is <u>first</u> on the commitee to draw up by laws for the society— Wrote to Oscar [Rix].

[Wednesday, January 23] I have at last finished my dress, which has been on hand for two weeks. Had a fine sleigh ride to school— through the snow. [Ephraim C.] Brown came to our room to settle for his bad conduct. Court over Harlow for whipping a boy—it is put off again for a week.[26]

[*ASR*] [Thursday, January 24] We waked up this morning with the following couplet in our heads—one had just about as much as the other to do in its production, for it is wholly and altogether a dream.

"Chastina dear, my thoughts on you seem not as others seem;
Nor flee away as others do a vague and empty dream."

[Friday, January 25] To [day] took place our 2d Review for this term—it came off in pretty good style. At 4 o'clock P.M. we set sail for Mr. L[yman] Pattridge's in company with Mr & Mrs. [David] Choate & Merrill. Had a fine visit and came home in good season.

[Saturday, January 26] Alf. was engaged all day in drawing up By-Laws for the Protection Union. Chastina Darned a darned pair of breeches—and began to make another rug of the "same sort" but gave it up on a promise of one from the store.

[Sunday, January 27] Attended church A.M. & listened to Mr. Carpenter of Littleton. Sarah [Walbridge Way] came Home with us

---

[25] The Wilmot Proviso passed the House but was defeated in the Senate.

[26] This court case involved a teacher's right to administer harsh punishment to students. According to Vermont State Archivist Gregory Sanford, the state statues at the time "did not get down to teacher conduct, outside of the requirement that they be of good moral character." Sanford, e-mail message to editor, January 26, 2009. There may have been a local ordinance.

N[oon] Staid till 5 when we took her to the Dr.'s & got a tooth pulled ASR
& all put for the East Part. Made a visit—lent Mr. Watts 10 doll[ar]
s & came home fat & saucy as ever. We are at present in a quandary
about what to do with our individual selves.

[CWR] [Monday, January 28] Have been washing and am somewhat tired. It seems to be a fashion for ladies in this village to make calls on Monday. Since school Miss [Mary] Calder, Weltha Cory, Mrs. [Sarah] Marsh & Mrs. [Eliza] Mattocks, the latter of whom called to beg as she said— That is to say the ladies have taken a notion to carpet the meeting-house & are raising money to buy a carpet &c. For my own part I do not think they have any business to call on us for we shall probably never have any benefit of it And therefore what I give is not from charity or because I wish to give. One does'nt like to be called "stingy." Alfred has gone to another union meeting & left me alone, a thing which he has never done since we were married until this union business began.

[ASR] [Tuesday, January 29] Yester eve we adopted the By-laws with no material alteration. Stormy to day. Wrote in connection with John Hendry for the Union to A. J. Wright of Boston to get Constitutions & blank certificates of membership & to make some dozen inquires. Got a letter & paper from Oscar [Rix]. Harlow's trial came off. Has to pay for ½ cost.

[Wednesday, January 30] Trimmed [Charles] Graham & others for absence.[27] Chastina has been copying French Rules. Played a game of chess. A. beat.

[Thursday, January 31] Made Miss [Louisa] Bradlee a visit. Got Rip Van Winkle.[28] Mr & Mrs [William] Mattocks present. Heard lots of Puzzles & riddles.

[Friday, February 1] Nothing of importance.

[Saturday, February 2] Regular exercises at school & Sewing at home A.M. P.M. Chastina visits Mrs. Laura Bennett & Mrs. Mary Weeks. Alf. attended a P[rotective] Union meeting—lead the case and made a speech or two. Paid it $10.00 and kept out of office. Talked with Dr. [Josiah] Shedd on school affairs and got a list of

---

[27]Charles Graham was listed as a student in the 1849 and 1850 PAC.
[28]*Rip Van Winkle* by Washington Irving (1783–1859) was published in 1820.

ASR rules from him.[29] Hired a piano & room for it—to pay .50 a month for one & 5.00 a term for the other & wood.[30] Headed also the Subscription for Harlow—the abused school-master—by putting down $1.00. Wrote to I. P. Dana of Danville.

[Sunday, February 3] Went to Church taken negatively. Because it stormed. Got a hundred Dollars of S[amuel] A. Chandler last evening.[31] Read newspapers and for the first time Rip Van Winkle.

[Monday, February 4] All as usual. Attended the N.E.P.U. Meeting and let it 93 dollars in addition to the 7 of last Saturday which makes in all $100 to the Union. This makes us 500. in all at interest. If we are prudent and in good health—I think we shall be able to make a live [living].

[Tuesday, February 5] Quite cold—some 16° below 0. Took supper at Schuyler Merrill's & attended the Temperance Meeting.[32] Met Mr Dana, J. P. at Dr [Josiah] Shedd's. Trying to make music.

[Wednesday, February 6] Cold still. Monthly Taken No. 40. Mr [David] Choate's folks preparing to go below.

[CWR] [Thursday, February 7] Mr [David] Choate & wife ready to go in the morning. I have assisted Mrs. C. in getting ready. Alfred received a packag from the Boston man, that Reports of the N.E.P.U. &c.

[Friday, February 8] Our folks were off this morning at five o'clock, leaving us asleep. Well we are masters of the domicil—excepting four children who have a better right than we. Quite warm. Played a game of chess

[Saturday, February 9] Warm & rainy. Mary [Choate] & myself have washed almost every floor in the house, besides <u>slicking</u> up wonderfully at other things. We get along nicely so far. Played a game of chess

---

[29] Dr. Shedd and Alfred may have been working on rules for the Academy. A section titled "General Regulations" was added to the pac in 1851.

[30] Music was offered at the Peacham Academy for the first time in the 1850 catalogue, with Miss Mary W. White listed as preceptress and teacher of music. It soon became a standard subject with an added fee.

[31] It is unclear why Samuel A. Chandler, the treasurer of the Peacham Academy trustees, gave Alfred money, although it may have been in payment for surveying.

[32] Schuyler Merrill (1803–92) had been Peacham's state representative in 1846 and a selectman in 1846–47 and 1850. Local temperance meetings, including this one, were not announced in the *Caledonian*.

[Sunday, February 10] We attended church—very bad walking— *CWR* that is no walking at all only for horses—rained almost all day— only a few at church.

[Monday, February 11] We intended to get up early this morning— but <u>jest did'nt</u>— But notwithstanding I did my own washing & the most part of Mary [Choate]'s besides doing all the chamber work. Went to school in the afternoon & then helped Mary again. <u>Lib</u>. Kavanagh took tea with us.[33] Had calls from Mr. [A. G.] Button & S[chuyler] Merrill. We cant keep house & do all other business as much.

[*ASR*] [Tuesday, February 12] Invited to Mr Eastman's. Did'nt go. Heard from Mr [David] Choate.

[Wednesday, February 13] Extremely Pleasant weather. So we laid in bed till 8½ o'clock and went to school without breakfast. Letter from Wm Graham Esq. N.Y. city.[34]

[Thursday, February 14] Nothing at all.

[Friday, February 15] A call from [Humphrey] Bennett and his wife. All about as usual.

[Saturday, February 16] Had no school. Read news papers all day. Weigh [1]83 pounds. Mr. [David] Choate arrived. Did not get my letter. Has bought some goods for Union Store &c.[35] Full of news & fun.

[Sunday, February 17] Wrote to Wm Graham Esq. N.Y. In great doubt what to do with ourselves. Trying to conclude to go to Boston. Hardly think we shall make it go.

[*CWR*] [Monday, February 18] Examination this afternoon. I have not been to school to day, but have been washing &c. almost all day— The workmen have commenced the room here for <u>the Store</u>. Alfred called on Dr. [Josiah] Shedd & I called at Miss [Mary] Calders to see the Misses [Weltha and Sophia] Cory.

[Tuesday, February 19] Finished off school this forenoon went off pretty well— Alfred settled with Mr. [David] Choate for our board.

---

[33]Elizabeth L. Kavanagh of Peacham was listed as a student in the 1846–47, 1849, 1850, and 1851 PAC.

[34]William Graham of New York City probably wrote about his son Charles, who had been "trimmed" by Alfred "for absence" on January 30.

[35]David Choate, who had owned stores in the past, probably went to Boston to learn more about the business of the Union store as well as to buy inventory. Bogart, *Peacham*, 273–74.

CWR I have ironed this afternoon & intend to go home to night, we are waiting for <u>our goods</u> to come. Just had a call from Mrs. [Sarah] Marsh.

[*ASR*] [Wednesday, February 20] Last night we went to the East Part after I had enjoyed a long talk with Brown & Weeks on the Union Store affair. They are going to drive us out of town—alas we! Tempest in a tea-pot! Went to the Corner and waited for the goods which came at last & Dustan [Walbridge] took the first lick in the shape of a new coat & trimmings. Attended the Temperance Meeting at Ewells.

[Thursday, February 21] Stormy day. Visited the E[ast] P[eacham] School A.M. P.M. At home. Visited Uncle Thoms.[36] Went to the Temperance meeting & Saw Alvah [Watts].

[Friday, February 22] Dustan [Walbridge] started for Montpelier. Very cold. Sent Isinglass by him. Regulated the Laboratory. Varney & Burbank from Danville on the Union business, &c &c.

[Saturday, February 23] Dustan [Walbridge] Returned—visited Aunt [Sarah] Stevens. Laziness predominant.

[Sunday, February 24] No go to church. Hear that Margaret Blanchard has quit off with her true-hearted [James] Morse. Attend a lecture by Mr [Beauman] Butler of Wells River on Temperance a very good discourse.[37] Alvah [Watts] Spent the night with me—at Mr. [David] Choates. Chastina went home.

[Monday, February 25] Played in the Laboratory &c. Wrote to [Owen] McLaren, T[haddeus] Stevens, C[harles] Smith, I[ra] O. Miller, J. Stevens. Recd a letter from McLaren.

[Tuesday, February 26] Played in the Laboratory. Agreed to pay Miss Louisa Bradlee $10.00 per term for hearing French. Went to E[ast] P[art] and got Chastina & Clarissa [Walbridge]. Clara got a letter from Wolcott saying that Harriet [Guyer] & Elizabeth [Taylor] have been exposed to the small pox & cant come at present. Mr & Mrs. [Asa] Brainard of Pottsdam, N.Y. visit Mr [David] Choate. Mr [Edward] Kilbourn of Littleton N.H. called.

---

[36]Thomas Watts, a brother of Chastina's stepfather, was the father of ten children, including Isaac and Alvah.

[37]Beauman Butler was then on a speaking tour. *Caledonian*, February 23 and March 9, 1850.

[Wednesday, February 27] Opened our school—have 43 scholars. *ASR* For the first time promulgated the rule that each Delinquency must pay 2 cts. whispers &c. Hardly know how the thing will work. Sent to Boston for books &c. Call on Clarissa [Walbridge]. Chastina begins her usual spring complaint of bad mouth and stomach. And In truth I am not over well myself.

[*CWR*] [Thursday, February 28] A few more scholars to day. I have been sewing. A call from Weltha [Cory]. Alfred received Mr [Henry] Clay's speech &c. from Mr. T[haddeus] Stevens.[38] Some of the scholars run off because they could not study & recite to please them— The goods for the Union came this evening. Mr. [David] Choate & [Uriah] Miner sat up all night marking & regulating the goods.[39]

[Friday, March 1] A real snow storm & blow last night. I have been trying to write a letter to Lizzie Fuller but dont succeed to my mind. Traded for the first time at our Union Store. A letter from Hale [Rix]. Answered it. So far our new system of fining scholars goes on most splendidly. Wonder nobody ever thought of it before.

[*ASR*] [Saturday, March 2] A fine morning. To day commenced the Union Store—its trade and prospects are flourishing. Received a call from Mrs [Mary] Weeks & Mrs [Laura] Bennett. Call from Clarissa [Walbridge] in the Evening. Played a game of chess. [*CWR*] Mrs. [Susannah] Chandler died last night about 11 o'clock.[40]

[Sunday, March 3] Attended church all day. Mr. [Erastus] Poor's funeral sermon was preached this forenoon. He was formerly a resident of Da[n]ville—but resided in Cincinatti Ohio.[41] After meeting we spend the time in reading. Mrs. [Susannah] Chandler is to be buried tomorrow. Mr & Mrs [John] Chandler were among the first

---

[38] Thaddeus Stevens sent Alfred a copy of Senator Henry Clay's Compromise of 1850, which allowed, among other things, California's entry into the union as a state free of slavery. *Caledonian*, February 16 and April 13, 1850. The legislation passed and was signed by President Millard Fillmore, despite satisfying neither Northerners nor Southerners.

[39] "Regulating" here means pricing. Uriah W. Miner (1808–60), the town auditor and superintendent of common schools, was known for his outspoken views. Obituary, *Caledonian*, June 15, 1860.

[40] Susannah Chandler, the wife of Hon. John W. Chandler, died at age seventy-eight. *Caledonian*, March 16, 1850.

[41] Rev. David Merrill delivered the funeral speech for Mr. Erastus Poor (1796–1850), a native of Peacham whom Merrill had known in Cincinnati, Ohio. Pearson, *Sermons*, 148–60.

CWR   residents of Peacham. Mrs Chandler had been deprived of her sight several years before her death.

[Monday, March 4] Very cold this morning, but pleasant. Had a large washing— Went to Mrs. [Susannah] Chandler's funeral at 1 o'clock P.M. at the house. Sophia Cory called this evening. Alfred read Henry Clay's compromise speech.

[Tuesday, March 5] Mother [Watts] came over this morning— I went into the Union Store with her. Town meeting to day— Alfred had books & drawing materials from Boston—cheap enough too. Went into school to see Miss [Louisa] Bradlee about drawing— Mrs. Phillips visited here. Called on Clara [Walbridge] & Mrs. [Sarah] Marsh. Town meeting.[42]

[Wednesday, March 6] Pleasant this morning— [ASR] Called on Dr [Josiah] Shedd and got leave to send for lectures. Wrote to Oscar [Rix]. Chastina not very well. Clarissa [Walbridge] has the teeth ache. Chastina Began to take lessons in Drawing of Miss [Louisa] Bradlee.

[Thursday, March 7] Got a letter last night from I[ra] O. Miller. He has concluded to accept our offer—i.e. to be our principal and give me 60 dollars a term for 3 hours work per day—while I study law &c. Chastina performed a large ironing to day and took a severe cold yesterday and is now quite sick—lame and sore throat.

[Friday, March 8] Chastina has been getting better. Co[l]. Blanchard & lady visited Mr [David] Choate's. Snowed & Blowed. Delivered the first lecture of the term on Heat.

[Saturday, March 9] Our new exercises of Discussion & Editing came off to day—very satisfactorily. We practice in Sketching. Play & Knit. The officers are making trouble with the Counterfeiters in Groton.[43]

---

[42] While men attended town meetings to set local government policy, Peacham women often made visits. Chastina's sister Clara was residing at Mrs. Sarah Marsh's when she was a student listed in the 1850 PAC. She also was listed in the 1846–47 PAC. The main item of business at this Peacham town meeting was a vote on whether to require that liquor licenses could be granted only for medical purposes, thereby prohibiting the retail sale of alcohol. This passed 180 to 10. *Caledonian*, March 9, 1850.

[43] Counterfeiters William Warburton (known as "Bristol Bill") and Christian Meadows had been recognized in the area and arrested. *Caledonian*, March 16, 1850; Clifford, *History of Danville*, 47–50.

[Sunday, March 10] Went to church A.M. Wrote to [Ira] Miller. ASR

[*CWR*] [Monday, March 11] All as usual. A few additional Scholars. Practiced drawing &c.

[Tuesday, March 12] Cousins Elizabeth Taylor & Harriet Guyer came to Mrs. [Sarah] Marsh's this morning.[44] All well & no small pox. Went into the drawing class. Had a call from Mrs. [Martha] Farr, & also from Dustan [Walbridge].[45] Alfred received from Mr T[haddeus] Stevens his speech on the slavery question in the house of representatives in Congress. Pleasant day— Clara [Walbridge]'s birth day, 20.

[Wednesday, March 13] Miss [Sophia] Leverette sick so she cannot go into school. Went into the drawing class. Like drawing well only it takes more time than I can well spare.

[Thursday, March 14] Wedding day—Daniel Foster & Miss [Mary] Carpenter are the happy pair who are to be made one.[46] Drawing some— Wrote part of a letter to John Way to go to California. Clara [Walbridge], Elizabeth [Taylor] & Harriet [Guyer] called on us. They had scarcely left when [Byron] Carpenter & [Zebina] Pangborn— some acquaintances of Alfred's at College boys called.[47] Alfred was enjoying himself right well, when <u>two ladies</u> called, <u>who somewhat</u> broke of[f] the conversation by amusing us with some of their <u>outlandishness</u>. We had rather not been here about that time. Received a letter from father Rix. Miss [Sophia] L[everett] unable yet to come into school— Alfred most sick. Sewing & drawing is my business.

[Friday, March 15] Messrs. [Byron] Carpenter & [Zebina] Pangborn visited the school this forenoon— Have been ironing— Went into drawing class. Finished my first piece this afternoon. Alfred wrote to father. Read a letter from John [S. Way] dated Panama N.G. Feb. 1st 1850. He was well then, & intended to start for San Francisco next day in the Steamer Oregon.

---

[44] Chastina's cousins Elizabeth Taylor of Alabama, N.Y., and Harriet Guyer of Wolcott were listed as students in the 1850 PAC.
[45] Martha Wheeler Farr (d. 1878) was the wife of Dr. Asahel Farr. PHA-MS, Farr, Asahel.
[46] Daniel Foster (b. 1820) of Peacham married Mary Carpenter (b. 1831) of Marshfield. *Caledonian*, March 30, 1850. He later went to California.
[47] Zebina Kellogg Pangborn (1829–1902), a Peacham native and a member of the University of Vermont class of 1850, and Byron Carpenter (1827–1909), who was from Marshfield and was a member of the university's class of 1851, had visited Alfred.

[*ASR*] [Saturday, March 16] Attended morning Duties at Academy. Then read the late speeches of Thad[deus] Stevens, Gov. [William H.] Seward and Dan[iel] Webster. Seward's the best and he will come out to[p] o' the heap.⁴⁸ Troubled with a cold. Last night read a lecture on <u>heat</u> &c. Another week is past and gone.

[Sunday, March 17] A.M. Went to church with Tine. P.M. At home where sick folks should be.

[*CWR*] [Monday, March 18] Washing. Mr. Ayer & Laura called. Laura on her way to Da[n]ville to take lessons in music. Alfred received a letter from Ira O. Miller. His answer favorable to Alfred's proposition in regard to the school— Alfred called to see Dr. [Josiah] Shedd, he also says good! Alfred Sent $50 to Oscar [Rix] in a letter. This pays off all his old college scores, except what Mr. [Thaddeus] S[tevens] assisted him.⁴⁹

[Tuesday, March 19] Went into the drawing class. To day commences the trial of the Groton Counterfeiters. Alfred commenced reviewing Blackstone.⁵⁰

[Wednesday, March 20] A very cold morning to begin with. Received a letter from Thaddeus Stevens.⁵¹ Went into the drawing class.

[Thursday, March 21] Cold weather. Ironing & fixing a dress, mending, and "other fixins" is my business, this day. We called to see the girls, that is Clara [Walbridge] &c. this eve. <u>Alfred & I</u> went <u>down</u> to the Union [Store] & bought ten <u>great big</u> apples. I took each

---

[48] Among the many senators who responded to Henry Clay's compromise speech were William H. Seward (1801–72) and Daniel Webster (1782–1852). The latter's speech was published in the *Caledonian* on March 23, 1850. Many Northerners found his speech "utterly false to freedom" because it favored non-intervention in slavery and the Fugitive Slave Act. *North Star*, March 23, 1850; Trefousse, *Thaddeus Stevens*, 78–82.

[49] Alfred's cousin Thaddeus Stevens helped Alfred financially in his studies at the University of Vermont as he helped educate his nephews. Trefousse, *Thaddeus Stevens*, 78. Alfred Rix, Burlington, Vt., to Thaddeus Stevens, Lancaster, Penn., March 18 and October 22, 1845, Thaddeus Stevens Papers, Library of Congress, microfilm reel 1. These letters, addressed to "Dear Patron," were requests "for more aid" to pay for "college tuition," "college incidentals," "board," and "books." I thank Beverly Wilson Palmer, co-editor of the Thaddeus Stevens Papers, for providing photocopies of letters.

[50] *Blackstone's Commentaries on the Laws of England* was the standard text read by all nineteenth-century lawyers and judges.

[51] No letters that Thaddeus Stevens wrote to Alfred have been located, only letters from Alfred to him.

of the girls one & went over again to their door, rolled them in & in common parlance, <u>sloped</u>.

[Friday, March 22] Commenced me a calico dress. Went into the drawing class— A lecture in the evening on Meteoric Stones & Shooting Stars, read by Dan Clarke—[52] Afterwards Alfred had some experiments with the Electerizing Machine.

[Saturday, March 23] Exercises as usual this forenoon— Miss [Sophia] Leverette & Emma Kilbourn made us a call—& also Weltha [Cory]. We called this evening to see Sarah A. Goodenoug who is sick.[53] That "Curiosity Box" has come at last, & in it we find copies of half Boston newspapers, the books that Alfred sent for— Oranges, figs, soap & even Oscar [Rix] himself in miniature. We sat up late to read the trial of Dr [John] Webster—with which all the papers are filled about this time—for the murdur of Dr [George] Parkman—[54] Adeline [Rix] is married.[55]

[Sunday, March 24] We attended church in A.M. & P.M. Saw Alvah Watts, he had a large school at Danville this spring.

[Monday, March 25] Washing— Clara [Walbridge] & Dustan [Walbridge] & Lyman [S. Watts] & also Mr Harvey Clarke Called—[56] We went to singing school part of the evening. Have just heard that Cousin Elizabeth Walbridge of Ohio is dead.

[*ASR*] [Tuesday, March 26] Tina cried to go somewhere—But no go. Dry time for news.

[Wednesday, March 27] Talked with Dr [Josiah] Shedd about [Ira] Miller's coming— He consents—but has a week to reverse his decision in. Wrote to Miller. Had a very bad day in school. Showed

---

[52]This and other lectures that Alfred referred to may have been among those that he mentions Dr. Shedd's having allowed him to send for in the journal entry for March 6. Dan Clarke of Peacham was listed as a student in the 1848, 1849, and 1850 PAC.

[53]Emily Kilburn of Littleton, N.H., known as Emma, was listed as a student in the 1850 PAC. Sarah Ann Goodenough (ca. 1832–65) of Peacham was listed in 1846–47, 1848, 1850, 1851, and 1852.

[54]John White Webster, a professor of chemistry at the Harvard Medical School, was on trial for the murder on November 23, 1849, of Dr. George Parkman, a wealthy Bostonian. Amory, "Dr. Parkman Takes a Walk."

[55]Alfred's sister Adeline Rix married Edward Bierstadt, the brother of noted painter Albert Bierstadt. A photographer, he was granted patent no. 174,893 in 1875 for "Improvement in Stereoscopes," with Alfred Rix listed as a witness.

[56]Harvey Clark was born in Peacham in 1826.

ASR the patch on my a— 2 or 3 times, and blew my nose on myself. Farewell!

[Thursday, March 28] Experimenting &c. Chastina has just finished her 3d drawing and she is doing wonders. She fitted a dress for Elsey [Choate].

[Friday, March 29] Read a part of Dr Webster's Trial.[57] Read a lecture of Horace Mann's to Young Men.[58]

[Saturday, March 30] Very interesting exercises at Academy. Read & Played. Visited at Mrs. [Sarah] Marsh's. Sidney [Rix] staid over night with us.[59]

[Sunday, March 31] The <u>head</u> of the family staid at home while the <u>tail</u> of it went to church. We are awfully tired out and weary.

[CWR] [Monday, April 1] Washing &c. Had <u>company</u>.[60] Alfred called to Dr. [Josiah] Shedd's.

[Tuesday, April 2] Very warm— Went in to the drawing class. This afternoon Mrs. [Aurilla] Choate & myself went to Mr [Uriah] Miner's to eat new sugar—the first we have seen— Mr. [A. G.] Button & wife & Mr Morse & wife were there— Alfred came after us. Dr. [Josiah] Shedd called & confirmed the bargain about Alfred's stay here another year on the conditions which he proposes. That is in company with Mr [Ira] Miller.

[ASR] [Wednesday, April 3] Wrote to [Ira] Miller & Mr Kilburn. About this time The Trial of Dr [John] Webster for the murder of Dr [George] Parkman closes with a sentence of death against Webster. We were somewhat surprised at the verdict—considering the character of the testimony.[61]

[Thursday, April 4] Bad walking. Chastina finished her 4th Drawing and had a tooth filled by Dr. Dearborn of Newbury.

[Friday, April 5] Chastina ironed & worked out. McCleran read a

---

[57]*Caledonian*, March 23 and 30, 1850.

[58]Horace Mann (1796–1859), an educator and statesman, was the author of *A Few Thoughts for a Young Man: A Lecture, Delivered before the Boston Mercantile Library Association, on Its Twenty-Ninth Anniversary* (1850).

[59]Sidney Redfield Rix of Peacham, a cousin of Alfred's, was listed as a student in the 1850 and 1851 PAC. In the journal he was usually referred to without his middle name.

[60]Chastina's menstruation indicated that she was not pregnant.

[61]*Caledonian*, April 6, 1850.

lecture on Whirlwinds & Waterspouts. Introduced with much good effect my long made crystals.

ASR

[Saturday, April 6] Chastina went home a-foot—smart as a skinned cat. I attended to our Saturday's exercise and followed. Called on Si. Way and got a call from the Young Curriers. Had a good visit and a good lick of lasses and laid ourselves up for refreshment till[62]

[Sunday, April 7] This is a pleasant day. Started for our home about sunrise and enjoyed our walk on the crust very much. We are two extremely lazy young folks. 28 Years ago to day our folks if I remember correctly had a fine time.[63] A few of the neighbors were called in and there was a very social time of it.

[CWR] [Monday, April 8] Washing day of course— Alice [Watts] came over with the girls this morning & stayed with me to day— This Evening we have spent the evening at Mr [William] Mattocks'—had a pleasant visit. Alfred spoke to Mr M. about studying law in his office. Alfred received a letter from Mr [Rufus] Case of St Johnsbury, asking him to deliver a lecture at the Teachers Institute of St. J[ohnsbury].[64]

[Tuesday, April 9] Went into the drawing class. Had calls from Clara [Walbridge] & Harriet [Guyer] & also from Margaret Calder & Weltha [Cory]— Commenced a dress for Mrs [Aurilla] Choate.

[Wednesday, April 10] Heard that Alvah Watts is crazy again. Miss [Louisa] Bradlee told of the improper conduct of Edward L[ee] & Charley Graham.[65]

[Thursday, April 11] To day finishes up the week for school as <u>Fast</u> is on hand— Alfred makes gas for his Chemistry Class— A lecture read by James Merrill on Weather Almanacks. Received a letter from [Ira] Miller.

---

[62] At the Watts farm, Chastina and Alfred appear to have been enjoying molasses, or maybe "lasses" was Alfred's word for maple sugar, an annual treat, as the weather had been good for tapping the trees. Bogart, *Peacham*, 70, 356.
[63] It was Alfred's twenty-eighth birthday.
[64] A Teachers' Institute was announced in the *Caledonian* on April 6, 1850, called by Vermont's first state superintendent of common schools, Horace Eaton (1804–55). Rev. Rufus Case (1809–87) of St. Johnsbury asked Alfred to speak, but he apparently did not accept. Comstock, *Congregational Churches of Vermont*, 170.
[65] Edward E. Lee of New Windsor, N.Y., was listed as a student in the 1846–47, 1848, 1849, and 1850 PAC.

CWR   [Friday, April 12] Fast-day—& a very pleasant one too. We had an excellent sermon from Mr [David] Merrill this forenoon from this text—"no man puteth new cloth upon an old garment,["] &c—[66] His discourse was principaly upon slavery— Suggested as he said, upon reading an advertisement—That the Rev. Mr. Jones of Virginia wished to sell his farm consisting of six hundred acres, with all the stock together with <u>forty servants</u> who are young & <u>increasing</u> in <u>number</u> & <u>value</u>, all these to be sold at the reduced price of $35,000, as he wished to be come a Missionary— Wrote to [Ira] Miller, Mr. [Edward] Lee & Mr. [Charles] Graham.

[ASR] [Saturday, April 13] At home. Dustan [Walbridge] called. Wrote a billet to Mr [David] Merrill to let Clarissa have the School at Littleton.[67] Bought a bottle green piece of cloth for a coat. Wrote to Oscar [Rix] for the Prot[ective] Union. Read Mr [Charles] Sumner's Lecture on White Slavery in the barbary States[68]

[Sunday, April 14] Alf. went to church through snow and blow and Storm—dreadful time for the farmers. We, that is Chastina and Alfred thot each shall write in the Journal alternately and if he neglects, he shall write from the time the Journal stops to the present moment. The last part of this agreement is what causes me to write for two days.

[CWR] [Monday, April 15] Wrote to Charles Smith— Washing. Alfred has been making ink. And if it proves good will be quite a saving— He had made about a "<u>quart</u> or a <u>quart</u> & a half or two <u>quarts</u>."

[ASR] [Tuesday, April 16] This is writ with the new Ink. Superior Rix Ink! Woke up this morning at 7 oclock and got up—thankful for that—worked & eat and at 9 o'clock P.M. went to bed again. This is the round we run. Among our labors may be reckoned—Drawing & Patching by the wife and gas making by the Husband. Reading The

---
[66] The Bible text is Matthew 9:16.
[67] Clara Walbridge had been teaching in Vermont and New York, and because Alfred knew her well, his recommendation was probably all that was needed for David Merrill to write the school committee in Littleton to recommend that she be hired. Bonfield and Morrison, *Roxana's Children*, 81.
[68] Charles Sumner (1811–74) was the author of *White Slavery in the Barbary States: A Lecture before the Boston Mercantile Library Association, Feb. 17, 1847* (1860).

first Vol. of Blackstone. This day the Snow lies in drifts from 1 to 6 feet deep in every direction.[69] Hay is $10. to $12. a ton. I am so anxious to finish this page [of the journal]. I will write once in two lines.

[Wednesday, April 17] Mr. [Lafayette] Livingston married.[70] People are getting out after the storm. All's well.

[CWR] [Thursday, April 18] Pleasant & somewhat warmer. Mrs [Sarah] Miner & Mrs [Mary Elizabeth] McClary visiting here.[71] Elizabeth [Taylor] came over to see the girls & bid us "Good bye" as she intends to go to Wolcott tomorrow.

[ASR] [Friday, April 19] Lecture Read by Geo. Clarke Jr. Gave Eugene Wheeler a lecture on his Duties & Prospects. Call from Mrs [Rhoda] Wheeler.[72] Chastina aided at the Academy in improving our Ink. The result is seen in the difference between the complexion of Yesterday and Today's Record.

[Saturday, April 20] Dreadful Lazy. Drinked Lemonade. Played & Visited the Girls. No Paper in School to day. Pleasant. This ink looks beautifully and I like to write with it. And fearing lest it may change its complexion & so bring our good taste in question with after-generations, we will just state that it is <u>now</u> a beautiful dark clear & deep blue! Chastina is very good looking to day!

[CWR] [Sunday, April 21] Attended church in forenoon & afternoon I have left my Sabbath school teaching, & took my place in my class again, which is much pleasanter.

[Monday, April 22] Rainy almost all day— Washing— We called this evening to see Weltha & Sophia Cory. They start in the morning for Methuren to work in the factory or at other work.

Received a letter from [Charles] Smith.

[ASR] [Tuesday, April 23] Gave Geo. Clarke Protoxide of Nitrogen and so tickled him almost to death. Chastina has finished her

---

[69]On April 20, 1850, the *Caledonian* reported one of the worst snowstorms of the year, adding, "we scarcely dreamed that winter would yet linger in the lap of spring."

[70]Lafayette Livingston (b. ca. 1825) married Amanda Livingston (b. 1824); both were from Peacham. *Caledonian*, April 27, 1850.

[71]The visitors were Sarah Morrill Miner and Mary Elizabeth McClary (1822–91).

[72]The Wheeler brothers of Peacham, Eugene (b. ca. 1834) and Jerome (b. ca. 1837), were students listed in the 1846–47, 1848, 1849, 1850, and 1851 PAC; Jerome is also listed in 1852. Their mother was Rhoda Skeele Wheeler (1794–1864).

ASR St. Bernard.⁷³ Welth [Cory] & Sister <u>did'nt</u> go to Lowell to day. Alix Johnson called to hire a school maam. Little Tassle! Snowing again!!

[CWR] [Wednesday, April 24] Things about as usual—only some a little more so. Miss [Louisa] Bradlee gave us a lesson "in perspective" which she has promised all the term— Commenced another piece in Crayoning—& also a dress for Mary Choate. The last one I think, that I shall cut for others asid from family concerns. Called to see Mrs. E[phraim] C. Brown & her baby—a very pretty one it is too—⁷⁴ Calls from Clara [Walbridge], Maria Blanchard, E. Harvey & Miss Parker.⁷⁵ Received a letter from Mr. Mighell, Amanda Morrills husband.

[ASR] [Thursday, April 25] Scholars are leaving for their farms & merchandise. Chastina made a string of Calls. To day has been the first real Spring day. Found out that solder added to Muriatic or Hydrocholoric acid to saturation will form a kind of flux for soldering—apply and wait—it is wonderful how it will cause metals to adhere.

[CWR] [Friday, April 26] Warm Weather—almost as warm as summer. I commenced a piece in colored crayons— Had a peep at the moon through the telescope.

[Saturday, April 27] Another warm day— Spring has come at last. Went with Clara [Walbridge] to purchase bonnet &c. We are <u>dreadful lazy</u> Saturday's

[Sunday, April 28] We have attended church half of the day. Listened to a sermon read by Dea[con] [Ezra C.] Chamberlain. Mr [David] Merrill absent on a visit West.⁷⁶ Read the "Merchant of Venice."⁷⁷ Alfred is pleased enough because I am obliged to pay the penalty of forgetfulness—by writing for three days.

---

⁷³Chastina's "St. Bernard" was probably a coat.

⁷⁴Betsey Brown had given birth to a daughter, Laura.

⁷⁵The callers were probably students from the Peacham Academy, but they are not easily identified without full names.

⁷⁶Since Rev. David Merrill was visiting friends in Ohio, Deacon Ezra C. Chamberlain (1799–1877) read a published sermon.

⁷⁷Shakespeare's comedy was published ca. 1595.

[ASR] [Monday, April 29] No Visitor as C. Expected!⁷⁸ Wrote for Mr [David] Choate to Mr [John G.] Kaulback.⁷⁹

[Tuesday, April 30] Some of our Scholars complain that their Preceptor attends more closely to Blackstone than to them. Dr [Josiah] Shedd made us a call & talked over things. Paid him 12 dollars for the Physiologies. Dustan [Walbridge] called & bade us Good Bye—he goes tomorrow to Montpelier. No mail—The Freshet has washed off the rail-road.⁸⁰

[CWR] [Wednesday, May 1] We did'nt go maying for two reasons, first because we were too lazy & second because in all reason there was nothing to pick except last year's leavings. And again it has rained a good part of the day. Called to see Mrs. [Elisabeth] Strobridge. She looks very sick indeed, & is really so—⁸¹ Commenced lining & trimming a bonnet for Clara [Walbridge]. [Owen] McLaren called & got a certificate of good behavior.

[ASR] [Thursday, May 2] Nothing!

[CWR] [Friday, May 3] I have nearly as much to write as Alfred had yesterday. Edward Kilburn called on us as did also Emma [Kilburn] & Miss [Sophia] Leverett. So did Jane & Katy Chamberlain & Miss Coburn.⁸² Alfred is almost sick with a cold.

[ASR] [Saturday, May 4] Chastina finished her "House" in colors. Alf. aided Mr [A. G.] Button in the Examination of the Summer School maams.⁸³ Pretty good luck with all but Abba Blanchard—she is not fit for a common scholar.⁸⁴ Here perhaps as well as any

---

⁷⁸Chastina was pregnant, and Alfred showed his enthusiasm with an exclamation point. He left two lines blank, as if he expected more to be written on the subject.

⁷⁹John G. Kaulback was named treasurer at the first meeting of the Working Men's Protective Union on October 6, 1845, and then took on the role as central agent of overseeing all the stores, known as divisions, as chairman of the Committee on Trade for the Protective Union. Rozwenc, *Cooperatives Come to America*, 29, 71.

⁸⁰Rain had followed the heavy snow, causing flooding that washed out bridges, so no mail arrived from the south for six days. *Caledonian*, May 4, 1850.

⁸¹Elisabeth Clark Strobridge gave birth to a son on April 6, 1850. He was given the name Lafayette, after his father.

⁸²Jane Chamberlain (1831–1914) of Peacham, a cousin of Catherine's, called Katy, was listed as a student in the 1846–47, 1848, 1849, and 1850 PAC.

⁸³On this date only women scholars applied for teaching certificates. The Peacham examining board consisted of the Methodist minister and Alfred.

⁸⁴Abba Blanchard of Peacham was listed as a student in the 1846–47, 1850, and 1851 PAC.

ASR where may be mentioned the circumstance that the good merchants of this village have been and are still doing all they can to do us and our school injury for the avowed reason that I belong to the N.E.P.U. The end is not yet.

[Sunday, May 5] Last night we took a long walk by way of Mr. [David] Merrills & [Uriah] Miners over the fields and home. To day we are at home resting.

[CWR] [Monday, May 6] Rainy & thunder in the afternoon— We took a short ride the first that I have been in a wagon— Received a letter from brother Austin [Rix] who is now at Dalton.

[ASR] [Tuesday, May 7] Mr Henry Stevens called and took dinner with us. Paid him $17.00 on the matter of Probate costs on the Stevens Estate.[85] Clarissa [Walbridge] & Mother [Watts] came over. Mr [Alix] Johnson brought back the Speaker's Guide. Chastina gone home. I am trying to find out some method of getting over the country in the course of a year or two in search of a location for us. Dustan [Walbridge] has returned from Montpelier all disheartened—for he expected to find employment there and is disappointed. Mr [Samuel] Chandler asked me to survey for him.

[CWR] [Wednesday, May 8] Our people all well as usual. Sewed for mother on a coat for Isaac [N. Watts]. Clara [Walbridge] fixing to go to her school next monday at Littleton N.H. Started from home about six A.M. for the corner & arrived there before seven, & stopped some time on the way. This was on foot. Alfred was real lonesome while I was absent. I found him at work on my drawing.

[Thursday, May 9] A very rainy day this has been— Went into the drawing class. Dan Clarke called at our room— Alfred quizzed him concerning the reports that Brown & Weeks have made about the school.

[ASR] [Friday, May 10] Gran'maam [Olive] Brown moved to Cabot. Harriet Guyer & Clarissa [Walbridge]'s room moved & gone. Prepared for Surveying. Mr [David] Choate & Newell [Marsh] transplant shade trees. Got a letter from Miss Helen T. Warner of

---

[85]Henry Stevens (1791–1867) of Barnet may have been a commissioner for the estate of Alanson Stevens (1792–1847), Sarah's youngest son and Thaddeus's brother. There are no probate records relating to this estate at the Caledonia County Courthouse.

Hardwick. The weather is cold and so are our friends. Here it will be ASR necessary to a clear elucidation of our subject to introduce
An Illustration of

A Backward Spring!

[*CWR*] [Saturday, May 11] I hardly dare commence under such a striking illustration— Alfred has been Surveying a good portion of this day— Received money of Mr. [Samuel] Chandler. For myself I have been half sick & more than half lazy— Have ironed & made a chair cushion. Had calls from the Misses. Eastman.

[*ASR*] [Sunday, May 12] Heard Mr [Rufus] Case of St. Johnsbury A.M. P.M. over at home & to[ge]ther at Thad Blanchard's funeral.[86] Pleasant day.

[Monday, May 13] P.M. Began Examination of my school. Finished Plotting & calculating Mr [David] Choate's farm. Made out two Deeds between Choate & [Hazen] Merrill. Chastina is about sick. Her Spring trouble, a kind of jaundice is upon her again. Some talk of moving to Aunt Nabby [Chamberlain]'s soon.[87] McLaughlin began to saw wood at the Academy. This is fairly Spring.

[*CWR*] [Tuesday, May 14] Alfred finished school this fore noon— I went up & paid Miss [Louisa] Bradlee for the services this spring— At noon Alfred paid Miss [Sophia] Leverett the amount agreed on—when in about an hour afterward down came Mr. [Nehemiah] Bradlee—Post-haste—Saying Alfred had cheated Miss L out of her

---

[86] Theodore Blanchard was born in Peacham in 1790. *Caledonian*, May 25, 1850.
[87] Abigail Chamberlain (1786–1861) lived in the newly rebuilt house next to the Choates at Peacham Corner, with an apartment to let on the second floor with its own entrance. Elderly unmarried women were commonly referred to as "aunt," even by non–family members.

CWR board—& worse that he meant to— He just called on the lady to see what it all meant. She could'nt say as she expected any more only she thought she ought to have more— She has proved herself a silly weak thing during this term—& to wind up with has been real ungenerous. Alfred Surveys for Mr [Samuel] Chandler in afternoon. came home all tired out—& got ready to go to Boston in the morning— He goes to see about the [Protective] Union business.

CHAPTER FOUR

"Boarding Ourselves" and Ending Alfred's Principalship
May 15–August 14, 1850

After mature deliberation we have concluded to quit boarding out and try whether it is not more economical to board ourselves . . . We are now living in a <u>family way</u> and hope to prosper . . . Our affairs with the Cal. County Gram. School are this day settled.
ALFRED

Things do'nt seem as they used to at home [at the Watts farm]. Probably it is because it is not <u>my</u> home now—only for a visit.
CHASTINA

BETWEEN THE PEACHAM ACADEMY'S 1850 SPRING AND SUMMER terms, Alfred took a train trip to Boston. He had two errands to attend to. The first was to purchase goods for the new Union store; the second was to buy household furnishings for the new living quarters that he and Chastina were preparing to move into. They had decided to move next door and try to "board ourselves" at the home of Abigail Chamberlain. Chastina and Alfred had enjoyed "boarding out" with the Choates, but sharing a house with the family's four children and with a new store that was receiving a steady stream of customers had given them little privacy and no quiet. At Miss Chamberlain's they would be able to save money by preparing their own meals, and Alfred would have a quieter place to study. But boarding themselves meant that they would now need their own cooking utensils and tableware. Alfred may also have wanted to make this trip to Boston in order to discuss with his older brother Oscar the locations he might consider in looking for a permanent home for himself and Chastina.

While Alfred was away, Chastina went back to the Watts farm in the East Part to help her mother. She was on hand when her sister Sarah gave birth to a healthy baby girl on May 18—making clear why the Ways had married so quickly the previous October. Chastina stayed in the kitchen during the labor and birth, probably looking after the younger children and feeding her father and brothers, who would have been busy with the spring work on the farm. The presence of a doctor was not noted in the journal, but the neighbors whom Chastina reported had come in may have been older women who helped with births. The father of the baby was mining in California.

When Alfred returned from Boston, he and Chastina began the process of moving next door. Most of Abigail Chamberlain's house was only four years old, and the upstairs rooms where the Rixes were to live had not yet been fully finished. Alfred and Chastina papered the walls, built a clothes closet, and purchased a cooking stove, pots, and kettles. "Aunt Nabby," as Miss Chamberlain was called with respect by townspeople, lived on the first floor. She had turned sixty-three on her last birthday and was from one of the most prominent early Peacham families. Like most residents at Peacham Corner, she welcomed Academy students as boarders. She must have taken particular pleasure in boarding the principal and his wife.

"After much toil of body and spirit," Alfred wrote, they were soon "pretty well established" in their new quarters. Although the $18 a year they were paying Aunt Nabby was a significant savings over the $3 a week they had paid the Choates, they were forced to spend a good deal of money furnishing their new home at a time when their income had decreased. So Alfred returned to a skill he had used to help finance his college education: he did some work for Samuel Chandler, surveying land on Cow Hill in Peacham's northwest section. He also added the job of handyman to his busy schedule, helping Aunt Nabby around the house.

In early summer, Chastina began to complain of poor health. On June 2, Alfred confirmed that she was pregnant. As the weeks progressed, he noted her continuing sickness and tiredness. She also continued to suffer from the "sick head ache" that had so often plagued her. Although it is not specifically noted in the journal, Chastina had been relieved from teaching at the Academy as she took on added work at home. And Alfred, with more time on his hands, occupied himself with his law studies but also read the local newspapers more closely. He followed the news on California's entry into the Union, and also on two New England scandals—one was local, concerning counterfeiters who were being tried in Danville, and

Rev. David Merrill, Vermont, ca. 1845
A son of one of the earliest families to settle in Peacham, David Merrill attended the Peacham Academy, Dartmouth, and Andover Seminary. He was called to the Peacham Congregational Church in 1841, where he married Alfred and Chastina in 1849. He wears a double-breasted velvet vest, an unusual cravat, and a coat with a wide collar. He may be wearing fall-front trousers; fly front appears in the 1840s. His sideburns were fashionable in the 1830s but not in rural areas until the 1840s. *Peacham Historical Association.*

the other was a sensational murder by a Harvard medical professor of a rich man to whom he owed money.

On July 22, David Merrill, the popular minister at the Congregational church, died unexpectedly at the age of fifty-one. The Rixes were among those who stood watch at his bedside during his last hours. Chastina helped prepare the church for the funeral, which she and Alfred both attended. Merrill was a Peacham native who had gone to district school with Chastina's mother. He had studied at Dartmouth and the Andover Seminary in Massachusetts. The Merrill family, among the earliest in Peacham, had maintained a successful farm at the foot of Cow Hill, where David's brother Hazen and his family still lived. In 1840, Hazen had negotiated the church's call to his brother, who at the time was a successful pastor in Urbana, Ohio. David Merrill had agreed to become the second Congregational minister in Peacham, following in the pulpit the long-serving Rev. Leonard Worcester, who had been pastor from 1799 to 1838. Merrill returned to his native town in 1841 with his wife and their ten children; those who were of school age attended the Academy. Merrill's commitment to abolition and temperance had long been supported by the church and by the majority of people in Peacham.

Alfred and Chastina were among those who shared Rev. Merrill's views on abolition. Alfred noted that they both watched Congress closely "on the subject of Slavery" and were interested in the admittance of California to the Union as a non-slave state. He viewed with indignation his fellow countrymen and townsmen who did not share the abolitionist stand. He hoped that "those who read this [journal] in after years" might "find all right."

Alfred had begun to note his dissatisfaction with Peacham's town leaders in the journal almost daily. On June 14 he expressed his displeasure with his fellow townspeople who were reluctant to speak out against these influential men. A young man full of ambition and confidence, Alfred wanted to change the way things were run in Peacham so that men could speak their opinions freely without fear of losing business and respect. He was frustrated with the resistance he encountered.

Alfred and Chastina got their first look at "some Calafornia gold" while visiting the Watts farm on June 2. John had sent the nuggets to Sarah with a letter written from the diggings in Hangtown, Eldorado County:

> I have been on prospecting Excursions in Company with four others . . . in persuit of Better diggins and spent one week among the Indians and Wild Beasts of the forest . . . I think I have seen the Eliphant now by this time . . . I suppose you will want to know how much gold we have found . . . recollect that I should tell you if I did not promise myself not to write one word about what the Company made.[1]

He was not silent, however, on his opinion of the mines: "Tell any one that wants to come to California to stay at home." But by the time his next letter arrived, written from the mines on June 21, he had changed his tune. He first assured his wife, and the many neighbors who he knew would read his words, that "all of the Vermont Company that is with me are all well." He then addressed the subject Sarah and her family had been anxiously waiting to hear news of:

> about the Claim that we bot here Paid 830 dollars for the Privilege of four men to work with 14 others on the bar we since have bot out 3 of them and that gives us all a chance to work on the bar I told him [Alfred] that we should get it worked out by the 4th of July but it will take one month longer than that . . . tell Alfred that the last 3 Saturdays have ben lucky ones and the last one

---

[1] John S. Way, Hangtown, Calif., to Sarah Walbridge Way, Peacham, April 7, 1850, private collection. The formal name for Hangtown was Placerville.

but the one before I wrote to him four of us took out $1150.00 and the next day after I wrote him only 7 dollars! But those strikes are few and far between.

He added, "I shall be home next Winter some time if I have my health."[2] As it turned out, however, he would not be gone that long.

On the first anniversary of their wedding, Chastina and Alfred had a daguerreotype made at a studio in Danville. They stood staring at the camera, he tall and confident, she small and unsmiling, holding a sign that read "July 1850," making it easy to date the photograph. To commemorate the occasion, at Chastina's insistence, Alfred composed a long poem on the day they had "entered upon the marriage state." His wife may have been hoping for some romantic sentiment, but he used his wit instead, describing the day's activities, including the six hours he had spent at school while she was at home "in dish & dough Or putting your darning-needles through." Alfred's sense of humor had helped to smooth the bumps in the road during the young couple's first year of married life. It would also help to carry them through the challenges that lay ahead.

[*CWR*] [Wednesday, May 15, 1850] Alfred started for Boston about 7 o'clock A.M. Had the pleasure of Miss [Louisa] Bradlee's & Miss [Sophia] Leveretts company part way—[3] He must give an account of himself while gone— As for me— In the first place I am just about sick. 2d It rains real hard & I start for home soon, notwithstanding— Went over with Mr [David] Currier in a wagon without a seat—that is only a box in it—got home at last—tired & sick enough—found the folks cleaning house &c. &c.

[*ASR, written later*] Alf proceeded by stage at the cost of 75 cts to Wells River. Thence by cars to Boston. Saw Mr Eastman of Littleton & Mr Carter Evans of Peacham.[4] At about ½ after 7 arrived in Boston—fare 4.50. Took Hack for No. 101 Pleasant St. the residence

---

[2]John S. Way, Hangtown, Calif., to Sarah Walbridge Way, Peacham, June 21, 1850, ibid. John's letters to Alfred have not been located.

[3]Alfred shared the stage to Wells River, the closest railroad station to Peacham, with Sophia Leverett, who was listed as a student in the 1850 PAC but was also a teacher at the Academy whose services he had not renewed; and Louisa P. Bradlee, who was listed as a teacher of drawing and painting in the 1846–47, 1848, 1849, 1850, 1851, and 1852 PAC.

[4]Carter W. Evans (ca. 1808–77) was a Peacham businessman. Bogart, *Peacham*, 266.

ASR of Brother Oscar [Rix]—found Mary Ann [Rix] at home all alone. Walked into Oscars store 430 Washington St. He seems to be doing a fine business all for No 24 Div. of N.E.P.U. At tea was introduced to Messrs [Galen] Coffin & Twitchell, both at work in Oscars Pattern Shop. After the Theatre Exercises, Sister Adaline [Rix] appeared & introduced her new husband, Mr. Edward Bierstadt—and a good fellow he is too—so I think. We spent the Evening in all manner of small talk.

[*CWR*, leaving space for above] I am here at home, did'nt sit up all day—

[*ASR*] [Thursday, May 16] Awoke in the attic of a five storied house—got up—got down, eat & got out at about 7 o'clock. Walked straight for [John G.] Kaulback's office 93 Water St.[5] Undertook a settlement & partly succeeded. Run about during the day—made some small purchases & brought at 7 P.M. my artillery to bear on Esquire Kaulback according to appointment. I find him a tough customer—he will have all his own way or not at all. But he at last came to a bearing and agreed that if our business was not hereafter done more to our satisfaction we were at liberty to choose a man on the ground & have him see that it was done. Here endeth the first Lesson. But it did not end till a perfect blow out. I sloped.

[*CWR*] Commenced sewing a little for mother [Watts]— Things do'nt seem as they used to at home. Probably it is because it is not <u>my</u> home now—only for a visit

[*ASR*] [Friday, May 17] Having completed yesterday the chief business that called me to Boston, to day I started out in company with Sisters Adaline [Rix Bierstadt] & Mary Ann [Rix] to hunt up a little toggery & furniture for Chastina. We succeeded very bravely & came back leg weary enough. 40 yds Calico—1 Muslin Dress—1 Berage dress—1 shawl—1 Astral Lamp—Knives & forks—Candlesticks &c &c.[6] In the Evening we all went to the Museum & saw

---

[5]Alfred negotiated with John G. Kaulback of NEPU, who oversaw all the Union stores, for products for the Peacham store. Rozwenc, *Cooperatives Come to America*, 71.

[6]In addition to household items that the Rixes needed for their new living space, Alfred purchased fabric for Chastina: calico to use in making an everyday dress; muslin, a fine sheer cotton for a good dress; and barege, an open-weave fabric generally printed with a floral or striped design, for another fine dress. Lynne Z. Bassett, textile and fashion historian, suggested how these fabrics would have been used; e-mail message to editor, January 4, 2009.

"London Assurance" & The Liar. Went home rather dissatisfied with the performance.

[CWR] Visited at Mr T[homas] Watts' to day.[7] Mrs. W. always has work enough for me to do when I go there—Trimmed & fixed four bonnets—that [is] one new & others not. Came home & found Sister Sarah [Walbridge Way] feeling bad & weeping over the miniature of her husband.

[ASR] [Saturday, May 18] The man what ought to have brought home our goods jest did'nt. I went after him—he thought a mistake had been made in change in my favor— I concluded he had made another about 2.00 against himself for not doing as he agreed in sending—he was glad to quit even & so was I— I loafed off down on to State St saw Wm Bradlee.[8] Went to Taylors on Merchants' Row & saw his Clerk—and as I went away met [John] Watts![9] Hurra! Alive! So off we scoured. Met Cosin Smith who introduced us to all the Courtrooms & Courts—&c &c till moonrise when we slunk.

[CWR] Awoke this morning at 4 o'clock & found there had been a <u>mess</u> during the night. Found some of the neighbors there. In short Sarah [Walbridge Way] <u>was sick</u> & continued to be very bad, until about 10 minutes before 5 o'clock P.M. when She was delivered of a daughter— I took my place in the kitchen & there kept myself all day.

[ASR] [Sunday, May 19] A.M. Went to the Melodeon & listened to Theodore Parker—and I think his discourse surpassed anything of the sort I ever heard.[10] I am most profoundly sorry we are so destitute of such men. P.M. Went to an Infidel Discussion on Hanover St. Rather a slim affair. Spoke on the Aff. of the Question, "Is there any Being, Agent or Thing in the Universe which is not Material?" Saw Abby Folsome & Mr Seaver &c. On our way home we discussed

---

[7] Sarah Bailey Watts married Thomas Watts in 1835, after his first wife, Sarah's, sister Jane died. They lived in the East Part on a farm northwest of the Watts farm.
[8] William Bradlee (1823–50), son of Nehemiah and brother of Louisa, was working in Massachusetts. He spelled his family name "Bradley" rather than "Bradlee."
[9] John Watts (1818–87) was the son of Thomas and Jane Bailey Watts. He married Esther Hidden in 1845 and moved to Boston.
[10] Theodore Parker (1810–60) was a well-known minister at the Unitarian church in West Roxbury, Mass., and a passionate advocate of abolition. Four months after Alfred heard him preach, he delivered a well-publicized sermon on conscience and law that focused on the moral issues raised by the passage of the Fugitive Slave Act.

ASR   the more practical Question of "Whether, as Beans <u>would</u> be eaten, there was any means to take the wind out of them?"

[CWR] The <u>baby</u> is a fine little plump thing—very pretty all getting along as well as could be expected. My health is some better though I am unwell yet.

[ASR] [Monday, May 20] Came Home.

[CWR] I have been sewing for the little <u>tot</u> nearly all day— Sarah [Walbridge Way] quite comfortable.

[Tuesday, May 21] Alfred came over after me— Rained like a shower— So I go back to the corner & here the scene changes. First I must see the new things which A. brought me—Dress, Lamp, Candlesticks &c &c. We <u>are</u> really going to keeping house. A Crate of crockery is being opened so we go in the first place—after returning to Mr. [David] Choates—and select our crockery—which consists of a brown tea sette—not very pretty—but it will do— Next we proceed to Aunt Nabby [Chamberlain]'s & commence papering our room. She finds paper & we put it on—work till dark—took tea with Miss Chamberlain, <u>alias</u> Aunt Nabby.

[Wednesday, May 22] Alfred got up & went up to Miss [Abigail] Chamberlains before breakfast. He took breakfast with Miss C. At about 7 o'clock I came up & helped him paper untill 8 o'clock when he was oblige to leave & commence his school— School opened with about 12 scholars— Gave out his lessons & then came agin to help me paper. We completed papering about 3 o'clock P.M. when Alfred got a horse & carried one load of goods—then went to the Hollow & got a cooking stove; for which he paid $12.00— After which he carried another load— Small loads & more of them. By this time we both are completely tired out. We stay at Mr [David] Choates yet.

[Thursday, May 23] Alfred carried the remaining part of the goods this morning before school—I staid at Mr [David] Choates & cleaned out our rooms— At 4 P.M. went to Miss [Abigail] Chamberlains— when we set up our bed & carried off a few things— Such a [poor] looking place I never saw— I am all discouraged & sick— Went to Mr Choates to tea—when after tea she—that is Mrs [Aurilla] C. mother like fixed us off with a loaf of bread some dough nuts & a pie—& to night we stay in our new home for the first time— How weary we are!

[Friday, May 24] Alfred was up early & at work with might & main—blacking our stove—which unfortunately got caught in a thunder shower last night— I[t] took till nearly nine to finish it. We took breakfast with Miss [Abigail] C[hamberlain]. I have busied myself as fast as possible in setting things to right. Got dinner for the first time. After school we went in pursuit of pots & kettles &c. But were not very successful.

[Saturday, May 25] Mr [Samuel] Chandler called before we had got our breakfast—to have Alfred go & survey with him. So off he goes with only eating a <u>bite</u>. Came back about 1 o'clock P.M. Our pots & kettles dont fit. So they must go back again— He finds the necessary articles at Mr [A. G.] Buttons the Methodist minister. How glad we are that Saturday night has come. At night what should we have sent to us but a nice mess of trouts—thanks to Mr. Button & his good lady!

[Sunday, May 26] We were disturbed in our slumbers at <u>about eight o'clock this morning</u> by Lyman [S.] Watts—who came over to have us go over home— Sarah [Walbridge Way] is not so well— Accordingly I prepared breakfast as soon as possible & we were ready to go a little before noon— Found her looking rather slim— She has a good deal of fever. We staid until night. Alfred went into the field & picked us a mess of cowslips for <u>greens</u>.

[Monday May 27] I had a large washing—besides my housework. It is wearisome business when one is unwell—to work so hard. Alfred is fixing up things as fast as possible.

[Tuesday, May 28] Had our <u>greens</u> for dinner. They went first rate. I have troubles & trials in the cooking line. Alfred is about making out his survey for Mr. [Samuel] Chandler— We have so many things to attend to we hardly know what we do.

[Wednesday, May 29] Have been sick almost all day— In evening however we went down to Mr [David] Choate's & settled with him— We are rather poor now days. Had so many things to buy that the <u>shorts</u> have nearly used us up.

[Thursday, May 30] Have done my ironing. Rather hard for me— Alfred finished the plotting of One of Mr [Samuel] Chandlers fields. We made us a <u>clothes room up garret</u> out of some pieces of boards & some sheets for walls— I said above we were poor— Well, we are not for we have a clothes room at any rate.

CWR

CWR [Friday, May 31] Did some baking &c. It takes us nearly all the time to fix! I hope there will be some end to it soon. I have forgotten to give a description of our rooms—or the place where we are—Alfred shall give the description Mother [Watts] called on us. I went home with her.

[Saturday, June 1] Alfred came over in the morning & we went to Danville. He to close up the settlement of the Stevens estate—& I for the ride— Took dinner at the Temperance Hotel—[11] We went to Alvah [Watts]'s Laboratory. Alfred fixed some of his aparatus which was in rather a bad state—Told him what & how to use a score of things which a preceptor ought to know the use of. Returned to father Watts' about 4 o'clock P.M. Took supper with them. Sarah [Walbridge Way] some better. Saw some Calafornia gold sent home by John [S. Way]—He says—after being at the mines about one month—Tell "any one who wants to come to Calafornia to stay at home." This speaks his opinion rather plain. Well we are at home at last We are at the tinkering again—There is no end to this. This journal so far as I have written may be somewhat in want of wit if not in words as I have written the last two weeks of this from memory.

[ASR] [Sunday, June 2] Attended church A.M. and heard Mr. Bullard. P.M. At home trying to mind our own business. We have now got pretty well established in our new Quarters—which last word reminds me that as yet we have not set down the particulars in this affair. After a fair offer from Aunt Nabby Chamberlain of 2 Rooms in her house 2d floor & all appurtenances thereunto belonging for the small sum of 18.00 a year, and after mature deliberation we have concluded to quit boarding out and try whether it is not more economical to board ourselves. Therefore we have accepted the aforesaid Aunt's offer and at the present writing we find ourselves snugly ensconced in the above mentioned rooms after much toil of body and spirit.

---

[11] The "Stevens estate" may have been that of Alanson Stevens, who died December 31, 1847. The name of the Danville hotel indicated that no alcohol would be served there. With lectures and meetings on temperance held frequently, a hotel welcomed the added business. Roth, *Democratic Dilemma*, 225–28; Bogart, *Peacham*, 215.

In the first place I went to Boston and made some few family ASR purchases (for a particular account of which see Acct Book of proper date)[12] and 2dly, a host of small home utensils were provided and fitted for their respective places and uses. We are now living in a <u>family way</u> and hope to prosper. Our present dwelling place is situated in the most busy part of Peacham Corner. Commands an extensive view of wooden buildings in front, green hills to the right and left and a generous range of exceedingly small houses in the rear. On the whole it is a very pleasant location. We are meaning at present to remain one year. Chastina during the whole <u>movement</u> has been quite unwell—hardly able to be about and yet continually laboring. We hope she is soon to be better. To day we wrote to I[ra] O. Miller and to sister Clarissa [Walbridge]. It rains almost constantly.

[Tuesday, June 4] Comes tomorrow, meanwhile we will say a word or two of

[Monday, June 3] Made [Humphrey] Bennett's folks a call. Quite Pleasant, Now

[Tuesday, June 4] No school to day. Training day—2 or 3 of the "bold sodgers" have been shot for their pains.[13] Wrote to T[haddeus] Stevens Esq. A meeting of the No 107 NEPU & determined to enlarge our capital to 16.00 & buy a new store at the Corner &c. 3 or four young gents from the East Part took dinner with us. This is the first right down altogether pleasant day we have had this season.

Forrid March! A—es to the Hog-pen & Faces to the fence!!

---

[12]The account book has not been located.
[13]The tradition of June training day originated in Peacham around the War of 1812. Intended as a day for men of military age to train, it became mainly a day of frolic and fun. Bogart, *Peacham*, 214–15, 248–50.

ASR [Wednesday, June 5] Mr [David] Choate &c. bought a store for the Union of Mr Wheeler.[14] We made out the writings. Chastina made a multiplicity of calls— The good people cleaned the church.

[Thursday, June 6] Recd a letter from [Ira] Miller. Went Briaring, & bought a sucker! Luther Parker & Louisa Martin = 1[15]

[Friday, June 7] Carpeted the meeting house. Warm weather. Chastina's health is poor and poorer.

[Friday, June 7] [This day] Has been disposed of once [above].

[Saturday, June 8] Chastina baked & worked on my linen coat, while I read and wrote and run. Mr [David] Merrill returned from his journey to the West.[16]

[Sunday, June 9] Went to church and behaved ourselves. Heard that Sally [Walbridge Way] is not so well, so got a horse and went over to see her.

[Monday, June 10] Rains & rains and we go into a Bear's den. [Dan] Foster fined $10. & costs for selling liquor contrary to law— fiddlestick![17] Paid Miss [Jane] Lang some 15 dollars for furniture &c. I am tired of buying trumpery only to be sold again.[18] It is my pen and not me what makes this hand writing. I spell it right but the marks dont somehow look nice.

[Tuesday, June 11] Cold weather. Wrote for Mr [David] Choate to Oscar [Rix] & Mr [John G.] Kaulback. Chastina washed. Here let

---

[14] The Union store moved from the Choate home across the street to the northernmost space in the row of businesses at Peacham Corner. Ibid., 274; Scott, *Pictorial History*, 47. *Walton's Vermont Register* in this period listed no store owned by Wheeler, but Bogart lists a Wheeler's Tavern (est. 1848); *Peacham*, 277.

[15] Luther F. Parker and Louisa Martin were married in Peacham. Both were well known to Alfred and Chastina as former classmates. There was no announcement in the *Caledonian*, but the marriage was recorded by David Merrill when he returned to town. Peacham Town Meeting Records, 1845–65, 220.

[16] David Merrill left Peacham on April 22, 1850, to travel to what later became known as the Mid-West, where he had served as a minister in Urbana, Ohio, from 1835 to 1840. He preached and visited friends on his trip, returning to Peacham on June 8. Pearson, *Sermons*, 12–14.

[17] Dan Foster, a tavern and livery stable owner at Peacham Corner, must have been found to be selling alcohol for non-medical purposes, and was fined in accordance with county law. Peacham voted to restrict liquor licensing to medical uses by a wide margin almost every year from 1845 to 1853. Bogart, *Peacham*, 215–16; Bonfield, "Work Journal of Albert Bickford," 129.

[18] Jane Lang lived at Peacham Corner and took in student boarders, according to the 1846–47 PAC. Chastina was frustrated with items she labeled "trumpery," probably meaning the pots and pans they initially purchased that did not fit their new stove and had to be replaced.

it be recorded that the Subscriber has received a beautiful present ASR from his wife of a green Kid Pocket Book—cost $1.50. It is no doubt a hint to me to put my money in it and keep it there rather than spend it as I do. We shall see how well I heed her monition. A. Rix A.H. (ass he)

[Wednesday, June 12] Got a horse at [Dan] Foster's and took a ride about the Country, & Home. Met Amos & Mary Norris.[19] Wm Strong and Lady arrived—in tall style.

[Thursday, June 13] A paper from Oscar [Rix]. Read Tribune— One of the very best papers in our Country. Chastina continues in bad health. [illegible symbol]

[Friday, June 14] Chastina still sick. She went to see H. Pattridge. Found my table covered with flowers. About this time Congress is wide awake on the subject of Slavery & the admission of California as a state. We take much interest at this date in public matters especially such as are now transacting at the Capital. Chastina and myself agree remarkably well. We are both free-Soilers.[20] We both are anxious to see by one means or another the territory of the country free from the possibility of Slavery. But we hardly expect this result at present. Those who read this in after years may, I hope, find all right. Notwithstanding all that has been said, written & done by Americans against intolerance and in favor of freedom of thought & opinion & the free expression of them, still I am certain that the desired end is not yet by any manner of means attained. I must confess that I am ashamed of my fellow countrymen and fellow townsmen. And this I say from no spleen or pique—but soberly. An honest expression of sentiment on many points of Religion & Politics would throw very many of my young brethren out of fair into very dark prospects of a livelihood. Too much is at stake to speak out—so silence or a cold approval of the established notions and customs is the almost universal result. These are the facts on the one side as all are able to bear me witness—and on the other hand that the number

---

[19]Amos Norris (1822–84) and his sister Mary B. (b. 1830) were both from Peacham. She was listed as a student in the 1846–47, 1848, and 1849 PAC.

[20]Free-soilers were those who opposed slavery in any of the new territories and states entering the union.

of these gagged ones is not by any means small may be ascertained by any one who will take pains to inquire. Put the plain question to your first door neighbor—whether he feels at liberty to state fully in all matters his opinions & whether he considers it as well for him to be perfectly sincere in all things? He will answer "No!" The truth is that there is at present altogether too much formality and insincerity, and I am no prophet if the time is not now rapidly advancing when men will quit it and each allow his neighbor to do the same. There is no one thing which so much clogs advancement in almost all things as this—and I mean that it shall not escape my future notice and candid comment.

[Saturday, June 15] Heard our regular exercises & then followed Chastina home—where the chief part of the forenoon was spent in discussing law with Mr [Lyman] Watts as to his title to his farm. Chastina took charge of Sally [Walbridge Way] and P.M. we made a short visit to Aunt [Sarah] Stevens.

[Sunday, June 16] At home—i.e. at the East Part. Read and talked. Wrote to John Way at Sacramento City, California. Came to the Corner & went to bed & slept nicely till

[Monday, June 17] Chastina washed & was tired all out. Poor thing. Visited the Academy. Present from Mrs. [Sarah] Stevens in the shape of a piece of cheese—we sent her a specimen of our Tea 1 lb.

[Tuesday, June 18] Had Boiled victuals for dinner. Scolded Chastina for trading at [Ephraim C.] Brown's. Chastina almost sick. Looked up Mr [Lyman] Watts case. Found that any interest whether vested or contingent may be conveyed. Finished Reading the 2d Vol of Blackstone.

[Wednesday, June 19] Began Aunt Nabby [Chamberlain]'s Well Curb. "Nothing more"

[Thursday, June 20] Letter from Oscar [Rix]—who sent rects &c. Shower. Got a paper from Oscar. These days are remarkable for want of news. After a calm there generally comes a storm, so I am mending my pen for some tall story what is to be heard.

[Friday, June 21] Finished Aunt Nabby [Chamberlain]'s Well Curb. To day in open Court at Danville "Bristol Bill" alias Wharburton attempted to cut the jugular vein of B[liss] N. Davis Esq. state's *ASR* attorney, with an old case Knife. Bill had just received his sentence of imprisonment for ten years at Windsor. Davis had labored with much zeal and some bitterness for this result, and Bill took this method to show how well he appreciated his efforts. Davis escaped narrowly with his life.[21]

[Saturday, June 22] Chastina wrote to Clarissa [Walbridge] by Emma Kilburn.[22] We had the privilege of seeing Bristol Bill & his coadjutor Meadows as they passed through our town ha[n]d-cuffed & fettered this morning on their way to the State Prison. Chastina is much better & I am worse, that is, lazier than usual. Slept a good part of the P.M. Bought Garden of Kavanogh at 2.00.

[Sunday, June 23] Went to church P.M. Alf. made Amos Norris a short visit and learned about the business of his agency.

[Monday, June 24] Tina Stewed beans & washed as a woman should.

[Tuesday, June 25] Letter from I[ra] O. Miller. Saw Addison Parker who Paid me 13.00 all right.[23] [*CWR*] Visit from Father & Mother [Watts].

[*ASR*] [Wednesday, June 26] Nothing at all. [*CWR*] Mrs [Aurilla] Choate called here. We called to see Mr [John M.] Martin who is sick Also called to Mr [Trustram] Sanborns

[Thursday, June 27] Had the sick head ache all night & this morning too, so Alfred had to get his own breakfast. However have so far recovered as to do my ironing & go visiting at Mr [David] Choate's

---

[21] *Caledonian*, June 22 and 29, 1850. Bliss N. Davis (1801–85) was the prosecuting attorney at the trial in the courthouse at Danville, and when the two criminals were sentenced, Bristol Bill pulled out a knife he had hidden in his clothes and stabbed Davis in the neck, just missing the jugular vein. Davis lived. Clifford, *History of Danville*, 47–50. After Bristol Bill served his ten-year sentence at Windsor, he was taken back to Caledonia County and was sentenced to six more years for stabbing Bliss. Blaisdell, *Over the River*, 200–205. His partner, Christian Meadows, served three years and two months before being pardoned and was soon employed by the U.S. Treasury in the engraving department in Washington, D.C. *Caledonian*, July 23 and August 6, 1853.

[22] Emma Kilburn, from Littleton, N.H., must have lived near where Clara Walbridge was teaching.

[23] Addison F. Parker of Coventry, brother of Luther F. Parker, was listed as a student in the 1846–47, 1849, and 1850 PAC. He must have been paying his Academy tuition. He went to California in early 1853 and returned by fall 1854.

CWR Had a good visit— Saw Emily Gould & Frances Miner there.[24] Elsa [Elsie] Choate gave me a dish of strawberries to bring home.

[Friday, June 28] Got all ready to go home when our folks did not come after me. So I feel somewhat disappointed. Isaac [N. Watts] & Alice [Watts] came over to see me. [ASR] Alf. got some beets at Mr [A. G.] Button's & planted them. Alf. Reading the 3d Vol. of Blackstone. He is nowadays very hearty & saucy and weighs 185 lbs. avoirdupois. [CWR] Alice & I went to the old Graveyard to pick some strawberries and got caught in a shower. Chastina [ASR] Letter from Clarissa [Walbridge] at Littleton by Miss E[mma] Kilburn. Laura Chandler began attending school.

[Saturday, June 29] Chastina went home and attended upon Sally [Walbridge Way] who continues to be poorly off and a fair prospect of more of the same sort. After the school exercises I followed her over. The day was warm and for the sake of a sweat I concluded to go over in ½ hour. I did it in 27 minutes.

[Sunday, June 30] At the Corner again. Mistake, stay at the East part. Pick a lot of straw berries. Eat and snort.

[Monday, July 1] At the Corner again. Rainy. Morris & Newton Clarke leave school.[25] Sort o' sick.

This is a cow.

The—Cow—is—a—very—use-ful—animal. She gives milk and brings calves. [Small drawing of a calf] A calf is a small animal. Calves are very numerous. Calves are properly very modest & innocent things. But they sometimes become very queer and behave quite unseemly. Thus—this

---

[24]Emily Gould of Peacham was listed as a student in the 1846–47, 1848, 1849, 1850, and 1852 PAC; Francis Miner (b. 1830) of Peacham was listed in 1850. Quimby, "*People of Peacham* Addendum."

[25]Brothers Morris and Newton H. Clark of Groton were listed as students in the 1849 and 1850 PAC.

animal will sometimes be found in "Hat-straps & boots" Dangling a gold chain, Ivory-head cane & an inverted [ink spot]. [Drawing of cow dressed in men's clothes] The word where the blot is means Shirt—Not Shit-Ass.

The above [drawings] are from life. The first in the Chapter is what Aunt Nabby [Chamberlain] milks, the 2d follows the first—the 3d follows the 2d and may be seen at this moment Doing the graceful on [Dan] Foster's Pizano.

[Tuesday, July 2] Last night received a letter from [Ira] Miller & the proposed Handbill, which I this morning Sent off to D. Kimball of Hanover N.H. to have printed 300 copies. Tina washes a great washing and I begin the perusal of the Vermont Statutes. Rains a little all along. I ache and ache most <u>fundamentally</u>.

[Wednesday, July 3] Dull day. Worked a little on the sofa.

[Thursday, July 4] All quiet. No school. Chastina went home. Worked all day on sofa. News of Prof. [John W.] Webster's Confession.[26] Eat my dinner & supper "in singleness of heart."

[Friday, July 5] At school as usual. Finished my Setee frame. Went to the East Part.

[Saturday, July 6] Finished the 3d vol. of Blackstone. Picked strawberries & played. Dr [Asahel] Farr opened Sally [Walbridge Way]'s Breast.[27]

[Sunday, July 7] Attended church A.M. after having dressed Sally [Walbridge Way]'s breast. She begins to feel better. Rather windy these days. Mr [Lyman] Watts' horse has got kicked almost to death.

---

[26] *Caledonian*, July 6, 1850. Harvard professor John W. Webster confessed to the murder of Dr. George Parkman, a Boston philanthropist, to whom he was heavily indebted. On November 23, 1849, Dr. Parkman went to Webster's chemistry lab demanding money. The professor killed him, carved up the corpse, and hid the body parts under the floor of his back room at the Harvard Medical School. This case remains one of the most frequently told Harvard stories from the nineteenth century; as Cleveland Amory began the tale: "To the student of American Society the year 1849 will always remain a red-lettered one. In that year two events occurred at opposite ends of the country, both of which, in their own way, made social history. At one end, in Sutter's Creek, California, gold was discovered. At the other, in Boston, Massachusetts, Dr. George Parkman walked off the face of the earth." Amory, "Dr. Parkman Takes a Walk," 119.

[27] Breast infections often resulted in fevers and were thought to be a medical problem. Should the second breast become infected, a wet nurse had to be found. Ulrich, "Women's Travail," 180–81.

ASR   [Monday, July 8] At school as usual. Board at the Tavern while Chastina is taking care of Sally [Walbridge Way]. Hoed my corn again & brushed my pease. Laura Chandler & Jane Marsh present me with a fine lot of Straw-berries.

[Tuesday, July 9] Recd a speech from T[haddeus] Stevens on the California Question. Got our Handbills from Hanover. Sent 50 to I[ra] O. [Miller], & 50 to E. H. Miller.

[Wednesday, July 10] Wrapped up and sent of[f] by mail some fifty letters containing handbills. Gave Dan Clarke & Hen. Martin a lot for Distribution also the Trustees.[28] The Trustees met & visited our school—all right. News from California—cant find out what. News that President [Zachary] Taylor's dead.[29] Letter from Oscar [Rix], sending rect of 83.00. Wh[ich] delivered to [David] Choate. "I grieve that I am all alone." H. K. White[30]

[Thursday, July 11] As usual. Dan [Clarke] left school. Went to the E[ast] Part to see how the "stock gets on." Remain over night & return early on

[Friday, July 12] Water our plants— Keep school—not cool for it has been a hot day. Reading Kent in School.[31]

[Saturday, July 13] Tina came home and spent from two till 8 in cleaning where I thought there could be no dirt at all. Women are some! Went a-fishing & caught five small fishes and was hungry enough to eat all the loaves what fed the five thousand.[32] Looks like rain. Mr. [William] Seward has made another speech—he is a man and the day is coming when New York will make him her Champion as he is almost at present.[33]

[Sunday, July 14] At home in the forenoon— Rains— Chastina has the sick head ache. Read in the state Trials the trial of Wm Penn

---

[28] Henry N. Martin (b. 1829) of Peacham was listed as a student in the 1849 PAC.
[29] President Zachary Taylor died on July 9, 1850, and was succeeded by Millard Fillmore.
[30] "Solitude," by the popular English poet Henry Kirke White (1785–1806), includes the lines "It is not grief that bids me moan; It is that I am all alone."
[31] Alfred was probably reading *Commentaries on American Law* (1826) by James Kent (1763–1847).
[32] Alfred was referring to the story of Jesus feeding the multitudes with five loaves of bread; Matthew 14:17–21.
[33] Senator William H. Seward (1801–72), a Northern Whig, delivered his famous "Higher Law" speech opposing Henry Clay's Compromise of 1850 as being unfair to the North.

for a Riot.³⁴ Funny. P.M. Alf. went to church and after a short nap awoke and found of those where he could make observation 24 were asleep or making desperate efforts from becoming so. This preaching to quiet folks to sleep is in my humble opinion shabby Gospel. The minister is an ass for not bringing his bunk to church. Sabbath is the day of rest!

ASR

[Monday, July 15] Rainy quite. Went to Mr [David] Choate's & [A. G.] Button. Bought trimmings &c for settee. Brought home Salad & Greens.

[Tuesday, July 16] Began to have milk of Brainard.

[Wednesday, July 17] Tried to get a Daguerreotype of ourselves but bad luck would not allow it. We found it hard work to keep cool & sit pretty half the afternoon of a day like this.

[Thursday, July 18] To day it set in Raining as if for a flood & Rained all day & all night.³⁵

[Friday, July 19] The same as yesterday only the raining was already begun. Letter from W[eltha] A. Cory.

[Saturday, July 20] Rains yet. Small bridges are pretty much swept off—roads gullied badly and no prospect of fair weather yet. So we concluded to go about making an ark in the shape of a Settee—the frame of which I made some days since during my widowerhood. Ergo, I went to the East Part and got hay & other fixins & we worked till dark & finished up as beautiful and easy an ark as ever walked the waters. It may be that our posterity may enjoy a snooze on it. I ought to have said a voyage to the land of Nod. We began to read Sparks life of Benj Franklin.³⁶

[Sunday, July 21] Attended church. For the first time this summer Chastina came out in her white dress and full Toggery. She

---

³⁴William Penn (1644–1718), the founder of Pennsylvania and an early champion of democracy and religious beliefs, was arrested in 1670 after speaking in the street when the Friends' Meetinghouse in London was padlocked. At the trial, the members of the jury refused to convict him; they were fined and imprisoned but were vindicated on appeal. This case established the principle of independence of the jury in British law.

³⁵David M. Ludlum characterized this "tropical storm" that reached northern latitudes in 1850 as "a rarity," and he noted that the *Vermont Chronicle* (Windsor) called it "the greatest storm and flood that ever occurred here within the memory of man." Ludlum, *Vermont Weather Book*, 136.

³⁶Jared Sparks (1789–1866) was the author of *The Life of Benjamin Franklin*, published in 1845.

ASR continues still to take the shine off from all the young fry in Town. As to myself—I eat, grow fat & read sermons when the minister is sick or the Deacon cant, all which "was" to day. This is the end of the present chapter!

P.S. At dark to day we learned that our minister Mr. D[avid] Merrill lay at the point of Death. We hastened thither and found it even so. We remained attending upon him as well as we could expecting every moment would be his last. His disease is Erysipelas—whether spelt right or wrong. The Physicians have all given him over. We wait.

[Monday, July 22] We continued watching the dying man till 10 minutes before one this morning when he ceased to breathe. His age 52.[37]

[Editor: Two lines were drawn here, maybe to indicate a change in Peacham life.]

At school as usual. P.M. Got our Daguerreotype in which Chastina is foolishly represented with her head bowed forward. But 8 trials would not better the picture on the whole so we take this and try to be content.[38] What right have we poor devils to complain? Farewell!

[Tuesday, July 23] No school to day. Letter from J[ames] K. Colby. Chastina aided in dressing the church in mourning. P.M. Attended the Funeral of Mr [David] Merrill. Mr [Rufus] Case Preached the Sermon. [Alvah] Watts finished his school. Call from Dan Gilfillan.[39]

---

[37] Because Rev. David Merrill was ill, Alfred was called upon to read a printed sermon at church. Chastina probably wore her wedding dress in celebration of their first anniversary. According to the *Caledonian* of July 27, 1850, "The death of a man so able, useful and influential as was Mr Merrill, is a public calamity . . . Mr Merrill leaves a wife and ten children."

[38] Alfred and Chastina went to Danville to have a daguerreotype made to celebrate their first anniversary. They held a sign with the date "July 1850." Chastina, who was three months pregnant, may not have been sure how to present herself.

[39] Daniel William Gilfillan (1825–85) was a member of the class of 1847 at the University of Vermont, where he knew Alfred. He married Helen Partridge (1826–85) at the Peacham Methodist Church on August 1, 1850, with Alfred and Chastina in attendance. Daniel and Helen went to the Mid-West to teach, and according to a local historian, he became "one of the early abolitionists of the Garrison school, an earnest advocate of temperance, and a leader in the cause of prohibition." Wells, *History of Barnet*, 432–33.

May 15–August 14, 1850   *143*

[Wednesday, July 24] Wrote to Mr [James] Colby & Mr. I[ra] O.   ASR
Miller. All as usual. Wrote off Rules for the Academy.[40]

[Thursday, July 25] Went on a short walk to the East Part and came back on

[Friday, July 26] Finished my Summer Term. Letter from John S. Way who is at George Town, California.[41]

[Saturday, July 27] Letter from C[arlton] J. Morrill of N. Orleans, La. Paid Mr [David] Choate the 25 dollars we owed him. Let him have a hundred more on interest. Got in Kindling. Picked cherries. Pulled weeds—made a bath &c.

[Sunday, July 28] Attended A.M. on Mr [Asa] Skeeles Reading at Cong. House. P.M. attended Mr [A. G.] Button's church. Sleep is great annoyance to him who is not over interested in church service. It has fallen on we of late with almost irresistable force. If we reckon by the week Today is the

First Anniversary Of Our
Wedding

But if we reckon by the day it comes tomorrow.

(See Aug. 1 Sequens)

[Monday, July 29] Reckoning by the day this is our 1st anniversary Wedding day. Pleasant A.M. P.M. Rainy. Chastina wrote Clarissa [Walbridge] & sent John [S. Way]'s letter by Mr [Edward] Kilburn who made us a call. Surveyed a little for Wm Marsh, got .50 for it and gave it to Tine to buy plums with. Chastina worked hard washing—tired and lame at night, but her health is quite good—So mote it be. She wants me to write a little poetry to day.

On the Occasion of having
Walking up the aisle and took a wife
Wat I never had before:
And felt so slick I thought I should fall
Flat on the Meeting-House floor!

---

[40]Alfred may have written to academy principals James K. Colby and Ira O. Miller concerning the rules he planned to add to the next Peacham Academy catalogue.

[41]John's location is unclear, as there is a George Town in Tuolumne County and a Georgetown in El Dorado County.

ASR [Tuesday, July 30] Made me a Saw Yoke. Dan Gilfillan called and invited us to his contemplated wedding. All's well that ends well.

[Wednesday, July 31] Painted my Saw Yoke. Call from Mrs. S[amuel] A. Chandler. Reading the 2d vol. of Kent & Life of Franklin. Slept about 2 hours P.M. Laziness, Laziness! I greatly admire the character of Franklin. Chastina thinks there is a slight shade of difference between Franklin & her husband—but I am obliged to differ from her. Got a horse & wagon for the wedding.

[Thursday, August 1] The following belongs of course to July 29, 1850.

I.

Dear Wife,
   One Year is pass'd since we
Resigned our natreal liberty,
And in pursuance of our fate
Entered upon the marriage state.
If I remember well, no change
That one could reckon very strange
Has fell on us. Our heads and faces
Continue in their proper places;
Our hands and heels, our bone & brains
Are ready for their round again.

II.

One year is gone since we were married;
Old Time has neither stopt nor tarried;
His flight is onward—so is ours:
The grass, the grain, the leaves & flowers
Have gone and come, just like the wave
Washing the sand grains to their grave.
Here let us pause and set a bound,
Constant and careful as the year comes round:
For days & months & years should not
Go off uncounted and forgot.

III.
Within the year which now is gone
Let's see, Chastina, what's been done.
First we have slept from 9 till 6!
Quite unbecoming thee and Rix!
Bright mornings passing, while in bed
A young, strong pair lie stretch'd stone dead!
Shame, Shame upon you! Get you out
Betimes and stir yourselves about,
Or Bed-bugs, lice and moths will crawl
Upon you and devour you all.

IV.
Next we have spent in fun and laughter
And in the scrapes that follow after,
Two hours each day—a loss of time
I cannot reckon quite a crime.
For I have thought and still am thinking
That fun will keep a man from drinking,
Women from scolding, Children well—
That's, Everybody out of Hell.
But then too much of game and giggle
Is sure to set folks on the wiggle—
Turns Hes to asses, Shes to hags,
Or both to utter nonsense bags.

V.
Two hours each day at least, I think,
We've spent upon our meat & drink:
To stew & stir—to taste & try—
To gulp & guzzle—wet & dry
Full-fill our maws, till we must take
Cathartics for the Belly-ache:
And consequent the splurge and sprawl—
The doze and donkey-state and all
The like attendants big and small.

VI.

Full three hours more each day we've lost
In adding to our neighbor's cost.
Visits and parties, calls and knocks
Emptying one's "pocket full of rocks."
Of all the useless and silly whims—
The Dandy of all Dandy Jims—
Is this, the leaving of one's proper labors
To go and stop those of his neighbors!
'Tis plain there ought to be a Law
That all by Sampson's Jackass' jaw
Should die, who spend their little breath
In "jawing" their dear friends to death.

VII.

Two full hours more in various ways,
As reading stories, short delays,
Uneasiness or dreaminess
Or something else that ends in s,
And we have left six hours spent well;
A shameful, shameful tale to tell!
Of these six hours, I've spent in school
The chief—or "must" rules any fool.
<u>Your</u> six at home in dish & dough
Or putting your darning-needles through.

VIII.

Thus hath our year been pass'd, Chastine,
Ar'nt it a pickter vorry fine?
Remember the sketching is'nt mine
At least no more than it is thine,
Amen. Let all the people "jine"
In prayer for change—but never whine
      At one bad fix
But halt! Wheel! Take a new line
For which you'll reckon this the sign

      From Alfred Rix.

[Friday, August 2] Read eat and play.   ASR

[Saturday, August 3] Nothing New.

[Sunday, August 4] At church A.M. Heard a very flat sermon from the Rev. Mr. [W. W.] Thayer of Lyndon. The more I hear of this sort of Preaching the worse I like it. In the P.M. we staid at home and read the life of Ben. Franklin by Jared Sparks.

[Monday, August 5] Washed and Read.

[Tuesday, August 6] Went to the East Part and began to help hay & do house-work.

[Wednesday, August 7] A.M. Reading &c. P.M. Went to mill with Chastina, Isaac [N. Watts] & a bushel of corn. Got the last ground and drove on with the rest to the Raspberry field on the New Road over the Pond—picked 6 qts & got some pond lillies & returned.

[Thursday, August 8] Visited Aunt [Sarah] Stevens.

[Friday, August 9] Mr [Lyman] Watts & Lyman [S. Watts] went to help Mr [David] Currier build a Hay stack. Guck [Augustus Walbridge] & I worked at Home.

[Saturday, August 10] [David] Currier & George [Currier] worked with us at Haying.

[Sunday, August 11] At home. Wandered over the old hill & picked up all manner of green things.

[Monday, August 12] Worked and played. Sent Advertisements to Caledonian & North Star.[42]

[Tuesday, August 13] Came home again to the Corner. Rainy.

[Wednesday, August 14] Wrote to stop the Caledonian. Wrote to subscrib for the Chronotype.[43] Mrs. [Deborah Shedd] Chamberlain

---

[42] Alfred sent the newspapers the announcement of the opening of the Peacham Academy on September 4, with Ira O. Miller as principal and teacher of Greek and the natural sciences; Alfred Rix as teacher of Latin and mathematics; Miss Mary W. White as preceptress and teacher of French and music; Miss Louisa P. Bradlee as teacher of drawing and painting; and A. Farr, M.D., as lecturer on anatomy and physiology. *Caledonian*, August 24, 1850.

[43] The weekly *Chronotype* out of Boston, founded in 1846 by Elizur Wright (1804–85), became a successful anti-slavery newspaper. While Alfred was principal of the Peacham Academy, he kept up his subscription to the *Caledonian*, to which he sent Academy announcements and other news. In the Rix Family Papers at the California Historical Society, there is a copy of the weekly *Chronotype* for November 28, 1849, with several ads featuring goods for California mining, including one for "Water-Proof Goods" made from "patent vulcanized rubber" that Alfred may have kept for an invention he soon was working on.

ASR Paid me for Sarah's tuition.[44] Our affairs with the Cal[edonia] County Gram[mar] School are this day settled. Mr [Samuel] Chandler paying me 30 dollars. Dr [Josiah] Shedd & Mr [Ezra C.] Chamberlain consult a long while on school affairs.[45]

---

[44]Sarah Ellen Chamberlain (1838–70) of Peacham was listed as a student in the 1846–47, 1848, 1849, 1850, 1851, and 1852 PAC.

[45]Dr. Josiah Shedd and Deacon Ezra C. Chamberlain were trustees of the Peacham Academy. Although they agreed to Alfred's plan to share the teaching with Ira O. Miller, they no doubt continued to turn to Alfred for reports on Academy affairs.

CHAPTER FIVE

Studying Law, Preparing for Baby, and Catching Gold Fever
August 15–December 31, 1850

> *I conclude to go* [*to California*] *as soon as I am ready . . .*
> *Chastina is making herself extremely busy now-a-days in*
> *prosecuting a certain branch of family manufacture.*
> ALFRED

> *I attend to the household duties which employ a good part of the time.*
> *. . . There is a great deal of labor in* work.
> CHASTINA

ON AUGUST 24, JOHN S. WAY MADE A TRIUMPHANT RETURN FROM California "with his pocket full of Rocks." It had been one thing to read John's letters from California, but it was quite another to hear firsthand about the miner's experience. The stories he told of his "adventures" must have made quite an impression, because within days Alfred had made up his mind to take his own trip to California, "as soon as I am ready," without any discussion of the subject with Chastina noted in the journal. After they talked about it, Alfred noted that she "seems to be willing to take the gold but is a little doubtful about taking the 'responsibility.'" His resolve was bolstered when the trunk containing the earnings of four of the returning miners arrived. He estimated John's portion to be about $2,700—"as much as a boy can lift," and enough money to buy a farm. Alfred was, as Chastina later noted, becoming "troubled with the California Fever." He was growing restless, feeling stifled in Peacham and ready for change.

149

Studying Law, Preparing for Baby, and Catching Gold Fever

Now that he was no longer teaching at the Peacham Academy, Alfred had more time to work on his inventions. With his curious mind and his talent for mechanics, he had always enjoyed "tinkering." Earlier that year he had made crystals and a paring machine, and now he was working on some waterproof armor, which he referred to as his "Dumfudgeon." Most of Alfred's experiments and inventions were for his own pleasure, but he may also have had dreams of making money, if not with this armor, then certainly later in the year with his adding-multiplying machine. But he also spent time with John, soaking up everything he could learn about California and the economic opportunities there. When his younger brother Hale arrived for a visit, with his own plans for a trip to California, Alfred fully supported the idea, hoping that "if all things are favorable in the spring," he would be able to join him there.

Through the fall, Alfred spent hours studying for his upcoming examination to gain entrance to the Vermont bar. There were times when his eyes were so strained that Chastina had to read the law texts to him. Chastina spent her time preparing clothes for the baby due at the end of the year and completing the household duties she was now responsible for, including the preparation of meals and housekeeping.

Alfred's feelings toward the town continued to sour as the weeks went by. Facing resistance from the local leaders to his way of thinking about such things as free speech, election by ballot, religion, and modern education, and no longer fearing recriminations now that he had stepped down as principal, he began to voice his opposition. At the Free Democracy nominating caucus in August, he suggested the use of a ballot for nominations rather than "the old mode of nominating by a committee." He also pushed to have candidates for justice of the peace selected from both parties. The "old blue partisans," as he called the town leaders, continued to resist such recommendations and were still winning out for the most part, but Alfred felt confident that the old way of thinking in Peacham had been dealt "its death blow."

Despite having given up the principalship, Alfred was still one of the town school superintendents, and in that capacity he led a campaign to adopt new readers for the district schools, a modern series that the new Academy principal, Ira O. Miller, had used at the Hinesburgh Academy in Chittenton County. In an article in the *Caledonian* published on November 16, Miller described the Town Readers he recommended as containing "valuable selections of a high moral character from our most classical English and American writers . . . suited to the wants of our Common

Schools." An interest in improving education increased as the first Vermont state superintendent of schools, Horace Eaton, issued a report at the end of 1849 praising teachers who showed more "interest and zeal in their work" instead of "indifference and apathy." No longer, he wrote, did teachers "pass their time of employment and receive their pay." Their purpose had become "to improve their pupils" and do away with "dull formal and lifeless routine." Teachers such as Alfred and Ira Miller supported better teachers and "improvement in their methods," as Eaton stressed. In an article in the local newspaper in December, Alfred gave his final word on the Mandeville's Readers series. He labeled them "silly," with "extracts from Joke Books and third rate newspaper," and found that the volumes for older children had "a very flat exposition on English Grammar" and were filled with "very bad commentaries." His last sentence called the readers "an *unmitigated humbug*."[1]

The vote on the district schools' readers was a county-level decision, and many old-time school superintendents, mainly ministers, were opposed to the idea of new readers. Alfred took on the fight with all his energy. He traveled to each town in the county and spoke person-to-person with school superintendents, trying to convince them of the need for a good new reader to properly educate the town's children. He eventually won his case, although he undoubtedly alienated some town leaders along the way. He voiced his annoyance at their old-fashioned ways and their immovable attitude toward young men like him with different opinions. It was another victory for Alfred, but it must have added to his dissatisfaction with his life in Peacham. In the past year, he had had fights with political party leaders, school superintendents, and local merchants. Another annoyance that surfaced, one clearly stated in the journal, was his dissatisfaction with the ministers at the church, many of whom were giving trial sermons in the hope of earning the pulpit that had been held by the late Rev. David Merrill. Alfred railed in the journal against the lengthy, often boring sermons and prayers. Even Chastina, who had been raised to be supportive of religious practice and belief, grew tired of prayers that required the congregation to stand for a full hour, especially as her pregnancy progressed.

The law cases that came Alfred's way as he studied for the bar examination were mainly petty robberies and unpaid debts, nothing of particular interest to his active intellect. The challenging cases all went to the

---
[1] *Caledonian*, January 5, November 16, December 21, 1850.

town's respected lawyer, William Mattocks, in whose office Alfred was apprenticed. He accepted the situation as he studied for the exam, but he knew that he would want to expand his range of influence once he had been admitted to the bar. The population of Peacham was decreasing, and Alfred was resigned to the fact that the town provided cases enough for only one lawyer. He would have to move to new territory if he wanted to earn recognition and have challenging and meaningful work.

With his license to practice almost in hand, Alfred moved to resolve his case with Ephraim C. Brown, who had taken out his anger about the Union store by criticizing Alfred's work at the Academy. Having stepped down as Academy principal, Alfred felt free to pursue a case against the merchant, so he had "called the delinquent to an account." Prior to confronting Brown, he discussed the matter with William Mattocks and two town leaders who knew him well, David Choate and Samuel Chandler, and interviewed another witness who had heard Brown's comments. Presented with this ammunition plus the threat of a lawsuit, Brown agreed to pay $100 in compensation to Alfred "for that ugly wiggle to his tongue." It was another victory for Alfred, but it did nothing to assuage his ill feelings toward the town.

Through the fall, Chastina wrote only briefly in the journal, listing her domestic duties—washing on Mondays, cooking their daily meals, sewing baby clothes, and calling on women friends, especially those with small children. It was the first time since their marriage that their journal entries reflected differing attitudes about their present situation and their future. She was focused on home activities while he dreamed of California, with its potential for new opportunities and wealth. Both knew that no firm plans could be made until the baby was born, yet there was clearly a widening rift in their relationship. Chastina was preparing to welcome their first child into the family even as Alfred was thinking of going west in search of a new life.

December was an eventful month for the Rixes. On the 6th, Alfred passed his exam, with no details noted in the journal, and "became a Lawyer at the Bar of Caledonia County State of Vermont." And on December 30, Chastina gave birth to Julian Walbridge Rix, with Alfred noting the details of the birth. "So ends the year 1850," wrote Alfred on New Year's Eve. And so the next chapter in their life began.

[*CWR*] [Thursday, August 15, 1850] I again introduce myself to the Journal, from which I have been quite a stranger of late, though I doubt not but that it will be more acceptable than it would have been had I been punctual in my part of the scribbling— Alfred had a long confab in politics with some of the old Whigs. Dr [Josiah] Shedd made us a call & highly entertained us with his stories of "quacks," &c. Alfred received a pamphlet of "Perforations" into Carlyles Latter day Pamphlet.

[Friday, August 16] Alfred finished his "stent" in law reading about eight o'clock, & then read to me the "Perforations" by Elizur Wright.[2] They are worth reading no mistake. Meanwhile I attend to the household duties which employ a good part of the time especially when we have green corn & string-beans for dinner— We live high these days because we are excessively fond of green things which are very plenty just at this time

[*ASR*] [Saturday, August 17] Wrote to Ballston Spa, N.Y. to learn about the New York Law School. Read Elizur Wright's Perforations in Carlyle and they seem to be pretty numerous and large—whereby we see daylight where we least expect to find it.

[Sunday, August 18] Wrote Oscar [Rix] & to Amanda B. Hodgsdon. Went to church & listened to a flat performance by Mr. Rev. Dr. Pious Underwood. It behooves us poor devils to take what is offered and not look a gift horse in the mouth, if it were not so I should swear the peace on that man & have him wound up in a sum of 1000$ not to torment us before our time. It is enough in all consciences to have a Hell in eternity and it seems to me we ought to be allowed to enjoy the Earth in peace. But Devils will come and disturb the best families now and then. I'll have these poor fools sometime—there is no edge to them at present.

[*CWR*] [Monday, August 19] Got up early for me and went to washing. There is great deal of labor in work. Alfred reads law & busies himself in various ways these long days.

---

[2]Elizur Wright, familiar to Alfred as the founder of the *Chronotype*, was the author of an 1850 pamphlet titled "Perforations," which critically appraised essays written by Scottish satirist and historian Thomas Carlyle (1795–1881).

CWR   [Tuesday, August 20] This A.M. Alfred & I went over to the Academy and tried to regulate things & sweep out. We raised a perfect specimen of a storm in a desert. I am trying to sew some these days but my domestic duties are so numerous, my sewing hours are somewhat limited. Alfred wrote to father Rix family

[Wednesday, August 21] Alfred is on hand this morning as he is preparing to take a walk to Danville a distance of about six miles— So I prepared breakfast with all possible haste and he started about six A.M. The supreme court is now in session at Danville & Alfred is anxious to avail himself of any advantages therefrom. I have been very lonesome to day & it has been a week almost since morning— Mother [Watts] called here a short time. Had a call also from Miss [Louisa] Bradlee— It is now after nine o'clock P.M. I am here all alone—the first time Alfred has ever been away & left me at home alone.

[ASR] I suppose Tina left this space for me to record my adventures in. At 8 o'clock A.M. I got to Danville and found folks there in abundance. Ch. Justice Royce, Assistants Redfield, Bennett & Poland on the Bench.[3] Listened with all my might. Mr Stoddard of Waterford asked a place for his daughter as teacher in our Academy. I writ to [Ira] Miller on the subject. Slept in the same room with Joseph Potts Esq of Barnet.[4] The smell of Tobacco was as strong as from certain vessels indicated by this gents name, by leaving out one t. Quite interested in court proceedings.

[Thursday, August 22] Talked over with B[liss] N. Davis Esq his adventure with Bristol Bill—saw the knife & the scar in his neck made by it. Attended court as usual—came off at the Adjournment which took place at 5 o'clock P.M. Walked home in two hours. While at Danville was introduced to most of the gentlemen of the

---

[3]Judges on the 1850 Vermont Supreme Court were Chief Justice Stephen Royce (1787–1868), Isaac F. Redfield (1804–76), and Daniel Kellogg (1791–1875). The Circuit Court judges were Robert Pierpoint (1791–1864), Jacob Collamer (1791–1865), Milo L. Bennett (1790–1868), and Luke P. Poland (1815–87). The Caledonia County Courthouse was at Danville until 1855, when the county seat moved to St. Johnsbury. *Vermont Legislative Directory.*

[4]Joseph Potts (1819–62) of Barnet was admitted to the bar in Danville in 1843 and opened a practice in Groton. Wells, *History of Barnet,* 581–83. Strangers often shared rooms and beds at this time.

ROXANA BROWN
WALBRIDGE WATTS,
VERMONT, CA. 1850
Print from daguerreotype made in St. Johnsbury, Vermont, when Chastina's mother, called "Mother Watts" in the journal, was about fifty years old. The books on the table next to her indicate that she was literate and proud of it. She wears a dress made from heavily glazed cotton chintz with capped sleeves and a pointed waistline, holdovers from the 1840s. Her gold bead necklace was a common accessory at the time. *California Historical Society.*

bar present.⁵ Think I shall like to douse in among them. Found Dan. Gilfillan & wife & Clara [Walbridge] here when I got home. All right.

[*CWR*] [Friday, August 23] Clara [Walbridge] with us today. She is almost sick with a cold— Alfred had letters from [Ira] Miller & Carlton J. Morrill. Clara walked home at night

[*ASR*] [Saturday, August 24] Our mouths made up for some honey, we started at a signal given from home—which was to be a white cloth in an open door in sight of us—⁶ As I said before we started at about one o'clock P.M. the sun scorching our backs me[a]n while.

After a scamper in the woods—cutting a huge tree—gloving & hooding—fire & straw & fight & frolic we came off gloriously

---

⁵Alfred may have gone to the courthouse to acquaint himself with the lawyers who would be examining him later in the year when he applied to the bar.

⁶The land between the East Part and Peacham Corner had been so cleared of trees that a white cloth held up at the door of the Watts farmhouse could be seen from a second-floor apartment at Peacham Corner.

ASR rewarded with 3 or 4 ounces of honey —— comb. After a terrible fright from a burning brush heap wherein a pan of milk was called in requisition to put out the conflagration but which in fact went into our maws, & after a slight political skirmish with Alvah [Watts] & Uncle Lyman [Way], we all went off to bed as become peaceful citizens. When it was midnight, that "witching hour!" our slumbers were broken by the clatter of a man's heels over our floor. The intruder brushed by our bed—fumbled over the table, found a match & lit it & came to hold it to our innocent noses, when we just raised ourselves up & cried out, "John Way, how do you do sir?" The Californian was at home again—with his pocket full of Rocks. We got ourselves up and listened to his adventures. Of all which more by & by. Recd a letter from C[arleton] J. Morrill.

[Sunday, August 25] Came home from East Part. Slept, read, played, & loafed all day long eating at regular intervals between the Exercises. Rainy & bad for wheat.[7]

[Monday, August 26] At work as usual—finished the reading of the Life of Patrick Henry.[8] He seems to have been a patriot & orator, but not remarkable for scientific or legal attainments—on the whole I am pleased with his character—but must say I do not entertain that profound respect for it which I feel for some other names. Whenever I think of Franklin or Washington or Adams or Jefferson—(and I might include many other names) I feel like uttering my thanks to them & bowing in meek approbation of their characters & principles. There seems little left me but adoration. Not so with Henry.

[Tuesday, August 27] Baking and brewing. Geo. Clarke made us a call. Talked over matters. Lent him Wright's Perforations. In the Evening the Free Democracy held a nominating Caucus.[9] A. Rix was called to the chair. The old mode of nominating by a committee was advocated strongly by most of the old blue partisans but the chair supported the mode by ballot and was backed up by a very

---

[7] Excessive rain in July and early August delayed the harvest and diminished the value of the hay. Yale, *While the Sun Shines*, 3–4, 18–19.
[8] Alfred may have been reading *Life of Patrick Henry* (1817) by William Wirt (1772–1834).
[9] The *North Star* of August 24, 1850, announced the meeting of the "Free Democracy of Peacham" for "the purpose of nominating a candidate for Town Representative, and seven candidates for Justices of the Peace." The two major parties in the county at this time were the Whigs and the Free Democrats. The latter included the free-soilers like Alfred.

respectable minority & although the improved method did not fully prevail yet it is believed the old mode has got its death blow in this town. Furthermore, an attempt was made by the chair also to select the candidates for Justice of the Peace—from both parties & succeeded so far as to have a committee appointed to meet a corresponding committee of the Whigs & concert matters. Nominated Wm Mattocks for Representative.

[Wednesday, August 28] Read during the morning— Chastina is busy Preparing for Company, which came about 11 o'clock in the shape of John Way & Wife. Just P.M. Comes Mrs E[phraim] C. Brown and baby—<u>Postquam</u>—Dr [Asahel] Farr & wife—also Mr Lance &c. Fine visit— Talk of California—[10] I conclude to go <u>as soon as I am ready</u>. These are vacation times. Warm. Father [Lyman] Watts called— Paid J[ohn] Way for a gold [Here Alfred draws a circle with "20" in it meaning $20 dollar gold piece]. Same Day Evening— The Whigs held their Caucus and after an infinite amount of fretting & fuming—blowing & bursting—amidst confusion and noise it was voted to accede to the Free Democratic proposal & so choose a committee of arrangement. The more I see of party movements the less I think of their worth.

[Thursday, August 29] Got one of Chase's Interest Tables & framed & varnished it for preservation. It seems to be perfectly accurate. Tina Sewing. At dark come I[ra] O. Miller 2 brother & sister to town—we i.e. I[ra] O. & Myself tried to get him a boarding place but did not fully succeed.[11] Introduced to the family, &c &c. The Political committees met & agreed on candidates— So we go!

[Friday, August 30] This is to one man, no doubt, an awful day, for it must be his last. Prof. [John W.] Webster is to be executed to-day & notwithstanding many believe him fully guilty & that he will make another confession, yet I venture to record here before it is known my decided opinion that he will leave no further confession & that if he is guilty the proof is not sufficiently strong to forbid the

ASR

---

[10] The *Caledonian* of August 31, 1850, reported the return of four of the "Peacham California Company" with about $3,000 each. Of the eighteen men who had left in January 1850, town records show that fifteen returned, one died in California, one disappeared mysteriously on the return trip, and one was unaccounted for. Bonfield, "Ho for California," 16.

[11] Ira O. Miller arrived with his brother, Stearns Robert Miller, and sister, Mary, both from Coventry and both listed as students in the 1850 Pac; Mary was also listed in 1851 and 1852.

ASR Gov. from commuting his sentence to imprisonment for life.[12] [Ira] Miller gets boarded at [Trustram] Sanborn's & goes to Montpelier. This is at 2 o'clock wait till night for the political news.

[Saturday, August 31] Finished the reading of Kent's Commentaries. Read news. My practice is to let the news be till Saturday—then into it for all! The news came by to night's mail that Dr [John W.] Webster was executed according to the most approved method. It seems that he left no further record of his guilt as was expected. For one I doubt the propriety of hurrying a man into the other world. I do not condemn capital punishment under all circumstances—it oftentimes cannot be avoided with safety to community. But in New England where there are prisons & jails & where all feel that a little delay is no escape, it were better to enforce this Sanction of the Law in a moderate way. In the present case, If he is guilty to the fullest extent claimed by any one still there is no necessity to urge his speedy execution. The idea that delay dulls the sense of punishment is too puerile and sounds too much like heathen reasoning to be entertained in these times. While on the other hand if in his confession he has told the truth it is terrible injustice to hang him at all. And it looks to me as if he had given the right version of the facts. Almost every circumstance which occurred previously to the homicide is in perfect keeping with this supposition, while they utterly forbid the opposite, i.e. the supposition of murder. Again, all that took place afterwards can be explained on one supposition just as well and no better than on the other. These are considerations worthy examination. But Webster was a fine man & was needed as an example!

[Sunday, September 1] Attended church & listened to a bore in the shape of old Johnson of somewhere. P.M. At home. Chastina went again hoping for better things but like to have died before she got away. Bad luck to a minister who thinks God so dull as to need an explanation in the shape of a prayer of an hour's length in order to understand our case. But perhaps the old fellow meant to worry the Lord with his long & voracious importunity—but this was a mistake in him for the Lord would turn his ear to shorter & keener prayers while old Johnson's would be considered as coming from an old ass who had got already more than he deserved. Simon Varnum's

---

[12]*Caledonian*, September 7, 1850.

oldest boy of 11 years died & was buried this afternoon. [Ira] Miller & myself walked out.

[*CWR*] [Monday, September 2] Alfred introduces [Ira] Miller to his future scene of action. My business is washing of course. Dustan [Walbridge] made us a call.

[Tuesday, September 3] Dustan [Walbridge] came for me to go over home. Mrs. Martin & Mary Gilfillan there visiting. Alfred came over to tea & then returned to the corner, while I stayed all night. "Town Meeting." Mr. [William] Mattocks free soiler elected representative, & also seven free-soil justices.[13] Received a letter from Oscar [Rix]. All well. Adaline [Rix Bierstadt] has got a little son.[14] Alfred is having Mr. [William] M[attock]'s office fitted up in order to be more decent to stay in.

[Wednesday, September 4] Came home this morning. Found Alfred just ready to start for school— The school opens with between forty & fifty scholars. The Misses Harvey have taken possession of their room here much to my annoyance although they are some of the best of girls.[15] It is not so pleasant to have persons unconnected with a family passing through a room at all times. Chastina [Brown] & Cynthia Brown made me a call.

[*ASR*] [Thursday, September 5] Began our school-recitations. Fine weather. Do a bit of lawyering now and then. Chastina is at work on shirts & chemise. Called on [Humphrey] Bennett in the Rix v [Ephraim] Brown case. Talked over the matter with [David] Choate & Samuel [Chandler].[16]

---

[13] William Mattocks was elected as Peacham's representative to the Vermont legislature at the September 1850 town meeting when statewide and local elections were held.

[14] Adeline Rix Bierstadt must have been pregnant at her wedding to Edward in 1850, which may be why their marriage year was usually given as 1849 after the Bierstadt brothers became well known. Rix, *History and Genealogy of the Rix Family*, 94–95.

[15] The Harvey sisters, students at the Academy, boarded at Abigail Chamberlain's using the same entrance as the Rixes, whose first room they had to go through to get to their own. The 1850 PAC listed seven girls named Harvey, two from Peacham, three from Barnet, and one each from Topsham and Ryegate.

[16] Alfred consulted with two town leaders who knew him well in regard to his case against merchant Ephraim C. Brown, who had criticized his teaching at the Academy. According to *Walton's Vermont Register*, Peacham had four merchants in 1850: John M. Martin at the Corner with the post office, Isaac Watts at the Hollow, Carter W. Evans (ca. 1808–77) with a woolen mill at Water Street, and Brown and Weeks also at the Corner. Only Brown seems to have spoken out against Alfred's leadership in the Union store.

ASR   [Friday, September 6] Employed Mr [William] Mattocks as counsel in the case of Rix v Brown and consulted others—find quite an amount of matter servicable as testimony.

[Saturday, September 7] Continue to consult neighbor by neighbor and am bringing the affair to a head. Made out a writ against Mr Davidson for old Bradlee. A few such cases as these where an old stingy mearchant sues on a balance in account where all he has as balance is interest on his own charges and a rejection of the other's—I say a few such cases as these will get me rather out of countenance with law affairs. [CWR] Called on the [Ira] Millers

[Sunday, September 8] [*ASR writing entry in the shape of an upside down cone*] No morning at all—Afternoon we eat breakfast and comb our heads—Clarissa [Walbridge] called. Mr Stone preaches—Good luck to him—we cant hear him—Preachers are rather doubtful stock—one lately run away with a Hardwick girl as wife when he had one already. Let us wait for further particulars. Sort of a cowery day. There seems to be a flat-ness of feeling about us to day which unfits us for either work or play and sort of makes every thing run to a point & so on to nothing at all at all

[CWR] [Monday, September 9] Alfred wrote to [Charles S.] Smith. Had a hard days work & "boiled victuals" for dinner. Alfred wrote to Mr Bartlette of Lyndon concerning <u>his case</u>.

[Tuesday, September 10] John Blanchard & James Merrill started for Wisconsin. Mother [Watts] called. Pleasant weather these days. Made Miss [Louisa] Bradlee a call. Camp meeting opened.[17] [Ira] Miller, sister & Miss [Ann Maria] Child called on us. Letter from Miss [Sophia] Leverett.

[ASR] [Wednesday, September 11] Wrote to Miss [Sophia] Leverett—would not give her what she asked—viz—a certificate of recommendation. Made out deed for T[rustram] Sanborn to Mrs Dana. Yesterday James Merrill & John Blanchard started for the

---

[17]The *Caledonian* of September 7, 1850, published an article from the *Christian Messenger* on a "Camp Meeting" for the Danville District at Peacham. Held on the farm of Hartwell Hooker near Cabot, it apparently was a Christian gathering where families could bring their tents and stay for a few days of preaching and praying.

west. Rained to day all over the camp meeting and scattered the saints most wonderfully.

[Thursday, September 12] Dont find anything worth recording.

[Friday, September 13] Received a letter from Bartlett & Bingham saying they are ready to go it in the law-suit. Tim Cowles & Steele had a fight for a horse. Made a little headway against my Law.

[Saturday, September 14] A Letter—and one of the long sort too—from [Charles S.] Smith arguing in favor of Theological Schools. Went over to the East Part—went fishing in the Afternoon with John S. Way down Elijah's Brook & caught about 70.

[Sunday, September 15] Went to Camp-Meeting with John [S. Way] and Guck [Augustus Walbridge]. Saw an acre of folks and an acre of fools. About 30 young men & girls came forward into the anxious seats and got confoundedly scared—good enough for them—no business there![18] Postquam went home & got Tina and a peck of apples. Dined at Orman Hooker's.[19]

[Monday, September 16] Chastina washed and went to bed tired all out. Charles S. Smith made us a visit—staid over night. Dr [Josiah] Shedd & [Ira] Miller all with us in the evening.

[Tuesday, September 17] [Charles S.] Smith left for Hardwick & his sister Mrs or Widow Lord started for the West. To day came on My First Case in Lawyering in Peacham, in the shape of counsel for the State v. Stone & Davidson, two young men who had been brought up before the justice on a charge of Burglary & theft. No good evidence could be found against them & they were discharged. The confession of Stone on account of its having been made under inducement was not admitted. So mote it be.

[Wednesday, September 18] Got in my wood— Called on Miss [Mary] White our Preceptress i.e.[20] Tina & I dug some potatoes & brought the hoe in for breakfast & left the potatoes leaning up by the fence.

---

[18] The *Caledonian* of September 21, 1850, published an article from the *Christian Messenger* stating that "quite a large" number had professed conversion at the "camp meeting."

[19] Orman Hooker (1818–85) owned the farm of the late Congregational minister Leonard Worcester (1767–1846) in the western part of Peacham.

[20] One of Alfred's duties was to check on his teachers, as he did with Miss White, the new music teacher.

Lawyer's First Case!

[Thursday, September 19] Nothing at all but rain.

[Friday, September 20] Had a serious confab with E[phraim] C. Brown, merchant, on the merits of the case between us. He seems to be very penitent and ready to make any reasonable reparation for the mischief he has done, which fact determines me to let him off at the very lowest mark possible. But it still remains to be seen whether he will adhere to his present disposition. Nothing but force, I am sure, could bring him down in this manner from his lofty & swelling pretensions. The chief facts in the case are shortly these. For a year and a half I went on with my school at the Academy in prosperous style. Not a word was uttered against me either as a teacher or a man. Perhaps few Preceptors have been more completely popular. But in the winter the subject of Union stores came up in our town for discussion. I plead & acted in their favor—aided in establishing one in Peacham. By this course Brown became my enemy—declared war against me & entered at once on the campaign and flagged not till he had lied & frightened off many students, kept more away & got the name of the school into bad repute in neighboring towns & brought it to be somewhat to be suspected in this. We kept our mouths shut till our time was out & then looked up the case & called the delinquent to an account. I give him till tomorrow to say whether he will pay up willingly or be squeezed to it.

[Saturday, September 21] [Ephraim C.] Brown promises to pay me a hundred dollars next week and be even. So mote it be. The case of Bradlee v Davidson was tried. Made out a writ v Geo. Colby of Bradford for Trover. Chastina & I went to East Part. The Gold from California, dug by [John] Way, [John and Chester] Martins & [Alex] MacLeran has come. John has got as much as a boy can lift all in 20s & 10s—he dont tell how much in value, but I guess it is $2700.00.[21]

[Sunday, September 22] Wrote to Oscar [Rix]. A.M. At church to hear Mr old [Austin O.] Hubbard of Barnet. If he ever gets to heaven it will be because, "Blessed are the poor in spirit for theirs is the kingdom of heaven."

[Monday, September 23] New Piano come & got a going—Music! Mr [William] Mattocks went to Boston. A meeting of our Union Division. Adjourned till one week. Bought some flannel &c.

[Tuesday, September 24] Visit from Aunt [Sarah] Stevens & Mother Watts.

[Wednesday, September 25] Geo. Currier Came along & I paid him 3.00 for the 21st of Vt. Reports, to be repaid on condition. Quite Cold & Fall-like.

---

[21]The transport receipt on the box, dated August 11, 1850, read: "One valise said to Contain Fifteen Thousand & Two Hundred Dollars in gold dust." It was made out to John Martin and shipped on board the steamer *Crescent City* from Panama to New York. Private collection. Bonfield, "Ho for California," 17.

ASR [Thursday, September 26] Finished the Reading of Stevens on Pleading. Began Swift on Pleading.[22]

[Friday, September 27] Mr [William] Mattocks returned. Worked on a paring machine. Cold & rainy.

[Saturday, September 28] Read and played football. C. visited Laura Bennett who is sick of a fever.

[Sunday, September 29] Went to church—heard an old fellow from the West—he preached without notes and got off two glorious sermons. John Way & wife & Clarissa [Walbridge] called on us at noon and so did Hartwell Hooker.[23] Went dow[n] & saw Laura Bennett again.

[Monday, September 30] Wrote a recommend for Jane Chamberlain.[24] Picked my corn & Bought ½ barrel flour. Saw a wonderful phenomenon in the heavens, a sort of broken down comet, with its head broke & its tail curled up. [Ira] Miller Spent the Evening with us & attended an auction.

[Tuesday, October 1] Had a husking & all its accompaniments.[25] Chastina is making herself extremely busy now-a-days in prosecuting a certain branch of family manufacture. Winter will be likely to bring with it a necessity for a large amount of flannel garments. It is to supply such a contemplated want that Chastina's fingers are now so nimble. Good luck to her! May every garment she makes find a wearer to fill it who shall be more than all she anticipates in her fondest & most Pleasing hopes.

[Wednesday, October 2] Awful Rainy day. The Congregational

---

[22] Henry John Stephen (1787–1864), *A Treatise on the Principles of Pleading in Civil Actions Comprising a Summary View of the Whole Proceedings in a Suit at Law* (1835). Zephaniah Swift (1759–1823) published several books, but Alfred was probably reading *A Digest of the Law of Evidence, in Civil and Criminal Cases and a Treatise on Bills of Exchange, and Promissory Notes* (1810).

[23] Hartwell Hooker (1797–1875), the farmer who owned the land where the camp meeting was held, had fourteen children, including two sons who were interested in going to California. Bonfield, "Ho for California," 28.

[24] Jane Chamberlain attended Mount Holyoke Seminary from 1850 to 1852 and was the first Peacham girl to graduate from college. Patricia J. Albright, Mount Holyoke College Archivist, letter to editor, January 22, 1988.

[25] Farmers invited people to their farms to husk the recently harvested corn, which would be fed to the animals through the winter. After the work, the group enjoyed refreshments. Alfred's small garden meant that the occasion was strictly a social event.

ministers gathered themselves together here to day in Conference.[26] Some find ready entertainment and some dont. One old chap stood in the street with his tail hanging down like any rooster's in a rainstorm, waiting for a "call" to dinner more than half an hour. The Deacons stood in a horse-shed and laughed at him. Aunt Nabby [Abigail Chamberlain] cant get nobody to eat & sleep with her. A couple of old coneys try to lecture at night. Chastina is a little cross. Dunned [Ephraim] Brown for his promised 100. Calves' tails have riz! Reading Cruise's Digest—Starkie's Evidence & Story's Equity Jurisprudence. Chastina has undertaken for two dollars a volume to read Russel on crimes to me evenings when my eyes wont allow I shall read myself.[27]

[Thursday, October 3] Rains still and cold. Attended with C. a lecture by Kimball & Co. on Electro Magnetism, illustrated by a variety of Experiments. Idem tomorrow.

[Friday, October 4] Attended and aided in our first Fall Review. With Chastina called on Mrs [Laura] Bennett who is getting some better. Also went to hear the rest of what old Kimball had to say on Electricity. There are a great many geeks in this world besides those that are eaten at thanksgiving.

[Saturday, October 5] Waited all the A.M. for a Surveying class to get ready to go into the fields, which they did at one P.M. Chastina is rather wee but means to walk to the East Part after Tea. Yesterday & Today have been most beautiful specimens of Fall weather. Mr [Ephraim] Brown still holds off about paying up his score and I should not be surprised if he wanted to back out of the undertaking. But we are bound to put him through if he does not. Mr [Asa] Brainard of Danville arrived last night who no doubt means to preach

---

[26] The semi-annual meeting of the Caledonia County Conference of Churches was to be held at Peacham on October 2 and 3. *Caledonian*, September 28, 1850.

[27] Alfred was reading law texts, including William Cruise et al., *A Digest of the Law of Real Property* (1849–50); Thomas Starkie, *A Practical Treatise of the Law of Evidence and Digest of Proofs, in Civil and Criminal Proceedings* (1824); Joseph Story, *Story's Equity Jurisprudence* (1835–36); and William Russell, *Russell on Crime [A Treatise on Crimes and Misdemeanors]* (1819). Alfred wrote of paying Chastina to read these to him, but since their finances were joined, this is probably a game they played. She never complained about a lack of money or spoke of money as "hers" or "his."

ASR here tomorrow.[28] I keep scratching on here, simply because I have nothing else to do— I am waiting for Tea. Peacham, Oct. 4, 1850. A. Rix

Went home to East Part and knocked at both doors at once which, led our folks to think the Rochester Knockings had come.[29]

[Sunday, October 6] At home resting from labor and eating a little for the stomach's sake. News that some of the Southern States mean to secede on account of the late act of Congress admitting the State of California.

[Monday, October 7] Cold and snowy—gathered squashes. Chronotype come.

[Tuesday, October 8] Wrote to Oscar [Rix] for the chronotype & sent two dollars. Dunned [Ephraim] Brown. Played a game of chess. [William] Mattocks went to Montpelier.

[Wednesday, October 9] At last [Ephraim] Brown has come forward and given me his note for one hundred dollars on demand in compensation for that ugly wiggle to his tongue. Warm and pleasant.

[Written later, after his return] Started in company with John S. Way for Montpelier to 'Lection—at about 2½ o'clock. Stopt at Marshfield and made Dustan [Walbridge] a short call, then drove to Plainfield and staid till morning. Chastina went home, leaving my bed and board all alone. Made a [Alfred draws here a wavy line].

[Thursday, October 10] Continued our journey to Montpelier village. I shall reserve for a future notice one or two rich scenes which we took in at the tavern and by the way. Put up at the Union House and went to the Capitol and looked over the property. Saw a silver plow & Mexican lances & the ordnance taken by the Vermonters at the Battle of Bennington. Saw also our old opponents Cottrill & Hayden. Saw also Mr Leavenworth & some other folks. Attended

---

[28] Rev. Asa Brainerd (1801–89), who replaced Alvah Watts as principal of the Phillips Academy in Danville, was helping to organize the upcoming teachers' convention in Montpelier. *Caledonian*, August 24 and October 12, 1850.

[29] "Rochester knockings" was a common phrase in the mid-nineteenth century, used to imply spiritual communication. Rochester, New York, was an early center for a new wave of spiritualism or occult philosophy in the United States; "knockings" refers to the rapping sounds through which mediums claimed to be communicating with the dead.

the opening of the Session in the House.[30] Bought some duddery & *ASR* toggery for our folks, attended an auction, took a lick of 'isters and went to bed & slept like an ass till next day. Chastina was all day engaged in the more useful and benevolent business of constructing small hoods for her bare-headed little sisters. Very Fine Weather.

[Friday, October 11] Rains. Start for home about 7 o'clock. Got there about 4 o'clock P.M. Saw some sights & scenes which must await a future leisure. Chastina continues her millinery. Cynthia Brown visits Mrs [Roxana] Watts' at night.

[Saturday, October 12] Stataturdudy Come to Corner. Rainy. I read news. Tina ironed and baked & worked and so forth.

[Sunday, October 13] Listened A.M. to a little minister from Waterford— Sarah B. [Walbridge] Way for the first time come out to church—first time since her sickness. P.M. At home.

[Monday, October 14] All things about as usual. Helped [Ira] Miller kill a party about to have been at Tavern.

[Tuesday, October 15] Wrote to D. Kimball of Hanover N.H. about Catalogue. [Ira] Miller starts for Montpelier.[31]

[Wednesday, October 16] Took charge of the school and worked hard. Some of the scholars wish [Ira] Miller would stay off and others want me to hear their classes <u>all the time</u>. Call from Dr. [Josiah] Shedd. Miss [Mary] White & Mrs [Eliza] Mattocks call and talk over a proposed ride by the women to St. Johnsbury. Letter from Mr Kimball.

[Thursday, October 17] [Ira] Miller on hand. Women off for St. Johnsbury. Fine day.

[*CWR*] We took a ride over to Aunt [Sarah] Stevens. Alfred wrote to Mrs. Hodgeden for Aunt S[arah Stevens].

---

[30] On the way to Montpelier, Alfred called on Chastina's brother Dustan Walbridge, who was in Marshfield serving an apprenticeship in the wheelwright trade. Bonfield and Morrison, *Roxana's Children*, 122. Alfred traveled to Montpelier to attend the state legislature, where William Mattocks represented Peacham, and he may also have gone to make some purchases at the Montpelier Protective Union No. 59, which was in business from 1848 to 1858. Rozwenc, *Cooperatives Come to America*, 126. He did not mention attending the teachers' convention, another indication that he was through with the Peacham Academy.

[31] Academy principal Ira O. Miller attended a teachers' convention in Montpelier convened for the purpose of organizing a State Association of Teachers. *Caledonian*, October 12, 1850.

CWR   [Friday, October 18] Rainy day. Alfred fixed our center table, commenced making a lamp-mat. Calls from Laura Harvey & Margaret Blanchard. Alf. begins to be troubled with the California fever.

[ASR] [Saturday, October 19] Made out writs for I[ra] O. Miller & Holton. Had a long talk with John Way & Dr. [Asahel] Farr on the subject of Gold hunting—who knows but we may all go off together. Chastina seems to be willing to take the gold but is a little doubtful about taking the "responsibility."

[Sunday, October 20] Alf attended church A.M. and heard Mr Jackson Abbot preach a very flat discourse.[32] Why wont ministers learn to preach to some effect and why wont churches act to some effect. I am sick of this everlasting preaching and no practice. When poor wretches, called fugitive slaves are chased by their southern masters into our state, why cant <u>good</u> folks lend a hand to help them? They dont. They wont! and so I have'nt much opinion of em.[33]

[Monday, October 21] Went to meeting in the evening.

[Tuesday, October 22] Recd 18 dol[lar]s of J. Carter for [William] Mattocks in the name of [Alfred draws here a wavy line].

[Wednesday, October 23] Omitted a recitation P.M. so as to let scholars go to church. Old Gallaher makes quite a stir among the piously disposed young women. Finished Reading 1 vol. of Cruise's Digest & 1 vol. Starkie on Evidence. Chastina got a loose dress started.

[Thursday, October 24] Attended to the book-business. Examined Mandeville's Series of Readers—condemned them.[34]

[Friday, October 25] Had our Second Review for the Fall-term.

---

[32] Jacob Jackson Abbott (1813–78) was from Groton. Comstock, *Congregational Churches of Vermont*, 159.

[33] Congress passed the Fugitive Slave Act in September as part of the Compromise of 1850, with a major concession to the Southern states as it mandated the return of runaway slaves to their masters and increased penalties for those who aided fugitives. Alfred expressed the views of the free-soilers who opposed this law. Vermont was one of the states that passed personal liberty laws, forbidding judges to fine or jail Vermonters who helped slaves and refused to send the fugitives back to their masters.

[34] Before the adoption of the Vermont School Law of 1849, each district school chose its own reading books, often keeping the same texts for years. Under the new law, town superintendents in each county were to meet as a board to examine and recommend suitable books to be used in the schools for a period of at least four years. Alfred examined Mandeville's Series of Readers and found them lacking; following the recommendation of Ira O. Miller, he favored Town's Series of Reading Books, published in 1848 by Sanborn, Carter, Bazin in Boston, which Miller had used while teaching at the Hinesburgh Academy. *Caledonian*, November 9, 1850.

Visited with Mr. [A. G.] Button, Mr [Thomas] Goodwillie, & Mr [Austin O.] Hubbard. Had quite a flourish of small armor & some little sharp shooting with the latter on the late convention. Chastina finished her dress. *ASR*

[Saturday, October 26] Concerted a plan with [A. G.] Button, Col. Porter & Mr Sawin to knock the Appleton clique all into [pi?].[35] Sawin & I went in a most horrible rain to Ryegate & Barnet, saw Beattie & McArthur and got them with us. Come up from Mackindoes by stage.

[Sunday, October 27] At home—Reading & Resting.

[*CWR*] [Monday, October 28] Alfred starts early in the morning about the book business. I, of course, am washing as usual. Find myself very tired after getting all my work done. Called on Mrs. [Betsey] Brown. Got <u>some patterns</u> of her. This evening has been unusually lengthy. I dont like to stay alone.

[*ASR, written later, after he returned*] Rix went to Sheffield & Wheelock & put up at Sutton with Daniel G. Shaw.

[*CWR*] [Tuesday, October 29] Very cold & some snow. Alfred gone yet. I do not like the fun of keeping house all alone, however, I make out to get along—but shall be glad to see Alfred's good natured face again— Have been very busy at my work all day & till ten o'clock P.M.

[*ASR*] Rix went from Sutton to Burke, thence to Newark, thence to Lyndon & Waterford where I put up.

[*CWR*] [Wednesday, October 30] Clarissa [Walbridge] came on a visit—Made Mrs. [Betsey] Brown a call.

[*ASR*] Rix came to St. Johnsbury & Barnet & Peacham. My object in this tour has been to reverse a Recommendation of Mandeville's Readers made by a few of the Superintendents—the thing has been handsomely done.[36] Found all well at home. A Ball at [Dan] Foster's. Consulted with Porter & Sawin. &&.

---

[35]Appleton was the publisher of Mandeville's Readers.

[36]Alfred visited school superintendents in neighboring towns to urge the adoption of the new readers. Some, including the Barnet superintendents, Rev. Thomas Goodwillie and Rev. Austin O. Hubbard, favored Mandeville's Readers, while others, including James M. Beattie and J. McArthur of Ryegate and Daniel G. Shaw of Sutton, supported Alfred's choice. Rev. Goodwillie and Rev. Beattie were Peacham Academy trustees from 1848 through at least 1860. Goodwillie was also listed in the 1846–47 PAC and as president from 1852 on, replacing David Merrill.

ASR   [Thursday, October 31] Closed business with P[orter] & S[awin] who seem extremely satisfied with the result. Took my classes again in the Academy. Wrote to [T. A.] Cutler, [T. W.] Duncan & Brigham.[37]

[CWR] [Friday, November 1] Received a letter from Hale [Rix]. Clara [Walbridge] & I very busy making things after our patterns borrowed from Mrs. [Betsey] Brown. We visited at Mr. [David] Choate's in the evening.

[Saturday, November 2] Clara [Walbridge] attended the forenoon exercises at the Academy. Alfred read newspapers, & for my own self, did a large ironing & attended to other domestic business.

[Sunday, November 3] Alfred went to church. In A.M. heard old Mr. Sutherland preach & in the afternoon went to the Chapel. Mother [Watts] called at noon. Clara [Walbridge] went home after meeting

[Monday, November 4] Alfred started early this morning with his surveying class for Cow Hill to survey some disputed land. I have been washing & am very tired. Had calls from Mrs. E[phraim] C. Brown Miss [Ann] Cameron & Ellen Morse. It is now after 9 o'clock P.M. & Alfred has'nt come yet.

[ASR] Alf. after numerous trials and tribulations got his corps of surveyors on the hill-top and set about operations. The clouds hung upon the mountain so thick & misty that it was difficult to run a line to suit us. We spent the chief of the day in hunting out old lines.

[Tuesday, November 5] Remained over last night at Mr. [Daniel] Bickford's in Cabot.[38] At sun-rise we were on the ground again and succeeded in our enterprize most admirably. Came home at dark and found Tina with Tea all ready & waiting for me—bless her! For a further account of this expedition see the plan of the land and the accompanying papers.[39]

---

[37]These were Vermont school superintendents T. A. Cutler of Waterford and T. W. Duncan of Burke; Brigham was not identified. *Caledonian*, November 9, 1850.

[38]Daniel Bickford (1798–1868) owned a farm on the Peacham-Cabot border. Bonfield, "Work Journal of Albert Bickford," 118. Among the area landowners who were involved in the dispute were David Choate, John Way, Sr., and Col. Blanchard; the latter's identity is not clear.

[39]None of these papers have been located.

[Wednesday, November 6] The above 6 [in the date line] is made larger because this is Chastina's twenty-sixth birth-day. She has got into a notion of late that on her birth-day she is entitled to some especial notice in the Journal—and some more out of it. Therefore,

ASR

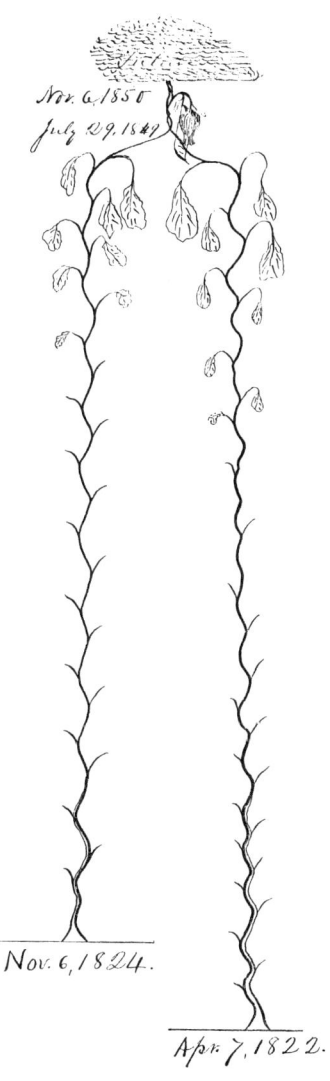

ASR   This is the state of man:
To day he puts forth the tender leaves
of hope, tomorrow blossoms.
                Shakespeare, King Hen. VIII
                    (Act III, Scene II)

Paraphrase.
This is the state of man
  To day
He goes a courting,
  Tomorrow
He gets married.
  The third day
There's a baby!

[Thursday, November 7] Before Breakfast we were favored with a call from Elder [T. W.] Duncan of Burke who read 8 pages of foolscap to prove that Mandeville was a fool & get his breakfast. Chastina did'nt feel very smart to day.

[Friday, November 8] Got our catalogues, black and white. Old Gallaher got back yesterday and went to making folks good with all his might. [*CWR*] Made minced pies & eat a boiled dinner.

[*ASR*] [Saturday, November 9] Made cement— Recd the school circulars— Dunned Dr [Josiah] Shedd & [Samuel] Chandler to give a set of Readers. Attended [Ira] Miller's Teacher's Class. Father & Mother Watts took tea with us. John [S. Way] called on us in the evening. John Way 1st asked me to get [William] Mattocks for their Lawyer in the case.

[Sunday, November 10] We attended church A.M. & heard Mr. Gallaher—rather a bore. Read Tribune, Bayard Taylor & Chronotype.[40] P.M. & looked out the window! At church again in the evening.

[Monday, November 11] Wrote to Oscar [Rix]. Chastina Washed &c. Planed out some boards for California &c.

[Tuesday, November 12] Talked over matters with Col. Blanchard, he seems to be unwilling to arbitrate.

[Wednesday, November 13] Saw [David] Choate & [Daniel]

---

[40]Bayard Taylor (1825–78) went to California in June 1849 as a reporter for Horace Greeley's *New York Tribune* and published the now-classic gold rush study *Eldorado* in the fall of 1850.

Bickford & [John] Way sen[ior]. Conclude to make Col. fair offers, then quit & go to law. I am appointed to make them. Col. Wont Listen—hard as a rock—he wants [Daniel] Bickford to go into law if he chooses. Laura Bennett spent the Afternoon with us. [Humphrey] Bennett at Tea with us. Held a council with Messrs Porter & [A. G.] Button on Parson [Austin O.] Hubbard's case & conclude it to be about desperate. But we cannot quite determine what remedy. "The mountain labored & got a mouse."

ASR

[Thursday, November 14] Mr. [William] Mattocks returned from Montpelier [*CWR*] 2 days since. Alfred full of business. Mrs. [Laura] Bennett here visiting.

[Friday, November 15] Nothing of note occurred. Col. Porter made us a call in the evening.

[Saturday, November 16] Examination of teachers took place at the School-house. Alfred attended. Finished part of my work which has occupied my time so closely of late— Read the Chronotype in the evening.

[Sunday, November 17] Snow on the ground this morning, stormy all day— Have not been to church Alfred wrote almost all day on a subject which he is to lecture on tomorrow evening

[Monday, November 18] To day examination commenced. very stormy. The house full of girls & pictures, that is drawings. I of course am washing as usual. I get very tired my health not being very good. Alfred's lecture went off first rate, as well as the examination. A party at Mr. Bradlee's. News came of Wm Bradlee's dangerous illness in Charleston Mass.[41]

[Tuesday, November 19] Examination closed, & with it Alfred's teaching. By the way he is far the most popular of the teachers & many of his old scholars say to him "well if you are not going to teach here I shall not come here to school—&c &c." John [S. Way] & Sarah [Walbridge Way] visited us in the evening. Their baby is a sweet little thing. Call from [Ira] Miller.

[Wednesday, November 20] Alfred started for Boston & I am left alone again. How I should have delighted to accompany him, but circumstances forbad. The girls have all gone, & now we can have a

---

[41]William Chamberlain Bradlee, age twenty-seven, died of typhus fever on November 20 in Charlestown, Massachusetts. *Caledonian*, November 30, 1850.

CWR   house or rooms by ourselves. I have been very busy indeed to day, & it is now almost eleven o'clock P.M. I suppose Alfred is having a good time with his brothers & sisters.

[*ASR, written after he returned*] Alf. proceeds to Boston—found Oscar [Rix] at the Depot—rode home & found a whole family waiting, viz Mary Ann [Rix] & son & daughter, [Edward] Bierstadt, wife & son, Morris & wife, Misses Richardson & Bressingham & various visitors. Talked over matters & Oscar declared if I went to California he should go it too.

[Thursday, November 21] At night Chastina went to East Part—where there was a Paring Bee which she did <u>not</u> attend. Alf. made inquiries as to Submarine Armor &c. At night attended the Boston Athaeneum.

[Friday, November 22] Wrote to Chastina. Visited Amos H. Brainard and tried to buy his armor. Bought various articles. At night attended Prof. Paige's Lecture on Electrophathy.

[Saturday, November 23] Concluded to get my own armor made and went about inquiring as to the cost &c. Attended another of Paige's Lectures.

[Sunday, November 24] Chastina received & answered my letter—sending a check for $100.00.

Attended Theodore Parker's church. P.M. Read Tom Paine.[42]

[Monday, November 25] Wrote to Chastina again. Recd her letter. Examined & bought my pumps of Asa White Esq. Dined with Mr. Whipple the Submarine man. Made patterns for Window frame &c. Got the Helmet maker & Rubber man at work.

[Tuesday, November 26] Kept the ball rolling.

[Wednesday, November 27] Chastina came home.

[Thursday, November 28] In Massachusetts Thanksgiving—so we eat Turkey & 'tater & went to Burr's 7 Mile Mirror which is a painting as is a painting.[43]

[Friday, November 29] Gathering my toggery together—Hose, Helmet, glass Rubber &c. &c. Ended labor at 10 o'clock.

---

[42]Tom Paine (1737–1809) was a nationally known pamphleteer and political radical during the American Revolution.

[43]This mammoth panorama of the Great Lakes and rivers, created in 1810, was exhibited in Boston.

[Saturday, November 30] At 7½ A.M. pushed for home. For further particulars, behold are they not written in the books of the memory of Alf & Chastina. Chastina says she has been <u>awful</u> lonesome, and so she came home Wednesday & left me to walk from Barnet to the East Part—then over to the Corner when I might have rid all the way jist as well as no how.   ASR

[CWR] [Sunday, December 1] At home. Call from Col. Porter. Read News & Scripture.

[ASR] [Monday, December 2] At night attended a discussion at Bachop's & argued for Town's Readers & in defence of our own course.

[Tuesday, December 3] Stormy. Attended Court Danville. Found the committee on examination &c.

[Wednesday, December 4] Went to Barnet & got my box of Duds. Dustan [Walbridge] got home. Spoke for a girl as help. Tinkered my Dumfudgeon.[44]

[CWR] [Wednesday, December 4] By mistake the above was written instead of

[Thursday, December 5] This is Thanksgiving in Vermont. One week ago Alf. had Thanksgiving in Mass. A.M. At home. Worked on our Dum Fudgeon. P.M. Went to the East Part and took Supper with Father [Lyman] Watts folks. In the Evening John [S. Way] & wife & Clarissa [Walbridge] went to a party at Mr Dana's & left we all alone with a pan full of apples & a mug of cider. For Thanksgiving day this passed off very quietly.

[ASR] [Friday, December 6] Went to Danville with John [S. Way]. Was Examined by the Committee and took the necessary oath and became a Lawyer at the Bar of Caledonia County State of Vermont. So far as the Examination was concerned I am confident I passed it well. I ached to examine my examiners. Returned home and found brother Hale [Rix] sitting up perfectly straight among the young women. He is in for California. We reckon over our standing and conclude that he had better go at anyrate—I to go if all things are favorable in the spring. Heard from home.

---

[44]Alfred apparently was making a waterproof suit or submarine armor, which he called his "dumfudgeon." He was fascinated with science throughout his life, often attending lectures on electricity and other subjects and working on inventions.

ASR [Saturday, December 7] Walked to the Hollow with Hale [Rix] & home after getting a hundred dollars of Ike [Watts] & sending it to John [S. Way].[45] Chastina came home & here we are tinkering on our Dumfudgeon again.

[Sunday, December 8] Cold, stormy, snowy—sleighs run for the first time. At home all day. Write out more minutely the analysis of Mandeville Reader. Called to be at Danville tomorrow to defend Town [Readers].

[*CWR*] [Monday, December 9] Had calls before breakfast this morning, from Mr. [A. G.] Button & Col. Porter. Alfred starts for Danville with Mr. [William] Mattocks. So I am left alone again. Had a hard days work for me. Took me almost all day to get through with my washing & cleaning. In the evening had a call from Mrs. [Lydia Chamberlain] Shedd & Miss [Abigail] Chamberlain.

[*ASR*] Rix attended court during the day— At night discussed the rival Reading books till 1 o'clock and then went home with Mr Webster.[46] Mrs. W. was frightened & would'nt let us in for some time. Cold reception—cold stove—cold sheets—cold beds—cold dreams & cold victuals, cold comfort.

[*CWR*] [Tuesday, December 10] Alfred not got home yet. I arose about eight o'clock this morning, got my breakfast and after my work was done up, thought I would step down cellar to see how our apples come on—oh dear me! "The rats & the mice had made such a strife" among them that I was forced to wash & wipe every apple of them. This most ridiculous affair cost me another days labor & a hard one too. After 9 o'clock P.M. & I am all alone. [*ASR*] Attended Court again and at night went over the same track as last night, save that I gave Hatch a most glorious setting up. Lodged at the tavern till

[Wednesday, December 11] Attended court A.M. was appointed notary public and took the oath. Saw Walker the inventor of the new gas—he let me into his whole secret—see Docket for Dec. 1850.[47] P.M. Rode home with Mr. [Dan] Foster & found Chastina All well who spended all day in sewing.

---

[45]Merchant Isaac Watts had repaid a loan to Alfred, who apparently turned around and lent the money to John S. Way, who was in the process of buying a farm in Hardwick.
[46]Mr. A. Webster was a minister in Danville, not a Congregationalist.
[47]The docket has not been located.

[Thursday, December 12] Tinkered on the Dum Fudgeon. Call *ASR* from Mr T. A. Cutler of Waterford, who came to make some apologies for having behaved like an Ass. [*CWR*] Had a call from Mrs. E[phraim] C. Brown.

[Friday, December 13] Alfred at work on the Dum Fudgeon. Dr. [Asahel] Farr helped him in the P.M. This animal looks like the very critter himself. Had calls from [A. G.] Button and Col. Porter. Received a small package from Oscar [Rix] containing some life insurance reports & papers.[48] Alfred wrote to T. A. Cutler.

[Saturday, December 14] Baking & brewing. Alfred at his tinkering again. Drs. [Asahel] Farr & [Luther] Parker called to see the Dum Fudgeon. Parker tried it on. John [S. Way] & Sarah [Walbridge Way] came over in the afternoon & spent the evening with us.

[Sunday, December 15] We have been at home all day. Alfred has written a criticism on Mandeville's Readers and the remainder of the time we have read papers &c &c. We have very pleasant weather these days. There is just snow enough to make it nice sleighing and people are improving it.

[*ASR*] [Monday, December 16] Went over to Mr French's & partly engaged Mary to be with us by and by. Felt rather blue about one thing & another.

[Tuesday, December 17] Chastina washed & I worked on my Armor. Stormy & Cold.

[Wednesday, December 18] Went over to the East Part with John [S. Way]— Eat apples. Spoke to I[saac] Watts for Pork &c. Got 43 lbs beef of L[yman] W[atts]

[Thursday, December 19] Chastina baked a hash of minced pies— I talked with Mr [Daniel] Aiken of California.[49] Finished my Dumfudgeon.

[Friday, December 20] Opened my office. One case came in—that of Wm Harriman v School Dist. No. 3 of Barnet. Gave as good

---

[48] Alfred took out insurance on his brother Hale, who was going to California. Bonfield, "Ho for California," 19, where an incorrect date is given for his obtaining this insurance.

[49] Daniel Aiken (b. 1814) went to California in January 1850 with John S. Way's company and made enough money to purchase a farm in Barnet in 1853. Bonfield, "Ho for California," 11, 17.

ASR advice as possible and sent my client of[f] rejoicing. Got the criticism of Mandevilles in Print in the Caledonian of Dec. 21, 1850.[50]

[Saturday, December 21] Long talk with Dr [Josiah] Shedd on Luck & Life. Bought a dead pig—called it pork and cut & froze it up for Winter. Almost another case from Dr [Josiah] Shedd. Another visit from my clients Mr [Wm] Harriman & [John M.] Graham. The chance is fair for another mess. Go it ye cripple! Nuts for Scrooge! Chastina is making a new cap so as to be an old woman in [e]very deed. She is a very industrious woman like her husband, but strange to say her industry does sometimes take a queer turn towards grannyism. Now if she happens to see what I have written about her I shall no doubt wish the ink I have been shedding was in the inkstand. For the sake of filling out this page I have concluded to write what you see I have written. Alfred Rix.

[Sunday, December 22] Wrote to Oscar [Rix] and Hale [Rix]. At home. Reading. Alf. was house maid—he washed dishes in good style while Chastina was resting herself.

[Monday, December 23] We awoke this morning and found it had snowed during the night about a foot—and had been blowing a regular old NorEaster for an hour or two and had filled up all the holy vents to be found in and about our tenements.[51] Chastina washed, but had a cold, hard time of it. I packed away our meat and found a barrel with a peck too much of corn in it. Another Law case presented itself—that of Geo. W. Clarke Jr. v. Hiram Kelsey, being an action on the case for negligence in letting the cold weather freeze up potatoes. I consider this a most opportune action. If this action can be sustained, as it no doubt can be, considering the eminence of the counsel engaged for the Plaintiff, then I shall bring a suit or suits against the weather, in nomine, and see if some stop cannot be put to the mischief it is doing— The Actions proposed to be brought are Trespass and Detinue— Trover & Conversion would not be much out of place and

---

[50]Alfred evaluated Mandeville's Readers, using his wit to point out their emphasis on delivery rather than reading and their lack of "high moral character" with examples from "joke books and third rate newspapers" rather than classical English and American literature. *Caledonian*, December 21, 1850; see also ibid., November 16, 1850, with endorsements for the Town's series from J. P. Fairbanks (1806–55) and James K. Colby, noted educators from St. Johnsbury.

[51]The *Caledonian* of December 28, 1850, reported on "the severest snow storm that has been witnessed in the valley of the Passumpsic for the last fifteen years, at least." The snow reached eighteen inches, and the temperature dropped to zero.

it would be in perfect accordance with my feelings that it should be indicted as a Nuisance and forthwith Abated. In Testimony whereof I have hereunto set my hand and seal the day above written at Peacham, in the County of Caledonia, State of Vermont.

        Alfred Rix   his
                            +
                         mark

Locum Signi: [Alfred's drawing of skull and crossbones]

[Tuesday, December 24] Yesterday's storm has made work for today. Shovelled snow and read law as fast as possible. [Ira] Miller proposes to get up something in the shape of a School Journal. We have not yet fully concluded to publish it this week! We have been trying to make each other begin in its preparation. Chastina has been trying out her fat and making her first family nut-cakes. In the evening Miller calls again to discuss the merits of our Journal Plan. No mails from any quarter and no nothing.

[Wednesday, December 25] Forgot to say yesterday that I froze both my Ears. Partly bargained with Eb[enezer] Blanchard for the sale of my Dumfudgeon. Wrote to John M. Graham: a client.

[Thursday, December 26] Chastina is rather poorly off now a days. Went into the water with my Armor—it works so far first rate—but lack a good arrangement for ballast. John S. Way and E[benezer] S. Blanchard aided me. I fear Eb will fail for want of pluck to go into and work it. Made a conditional sale of ½ of the armor to Eb. I am to know if he sticks in one week. Set [E. F.] Brainard to making ballast harness. Wrote to Brother Hale [Rix] and to Geo. H. Hale, Esq. of Boston. Weather moderate. I rather think Eb. wants to speculate—time will show.

[Friday, December 27] Mr. [William] Mattocks returned. Wrote to O[scar Rix]. Visit from Father & Mother Watts— Union meeting at the Union Store. Mr [David] Currier flares up a little. Great fight at the East-Part School and tremendous excitement. Rob Gilfillan & Chandler Blanchard.[52]

[Saturday, December 28] Talked over matters with Mr [William] Mattocks—A new case of Brown & Weeks v. Arch. Bachop. Visit

---

[52] Robert W. Gilfillan (1833–72) and Chandler Blanchard (b. 1829), both of Peacham, were listed as students in the 1850 PAC; Chandler was also listed in 1849. Both soon left for California.

ASR from Frank Eastman at the office. Wrote to Mr [A.] Webster of Danville. Chastina is growing worse every day.

[Sunday, December 29] Snow fell to the amount of 6 or 8 inches. Chastina is growing worse.

About 2 o'clock P.M. We got it somehow into our heads that if we had any thing to do "'twere well if 'twere done quickly." So Chastina goes about some little cooking which <u>must</u> be done. A couple of chicken pies and a pan of Nut-cakes were summoned forth in short order. About dark unmistakable signs appeared of - - - we shall see what. At 10 o'clock Rix shovelled out the path that goes into the street & just asked the Dr. & his wife to come over—Dr. [Asahel] Farr. We had a very pleasant and sociable time till

[Monday, December 30] By invitation, at 1 o'clock A.M. Mrs [Aurilla] Choate and Mrs [Cynthia] Morse joined our circle.[53] Pain_____ Pain_____ Pain_____ Pain_____ 10 o'clock P.M. Chastina became the mother of a little Son, whose name is Julian Walbridge Rix.[54]

[Tuesday, December 31] Went after help—to Mary Gilfillan—Perley Sampson—Mary Sheppard & Elizabeth Bovee—all these save the last were engaged otherwheres—the last named came at 2.00 a week.[55] This has been the coldest day of the Season. We are now pretty well employed in taking care of our little "responsibility." Chastina is quite smart, laughs and talks as loud and funny as ever. She has, however, been very sick and for a long time as the record of Yesterday will show. She thinks it is paying pretty dear for the whistle-r! So ends the year 1850.

---

[53] Aurilla Choate and Cynthia Blanchard Morse (ca. 1800–81) assisted in the birth. Both were mothers themselves; Aurilla had four children, and Cynthia had five. Although medical doctors were often present at a birth during this time, women continued to help, especially older women who had practice delivering babies. Dye, "History of Childbirth," 100–103; Leavitt, *Brought to Bed*, 5, 97–100.

[54] Roxana Walbridge Watts, Peacham, to Hubbell Gregory, unidentified location, January 3, 1851, Walbridge-Gregory Family Papers. "Chastina has had a fine son and is quite comfortable, we are having the hardest winter that we have had for many years cold enough to freeze us all the time besides the snow is very deep and drifted beyond all calculation."

[55] None of the young women, Mary Gilfillan (1829–62), Perley Sampson (1829–1920), and Elizabeth Bovee (b. ca. 1830), had attended the Peacham Academy. Elizabeth was hired at $2 a week, a higher wage than most women teachers made at this time. Bonfield and Morrison, *Roxana's Children*, 81–82.

CHAPTER SIX

Practicing Law and Caring for Baby and Home
January 1–September 14, 1851

Chastina sewing & Baby-tending. Alf engaged all day in 2 trials.
ALFRED

The little Julian is quite cross & grows so fast that it tires me all out to take care of him.
CHASTINA

THE RIX HOUSEHOLD CHANGED DRAMATICALLY WITH THE addition of baby Julian. Chastina slowly recovered from childbirth with the help of a part-time hired girl, while Alfred set up a formal law partnership with William Mattocks. He continued to work on cases of little consequence, typical small-town conflicts of theft, deception, and land disputes, enough to keep him fairly busy but not intellectually challenged.

Alfred wrote most of the journal entries for the first six weeks after Julian was born, and even after Chastina regained her strength, she rarely wrote until the summer. Alfred no longer seemed inspired to show off his intellectualism and wit; instead, he listed their daily activities with few details, as Chastina had always done. He made no mention during the spring of going to California, although there were hints that he was continuing to plan for the trip and was waiting for the right moment to present his plans to Chastina. In the meantime, he talked with returning gold miners about their experiences, no doubt interviewing them with lawyer-like precision. He also read the local newspapers, which had at least one article in every weekly issue titled "From California."

In the third week of the new year, Hale Rix arrived for another visit, this time fully prepared to start off for California. But at the young age of twenty-two, he was having trouble raising enough money to finance his venture. After talking it over with Chastina, Alfred agreed to help fund his brother's trip. He used the occasion to learn what would be involved in undertaking a similar journey of his own. He investigated the cost of steamer tickets, life insurance, and the needed tools and clothes. In total he paid out $475 for Hale's trip. On January 22, Alfred saw Hale off from the Barnet station, fully understanding his brother's desire to seek his fortune, but wishing, as he wrote in the journal, that "every noble and big hearted young man like Hale could find honorable & comfortable homes without running such risks" as were involved in going to California. Alfred may have written those words for Chastina's eyes, choosing to temper his own enthusiasm for the California opportunity until she was ready to accept his plans.

In April, Chastina and Alfred moved again, this time to a house at the south end of Peacham Corner, away from the Academy and town activities. They rented the front rooms of a two-story house from Mrs. Sarah Marsh, a recent widow.[1] Alfred had become a director of the Union store in February and was busy with his law practice. He was continuing to work on his "Dumfudgeon," as well as learning how to construct an accurate adding machine. Away from the busy part of town, Chastina felt isolated and complained about having to carry Julian as he grew heavier. Mainly she stayed close to the house, attending to her many domestic and child-tending chores. With the birth of their first child, the couple who had previously shared activities and thoughts had fallen into more traditional gender-defined roles. Chastina, an educated woman, a practical and frugal partner who enjoyed her husband's humor and shared his political views and intellectual curiosity, was now confined to women's traditional role.

At the end of July, when Alfred left for a six-week business trip to Boston, Chastina no doubt believed that he had more in mind for his journey than just taking his adding wheel for others to review. Another reason for going may well have been to talk with his older brother, Oscar, about going to California. In the same month, Thaddeus Stevens visited his mother in Peacham and got together briefly with Alfred. Alfred does not mention

---

[1]Chastina, Peacham, to Clara Walbridge, Oakfield, N.Y., July 13, 1849, private collection. She reported that the family of the late Jonathan Marsh (1798–1849) was "building a new home below McClarys."

what they talked about, but in all probability he asked his cousin's opinion about going to California.

In early September, Josiah Shedd, a retired local physician, died at the age of seventy after a short illness. Dr. Shedd, the active president of the Peacham Academy trustees, was one of the wealthiest men in town and enjoyed great influence. Through the years he had became a close associate of Alfred's, and the two men had often met to discuss philosophy, politics, and education. Dr. Shedd's death was a great loss to Alfred and further increased his feelings of alienation from the town.

The first-time parents adjusted to having a child, finding it both a delight and a chore. The "new member" of the family was soon given the nickname "Bub" or "Bubby," meaning "brother," in the New England tradition of the firstborn son. The introduction of a child changed Alfred and Chastina's relationship, giving it an element of separation and a new clarity on the division of labor. Alfred wrote that Chastina, who was breastfeeding, was "alone with her baby and her Work." He worked on law cases, went to meetings, and continued with his inventions, pretending to complain that he had "to spend too much time with him to the evident neglect of some of my older clients." The parents recorded Julian's progress in the journal. By the end of January, he had gained a pound a week. By February 23, he weighed fourteen pounds; by June 13, twenty-five. They also documented his changing moods: "The boy bawls" and "Baby cross," they wrote in late January, but at other times he was "giggling like a clown" or "quiet as a kitten." In May he had "a bad boil . . . just on the point of his right buttock precisely on the sitting down place," and a month later he "got the chicken pox . . . broke out in forty thousand blotches." By the end of summer, Bub had his first tooth, and in the fall he had "got so he creeps all round the floor." Their "little responsibility" changed their daily schedule radically, providing both pleasure and anxiety. Chastina summarized their feelings well when she wrote that Bub "is on the whole rather a great chap."

With Alfred's growing discontent with living in Peacham and with Chastina totally occupied with household work, they played out the traditional roles of men in the public arena and women in the home. Both came from families in which this was the norm, but unlike their mothers, Chastina had become well educated and had earned her own money. She was not alone in this expanded role for women in society, as girls became better educated and turned to teaching to make a living. New England towns such as Peacham hired women teachers especially because women were paid less than men. As early as 1850, more than half of Vermont district school teachers were women.[2]

Not surprisingly, most women at this time left teaching once they were married. For Chastina to have even taught academic subjects at the Academy as a married woman was an unusual event that both she and Alfred readily accepted, but when she became pregnant, her teaching days were over. In 1847, when Alfred was a student at the University of Vermont, he had conveyed his view of women's place in the home in a letter to Chastina's sister Sarah, who was working in the mills at Lowell, a position he had tried to persuade her from taking.

> Woman's life is not in the world but at home. Woman's physical power is comparitively small— Her intelect almost as great and her heart is greater than those of men. What does this mean? Merely that her <u>life</u> is the life of inward joys and hopes and loves. Man's <u>life</u> is the life of <u>action</u>—his head and his arm must give their energy and strength to the great works which are calling for their exe[r]cise. But women cannot and should not be on a level with him in these labors. I speak as I think—<u>A woman is a wretched thing unless she may bring into exercise the peculiar powers and be allowed the development of the peculair suseptibilies of her woman nature.</u> She <u>must</u> have a home—an arm to lean on & a heart to trust in. Her growth ought to be the growth in the appreciation of the Beautiful—the True and the Good—[3]

Although his views had changed somewhat after college, he still believed that a woman's place was in the home. This became even clearer after the birth of their son, when he opened his law office and worked on his inventions while Chastina's schedule revolved around caring for their child and housekeeping. Alfred had always treated women with respect and enjoyed their company. He loved his wife, valued her industry, and shared ideas with her, but he truly believed that she belonged at home. Chastina, for her part, made no reference to her view on the man's role as husband, provider, or father. Her views became clearer later in their story. In the meantime, no mention was made in the journal of any possible changes in their future—they were busy with the present. But changes were coming.

---

[2] Nelson, "Vermont Female Schoolteachers," 8–9. A quarter of all New England–born women taught school at some point in their lives between 1835 and 1860.

[3] Alfred, University of Vermont, Burlington, to Sarah Walbridge, Lowell, Mass., November 6, 1847, private collection.

[*ASR*] [Wednesday, January 1, 1851] Chastina feels pretty smart— A storm—[4] Mother [Watts] on the ground to aid us. Made out deeds for [E. F.] Brainard &c.[5]

[Thursday, January 2] Taking care of Chastina.

[Friday, January 3] Chastina is not quite as well. Operated again with our Dumfudgeon in the forenoon. P.M. Brainards & [Lafayette] Strowbridge & John Goodenough all come for advice and for writings.[6] Father Watts and Sally [Walbridge Way] come over in the even'y.

[Saturday, January 4] Sally [Walbridge Way] remained with us. [William] Mattocks in office—made him a proposal to partnership in Law.[7] Got a little testimony from Uncle George Clark.

[Sunday, January 5] At home where I belong—taking care of Chastine along with Sally [Walbridge Way], who goes home after church service. Old Hubbard Preached.[8] Chastina is well enough to walk out into the kitchen and take breakfast with us and to make objections to my using the Adjective I have in Speaking of Mr. Hubbard. Clarissa [Walbridge] called & saw her little nephew and says "on the whole he looks much better than she expected he would!"

[Monday, January 6] At home all day taking care of the baby while the maid washes— Calls from Laura Bennett & Sarah Martin. Borrowed a facet of paper &c. Spent some time on the subject of Phonography—now while I have but little to do. Chastina is getting along pretty fast and the little lion still faster. Weather moderating.

[Tuesday, January 7] Chastina got up in the morning—put on her

---

[4] "Smart" here means witty and quick at repartee, another sign of the fun the Rixes had in their relationship, although in the journal it was mainly Alfred who expressed his wit. According to the January 4, 1851, *Caledonian*, the temperature on Tuesday had been thirty-four degrees below zero, but it was more moderate on Wednesday.

[5] E. F. Brainard (b. 1821) was a saddler and harness maker in Peacham.

[6] Among the advice-seekers were Lafayette Strobridge and John C. Goodenough (b. ca. 1823).

[7] Alfred had done his apprenticeship with William Mattocks and was now asking to be his law partner.

[8] Anson Hubbard (1791–1876) was a preacher from Lunenburg. Comstock, *Congregational Churches of Vermont*, 194.

ASR clothes and did not take them off again till night or lie down but a short time during the day. At the office and studying.

[Wednesday, January 8] Concluded a treaty of partnership with [William] Mattocks. Went to the Temperance meeting in the evening and put over the chief business for a fortnight. Chastina is smarter than ever.

[Thursday, January 9] Made out and signed with Mr [William] Mattocks an agreement for copartnership between us. 2 new cases. Chastina is about as usual.

[Friday, January 10] Chastina is very much worse—her breast is swolen and grown hard, but we hope she will master it without having a broken breast. Her head is also cracking with a severe pain—I fear she has taken cold. Mr Rufus C. Davenport has appeared to day as client. It has been thawing to day somewhat—perhaps for the January thaw. All else as usual.

[Saturday, January 11] Made out my first Bill in Chancery. Miss [Margaret] Calder, Mrs [Sophia] Chandler and Clarissa [Walbridge] Made us calls. Chastina is some better.

[Sunday, January 12] All in a flirt comes [E. F.] Brainard and charges one Steele with Theft of an overcoat— We rush around and scare up the Documents and send off E[benezer] S. Blanchard and Brainard himself after the thief who as it is said has gone for Canada. Call from Mother [Watts] and the children. Old Gallaher preaches here no doubt for the last time. Weather moderate and all well.

[Monday, January 13] Before daylight comes [E. F.] Brainard aforesaid, and use with force and arms, beats, pounds, and ill treats till he gets me out of bed. It seems they got their prisoner in Walden and now have him for examination. The matter is compromised and Steel is let off by returning the coat and paying costs. Afterwards on the same day—writs of attachments are issued against Steel in abundance & because of his resistence to the officers. Early on the morning of

[Tuesday, January 14] A complaint is entered by the grand juror of Peacham & at the sd Steel, but on the warrant issued thereon, the officer returns <u>non est inventus</u>. The old chap is off for Canada. Nothing new or interesting except the operations of the New

Member. Tried an experiment with [Ira] Miller to see if Hydrogen passed thro' turpentine becomes illuminating—No Sir.

[Wednesday, January 15] Looking up Authorities. Chastina is growing very smart—She went visiting this P.M. and carried the boy and took the lead in a regular old women's caucus. Go it while youre young!

[Thursday, January 16] Wrote to Weltha Ann Cory & to Hale [Rix] or Father [Rix]

[Friday, January 17] Very cold and stormy—after a small thaw. Chastina up all day & sewing & laughing funny as ever.

[Saturday, January 18] Made out a cord of documents in a case of Bastardy—Mary Paul v Francis Venor of Danville. Continues cold. [Ira] Miller promises he will board with us next Summer & thereafter if we want him. John Way makes us a short call.

[Sunday, January 19] Calls from Mother [Watts], Mrs Clark, Mrs Bovee & Mrs Charles Varnum.[9] No go to church yet. Calls also from Clara [Walbridge] & Lyman [S. Watts]. From appearances we judge that our putative father is in the place ready for some fun tomorrow. Chastina may be considered as now perfectly restored to her wonted health and good nature, though still rather weak for all sorts of business.[10] The baby grows like a weed and makes all stir— he is an early riser & therefore a reformer in our family.

[Monday, January 20] Attended to the commitments of Francis Moreau for want of bail. Had quite a tussle with one Edwards of Walden as to the propriety of the thing. He seemed to be very benevolent in words but had no money to bail the prisoner, though a wealthy man. In the afternoon came brother Hale [Rix] from Dalton all in a puff for California, but as yet no money for expenses. Hereupon, after all the rich men in the place had refused to run the risk, I took it upon myself with Chastina's Consent, and so made him out $260 in gold, reserving $40 to pay the premium on the policy of insurance which I am taking out on his life in the Hartford Conn. Company. We packed up the armor the value of which is about $150,

---

[9]Among the callers was Betsey Clark Varnum (ca. 1833–83), who married Charles Varnum (1822–1907) in 1849.

[10]Alfred may have been hinting to Chastina that he was ready to resume sexual intercourse.

ASR and had Hale examined by the examining physician. In all, I have been to an expense for Hale of about 475 dollars.[11] But if he is but successful for himself I cannot regret all I have done for him. He is now full of energy & hope & health. God bless him.

[Tuesday, January 21] Early in the morning Hale [Rix] starts home & takes the armor to Stevens' village. P.M. Chastina & Baby take a ride home to the East Part. An important case submitted. Spent chief of the day in making out a bill of what Hale will need & what he must do. Spent the night at Grandmothers.

[Wednesday, January 22] Stormy— Went to Barnet & carried a Carpetbag for Hale [Rix]—his money & pants—met him a moment, shook hands with him & sent him on I know not whether to fortune or poverty or death. Though we may be anxious to see our brothers & friends well off as to gold, yet it is painful to part with them on occasions like the present. I wish to Heaven every noble and big hearted young man like Hale could find honorable & comfortable homes without running such risks as he runs. Home in the storm— and attended the adj'd discussion of the Temperance Law—had a very good time. Letters from G. A. Burbank, brother Austin [Rix], Sutton Post Master & Sheriff Bartlett.

[Thursday, January 23] P.M. Went back to the East Part. Found there John Martin, Chester Martin, John's wife & baby also Nathan Harvey & Sister Martha.[12] We promised to visit Jno Martin's.

[Friday, January 24] Read Law and P.M. came home and set things in order. Chastina gets along finely. Talked over Chandler Blanchard's troubles with him.[13]

[Saturday, January 25] Had considerable courting business. Got $200. of Union [Store] folks.[14] Chastina came home and laid hold of

---

[11]Hale Rix's expenses for his trip to California included about $300 for transportation. Because of the high cost, most men going to the gold mines did not take out life insurance. Bassett, *Growing Edge*, 76, describes the policy of the National Life Insurance Company of Montpelier, chartered in 1848, where few dollars were ever collected on California death claims.

[12]Brothers Chester Martin (1825–1910) and John Martin (b. 1820) from Danville went to California in early 1850 with John S. Way's company, and both moved their families to Minnesota when John moved his in spring 1855. Bonfield, "Ho for California," 10, 17.

[13]It is not clear what troubles Chandler Blanchard had, but he did go to California in the fall of 1851. Ibid., 27.

[14]Alfred spoke with the organizers of the Peacham branch of the New England Protective Union store. He had helped organize the store, lent it money, and purchased inventory in Boston. The $200 may have been payment for this.

work in the old fashioned style—Ironed, baked & washed floors &c &c. She is now alone with her baby & her Work.

[Sunday, January 26] Alf. went to church for the first time for a long while. Chastina at home with the small folks. At Noon Mrs. [Sarah] Stevens called together with Mr and Mrs Harvey of Stanstead who seem to be down on a visit. To relieve the monotony of the times Miss Aunt Nabby [Chamberlain] & ourself had a few sharp words about some sharp sticks &c &c.[15] This is very fine weather & fine times. Our little "responsibility" has come on at the uniform rate of 1 pound a week—7 lbs. to begin with—now 4 weeks & 11 lbs.

[Monday, January 27] Got the women started in their work. Then attended to the trial of [E. F.] Brainard's case. Chastina is very smart. The boy bawls.

[Tuesday, January 28] Looked up Dr [Josiah] Shedd's case somewhat and in the evening attended with all the family a party at Mr [David] Choate's. Talked with Mr Hill of Sutton about Reuben Vance & the Rum barrel.

[Wednesday, January 29] A.M. quite Thawy—P.M. cold—snow—blow. Dr [Josiah] Shedd on the rack. Letter from Oscar [Rix]. Paid Mr [John M.] Martin 41.30 as premium on a policy of insurance on Hale [Rix]'s life which policy had not yet appeared.[16] Baby cross.

[Thursday, January 30] Chastina quite unwell—a little cold—liquored her up & cured her. Cold weather— Wrote to Oscar [Rix]. Call from Mr [A. G.] Button on schools.

[Friday, January 31] The coldest morning of the season. Cutting seal-papers. Chastina ironed. I've a cold for my comfort. Nothing else of note.

[Saturday, February 1] Weather moderated. Calls from Miss Bovee & Mrs Hutchins.[17] Court & Decision for Hopkins. Chastina & the baby are all right as a book. We think of taking out a patent on a new fashioned Baby—that is on one that Knows Beans when only 1 month old—the old sort not arriving at this interesting state till full grown & many, never. We have pretty good times with our

---

[15] This was the first indication of trouble between the Rixes and their landlady, Abigail Chamberlain. "The sticks" refers to the loads of wood being delivered for them.

[16] Peacham merchant John M. Martin must have served as an agent for the Hartford Insurance Company.

[17] Fenton Hutchins (b. 1821) and his wife lived in Peacham.

ASR boy—only I have to spend a little too much time with him to the evident neglect of some of my older clients. Chastina, however, is dissatisfied unless she can do just as much more than she used to, as she ought to do less. My pen has now shed ink enough for tonight.

[Sunday, February 2] At home.

[Monday, February 3] Mother & father [Watts] here in the evening. Union [Store] meeting—I was chosen one of the Directors. Letter from Oscar [Rix]. After we had laid ourselves out for night—then comes a "rapping, tapping at our chamber door!" So out I bounded on't the floor, "and nothing more" Except that I found I was wanted tomorrow at Walden to defend one Royal Woodward who had been charged & brought up for theft. Examined documents & authorities all night and was on hand in the morning and, though the man was guilty, he got clear & I got cursed & blessed both & got a hard d[a]y's work & a good fee!

[Tuesday, February 4] For to day's Exploits see yesterday's Record. I got so engaged in writing that I went over the line.

[Wednesday, February 5] John [S. Way] & Sarah [Walbridge Way] came out to get teeth filled & staid all night.[18] Sent John Goodenough $50.00.

[Thursday, February 6] Temperance meeting at Barnet. Made Hair oil with John [S. Way] & listened to a case presented by Mr Gregg of Danville & Wife. Hard case. Invitation from Mr [Charles G.] Burnham, State Superintendant of Com[mon] Schools to lecture at Danville.

[Friday, February 7] Wrote to [Charles G.] Burnham. Father Rix came from Haverhill, Newbury &c.

[Saturday, February 8] Father [Rix] left—Cold day—Dr [Josiah] Shedd's case adjourned. T. C. Goodenough v Steele continued for notice. Wrote to Rob Hale for Damages on accounts of Rail Road leaving our baggage—&c.

[Sunday, February 9] At home—reading Taylor's Diegesis.[19]

---

[18]Chastina's sister Sarah and her husband, John S. Way, had moved to a farm in Hardwick that they bought with John's gold rush earnings. Bonfield, "Ho for California," 17.

[19]Robert Taylor (1784–1844), *The Diegesis: Being a Discovery of the Origin, Evidences and Early History of Christianity* (1832).

[*CWR*] [Monday February 10] Attended to usual business. And at night Alf went to Danville to attend the adjourned term of the court.

[*ASR*] [Tuesday, February 11] Court opened—I went to Gregg's & heard his case. Chastina went over to the East Part. At night Alf attended Sunday School Exhibition.

[Wednesday, February 12] At court— Heard that the Cherokee is wrecked and all on board gone down save five.[20]

[Thursday, February 13] Court adjourned—Mock court—Went to Gregg's again.

[Friday, February 14] Attended court as counsel at Kelseys—took lots of testimony & adjd to next Tuesday. Rode to E[ast] Part with John [S. Way].

[Saturday, February 15] Wrote for John [S. Way] to Mr. [Rob] Hale—report of Cherokee contradicted. Came home—Call from Lance who left papers.

[Sunday, February 16] At home—Mother [Watts] calls.

[Monday, February 17] Chastina Washed for the first time— Got a new Boiler. Rix laboring in preparation for the Gregg case. P.M. Gregg came & gave notice that the trial must be put off on account of [William] Mattocks' sickness.

[Tuesday, February 18] Chastina Bakes & Splurges about in smart style. Attended to a new case or two.

[Wednesday, February 19] Chastina packed up & went a visiting Mrs [Laura] Bennett—talk of having a place with them. The record of Monday is wrong—Chastina did the washing to day— had company & went abroad—and got cold herself & got another for the Boy.

[Thursday, February 20] Chastina sewing. Alf. & John went to Danville & Walden, hunting for Evidence. Saw Mrs McDonald & the Woodwards. Snowy—Saw Keezer Pond & Lyman's Wood Farm & came home & found that Si Way had been kicking the

---

[20] Plimpton, "The North Fork," vol. 2, 559, reported that Hale Rix left New York in 1851 on the *Cherokee*, crossed the isthmus, and boarded the *Tennessee* at Panama, so his steamer did not wreck as was rumored. The *Cherokee* arrived safely in New York from Chagres on the last Saturday in February, "bringing $500,000 in freight and in the hands of passengers." *Caledonian*, March 1, 1851. I thank Carmel Barry-Schweyer for pointing out the information from Plimpton.

ASR school-master's a-s—that the latter had got a warrant for the former's arrest & that Si had taken leg bail and gone high & dry for Canada. Oh! Dear!

[Friday, February 21] Chastina Ironed for the 2d time this week. Aunt Nabby [Chamberlain] ordered Jim Kinerson who had brought us 7 cords of wood not to bring any more—said it was enough. We reckoned he might bring all we wanted & so he did. The old woman getting dreadful squally. Gave notice that we should quit at the end of the year.

[Saturday, February 22] Chastina cleaned the extra room. Alf. attended to Courting—looked up a new case or two. Worked like a slave all day.

[Sunday, February 23] The Baby in high spirits all save his cold. He weighs about 14 pounds not quite 8 weeks old. Went to church A.M. Hear a sermon from Prof Putnam. Clarissa [Walbridge] & Alvah [Watts] called at noon. P.M. Read Dr Taylor's Diegesis.

[Monday, February 24] Dreadful rainy. Chastina washed & recd all in her washing apparel—Mr & Mrs Gregg, Louisa Bradlee, Katy Chamberlain, Sarah Chamberlain & Mrs [Lydia Chamberlain] Shedd. Rix running after chips & clothes-pins.

[Tuesday, February 25] Chastina sewing & Baby-tending. Alf. engaged all day in 2 trials—[E. F.] Brainard v Hutchins & [E. F.] Brainard v. Steel in Review. A hard case the last & one where I felt ashamed of myself & my client. Brot in one & got brot in the other just as we ought. While in court there the cry of fire—& lo the smoke was streaming out of Col. Jake's house. All ran & in 10 minutes we put out the fire!

[Wednesday, February 26] Preparing for Tomorrow's effort. Concluded a contract with Mr Lance & the Walbridges as to the Panama murder—[21] We are to be counsel & look it up.

[Thursday, February 27] A.M. Went to see Mr Bolton & Adams about their case at Barnet—had to turn them off for want of time.

---

[21] James M. Walbridge (b. 1819) went to California in January 1850 with a company of men from the area, including John S. Way. He disappeared mysteriously on the return trip across the Isthmus of Panama. According to his biography in the family genealogy, "he was persuaded to leave his company and go on ahead. He was never heard from again, and was probably murdered for his gold." Wallbridge, *Descendants of Henry Wallbridge*, 121–22.

Went into the Gregg case with all my might. Made a plea in the afternoon of some 1½ hours length and did what was reckoned pretty well.

[Friday, February 28] To day we are on the other branch of the same case—i.e. as to the accounts brought in by the Greggs against the estate for her labor. Worked all day with might & main & came home with Alvah [Watts].

[Saturday, March 1] [listed as] Saturday 29 I.E. March 1 John [S. Way]'s folks here & Clara [Walbridge]—They made us a present of a large glass sauce dish.

[Sunday, March 2] Chastina & I went to church in A.M. P.M. we went home to East Part and eat apples. Read in Diegesis.

[Monday, March 3] Went to Walden to take charge of a case—Stone v Woodward—they licked us high and dry and would have done so if the case had been that of God v Satan or rather Satan v God. Quite stormy—John Way was on the ground. Chastina Sewing—which she says she always does when she is doing nothing else.

[Tuesday, March 4] Woke up at Walden for our jury did not come in till 2 o'clock this morning. Came home & warmed up after making my client a call & visiting Danville.

[Wednesday, March 5] Chastina Washes & a hard one at that. We sue School District No. 3 in Barnet. A new client or two. Recd letters from Morrill S. Rix last night & Oscar Rix—answered the latter. A long visit from Royal Woodward.

[CWR] [Thursday, March 6] Alfred tries to get a place for us to live. We can go to Mrs. [Sarah] Marsh's if we choose. I am busy all day & accomplish but very little. The little Julian is quite cross & grows so fast that it tires me all out to take care of him. The weather these days is warm & spring like. To day is rainy. Hannah Spencer a girl of eleven was buried to day.[22]

[Friday, March 7] We were awakened this morning about 4 o'clock by the cry of fire. Alfred sprang out of bed as soon as possible & dressed himself. We could not tell where the fire was, until Alfred

---

[22] Eleven-year-old Hannah M. Spencer was the tenth child of Ebenezer and Sarah Robinson Spencer, who lived near the Watts farm. *Caledonian*, March 22, 1851.

CWR went down. He came back & told me that the tavern, a building just across the street was on fire.[23] It was but a few moments before the flames burst out in every direction. Those in the hous had bare time to escape. Mrs. Weeks was oblige to dress herself out doors. The ladies in the village did themselves honor by their assistance in carrying water & goods out of the N.E.P.U. Store, which all thought must burn in spite of every thing—but which was saved only by the utmost exertion— Alfred is quite a hero in such an emergency. He stuck by the hottest place in store & poured water until the danger was over. Mr. & Mrs. Weeks & Abel Morse lost all their clothing excepting what they had on. Weeks loss he estimates at $300. They were boarders at the Hotel. The building was insured for as much as its value. Only a few things were saved out of the house. Mr. [Dan] Foster was gone at the time. The building took fire it is though[t] in the dress room of the ladies as there had been a dancing school there the night before. I picked up all our <u>duds</u>—that is the most valuable—ready for a start. I expected our house would burn too, but it just did'nt & glad enough we were that the fire was held in check. So much for the old tavern. Alfred started of[f] as soon as he got his breakfast on a surveying tour—to Danville. I have been ironing, but am so lame that I can scarcely move. Took cold & lifted too much. Ellen Morse made me a call & also old Mrs. [Polly] Sanborn. At night. We had fairly got to sleep when <u>Nate</u> Way & a Woodward made their appearance as clients— So ended the day & began another.

[Saturday, March 8] Alfred engaged at the Union Store in taking the loss & damage of the goods occasioned by the fire. The baby very cross & I [have] lots of work to do, & Alfred says I am cross……… ……………………….too. I did'nt expect to write <u>poetry</u> when I commenced but "some folks" cant say any thing without being poetical. Augustus [Walbridge] here & made me a visit.

---

[23] The Tavern House at Peacham Corner was built around 1803 and was owned in 1851 by Dan Foster. According to the March 15, 1851, *Caledonian*, "there had been a ball at the House the night previous, which broke up about 3 o'clock, and soon after the occupants had retired the fire was discovered. The inmates had barely time to escape. Not much of the property in the House was saved."

[Sunday, March 9] We have not been to church— George & Alma Currier called here at noon— The bell has just tolled one at about 5 o'clock P.M. I expect for cousin Leonard Browns little girl.[24] The little Julian has been as quiet as a little kitten.

[*ASR*] [Monday, March 10] Washed and played with the baby. Mrs Laura Bennett delivered of a fine fat boy at 1 o'clock P.M.

[Tuesday, March 11] Town meeting—Advocated two or three new measures. Was chosen one of the Superintendants of Common Schools.[25]

[Wednesday, March 12] Most terrible cold. Went to Palmer's Mills and Mr Woodward's—left a writ against Stone. Chastina visited by Mrs [Laura] Bennett.

[Thursday, March 13] At Home. Agreed with Mrs [Sarah] Marsh for house.[26]

[Friday, March 14] Worked at making a multiplication table. Sent [Humphrey] Bennett 25.00.[27]

[Saturday, March 15] Chastina went again to see Mrs [Laura] Bennett—I got frightfully angry at [Humphrey] Bennett & wife for trying to get our Julian to suck off the first nasty bizlings from

---

[24] The seven-month-old daughter of Chastina's cousin Leonard W. Brown and his wife, Maria Kittredge Brown, had died. *Caledonian*, March 22, 1851. Leonard and his family lived in Peacham Hollow. He sometimes served as a teacher in the district school.

[25] In addition to Alfred, the town appointed Congregational minister Asaph Boutelle (1804–66) and Methodist minister A. G. Button to serve as superintendents of common schools. Peacham Town Meeting Records, vol. 2, 44. Although Alfred was no longer the principal of the Peacham Academy, the town's decision to keep him on as a superintendent indicated that the town leaders valued his experience.

[26] The Rixes had decided to move from Abigail Chamberlain's house at the center of Peacham Corner to Sarah Marsh's house, which was south on the main road toward Water Street. Sarah Marsh, a widow, had at least three children who attended the Peacham Academy, including Newell, who eventually went to California in March 1852 and died there in November. Russell Clark, Peacham, to his son Ephraim W. Clark, California, February 8, 1853, PHA-MS, Clark, Ephraim W. For the funeral sermon for Newell Marsh, see Boutelle, *Sermon*, 5–21; entry in Kurutz, *California Gold Rush Bibliography*, item 70. In Boutelle's sermon, he presented this chilling statistic: "The proportions of deaths in Vermont was in 1850 about one in 100, while those who went out from us to California, one in 20 died last year."

[27] It is not clear whether the payment to Humphrey Bennett was for furniture, for his cooperation in reporting the critical remarks he had heard Ephraim C. Brown make about Alfred, or for something else. Alfred later sent his multiplication table to Chastina's brother Augustus, who was living in Hardwick with the Ways, so that he could fill in twenty-five columns. Alfred, Peacham, to John S. Way, Hardwick, March 23, 1851, private collection.

ASR Laura & let their little puke have our boy's clean milk—they dont make that work.[28] Working still on X table. Recd 2 Vols Greenleaf on Evidence from Sanborn & Carter.[29]

[Sunday, March 16] At Home. Reading Diegesis. Playing with Baby— By the way, the Boy is growing old so fast that we can scarcely keep track of him. He began about the middle of last week to know folks so as to laugh & play—he is now giggling like a clown. He kicks his father & strikes his mother & makes mustard paste by the acre.

[Monday, March 17] Worked at the Union Store, taking Inventory. Chastina Washed & about half Ironed—She grows smarter than ever. Call from father & Mother Watts.

[Tuesday, March 18] Work still at Union [Store].

[Wednesday, March 19] Looking up Harriman's Case.

[Thursday, March 20] Chastina mending— Aunt Nabby [Chamberlain] makes soap.

[Friday, March 21] Work on X table— Letter from Father [Rix].

[Saturday, March 22] Went to Aunt [Sarah] Stevens & Father Watts—who [s]topped & gave us to drink— Uncle Simeon [Brown] & wife there on a visit.[30]

[Sunday, March 23] Wrote to Father [Rix], Morrill [Rix], Oscar [Rix], Mighell & John S. Way & Augustus [Walbridge].

[Monday, March 24] Up Betimes—Washing—Directors met—fixt cradle.

[Tuesday, March 25] Up & off on a Survey for Thad Carter Esq—who found he was selling 10 instead of 16 acres. Chastina Ironed—Calls from some dozen—Alice [Watts] came over & remained over night.

[Wednesday, March 26] Fixing Stove—Writing Deed— Call

---

[28]This is not a reference to either mother being a wet nurse. Old friends Chastina and Laura were simply seeing whether their babies would accept another woman's breast. Alfred was offended by this experiment, wanting his son to have the most nourishing milk.

[29]Simon Greenleaf (1783–1850) published *Greenleaf on Evidence* (1842), which became a classic of American jurisprudence.

[30]Simeon Brown, one of Chastina's mother's brothers, and his wife, Clarissa Blanchard Brown, had moved from Peacham Hollow to Cabot. Chastina was especially close to their daughters Chastina and Cynthia, both of whom attended her wedding.

from John S. Way, who took our notes against I[saac] Watts & 55.+ *ASR* besides.[31]

[*CWR*] [Thursday, March 27] A vendue at the widow Dana's.[32] Alfred purchased a table, some Lamps, sauce plates & an old ax— Mrs [Aurilla] Choate called. Mr [David] Currier here to supper— Alice [Watts] went home. We had some new sugar for the first time.

[Friday, March 28] Very windy— Alfred caught a bad cold being out. Our rooms are being fixed about this time at Mrs [Sarah] Marsh's. Our little boy is very good natured of late. I think he is going to be a good boy.

[Saturday, March 29] A Law case came off here to day. [Josiah] Shedd against Hutchins. Bliss N. Davis for Shedd, [William] Mattocks & Rix for Hutchins, which latter got their case.[33] Pleasant day. Snow leaving us very fast. A visit from [Ira] Miller in the evening.

[Sunday, March 30] Went to church in A.M. Alfred took care of Julian

[*ASR*] [Monday, March 31] Run about. Got Tina a Rolling pin. Washed with new Soap. Evening, Mr [Isaac] Watts calls & settles & between J. S. W[ay]. & Ike Watts & us.

[Tuesday, April 1] All fools' Day. Chastina baked pies.

[Wednesday, April 2] Clarissa [Walbridge] came over to help us move. Concert.

[Thursday, April 3] Invented & completed what I call my "time table" last Tuesday which I forgot to record on that day. It seems to me to be a Table of much importance, but time will show. By sim[p]le inspection the length of time from one date to another can be at once determined.

[Friday, April 4] Fast day. Mr [A. G.] Button Preached a good sermon against the fugitive Slave bill in the fore noon & P.M. was held a temperance meeting at which we made a lot of dull speeches.

---

[31] Alfred often loaned money at a good interest rate. Here he had sold a note from Isaac Watts, a merchant in Peacham Hollow, to Chastina's brother-in-law John S. Way.

[32] The system of "vendue" was used to sell tax-delinquent lands. Bogart, *Peacham*, 293.

[33] In addition to being a prominent Danville lawyer, Bliss was a trustee of the Peacham Academy from 1847 to 1852. He later served as state's attorney and judge. Danville was the shire town (county seat) of Caledonia County at this time. Clifford, *History of Danville*, 64.

ASR   [Saturday, April 5] Studying on the Harriman case. Got into pretty good shape. Sawing wood a little. Oscar [Rix] neglects for some reason to answer our letter. Wrote to Hill & Samp[son]

[Sunday, April 6] Chastina & myself went to church A.M. & listened to a sermon from parson [Asaph] Boutelle on Music.[34] Because I am no Singer it is possible I have got a prejudice against music. But it seems to me a secondary instrument of usefulness. I never saw a scholar but he was a <u>man</u>—I never saw a singer but he was a <u>woman</u>. The weather is quite fine for the season. A little rainy to day. I am sometimes almost tempted to rise in rebellion to the false & foolish & wicked fashions and philosophy which seems to be all but universal. The idea that men are to become angels on earth & seraphs in heaven because they can or do contrive to get themselves into periodical excitements & spasms, is one of the very most preposterous ones which it is conceivable a sane man could for a moment entertain. Physical means—Sensuous means—& imaginary means are almost altogether resorted to in order to operate on the actions men [do] for their good. Pshaw! Far better advise them to use rain water & soft soap every morning for their purification.

[Monday, April 7] This is the anniversary of A. R.'s Birth.[35] Chastina went home with Clarissa [Walbridge], & a visit from [Ira] Miller. Tina & Bobble [Bubby] like to have tipped over—they went in wagon. Julian grows so fast that his mother cant keep him in shirts.

[Tuesday, April 8] Tina had new Sugar—rainy—Alf a bachelor again. Writing to certain publishers as to the Figure Table.

[Wednesday, April 9] Chastina came home P.M. after visiting Aunt [Sarah] Stevens.

[Thursday, April 10] Came on the long expected trial of Harriman v School District No. 3 in Barnet—in which case it was determined who gave good counsel to their clients. Rix & [William] Mattocks for Plffs—who recovered.

---

[34] Asaph Boutelle succeeded David Merrill as pastor of the Peacham Congregational Church, where he served from January 19, 1851, to November 7, 1865. Bogart, *Peacham*, 181; Comstock, *Congregational Churches of Vermont*, 16. Rev. Boutelle also replaced David Merrill as secretary of the trustees of the Peacham Academy.

[35] Alfred was thirty years old on April 7.

[Friday, April 11] Made writings for Eastman &c. Aided in the examination of Jane Marsh for School Teacher—doubtful pass.

[Saturday, April 12] Wrote a whole page of the Multiplication Table.

[Sunday, April 13] At home & at Rest. The little birds are hovering about our window for the old berries on the mountain ash—Beautiful things.

[Monday, April 14] From this day for one week we made shirts & mathematical Tables & prepared to move. Settled all up with Aunt Nabby [Chamberlain] & no trouble.

[Monday, April 21] Washed—Ironed—baked. Went after Clara [Walbridge]—& found out a new wrinkle in my table &c— learned that Alvah [Watts] is crazy again.[36]

[Tuesday, April 22] Chastina & Clara Cleaning House—Alf. carrying Crockery. Warm day.

[Wednesday, April 23] Moved bag & baggage from Aunt Nabby [Chamberlain]'s back end to Mrs. [Sarah] Marsh's fore end—left about 10 o'clock A.M. Hard day's Work. P.M. Alf. attended the Examination of teachers &c.

[Thursday, April 24] Prepared our Sitting Room—&c.

[Friday, April 25] Laid down the Carpet & put things in order. Letter from Oscar [Rix].

[Saturday, April 26] Sawed wood & baked.

[Sunday, April 27] At home in the forenoon. P.M. we went to the East Part to see Alvah Watts who is now deranged & raving—has attempted to cut his mother's throat. Succeed to some extent in keeping him in the ordinary trains of thought.

[Monday, April 28] Attended the Convention of Superintendants for the County at Danville—We had a glorious day of it—carried out points every one & altogether. Chastina Washes alone.

[Tuesday, April 29] Write the report of Yesterday's proceedings, being Secretary & send them to Danville & St Johnsbury for publication.[37] Sawed Wood.

---

[36] Alvah Watts suffered from mental illness and was eventually confined to the Brattleboro Retreat, an asylum for the insane, where he died.
[37] Alfred's report appeared in the *Caledonian* on May 3, 1851.

ASR [Wednesday, April 30] Ben Sawed wood for us— July Cross— Mother Baked. [Ira] Miller took tea with us.

[Thursday–Friday, May 1–2, 1851] Made Shed— Snowed—rained. Wood fell down & did'nt kill the head of the family— Attended the Reading Club at Dr [Josiah] Shedd's & left July at home.

[Friday–Saturday, May 2–3] Cut a pole for the Clothes Whirl & mounted it high on the Wood-Shed. Red news papers & played [with] Baby & Called at Mr [David] Choate's.

[Sunday, May 4] Rainy. Both at home. A lot of small trash united themselves with the Congregational Church to day. We have no sympathy for such operations. It is at best a foolish mockery—to call on the youth who has just come to the age of feeling & excitability to unite with a lot of old hard hearted hypocrites & bury his fun & frolic & his life of life in the grave of empty devotion. And this too on the strength of 3 or 4 stormy sermons & twice that number of windy prayers from such a fool as old Gala[g]her. Not a youth lives, of the common temperament, who may not be practiced upon by the most cruel & absurd cheats that the earth Ever saw—why then will men who profess to be guided by good motives employ the same means as the cheat to effect his purpose when a better is at hand? If reason—and that of the strictest sort fails to make me a christian— God Knows—I shall die a sinner— And if reason & that of the best sort cannot win me deciples, then may I go to the grave without a follower.

[Monday, May 5] Washed—Baked &c. A new wrinkle in Table.

[Tuesday, May 6] Baked cakes & tarts & pies for company.

[Wednesday, May 7] Chastina was sent for to go to E[ast] Part to see John [S. Way] & Sally [Walbridge Way] who had come from Hardwick. Rix wrote on Tables. Alvah [Watts] crazy as ever.

[Thursday, May 8] Had a tea party consisting of Mr & Mrs [William] Mattocks & Miss [Mary W.] White. Sent Fent Hutchins after [E. F.] Brainard.

[Friday, May 9] Attended the Reading Club at Mr [David] Choates

[Saturday, May 10] Looked up Law & Talked over matters with Directors & [John] Cowles &c. On the watch for [E. F.] Brainard.

[Sunday, May 11] Rainy— At home— Call from [William] Mattocks & [illegible]. Made out a batch of Writs

[Monday, May 12] The Woman Washed & the Man held Baby & made 4 Bills of Foreclosure in Chancery.

[Tuesday, May 13] The Young people had a pick-nick & Bubby rode out for the first time in a little hand wagon—he weighs 19½ lbs.

[Wednesday, May 14] At the office—into making Writs &c

[Thursday, May 15] Made garden— Settled with John Cowles to remain in Union Store at least 6 mos longer—&c.[38]

[Friday, May 16] Worked on Tables— Visited District School.

[Saturday, May 17] Call from [Humphrey] Bennett— Finished the Numbers Columns. Rainy.

[Sunday, May 18] Rix he went to church A.M. & Rix she went in the afternoon, both listened to dry discourses from Rev John Dudly of Danville, where he ought to stay.[39]

[Monday, May 19] Chastina Washed & Rix went to Danville. Saw B[liss] N. Davis v the Eastmans &c

[Tuesday, May 20] Finished the 14 lines of our table & Went over E[ast] P[art]

[Wednesday, May 21] Papered rooms for mother Watts. Geo Gill & Elvira Hidden were married.[40]

[Thursday, May 22] Worked in the office. Chastina Sewed & took care of Bub who has a bad boil & it is distressing enough for the little fellow—it is just on the point of his right buttock precisely on the sitting down place.

[Friday, May 23] Rix he did a good day's work on the table— Tina took care of July who is worse.

[Saturday, May 24] Attempted to have a court—got up about 3 o'clock with Bub—he is bad off—Doctor called to see him— Cynthia Brown called on us & was examine[d] for a teacher.

---

[38] John O. Cowles (1816–85), a hatter and watchmaker, was the clerk in the Union store.

[39] John Dudley (1805–98) was pastor of the Danville Congregational Church, where he commented in an 1851 sermon that there was "no season of especial religious interest" that year. Clifford, *History of Danville*, 76; Comstock, *Congregational Churches of Vermont*, 57, 178.

[40] George Gill "of the firm I. Watts & Co." married Miss Elvira Hidden (b. ca. 1829); both were from Peacham. *Caledonian*, May 31, 1851.

ASR [Sunday, May 25] All at home. July is a little better—his sore has discharged very copiously & we hope he will soon be well again. We hardly know how to get along with our much business in doors & out with our little help. Chastina wants Alf for a maid & he wants her for a man & which will succeed or whether both will do so, as yet remains uncertain. Yesterday we got a letter from Gov. [C. K.] Williams.[41]

[Monday, May 26] Washed & visited at Mr [David] Choate's—looked up the case of Richardson pauper.[42] Heard that the Kavanaugh girls are thieves.

[Tuesday, May 27] Sawing Wood & making table.

[Wednesday, May 28] Invitation to Wedding— Bub worse— Cogitating on an adding machine

[Thursday, May 29] Attended the Wedding of Abba McClary to [Martin C.] Chamberlain at 7 o'clock A.M. Rainy all day. Call from Friend Lance— Made cake!

[Friday, May 30] Worked on Add-er— Expected to go to Hardwick but could not for the rain.

[Saturday, May 31] Settled with Mrs [Sarah] Marsh on milk.[43] Worked on Ad. Bub is better.

[Sunday, June 1] A.M. Chastina went to church—I at home all Day.

[Monday, June 2] Worked on Adder. Washed &c.

[Tuesday, June 3] Attended Court at Danville—all night.

[Wednesday, June 4] Still at Danville—home P.M.—found Oscar [Rix]'s folks all here— talked over matters & things.[44]

[Thursday, June 5] Visited with the visitors

[Friday, June 6] At Danville again & Oscar [Rix] returned to Boston & left his family

[Saturday, June 7] Came home P.M. Chastina quite unwell. Call from Dustin [Walbridge] & Augustus [Walbridge]

---

[41]Charles Kilborn Williams (1782–1853) was the governor of Vermont from October 11, 1850, to October 1, 1852, during which time the Habeas Corpus Act passed, reflecting the strong anti-slavery movement in Vermont. It is not clear why he wrote to Alfred.

[42]As overseer of the poor, David W. Choate was authorized "to farm out to some suitable person . . . the poor belonging to the town of Peacham." Bogart, *Peacham*, 293.

[43]Sarah Marsh had four cows. Peacham Grand List, 1851.

[44]Alfred's brother Oscar visited from Boston with his wife, Mary Ann, and their two children. The men discussed Alfred's multiplication table and the business of the Union store. No doubt they touched on going to California, but Alfred did not note this subject in his journal entries.

[Sunday, June 8] At Home &c. [*CWR*] —all day, the whole posse of us. *ASR*

[Monday, June 9] Very rainy so we did not wash. But I had enough to busy myself about. I have to work very hard an addition of three to our small family makes a vast difference.

[Tuesday, June 10] washed. Got done before noon— Took a ride to Danville. I called at Mr Browns on account of a shower, while Alfred went to the Green. We went home & took tea, Father & mother [Watts] gone to Hardwick. Jule enjoyed his ride first rate, & so did his mother, only she scolded some about the <u>lookin old team</u> we had to go with and then pay a half dollar for it.[45]

[Wednesday, June 11] Alfred at work on his tables, & a machine for adding which he sent to Oscar [Rix] yesterday. Made the skirt of my dress, besides my other wash. Mary Ann [Rix] rather homesick She does not like the country The children are bruising about as though they enjoyed it

[Thursday, June 12] Cook, cook, cook, & eat is my business. I am just about tired out. Alfred had a letter from father Rix. He has heard from Hale [Rix]. He is well.

[Friday, June 13] Fixed a dress for myself. Everything as usual.

[Saturday, June 14] Alfred had a court this forenoon. Sidney Rix & his brother George gave us a call. I get real discouraged about these days

[Sunday, June 15] Alfred waited on Mary Ann [Rix] to church in the A.M. & me in the P.M. Mr. [Edward] Cleaveland from Cabot preached & preached rather slim too.[46]

[Monday, June 16] Washed and baked &c. Alfred worked on his tables.

[Tuesday, June 17] Pleasant. Alfred goes to Danville to attend to his Gregg clients. They had a fine time over to the Widow Hunts. Mary Ann [Rix] and myself visited at Mr [Humphrey] Bennetts. Had a good visit. We carried Julee and a real lug he is, nearly a

---

[45] Not owning a team and carriage, Alfred must have rented the outfit from a livery stable at Peacham Corner.

[46] Edward Cleveland (1804–86) served in churches in Cabot, Barnet, and Barton. Comstock, *Congregational Churches of Vermont*, 173. He was listed as an Academy trustee in the 1852, 1853, and 1854 PAC.

CWR twenty-five pounder. Mrs [Laura] Bennett is rather poorly off her babe 14 weeks old & she able to do but very little.

[Wednesday, June 18] At 9 oclock A.M. Father Watts came over with a horse and wagon, and took Mary Ann [Rix], myself & our Children—in all five of us—and carried us home we stayed all night. Had a good visit. Mrs [Alma] Currier visited there in the afternoon.

[Thursday, June 19] Grandmother [Olive Brown] & Chastina Brown came to fathers. We visited Aunt [Sarah] Stevens in the P.M. Had a very good time though not so good as sometimes. Alfred went to Danville. Lyman [S. Watts] brought us home.

[Friday, June 20] Ironing and baking &c. Alfred writing as usual. Jule rather cross.

[Saturday, June 21] Alfred & [Ira] Miller went a fishing to Ryegate They caught about sixty nice Pickerel—we sat up until 11 o'clock at night to dress them. Mother [Watts] sent us a pail of hulled corn. Quite a treat that. Together with our fishes. Mary Ann [Rix] & I took tea in Mrs [Sarah] Marsh room. Had a nice supper.

[Sunday, June 22] We have none of us been to church. All too tired & lazy to do so. For my part I am "chief cook & bottle washer" & cannot go. John [S. Way] & Sarah [Walbridge Way] & Clara [Walbridge] made us a call at noon. Very warm. Thunders while I am writing. Little Julian sits by my side in his high chair while I have been writing for the past week.[47] He makes a real mess among the pens and pencils. He is a pretty good boy considering all things.

[ASR] [Monday, June 23] Washed & worked on an adding machine. At office &c.

[Tuesday, June 24] Idem.

[Wednesday, June 25] John [S. Way]'s folks here to Dinner— All went to E[ast] P[art] P.M. John's baby sick

[Thursday, June 26] Went to the County Democratic Convention—& served as Secretary & Committee on Nominations.[48] Killed 2 squirrels with Stones & Sticks one a gray.

---

[47]This entry makes it clear that on occasion the Rixes skipped days and then wrote a number of journal entries at once.

[48]The *Caledonian*, a Whig paper, reported on the state and Caledonia County Whig conventions but nothing on the Democratic convention that Alfred attended. *Caledonian*, June 7 and 28 and July 5, 1851.

[Friday, June 27] Worked on Machine ASR
[Saturday, June 28] Settled with [E. F.] Brainard & Inventoried at the Union [Store].
[Sunday, June 29] At home. Bub has got the chicken pox on him— most horribly—broke out in forty thousand blotches— Mother [Watts] here P.M.
[CWR] [Monday, June 30] Sat up almost all night with bub. He is real sick Did a small washing. It is so warm that one cannot keep comfortable Alfred to work at the Union Store.
[Tuesday, July 1] A very little cooler on account of the thunder last night— Aunt [Sarah] Stevens here visiting— Julian is a very little better though he has a severe cold.
[Wednesday, July 2] Mary Ann [Rix] & the children gone to Dalton NH Mother [Watts] here visiting, brought us some straw-berries— Julian still very unwell.
[Thursday, July 3] Alfred has worked at Hial Weeks' shop making parts of his machine.[49] Suceeded very well. Julian more unwell. His cold is very bad, so hoarse he can scarcely make a loud noise. About 9 P.M. the boys commenced their operations preparatory for the 4th.
[Friday, July 4] Got up about 1 o'clock A.M. or rather got down having been up stairs, & up most of the time with July. He was so restless & sick that I could get no sleep with him. Commenced washing about 5 o'clock, did a large washing & cleaned house some— Such a rainy day we hardly ever witness. There was scarce a moment's cessation all day—it rained like a perfect shower. There has been many a sad heart & long face this day. Preparations had been made at St Johnsbury for a grand celebration but as a matter of course a rain would spoil all the fun.[50] Alfred is almost sick to day.
[Saturday, July 5] Bubby some better— Alfred at work on his machine but so lame he can scarcely get up & down.

---

[49] Hiel B. Weeks (ca. 1811–82), a Peacham tradesman, later went into the business of making sash, blinds, and doors. Bogart, *Peacham*, 371. Alfred misspelled his name here.

[50] Alfred was appointed as Peacham's representative on the St. Johnsbury Committee of Arrangements for the seventy-fifth anniversary of the Declaration of Independence, but it is not clear that he served. The local paper reported that despite the rain, between six hundred and seven hundred people attended the celebration, although the fireworks were put off until a clear evening. Apparently the Rixes did not attend any of the festivities. *Caledonian*, June 14 and July 12, 1851.

CWR [Sunday, July 6] Rainy in the morning. Mother [Watts] came down at noon. We have not been to church. [ASR] And we dont mean to go again till we can Sleep o'nights & be good natured day-times.

[Monday, July 7] The Grand Display of Fire-Works appointed for the fourth came off to day at St Johnsbury.

[Tuesday, July 8] Made out papers for Harrington of N.Y.

[Wednesday, July 9] Alls well! Got a Model Adding Wheel from Oscar [Rix].

[Thursday, July 10] Worked on the Adding Wheel to improve it.

[Friday, July 11] Chastina Washed & picked up her things in preparation for our Journey. Settled with Mrs [Sarah] Marsh for milk & room pd $1.65. Wrote to Chauncey Boardman of Bristol Conn. Last night had a long discussion with [Ira] Miller. Completed the plan for a Model Adder. We expect, both of us to be gone for some weeks & we here take leave of our big Journal & enter in short hand our minutes on the small.[51]

[Saturday, July 12] Went to the East Part & got a horse & Wagon. Saw Thad Stevens of Pa. for a few minutes.[52] Came back & talked over matters with [William] Mattocks & together with Chastina & Bub went to Hardwick. Found all folks right. Went a-fishing with John [S. Way] & caught a small string.

[Sunday, July 13] Visited & played with babies. At 3 o'clock got caught in a shower. At 4 P.M. Alf. started off for Boston. He met E[benezer] S. Blanchard & Clarissa [Walbridge] at the fork of the road to Hardwick Street.[53] A dark cloud & thunder in it came up over the hills &

---

[51] As Alfred prepared to go to Boston and Chastina to Hardwick, he wrote that they were leaving "our big Journal" at home and would be keeping notes in "the small" ones they were taking with them. No other journals have been located. The next entries were written by Alfred after he returned, sometimes from notes kept by Chastina, and sometimes from memory. In the past when Alfred had left Peacham, Chastina had kept the journal, but this time they both left, so the journal stayed in their house. He teased Chastina in these entries but probably guessed correctly that she was annoyed about his trip.

[52] Thaddeus Stevens spent a few days in Peacham "visiting his venerable mother who is 84 years of age, yet as vigorous as most ladies 20 years younger than herself." The newspaper added that Stevens was "in favor of Gen. Scott for the next president," a recommendation the editor found suitable for "a man of political sagacity." *Caledonian*, July 19, 1851.

[53] Clara Walbridge and Ebenezer Blanchard may have been courting. In an earlier letter to relatives, Chastina wrote about "a young Blanchard that walks home with Clarissa whenever she goes out and comes home so he can wait on her though there is nothing in it I suppose for he never stayed with her." Chastina, Peacham, to Hubbell and Martha Walbridge Gregory, Jackson, Mich., January 18, 1846, Walbridge-Gregory Family Papers.

made us scud onward a little faster. At this present writing the family are at home & Chastina has put into my hand her pocket journal, which it will be necessary for me at least in part to transcribe.[54] She describes John S. Way's farm thus: It is situated on Lamoille River—with a fair view of the Stream from the house. In front of the house towers Mount Pisgah & a little north Mount [illegible]. The stream is filled with fine trout & gravel—one a great luxury, the other a small one. The buildings of the <u>Ancient</u> Order of Architecture—still they have an air of comfort, except in cold weather when the air is too cold for comfort—though even then, I suppose, it will bear the name of cold comfort. I think, on the whole, John [S. Way] & Sarah [Walbridge Way] are very favorably situated for enjoying life—seeing as how they cant have much else to enjoy. Alfred started off about 4 o'clock P.M. I do not know when I shall see him again—(nor care). A thunder Shower has come up. Perhaps Alfred is caught in it (hope he is). Crops look very promising—except the crops of the last brood of chickens. Bub is cross—that is across my knee—one reason for which is, that I am free to write, & another is that it helps his belly-ache—if he has got it—but if he has'nt—he will be likely to get it.[55]

[Monday, July 14] Up with Julian all night nearly— Worrisome— Washing. Alf. Stopped over night at Father Watts's & in the morning was up and off—by two o'clock. Heard a dreadful Screaming on the mountain side like that of a man in distress—could'nt stop to get him out of trouble. Walked to Stevens Village—7 miles—having sent forward the baggage beforehand—took the Cars a little after 4 A.M. & got into Boston at 1 o'clock P.M. Went to Oscar [Rix]'s Shop & found him all right. Went into some explanations on the Adding Wheel & other matters. Engaged the Boston Stereotype Foundry to do us a small job in their way in furnishing a plate of Tables Mathematical &c.

[Tuesday, July 15] Julian Sick—gave him medicine—eat too much. Alf. finds his home at Oscar [Rix]'s boarding place at No 8 Lee

ASR

---

[54] The entries from here to August 16 were written by Alfred when he returned. Chastina gave him some notes so that he could describe her activities.

[55] Although Alfred was showing his wit here, he may have been aware of Chastina's mood about his going to Boston for a lengthy stay. The trip was to have been three weeks, but it turned out to be six. It may have been those "other mattes" that he planned to discuss with Oscar [Rix] that she worried about.

ASR [Grange?] place—Widow N. P. Ryder. A whole house full of boarders, & Oscar to make fun for them all.

[Wednesday, July 16] Extremely Warm— In shade at Boston Thermometer at 97°F. Bub well. Sewing on Bub's dress. Alf. begins his Adding wheel, which employs him all day, while at evening he writes or walks or eats as the case may be for some 3 weeks.

[Thursday, July 17] Chastina Sewing a little—very warm.

[Friday, July 18] Hulled corn— Ironed— Rode to Lambert Watts's on the hay-cart—rained— Bub full of fun & pranks—little Scamp he learns some new roguery every day.

[Saturday, July 19] Bub tore his mouth or rather throat with a long comb & was unable to nurse for the most of the day. This has been to me a long week— I have been greatly disappointed in not hearing from Alfred.

[Sunday, July 20] Sarah [Walbridge Way] & John [S. Way] Went to church— Augustus [Walbridge] went to Marshfield to see Dustan [Walbridge], while I stay at home & take care of the babies. Alf went to the Melodeon & listened to a discourse from Theodore Parker. Parker is one of the best teachers of our times—he is not, however, fully appreciated. His fault is too much study—too ideal.

[Monday, July 21] Hard washing— Sarah [Walbridge Way] unwell. A letter & two papers from Alf. Call from two ladies in Bloomer.

[Tuesday, July 22] Bothered to death with a call from John [S. Way]'s sister & her friend.[56]

[Wednesday, July 23] Went a pluming—got 4 qts—tired enough—papers from Peacham— Wrote to Alfred— Letter from Hale [Rix].[57]

[Thursday, July 24] Bad luck to this day— Sarah [Walbridge Way] sick— Bub cross—& I too!

---

[56] The identity of John S. Way's sister is difficult to determine, as his grandfather had children by his wife and also by a hired girl; John is from the latter branch. Bonfield and Morrison, *Roxana's Children*, 44. In any case, Chastina would not have looked favorably upon women in bloomers, a fashion made popular in the winter of 1850–51 in Seneca Falls, N.Y., consisting of Turkish pantaloons with a short overskirt. According to the May 31, 1851, *Caledonian*, "The bloomer costume has made its appearance in Vermont" in Windsor, and the editor joked that the wearers "appeared well."

[57] None of the letters from Alfred's brother Hale have been located. Plimpton, "The North Fork," vol. 2, 559, reported Hale Rix as an early miner at the "Oregon Bar (Ferry)" on the North Fork of the American River between Auburn and Folsom, where he mined for nine months.

[Friday, July 25] Ironing— Geo Currier made a call— Letter from Alfred— Glad enough to hear from him— Sent him Hale [Rix]'s Letter.

[Saturday, July 26] Rainy— Washed a little— Head ache all day— C[arlos] Sampson & J. Way here all day & all night—[58] All the wives & babies slept together. Sick-headache all night.

[Sunday, July 27] Alf. making the Dial to his Wheel. Chastina unwell— At home—lonely—little time for herself.

[Monday, July 28] Sarah [Walbridge Way] sick— Chastina washes for the lot—tired. Rainy. Call from two Bloomer ladies.

[Tuesday, July 29] This is our Wedding Anniversary— We have now been married two years— Two years have gone happily & rapidly away—we are now all well & should be happy as ever were Alfred with us.

[Wednesday, July 30] Took care of Bub— Three papers from Alfred.[59]

[Thursday, July 31] All as usual. Lots of work & workfolks— Bub cross & Sarah [Walbridge Way] sick & I homesick—cant help it. Suppose I must head it off.

[Friday, August 1] Pleasant— <u>Haying</u>—bought raspberries—picked currants.

[Saturday, August 2] Letter from Alf. Up till midnight with our plums.

[Sunday, August 3] Went to church. Up again till midnight writing to Alf.

[Monday, August 4] Washed for all or nearly so— Sent letter— Up with bub sick.

[Alfred—written later] Alf. rejoiced to be free once more bids adieu to Boston & proceeds by the morning train to Lawton Mass. The Adding wheel which he attempted to produce he did produce & to the perfect satisfaction of all parties. It adds with great ease & accuracy. Go it. The Interest & Time Tables are done & out. Good!

---

[58] Carlos Sampson (1831–1916) was the son of Sarah Bailey Sampson Watts and the stepson of Thomas Watts. I am grateful to Stephen Bloom for providing vital dates for Thomas Watts, Jane Bailey Watts (1792–1830), Sarah Bailey Sampson Watts, and their children.

[59] It was common to send newspapers from the place one was visiting, as the postage rate for them was less than for a letter. Henkin, *Postal Age*, 49.

ASR After a stop of some hours at Lawton Alf proceeded to New Bedford where in the midst of a horrible shower he finds his brother Edward & Sister Adaline [Rix Bierstadt].

[Tuesday, August 5] After so many trials I come at last to the records of this day. Chastina gets Alf's letter. This day a Mis Thompson marries one of Edward [Bierstadt]'s brothers & goes off with wife & in company with Ed & Adaline to Boston & leaves me to hunt my way the best I can. Visited Jesse Gifford & took down his story of the [James] Walbridge case.[60]

[Wednesday, August 6] Like an Ass neglected to accept an invitation to go to sea for a day or two. Travelled. Saw New Bedford. Over night with old folks.

[Thursday, August 7] Chastina went to the village. Alf went to Fall River. Put up at the Mount Hope house I think. Rather a shiftless place too.

[Friday, August 8] Worked all day for Sarah [Walbridge Way]—Recd a letter from Alfred at New Bedford. Alf left Fall River in the Steamer Bradford Durfee & went to Bristol R.I. where he remained till 4 o'clock P.M. when he took the S[t]eamer for Providence where he put up at the What Cheer house till

[Saturday, August 9] Met Charles Bierstadt & was over persuaded by him to take up my abode with him during my stay [in] Providence.[61] His house is on the hill N.E. of the main town. Bub up betimes—wrote to Alf. John [S. Way] Finished haying.

[Sunday, August 10] Had a fine mess of Pease for the first time this year. Lambert [Watts] & his wife at tea—a ride with the babies. Alf. walked through the pleasant part of Providence in Company with [Charles] Bierstadt & brother Thompson.

[Monday, August 11] Washed. Alf. at large.

[Tuesday, August 12] Bub wakes up with his first cunning little tooth. Alf sends Chastina $5.00 & leaves Providence. Stops at Greenwich till 4 o'clock & goes on to Stonington where he remains over night.

---

[60]Alfred continued his investigation into James Walbridge's disappearance in Panama.

[61]Charles Bierstadt (1819–1903) went into the photography business with his brother Edward and later became known for his stereoscopic views. The brothers were helped by their younger brother Albert (1830–1902), the famous printer.

[Wednesday, August 13] Alf. started for New London where he arrived at 10 o'clock A.M. *ASR*

[Thursday, August 14] Chastina ironed & went plumming. 5 qts. Alf went to Willimantic—staid till 2 P.M. went to Hartford— Put up at Exchange on State St— Visited the insurance office—wrote Chastina & [William] Mattocks. Saw Edward Goodman—Atty at Law.

[Friday, August 15] Circulated in Hartford till four o'clock, then went to Springfield. Got Lombard's Deposition & put up after getting Oscar [Rix]'s package from Express office. Chastina visited at John Watts's.

[Saturday, August 16] John [S. Way] Got a letter from Alf—that he should be home soon. [*ASR*] Alf Started from Springfield for home at 8 A.M. Met Bob Benedict aboard the Cars—he came on to Barnet. Met Frank Rix also near Bellows Falls—out with the Lowell Band—concerting—Funny time. Came from Barnet towards the Hollow with Frank Morse then turned at Stuarts & went over the hill to Mr [Lyman] Watts's where I remained over night—then

[Sunday, August 17] Put for Hardwick—where on the top of the hills I met John [S. Way] & Sarah [Walbridge Way] going to Peacham &c. Chastina Says she & Bub were tickled most to death to see the old man again. Bub in my six week's absence had almost forgotten me—but enough of rememberance remained to make him stare & smile & clapper-claw me & jump & hoot like a little devil. We eat & laughed all day.

[Monday, August 18] Chastina washed for the whole lot & I took care of Bub. John [S. Way]'s folks came at 5 o'clock.

[*CWR*] [Tuesday, August 19] We started on a short visit to Wolcott. Staid over night at Uncle Ira [Walbridge]'s. Saw Harriet Guyer there.

[Wednesday, August 20] Visited Harriet [Guyer]'s school—she's got a good one. We spent P.M. at Uncle Lyman Titus'—saw Grandfather [Oliver] Walbridge who is well & smart. Over night at Alger Jones.

[Thursday, August 21] Left [Alger] Jones in the morning & went to Uncle Hiah Guyer's. With him & Aunt Martha we went to Mr Whitings— Spent the afternoon there & the night at Uncle Guyer's.

CWR [Friday, August 22] Had as much as we could do to get back to John [S. Way]'s on account of the rain. Obliged to stop—it chanced to be at Old Waterman's. [ASR] At night John brought me a client—in the person of Erastus Howard. Stated his case & left.

[Saturday, August 23] Left John [S. Way]'s—came to Mr [Lyman] Watts—staid till night—then to our own home at Peacham Corner & again went into living on our own hook. Righted things a little & went to bed.

[Sunday, August 24] At home where we belong eating & growing especially Bub.

[Monday, August 25] Looked up [Erastus] Howard's case— Tina washed & baked & cleaned.

[CWR] [Tuesday, August 26] Alf started for Hardwick—went to John [S. Way]'s—got there at 9 in forenoon. [ASR] Killed a grey squirrel & went to Hardwick Hollow & Defended so they got but one cent cast on to us for Trespass. Great Time.

[Wednesday, August 27] Came home from Hardwick. [CWR] Tina & Bub took dinner at Mr [David] Choate's. Ironed in the afternoon.

[Thursday, August 28] Alfred is all tired out so he is resting & doing up little chores.

[Friday, August 29] Alfred at the office. I have took care of baby some, baked some & ironed some. have enough to keep me busy. Called at Capt. [Trustram] Sanborns after tea.

[Saturday, August 30] Bub is eight months old to day. He has got two teeth, begins to creep & get up by things, is on the whole rather a great chap. Alfred had a letter from Austin [Rix].[62] He is going to Calafornia

[Sunday, August 31] Alfred attended church in the forenoon. I went this afternoon. Heard Mr Jackson Abbott preach.

[Monday, September 1] Washing. Alfred has been surveying for Mr [Samuel] Chandler. Very pleasant indeed though exceedingly dry— Wells all most all dry. [ASR, *written later*] Dr [Josiah] Shedd taken sick.

---

[62]Another of Alfred's younger brothers, Austin Rix, went off to California.

[CWR] [Tuesday, September 2] Raining this morning when we awoke. Election day. Great excitement. Alex. J. Johnson took dinner with us. Mother [Watts] & Ella [Watts] come over to visit us this afternoon. Dr. [Josiah] Shedd not expected to live

[ASR] [Wednesday, September 3] Had a long confab with Dea[con] Martin, [Samuel] Chandler, & District No. 2. Watched with Dr [Josiah] Shedd— Dying all night. Stroke of Paralysis. Went to bed at 5 A.M. on

[Thursday, September 4] Dr [Josiah] Shedd died at 5 o'clock P.M. He was a fine old fellow in many respects—hard business man but a good neighbor, citizen & philanthropist. We all made a short visit at [Humphrey] Bennett's.

[Friday, September 5] Went to Groton post haste to attend a law suit—got there & found the case decided without Jury or argument. Looked up the facts & came home. Ironing by the women.

[Saturday, September 6] Wrote to F. J. Eastman & John Taisey. B[o]iled beens & baked taters. Put up notice for meeting of old Juvenile Society.[63] And So Forth.

[Sunday, September 7] Chastina & Alf go together once more to Church—where the Funeral Services are performed over the remains of Dr. [Josiah] Shedd. Prayer &c by H[arvey] Hitchcock— Sermon by A[saph] Boutelle.[64] Quite solem & appropriate. If there were in this world no worse men than Dr Shedd I should like to stay in it considerable longer than I shall be likely to. If a poor man dies nobody has a word to say against him if he has kept clear of the State Prison—while if a rich one dies he is cursed anyhow & sent to hell if

---

[63]Alfred was apparently trying to rejuvenate the Juvenile Society, a debating group begun in 1810 by Thaddeus Stevens and other male students at the Peacham Academy. Alfred saw that a library was needed in order to prepare for debates, and this was accomplished with financial gifts from Thaddeus Stevens in 1854 and 1855, plus a legacy of $1,000 at his death in 1868. Bogart, *Peacham*, 195–96. By 1851, only twelve circulating libraries had been established in Vermont. The Peacham Library continues into the twenty-first century. Belding, *Where the Books Are*, 27–28.

[64]Rev. Harvey Hitchcock (1814–89) had succeeded Rev. A. G. Button as Methodist minister; he served from 1851 to 1854. He and the other minister in town, Asaph Boutelle (Congregational), conducted the funeral service. The *Caledonian* published an unusually long obituary on Dr. Shedd on September 13, 1851. A follow-up article on November 18, 1851, listed the "legacies" he had left to "benevolent societies," including $2,000 to the Peacham Academy.

ASR he has not acted in all things like a Saint. This is unjust. Give Satan his due & rich men too. See if the world on the whole would not have got on worse without him, & if it dont miss him now he is gone & judge him accordingly. Dr Shedd has left a blank which could not be fairly filled by all the tribe of snivelling shit-asses who are now barking over his grave. Let them go to work with the same energy & faithfulness as he did & they will have less leisure for & less inclination to indulge in envious gab at the Dr's memory. To night we have eat some dozen peaches & a large amount of green apple pie & feel extremely well fitted to snort off a few lazy hours <u>in feathers</u>.

[CWR] [Monday, September 8] Got up early & went to washing. Left Alfred & the baby snoring soundly. Had a large washing. Extremely warm. It is more than one can do to keep cool in such weather. Mary Merrill & Jane Clark called at noon & Margaret Jane Harvey after tea. Alfreds old scholars love to call on him.[65]

[Tuesday, September 9] Had a "boiled dish" for dinner notwithstanding the heat. Dustan [Walbridge] came and made us a visit. He is getting along well I should think. Alfred away from home this evening. They are trying to revive the old Juvenile Society which has all run out.

[Wednesday, September 10] Alfred about sick with a kind of summer complaint. The hot weather holds on yet. Elizabeth Harvey made me a call. Alfred gone again this evening. Thunders & lightins real hard now while I am writing. Bub has got so he creeps all round the floor. It is hard work to take care of him It tires me all out to do my work in this hot weather & take care of baby too.

[ASR] [Thursday, September 11] All's well! And Chastina & July visit the Lion in his den. Fine weather.

[Friday, September 12] Looked up the merits of the Fugitive Slave Bill & discussed them in the evening with [Ira] Miller & [William] Mattocks & others in Juvenile Society.

[Saturday, September 13] Sent Bill to J. Scott. Watts & [William] Mattocks have a splurge on a certain note. Met [David] Choate &

---

[65]Mary P. Merrill of Peacham, the eldest daughter of Rev. David Merrill and his first wife, was listed as a student in the 1846–47, 1848, 1849, 1850, and 1851 PAC. Margaret Jane Harvey of Ryegate was listed in 1846–47, 1850, 1851, and 1852.

[Uriah] Miner & discussed our business as Directors of the Union [Store]. *ASR*

[Sunday, September 14] Alf. attended church A.M. Chastina P.M. Father [Asaph] Boutelle made out that all sin was murder. A Dreadfully logical Discourse. Even unkindness was a species of murder—for which God in the Great day will take terrible vengeance. He will be seen opening his great book at the place where one is recorded as having made faces at his Granny when a child, & there will follow in tones of an Earth Quake— "Murderer! Go howl!" Call from Mother [Watts] & Aunt Thos Watts. A letter from Hale [Rix] Stating that he had sent us on a bag of rocks. Let 'em come! "Yet there is room!" Bub eat a lot of sweet apple & dont sleep very well this evening. Chastine enjoy a small Bust in the shape of 4 roasted ears of green corn. Last night there was a slight frost & I fear a worse [one] to night. Strange change in the weather within a day or two. It is now extremely dry these days. We bring our water from Mr. [William] Mattocks's.[66]

Remark. A man with gumption goes by it—one without any goes where his father did.

Family Conundrums.

Why are our Curtains like an old lady?
   'Cause they wear "specks." (Fly shits.)
Why is our husband like a barn-frame?
   'Cause it costs a good deal to board him.
Why is our boy when falling head foremost, like smoke?
   'Cause we behold him "Ass-end-upwards!"

---

[66] The well at Sarah Marsh's must have gone dry because of a lack of rain that summer and fall.

CHAPTER SEVEN

Alfred Prepares for California
September 15–October 4, 1851

Begin to make some preparations for Cal.
ALFRED

*Never Shall I forget our parting; if it be our last
there is a sweet consolation in the thought that we were &
ever have been the happiest of the happy in each other's society.*
CHASTINA

"CONCLUDED TO GO TO CALIFORNIA," ALFRED WROTE IN THE journal on September 15. The decision had been made. For the next week, they detailed the activities involved in preparing for the trip. Alfred interviewed returned miners and encouraged others to join the group of men who had agreed to travel with him. He investigated the travel options and the necessary outfitting. He made arrangements with his law partner and settled his account with a local store owner. He laid in some winter provisions for Chastina and made sure she had plenty of firewood. For her part, Chastina made clothes and blankets. She served as his liaison with the men who came to the house wanting travel information. And she accompanied him in his rounds of saying goodbye to family. At the Watts farm, she had her own farewells to say to her brother Dustan, who would be making the trip with Alfred. For two and a half weeks, the couple readied themselves for Alfred's departure, and then "he has gone," Chastina wrote. Their lives had changed forever.

More than two hundred men from the Peacham area are known to have gone to California to seek their "pile" between 1849 and 1853, the height of the Gold Rush.[1] The cost of the adventure varied from $250 to $400.[2] The

---
[1] Bonfield, "Ho for California," 40; Bogart, *Peacham*, 226–27.
[2] Bonfield, "When Money Was Necessary," 130–31; Lewis, *Sea Routes*, 10–11.

Caledonian, citing ads from the New York papers, estimated the price of the trip by sea with crossing at Panama or Nicaragua at about $350 in 1851.[3] That was the equivalent of about $10,100 in 2009 dollars, a sum nearly impossible to raise when the annual income for Peacham farmhands was around $150.[4]

Alfred was unlike most of the men from Peacham who left for California. He had sufficient money in savings from teaching, surveying, and handling law cases, and thus he had no need to borrow for the trip. He also had a secure family—a wife and child who would have strong support in his absence from both of their families. Chastina was reluctant about his leaving, but he knew that she was a capable and thrifty woman who could take care of herself while he was gone. Others were not so fortunate. Chastina's younger brother Dustan had trouble raising the needed funds. He had recently completed his apprenticeship as a wheelwright but had not yet settled into a job in Vermont. His mother was unhappy about his plans, thinking he was too young to leave home, but she eventually relented, having decided that it was better for him to go with Alfred now than to go alone later.[5] In the end, Dustan's stepfather, Lyman Watts, made him a loan to cover the cost of his trip.[6]

Chastina, with baby Julian, was to remain in the house that she and Alfred had rented the previous spring at the south end of Peacham Corner. She knew that she would be lonely from the moment her husband of two years and two months walked out the door, but her love for him and her respect for his abilities would sustain her. She well understood both the risks and rewards of the adventure. The journal stayed in her hands, and she immediately resumed the practice of writing daily entries. The

---

[3] Figures for the cost of "passage and outfit" for California appeared in ads. *Caledonian*, February 9, 1851.

[4] The value of money at different times can be seen in the Consumer Price Index at http://www.measuringworth.com. The income for a Peacham farmhand in 1854 comes from Bogart, *Peacham*, 282. Average American wages at the time were between $200 and $300, leading historian Brian Roberts to conclude that miners were, like Alfred, whom he included in his book, mainly men from the middle class who could raise the necessary funds. Roberts, *American Alchemy*, 22, 82–87.

[5] Dustan's sister Clara described his situation in a letter to their brother Augustus. Clara Walbridge, Peacham, to Augustus Walbridge, Hardwick, October 4, 1851, private collection.

[6] This loan was not mentioned in the journal but was disclosed in a letter that Alfred included when he sent Dustan's "bill of exchange" for $200, repaying his stepfather. Alfred, San Francisco, to Lyman Watts, Peacham, June 30, 1853, private collection; Bonfield, "When Money Was Necessary," 144.

journal of two voices was now reduced to one, conveying only her perspective on the Gold Rush.

On the day Alfred left Peacham, Chastina listed the names of the men who would be traveling with him. There were sixteen from Peacham, four from Danville, three from Ryegate, and one from Barnet, plus Alfred's brother Oscar from Boston, who would be joining them in New York. Almost all had attended the Peacham Academy, and two of them—George C. Dana, Jr., and Sidney Redfield Rix, the latter a cousin of Alfred's—were listed in the current Academy catalogue as enrolled for the fall term. They all must have looked to Alfred, their former principal, for leadership. Three sets of brothers were making the trip: Alfred and Oscar, Mark and Chandler Blanchard of Peacham, and Ambrose and Henry Knight of Ryegate. Chastina was not the only wife who was staying behind; five of the men in the group were married, including John Gracy, who was the father of five children.[7] Four other women would be left "lonely and sad" as their husbands went to California in search of their "pile," hoping for a better life for their families. Four other women would soon share the "sore trial . . . of parting with a husband for so long a time."

[*ASR*] [Monday, September 15, 1851] Washed as usual— Concluded to go to California. Talked with some of the friends to the measure—Mark Blanchard & brother.[8]

[Tuesday, September 16] Begin to make some preparations for Cal. Went to see Seth Stuart—Accompanied by Chastina & July.[9] Fine ride.

---

[7] Much has been written about the departure of men who were leaving their families. An English woman traveling in America in 1849 and 1850 reported this response to the gold rush: "What misery has this California emigration brought on thousands of families—unknown, incalculable, wretchedness! There was, as may be supposed, a melancholy chorus of wailing and sobs when the dreaded moment actually arrived." Wortley, *Travels in the United States*, 108–109. I thank Gary F. Kurutz for this citation. See Yalom, *History of the Wife*, 228–29, for stories of men who unilaterally decided to go off, leaving their wives to fend for themselves.

[8] Brothers Mark Blanchard (1821–98) and Chandler Blanchard, both Peacham natives, agreed to join the group going to California.

[9] Seth W. Stuart went to California in January 1850 with the John S. Way company and returned with little in the way of financial gain. Bonfield, "Ho for California," 11–12; Peacham Grand List, 1852.

ASR [Wednesday, September 17] Wrote to Arnold Buffum & C. Vanderbilt of New York City as to passage &c. Regulated as to boots, pants &c—wrote to 20.[10]

[Thursday, September 18] Settled off with [William] Mattocks & [John M.] Martin. [Humphrey] Bennett's folks here on a visit.[11]

[Friday, September 19] About these days there is a terrible stir to get money for Cal. Some 20 young men & some old ones are after the wherewith to go with us. Some will fail. Went to see Seth Stuart again & got all possible particulars from him. Settled with Lyman Watts.[12]

[Saturday, September 20] Worked at furnishing Chastina her winter Stores of Sugar, flour & other provisions—filled bed[,] split wood &c till Stage came in & brought a reply from [Arnold] Buffum in full. Had a California meeting at [William] Mattocks office—some dozen agreed to go—to start next Steamer. Chose A. Rix to go to New York & get tickets. To go next Thursday & return on Saturday.

[Sunday, September 21] All the family at home all day— Rained this morning for the first time for a long while. Ira O. Miller called & spent the evening with us. Wrote to Ira O. Rix yesterday.[13]

[Monday, September 22] Settled with Mrs [Sarah] Marsh up to tomorrow & passd rects. She agrees for the future to let Chastina use water from her water pail till the well is full again & to let Mr R. ride out with her any where, & to meeting & I am to find whip.[14]

---

[10]Buffum and Vanderbilt of New York ran steamers down the Atlantic and up the Pacific. Alfred wrote to companies in Boston and New York that had advertised in the local newspapers promoting items to outfit those going to the California gold fields.

[11]Alfred was now in a law partnership with William Mattocks, with whom he had apprenticed in Peacham. John M. Martin, one of the local storekeepers, probably kept a tab for the Rixes. Bogart, *Peacham*, 274, 284. Chastina often met with Laura Blanchard Bennett, a close friend from school days, to compare their young sons.

[12]It is not clear what Alfred and Lyman Watts had to settle. It may have been a legal fee paid to Alfred for checking the ownership of the Watts farm, or possibly payment to Lyman for the meat that he had provided earlier in the year.

[13]Ira O. Miller, now principal of the Peacham Academy, was to continue without Alfred's help. Alfred's younger brother Ira wanted to go to California and eventually did, but not with Alfred.

[14]Chastina and Julian were to continue to live in Peacham at Sarah Marsh's while Alfred was in California. Mrs. Marsh had taken a liking to Alfred, probably because he had taught her children and also because he had high status in town. Alfred showed his sense of humor here, teasing about the situation. Because of the lack of rain that summer, the well the Rixes used for water had run dry, so Alfred arranged this alternative solution.

[*CWR*] [Tuesday, September 23] A very rainy day. And very welcome the rain is too for it is exceedingly dry. Alfred is doing up his business as fast as possible. I dont know what will become of poor me, when Alfred goes. A lot more boys have come home from Calafornia. Letter from brother [Edward] Bierstadt.[15]

[Wednesday, September 24] The boys fourteen in number have paid in each $50.00 to Alfred to purchase tickets in N.Y. We sat up very late to arrange matters & money for an early start tomorrow. A letter from Oscar [Rix]. He is going to Calafornia. They have a nice new son. All well.[16]

[Thursday, September 25] Got up at two o'clock and got breakfast for Alfred to s[t]art for N.Y. Did not go to bed again Wrote duning letters to John Watts & D[avid] Currier & carried them to the P[ost] O[ffice].[17] Letter from Ira Rix. He wants money to go to Cal. Bubby is real troublesome creeps all over the house & cries after me if he looses sight of me a moment. He has got three teeth & another coming. I am busy about nothing as usual.

[Friday, September 26] Very cold weather. Bub & I are rather lonesome. At work on Alfreds things.

[Saturday, September 27] Baking. Alfred does not come yet a long time it seems. [Ira] Miller called a few moments in the evening.

[Sunday, September 28] Went to meeting in the afternoon. They had a deacons meeting. Mother [Watts] Charles [Watts] & Augustus [Walbridge] called at noon.[18]

[Monday, September 29] Got up about six o'clock & went to washing, but strange to say did not get done till afternoon. Dustin [Walbridge] came here this forenoon. He is all in a fever to go to

---

[15] Chastina may have been referring to some of the California company who left in January 1850, fifteen of whom returned to Vermont. Bonfield, "Ho for California," 16–18. Edward Bierstadt, the husband of Alfred's younger sister Adeline, spent time in California in the 1870s, as did one of his brothers, the noted painter Albert Bierstadt. Bonfield and Morrison, *Roxana's Children*, 107.

[16] When Alfred's older brother, Oscar, joined Alfred in New York, he left his wife, Mary Ann Burton Rix, and three children in Boston. A catalogue card at the Society of California Pioneers says that Oscar Rix was "Buried Oct. 5, 1858," but the family genealogy by Guy Rix lists his death year as 1859.

[17] These men had borrowed money from the Rixes.

[18] Rev. Asaph Boutelle must have been away, so a deacon read a printed sermon. Chastina's mother and her sons came visiting after morning meeting.

CWR Calafornia. He & Clara [Walbridge] came over in the evening.[19] The Aurora Borealis presented a splendid appearance this eve. Alfred got home about ten o'clock P.M. Dustin & Clara waited till he come. Did not go to bed untill after midnight

[Tuesday, September 30] We were disturbed by Calafornia Boys this morning they kept coming untill they all heard what success Alfred had in N.Y. He did not buy tickets. Alfred had to be away from home most all the time. Another meeting this evening. I am at work on his flannels.

[Wednesday, October 1] The company have concluded to go Saturday this week. Dustan [Walbridge] is going. Alfred doing up his jobs fast as possible. Mrs [Elizabeth] Varney & Mrs [Laura] Bennett called this morning. Mrs V. has got [t]he Cal. fever pretty high. Dustin & Sidney Rix were here to dinner.[20]

[Thursday, October 2] We went visiting at Dr. [Asahel] Farr's in afternoon. In the Evening we went to see a Panorama of the garden of Eden &c.[21] Yuba Ricker took care of bub.

[Friday, October 3] Alfred got his things all ready. We went over to the East part. Called on Aunt [Sarah] Stevens. Took tea at our house, bid Dustin [Walbridge] good bye & came home to complete the packing of Alfred's things.[22] A sore trial it is to think of parting with a husband for so long a time

[Saturday, October 4] Got up about half past one & got Alfred some breakfast. At two he was oblige to start.[23] It is hard to part

---

[19]Chastina's younger siblings Clara and Dustan Walbridge were probably asking her to help them change their mother's mind about whether Dustan should go to California.

[20]Elizabeth Varney (ca. 1820–1904), a classmate of Chastina's, lived in Danville with her son Henry (1850–1920). Her husband, Robert (ca. 1822–94), had already gone to California. Ready to go to California besides Dustan Walbridge was Alfred's cousin Sidney Redfield Rix of Peacham.

[21]Artists often exhibited their work for the public to view, sometimes charging a fee. The showing of the oil painting *Expulsion from the Garden of Eden* by Thomas Cole (1801–48) was not announced in the local papers. Alfred and Chastina shared an interest in painting. She had taken lessons from the Peacham Academy drawing teacher, and Alfred often added drawings to their journal.

[22]They stopped first at the farm of Alfred's great-aunt Sarah Morrill Stevens, where Alfred had lived when he first came to Peacham. Then they went to the Watts farm for Chastina to say goodbye to her brother and for Alfred to say goodbye to Chastina's family.

[23]It is not known who drove the wagon that took Alfred and some of the others to the nearest railroad station, at Barnet, seven miles from Peacham.

with a friend when the hand of death is laid upon them. And hard too it is to part with one where danger lies in their track. Never Shall I forget our parting; if it be our last there is a sweet consolation in the thought that we were & ever have been the happiest of the happy in each other's society. He has gone! The hours are days. Lonely and sad am I, & our little boy he misses his papa.

List of those who went to Cal.[24]

Chandler Blanchard of Peacham		John C Blanchard of Peacham	
Sidney Rix	"	Dustan S Walbridge	"
Wm. D. Hooker	"	Alfred Rix	"
John Ewell	"	Oscar Rix	Boston
Harvey Varnum	"	Benj H Fuller	Ryegate
Michael Kavanagh	"	Ambrose Knight	"
Timothy Cowls Jr. of Peacham		Henry T Knight	"
George C Dana	"	[Robert] Harvey	Barnet
John Gracy	"	A. S. Allen	Danville
Sprague Harriman	"	John S Ladd	"
Asa Livingston	"	Erastus S Libby	"
Chester Brown	"	Henry M Howe	"
Mark Blanchard	"		

---

[24]Alfred must have provided Chastina with this list of men who originally planned to go to California with him. See appendix 3. Bogart, *Peacham*, 226–29, provides an incomplete list of the names of the men from Peacham who went to California in 1849–50. Few Vermont state histories or town histories mention the gold rush, despite the scores of men who went.

CHAPTER EIGHT

Chastina in Vermont and Alfred in California
October 5, 1851–August 22, 1852

> *Long & wearisome days they are to me . . .*
> *I live almost on my letters, at any rate I should not stand it long*
> *if I did not hear often . . . If ever Alfred returns I think he will have*
> *hard work to get my consent to leave me alone again.*
>
> CHASTINA

AFTER ALFRED LEFT FOR CALIFORNIA, A WAVE OF LONELINESS swept over Chastina. She was "busy all the time," running the household and taking care of Julian, but no amount of housework, visiting, sewing, or reading could alleviate her constant sadness. She found it hard to be alone, and she worried about Alfred so many "thousands of miles across the trackless ocean." Everything reminded her of their busy, happy days together; even a visit to her parents' farm in the East Part brought back memories of their early courtship. Sundays especially "are long days to me," she wrote, as she recalled their former "pleasant times reading & conversing together." She turned for comfort to the journal, where she could express the feelings she was experiencing. "Some times it is a relief to one to commit to paper his thoughts," she wrote. "It is next to talking over with a dear friend."

Chastina's daily life in Peacham was similar to that experienced by many women in New England whose husbands went off to California without them.[1] Women were often left to run the family farm, some with many

---

[1]Bonfield, "Ho for California," 22–23; Rohrbough, *Days of Gold*, 233–35, 243. Holliday, *World Rushed In*, was one of the first works to present the family drama of the gold rush, publishing both sides of the correspondence of California miner William Swain and his wife, Sabrina Swain, in Youngstown, N.Y., from April 1849 to January 1851. The phrase "California widow" was never used in reference to Chastina, but other wives who waited at home for their husbands' return often were labeled as such.

children to handle alone, some with no family or friends to help, and some with little money to meet the necessary expenses. Chastina was more fortunate than many in having close family and enough money to keep her comfortable, but she still felt neglected and alone. She noted a loss in her status in the community. "I must fight my battles alone," she wrote in the journal after being poorly treated by her landlady. And she felt mistreated by neighbors and even the daguerreotypist. Chastina's view of men's role became clearer in those months without Alfred as she realized that it was a husband's responsibility to protect his wife and family. She found herself diminished in the community without Alfred. Her views may have been conveyed in her letters to him, none of which have been located, but she expressed them clearly in the journal, knowing that Alfred would read the words when they were reunited.

Chastina repeatedly wrote that Julian needed his father. Fathers away in California were not home to share in their children's care or to witness their growth and childhood milestones. Alfred missed their son's first haircut. He was not there to help nurse Julian back to health during a bout of sickness. He was not there to celebrate his little boy's first birthday, even though he sent a birthday poem. He did not see Julian's first "steps alone" or hear his first words. Most of all, he was not there to give his son a father's attention, discipline, and love. "If it is hard for lovers to be separated," wrote Chastina in the journal, "how much harder is it for a husband & father to be away from his wife & child."

In January, Chastina and Julian went to see Alfred's family in Dalton, New Hampshire. Within days, however, she was called back to Peacham, where her mother had been taken seriously ill. Roxana slowly recovered, and Chastina decided that she and Julian would remain at the Watts farm until Alfred's return—where at least they would not be on their own, and she could help her mother with the endless chores. While there, she focused her attention on housework and settled into a busy routine. She made pies and doughnuts and bread, helped with the Monday wash, made clothes for her younger sisters and brothers, and did "some of the forty unnamable things which belong to house hold affairs."

Chastina found emotional solace in her letters from Alfred. They came twice a month—a total of twenty-two between October 8 and August 22. The first letter was mailed from New York before he boarded the *Prometheus*; the second was sent from Delaware, where the steamer had docked to let off a wounded passenger. Subsequent letters written en route described Alfred's life on the Isthmus of Nicaragua, on the Pacific, in San Francisco, and then finally in the gold fields. In January she mentions some journals that he had sent her from the trip.[2] She anxiously awaited the arrival of the mail, but retrieving it was not as easy while she was staying in the East Part as it had been at Peacham Corner. It was hard for her to get to the post office herself, so she depended on others to bring her mail to her. Everyone in town seemed to know when a letter from Alfred had arrived, and neighbors often stopped by to learn the news, even before Chastina had had a chance to read the whole letter herself.

Alfred's trip to California was not turning out as well as he had hoped. By February he was "not in so good spirits" at the mines, where he was failing to find much gold. His luck apparently did not improve, because by early April he had left the fields and returned to San Francisco. Initially his prospects did not look any brighter in the city. "Thousands upon thousands" of people were there, he had written Chastina, competing "to catch at every opportunity of making any thing." But by the next month, things were looking up. In May he wrote to say that he had accepted a teaching position at the newly opened public school near Mission Dolores that would pay him $150 a month. It was not the "pile" he had dreamed of earning, but it was a substantial increase over his $500 annual salary at the Peacham Academy.

Alfred had now decided that he would need to spend at least two years in California, and he wrote that he badly wanted Chastina and Julian to join him in San Francisco. Chastina was astonished at this unexpected request, as she had counted on his return and assumed that they would decide together where to move to settle. It had never occurred to her that he would not come back. Of course she wanted to be with him, but she could not imagine how it could happen. The idea of traveling so far on her own seemed impossible. It was not common for women at the time to travel long distances without their husbands or brothers. In 1849, when Clara had left upstate New York, where she had gone to school and was teaching, to return home traveling by herself, Chastina wrote of their mother's feeling "anxious, for it seems rather a long journey for one to go alone without some friend to look to for protection."[3] But as Chastina pondered Alfred's invitation over the following weeks, her thinking slowly shifted from being sure that she could never leave home, making such a long journey with a baby in tow, to wondering whether it might in fact be possible. California was becoming less of a strange land as men returned to Vermont and described the transformation of San Francisco into a civilized place.

---

[2] The journals she mentions have not been located.
[3] Chastina, Peacham, to Clara Walbridge, Oakfield, N.Y., July 13, 1849, private collection.

For his part, Alfred was pleading his case with Chastina's family. In June he wrote to her parents, reassuring them that he was doing well in San Francisco:

> I am still teaching—have about forty pupils—everything passed on pleasantly and very much to my satisfaction. I am moving to the Mission where I shall have a small garden to work during my spare hours. I calculate an income from it equal to about eighty dollars per month the terms are that I am boarded and have one half the clear income from the ground. The board is equal to about 30 dollars per month and the half produce about 50 per month which together with what comes of the Spanish classes I am hoping will not fall much below 200 per month for my clear savings . . . There is only one thing to make me uneasy—that is the absence of Chastina & Julian. My health is excellent, my spirits good, my prospects fair enough, but what of all that when I am so far from home? To be sure I have given my <u>home</u> a pretty strong invitation to come out here & am indulging a small hope of its being accepted.[4]

Weeks later, he also wrote to John and Sarah in hopes that they would help him convince Chastina to come:

> I am well and doing a fair business at present. I have invited Chastina & Clarissa to come out here—now you must not hinder them but help them off as soon as it seems proper. No healthier climate can be found on the world's outside than this same. We escape the hot weather of the interior and that was all you saw [in the mines] . . . the common idea in the east that California is a temporary spread and will soon blow up is all wrong—all gas and gammon. Any man of sense after looking for a moment at some of the facts in the

---

[4] Alfred, San Francisco, to Lyman and Roxana Walbridge Watts, Peacham, June 26, 1852, private collection. Alfred added another story to this letter, even though it does not say much about order in California: "You needn't tell Chastina that while coming down the Sacramento [after leaving the mines] I lost <u>all</u> I had except what was on my back at the time. My blankets (4 nice ones as ever covered a miner) were rolled around my entire stock of earthly effects, consisting of shirts, shoes, pant, vests, stocking, hankerchiefs, letters, writing apparatus and countless other 'fixins,' and deposited over board the steamer with other baggages. I always keep a pretty good look out for my extras but this time I was too keen for some rascal no doubt thought from my affections I seemed to exhibit for my pack and from the hand and weight of the thing that I had a 'pile' in it—so while the boat was touching at Benicia, he watched his chance & as I stepped forward for only two or three minutes he walked ashore with my flannels—it was in the night and by the time I found my roll was not aboard we were well on our way to San Francisco. That's the man what I curse every night and morning. But when Chastina asks me how my flannels and hosiery wear & last—am I to be blamed for smiling & answering her that she need expect nothing else but that shirts & stockings mad like <u>them ar'</u> will last well and do good service anywhere."

case will see that California is bound to shine a while longer yet. In the first place she has her gold mines which will give work to a great many for some time at the worst— Quartz mining will be a great business soon. But this is only one branch of her natural wealth. A large part of the state is land capable of agricultural improvements and it is being taken up for that purpose very rapidly. Some as fine crops have been produced here as in any part of the world . . . I should be happy here as man can be if my family was with me.[5]

Alfred was serious; he wanted Chastina and Julian in California, and he expected his wife to travel there without him. Nowhere does he write that they could not afford the cost of his returning to accompany them. He now had a position in the school system, earning a good living, and he envisioned their life together in the new flourishing city. Finally, after a visit in August with his family in Dalton, where she felt Alfred's absence more than ever, Chastina wrote, "I may go. Time will tell." As Alfred pushed harder, Chastina's resistance wore thinner. In time, she decided.

[CWR] [Sunday, October 5, 1851] Did not go to church. Clara [Walbridge], Mrs. Thomas Clark & Mrs McLeran called at noon.[6] Went to evening meeting

[Monday, October 6] Got up at six o'clock. Have done a large washing for me. Got done about two P.M. Took bubby & went up to the corner. Called on Mrs Blanchard & Mrs. Livingston.[7] Came home got my supper, ironed my colored clothes & had calls from Mrs [Sarah] Marsh & "brother Brewster."[8] All this alone with my baby.

[Tuesday, October 7] To day has been a lovely day warm & pleasant, but I cannot enjoy it. This afternoon I suppose Alfred sailed for Calafornia. And now while I am at home with our boy by my side, he is borne onward & away on briny sea. May heaven prosper & protect our beloved ones & return them once more to their homes

---

[5]Alfred, San Francisco, to John S. Way, Hardwick, July 25, 1852, private collection.
[6]Marietta Blanchard Clark (b. 1819) lived in the East Part near the Watts farm.
[7]Harriet Partridge Blanchard (1821–1902) was the wife of Mark Blanchard, who left for California with Alfred.
[8]This was probably Rev. Loring Brewster (1789–1860), minister at Wolcott, where Chastina spent her early years. Comstock, *Congregational Churches of Vermont*, 167.

CWR [Wednesday, October 8] Another day is passed. Long & wearisome days they are to me. Bubby is pretty troublesome. he keeps me fussing with him all the time. Mrs. Hichcock called on me.[9] Received a letter from Alfred at N.Y. He was well. They sailed yesterday, their company numbered nearly forty.[10] They sailed in the Prometheus. Alfred sent Oscars note of one hundred & twenty five dollars.[11]

[Thursday, October 9] Expected our folks over after me, but they did not come. Took tea at Mr [David] Choate's. Margaret Jane Harvey & Miss [Julia] Laughlin called on me.[12]

[Friday, October 10] Lyman [S. Watts] came after me to go home. Had quite a spat with the Lady of the house, or rather she got mad & was real insulting to L & myself before we left, all concerning the price of some apples.[13] Got home about noon. Helped Clara [Walbridge] some on her dress.

[Saturday, October 11] Worked on Clara [Walbridge]'s dress what time I could get besides taking care of bub in the forenoon. This afternoon mother [Watts] & I went visiting to Mr [David] Curriers. Called to see Mrs. Harvey Blanchard's folks.[14]

[Sunday, October 12] Did not go to church. The days are lonesome days to me.

[Monday, October 13] Have'nt done much of any thing excepting take care of baby. He is as much as one person ought to take care of. Into all manner of mischief. Had a letter from Alfred, when they had been out about two days. The Steamer was obliged to put in to Delaware to leave a young man who was accidentaly wounded by another. They were all well, & having as good a time as could be expected.

---

[9] Mahala Hitchcock (ca. 1815–52), the wife of the minister, lived across the street from Mrs. Marsh in the brick house designated as the Methodist parsonage.

[10] Chastina listed the names of twenty-five men who were going with Alfred to California. In his first letter Alfred reported that the number had grown to forty, so others must have joined the original group along the way.

[11] Alfred lent his older brother, Oscar Rix, money for the trip, and sent the note to Chastina to ensure that Oscar would pay it if anything happened to Alfred.

[12] Julia Ann Laughlin was listed in the 1848, 1850, and 1851 PAC.

[13] Chastina had probably helped herself to apples on the property, and the landlady, Sarah Marsh, objected.

[14] The Curriers and Blanchards lived in the East Part near the Watts farm.

[Tuesday, October 14] We were all somewhat startled to hear that A[lvah] Watts had come back to Peacham & but little better of his insanity. Mother [Watts] especialy is afraid of her life almost. My business each day is nearly the same I have fitted each of the little girls a dress & sewed some for Clara [Walbridge].

[Wednesday, October 15] We are having some very pleasant weather these days. Mother [Watts] & I visited Mrs. [Sarah] Stevens to day. The old lady said she was almost eighty five years old. She had washed five woolen blankets this forenoon. She does her work all alone.[15]

[Thursday, October 16] Grandmother [Olive Brown] sick, so mother [Watts] had to move her into her room. I assisted mother in making the change & in cleaning the rooms.

[Friday, October 17] Cynthia & Jane Brown came here this morning stayed until 3 o'clock P.M. In the evening Phineas & Abba Blanchard came to our house.[16]

[Saturday, October 18] This forenoon Clara [Walbridge] & I have been picking up to go back to the Corner. It takes a good deal to get us started I think sometimes I will not try to go any where it is such a job for me to <u>rig off</u> & come home & <u>un rig</u>. We got back to the Corner about three P.M. Charles [Watts] dug my garden sauce for me.[17]

[Sunday, October 19] It has rained almost incessantly all day—a lonesome time to me. If I could only know how & where Alfred & the rest of our friends were it seems as though I could feel some better. They have not been out of my mind a moment to day

[Monday, October 20] When we awoke it was raining very hard. The storm comes from the north east, it makes us think of our

---

[15] Monday was wash day in New England and involved much physical labor. It required filling large vats with water, adding shaved-up soap that she had probably made, heating the water, plunging the dirty clothes in the soapy water with a "clothes stick," wringing the clothes, rinsing them in clean water, wringing again, and finally hanging the clothes in the sun to dry. Blankets, quilts, and other large items were especially heavy and awkward to handle. For eighty-five-year-old Sarah Stevens to do her washing alone was quite a feat.

[16] Cynthia and Jane Brown were Chastina's cousins. Phineas Blanchard (b. 1834) and his sister Abigail lived in the East Part near the Watts farm. Phineas went to California in 1854.

[17] Chastina's brother Charles Watts turned over her vegetable garden for winter. "Garden sauce," often called "garden sass," is a reference to edible greens, with "sass" meaning salad. Phyllis Craig Graves, St. Johnsbury, letter to editor, April 18, 2010.

friends on the bounding deep. I have done a good large washing for me. Went up to the store made various little purchases, among the rest a cloak for bub.

[Tuesday, October 21] Doing house work, making candles, taking care of baby & sewing some. quite warm. A thunder shower this evening. A letter from Mr Carpenter of Waterford to Alfred, concerning the plan of a school house. I have the Knickerbocker No. 1. July, of the Reading Circle.[18] Alfred supposes that he has his life insured, but they would not accept of him or his money, on account of a trouble about his throat. Mr. [John M.] Martin did all he could to make them understand that it was not considered dangerous, but to no effect[19]

[Wednesday, October 22] Father [Watts] came over this morning & tells us that Lyman [S. Watts] is very sick with the bowel complaint. He did not take Clara [Walbridge] home with him. We get along pretty well. It takes one of us most of the time to take care of bub

[Thursday, October 23] I finished bub's cloak and cap to day. Nothing particular occured.

[Friday, October 24] To day like all the others has passed away. There is nothing that I can note that has taken place & yet I have been busy all the time. Alfred almost made me promise that I would run about a good deal, but as yet I have not nor do I feel any spirit to start out. Had the Eclectic Magazine[20]

[Saturday, October 25] Baking this forenoon— In afternoon rode to the Hollow with Jane Marsh. By the way Alvah Watts has been home from the "Insane Hospital" about a week He is some better than when he went away, but very far from being a sane man. The very first night he came home he ran away to the corner and put up at the tavern.

---

[18] The *Knickerbocker* was a magazine published in New York from 1833 to 1862. The Reading Circle must have been a system for circulating magazines. Chastina used it regularly.

[19] Alfred had signed up for life insurance with the Hartford Connecticut Company, but he was not accepted despite assurances from the company's agent, Peacham storekeeper John M. Martin. It is not known what Alfred's throat problem was. Insurance companies carefully selected their clients. Bonfield, "Ho for California," 19; Bassett, *Growing Edge*, 76.

[20] The *Eclectic Magazine of Foreign Literature, Science, and Art* began publishing in 1844 in New York.

[Sunday, October 26] Went to church in the forenoon. Listened to the preaching of the Rev. Mr [William] Bond of St Johnsbury plain[21] Lyman [S. Watts] is better. There is a report abroad that the Steamer Prometheus has been burnt. I do not credit the report. But if it should be true!! What misery and anguish of heart it would cause among the families of those left behind. The Sabbath is a lonely day for me We used to have such pleasant times reading & conversing together, that it makes me sad hearted when the Sabbath comes.

[Monday, October 27] We awoke this morning & found it snowing and as cold as Greenland in the winter. Notwithstanding we washed and cleaned house all day. John Way came here in the afternoon. His family are all well

[Tuesday, October 28] A little warmer. I fixed me up & carried our winter bonnets to Miss [Mary] Calder to be fixed. Got Harper June No. 6.[22] Came home & went to cleaning house again, it took all day to finish. Mrs. [Aurilla] Choate called

[Wednesday, October 29] Baking & Cutting apples. In the evening Jane [Marsh] had what she called a <u>sing</u>. I should call it a party. Mr. [Ira] Miller, Miss [Josephine] Stodard & Miss [Phebe] McKeen, the teachers were here & some fifteen or twenty students were here.[23] We had a very good time. Bub was awake the whole evening he behaved first rate for man of his age & of course attracted considerable notice & got lots of compliments.

[Thursday, October 30] Warm this morning & raining very hard It has rained steady all day & part of the [night] very hard. If it were not for the promise, we might think there was going to be another deluge. I have spent my time about as usual doing house work & cutting apples taking care of baby &c.

---

[21]William Bond (1815–94) was a pastor from St. Johnsbury. Comstock, *Congregational Churches of Vermont*, 166.

[22]*Harper's* was a popular literary magazine first published in New York in 1850. Chastina was reading the June 1851 issue, which had an article on shipwrecks. I thank the staff of the St. Johnsbury Athenaeum for preserving the issues from vol. 1 (1850) through today, plus an index.

[23]Teachers at the Peacham Academy listed in the 1851 PAC were Ira O. Miller, principal; Miss Phebe McKeen, preceptress; Miss Josephine M. Stoddard, teacher of French and music; and Miss Louisa P. Bradlee, teacher of painting and drawing. The November 22, 1851, *Caledonian* reported 97 scholars for the Academy in the fall 1851 term, bringing the total number to 226 for the year. Attendance had fallen off around this time because of competition from schools in neighboring towns and the decline in Peacham's population.

CWR [Friday, October 31] Pleasant this morning. Nothing of note has occured. I have been sewing principally to day. Clara [Walbridge] & I are fixing up our winter bonnets

[Saturday, November 1] This morning is very chilly. Mr [Samuel] Chandler called & paid Six dollars and eighty five cents of Hale [Rix]'s money. This is a lock of bubby's foretop [Chastina pasted a lock of his hair to the journal page], the first that was ever cut from his head. I wish to preserve it as a memento of his baby hood For since it was cut he seems no longer a baby—it has changed his looks so. He is now ten months old. He has no signs of walking yet. We hear nothing yet from our absent ones. The late rains have done a great deal of damage on the rail roads, & we have not got the mails regular. Got an Eclectic No 18 Nov.

[Sunday, November 2] Rainy again. However I went to church in the forenoon & Clara [Walbridge] in the afternoon Mother [Watts] tells me I can have an opportunity to send to Calafornia by Charles Varnum, s[o] I shall improve it by writing[24]

[Monday, November 3] I have done quite a large washing job for our family. Clara [Walbridge] wrote a letter to Dustin [Walbridge] & we sent them to Charles Varnum to carry to Calafornia.

[Tuesday, November 4] very cold this morning. It seem as though we should freeze in the morning. Bubby wakes up before daylight warm or cold & he first sits up as strait as a candle, in the bed. His next operation is to dig our eyes open with his thumb. A very funny way he has of using it. The little fuss I am afraid he will freeze some of these cold mornings. No news yet from our California folk.[25]

[Wednesday, November 5] I have been baking mince pies & bread. it takes me nearly all the time to do my work & take care of the baby what I do. I am almost discouraged when there is so much devolving on me & no one to aid me Called to Mr [David] Choate's the first call I have made since Alfred went away It is hard to be left alone.

[Thursday, November 6] This is my birth day, & a gloomier one I do not ever remember of spending. First it is a very cold day.

---

[24]Charles Varnum went to California, leaving a wife and daughter in Peacham. He stayed at least two years. Long, "Yankee Argonaut."

[25]This is the first time Chastina spelled "California" correctly in the journal.

Secondly Mr. [David] Choate came to set up our stove in the parlor, so we were oblige to be without fire all the forenoon. Then came a rumor that the Prometheus had her captain in irons & was on her way home. How anxious we are to know the worst. The agony of suspense is almost unbearable. What can the matter be? Why this delay to return? are things which have taken a thousand different forms in my mind I have fancied all sorts of misfortunes which they are undergoing And more. Can it be that the first report is true? Such a birth day may I never witness again

[Friday, November 7] A beautiful sunny morning has dawned upon us but I cannot feel happy. Ah yes. Another report says our steamer is coming home & all right notwithstanding the captain is in chains. This makes me feel better for we shall hear something soon. I went to the Hollow on foot to get bub a pair of shoes. Saw Charles Varnum there. He starts tomorrow morning for Cal. Came home & Clara [Walbridge] & I took Bub & called on Mrs. [Elisabeth Clark] Strobridge Mrs. [Mary Blanchard] Dana & Miss [Abigail] Chamberlain. In the evening Mrs [Martha Wheeler] Farr & Miss [Mary] Miller spent the evening here.[26]

[Saturday, November 8] Another pleasant day. Moses Currier & Lyman [S.] Watts were here to dinner. I have done scarcely anything to day. Anxious am I to have night come & the mail come too. 7 o'clock it comes! & O! good good, a letter. A great long letter so long that could not get the last read until nine o clock not however so long a letter that it would take two hours to read it, for bub the little scamp would'nt let me read all the time. They are at the Isthmus. Have had a storm & rather a hard time. But I am thankful to hear that they are alive & so well. For particulars see Alfred's Journal kept during the voyage.[27] Dr. [Asahel] Farr & wife came to hear the letter before I had looked it over myself

---

[26] Chastina and Clara had visited some women at Peacham Corner, including Elisabeth Clark Strobridge, whose brother soon left for California; Mary S. Blanchard Dana, whose family were neighbors of the Watts'; and Abigail Chamberlain, the Rixes' former landlady. The evening callers were Martha Wheeler Farr, the wife of the doctor who had delivered Julian, and Mary Miller of Coventry, the sister of the Peacham Academy principal and a student listed in the 1851 and 1852 PAC.

[27] Alfred's travel journal and his letters written on the trip have not been located; nor have Chastina's letters to him.

CWR [Sunday, November 9] A beautiful autumn day. Clear, cold, & pleasant. I went to church in the forenoon. Heard Mr [John] Mattocks preach. I love to hear him preach. He is always interesting and instructive. Clara [Walbridge] went home after meeting & left Alice [Watts] with me. I love to stay alone part of the time at least, and were it not for bub I should prefer to be alone a good part of the time. I have enjoyed myself very well this evening <u>thinking</u> reading writing in the journal & taking care of baby. I love to think over build castles & then let them fall— I know however that one gets gloomy by staying alone a great deal & I think this would be the case with me.

[Monday, November 10] I awoke & found the ground white with snow. & still snowing. There has fallen quite a lot of it to day. I have done my washing & work as usual. It is rather hard for me to do every thing alone. I have my water to dip out of a high cistern & bring out of the cellar. Alice [Watts] has taken care of the baby a good deal or I could not have done so much. This evening I have ironed my colored clothes. I make a practice of ironing my colored clothes monday after washing.

[Tuesday, November 11] I was awakened last night after I had retired by a most hideous noise, which frightened me half out of my wits for a few moments. I sprang out of bed & went to the window the moon was shining brightly so it was almost as light as day, but I could discover nothing but still heard the same dismal sounds. All at once an idea struck me. "A students tin horn," I guess. I then went back to bed, but soon the noise increased & upon a second look out of my window saw five youngsters, with a big brass drum & their tin horns marching along in martial array— Their music was fine! & they no doubt felt better than when those of them who belonged to the school got expelled this morning.[28] Jane Marsh "though[t] the day of judgment had come & she looked out to see if she could see any fire." It has been a real wintry day. I do not know but we are going to have winter in earnest. I have been baking pies & bread to day.

[Wednesday, November 12] Have been alone with my little boy almost all day. Knitting the little chap some stockings. He is so hard

---

[28] Under "General Regulations" in the 1851 PAC is this statement: "Scholars will be subject to the supervision and direction of the Principal, not only the school-room, but in respect to their study-hours, recreations, and conduct out of school."

up that I have been oblige to sit down in the day time & knit, a thing which I have not done before for a long time. Mrs [Fenton] Hutchins spent the evening here. Got the Sep. No of Knickerbocker. We keep pretty well posted up in the reading matter of the "Reading Circle." Some of the reading I like very much

[Thursday, November 13] Clara [Walbridge] come back in the afternoon. very cold indeed. I have made out to finish Bub's little stockings.

[Friday, November 14] Days pass on, & each brings the same routine for me. No one is more busy than I am & but few that accomplish more. I have been making bub an apron to day besides doing my work.[29] I have had rather a lonely day. Somehow I feel a kind of sickness & faintness whenever I think of both my own & Alfred's situation. I am here situated comfortably in our rooms & seem to have every thing to comfort me, or more properly to be comfortable— Yet the one object, which is necessary to my happiness, is away far away. And how is he situated? Could I answer that to my own mind it would be some consolation. Julian is beginning to be more & more company to me, for he begins to do & say those cunning things. One thing however is not quite so cunning for he has kept me up till nearly eleven o'clock.

[Saturday, November 15] Another stormy day. When we awoke it had been raining and then frozen over every thing so the trees presented a fine appearance, stretching their icy limbs abroad as if in pity, at their frozen condition. First it rained then commenced snowing & such a stormy day we seldom have though we have them more blustering. The day has passed with me just about as usual. Our Shed is not covered yet, & such storms as to day has brought makes sad work for me. It is no use for me to relate what thoughts & feelings a Saturday eve. brings to me. A dunning letter came to Alfred from one [Thomas S.] Hall of Lancaster N.H. to pay a debt of Hale [Rix]'s.

[Sunday, November 16] A fine batch of snow, nearly six inches I should think Had a sleigh ride to church this afternoon. Mr [Asaph] Boutell preached rather to the young, at the close of school His

---

[29]A pinafore-type apron was commonly worn by small children of both sexes. Lynne Bassett, fashion consultant, e-mail message to editor, March 16, 2009.

CWR subject Joseph of old, & his perfect character.³⁰ Clara [Walbridge] gone to meeting this evening— We have been writing to Harriet Guyer. How delighted I should be if Alfred could sit down by me this evening. I am lonely. Our little boy is sleeping quietly by my side in his snug little cradle, & now we want dear papa to make us happy. I have just been cracking the nuts he bought for us in N.Y. <u>How</u> can I take pleasure in such things alone. Even the smalest thing which I have my first thought is "Alfred loves it," or "he admires such things" would he could taste, or see, or hear with me. But I am filling this book with trash. Each day as I write & look over what nonsense I have put in I wish it were never written, & yet it is a real comfort to me to write even poor as it is. I never enjoyed it so much before. Some times it is a relief to one to commit to paper his thoughts, it is next to talking over with a dear friend.

[Monday, November 17] I have done my washing once more. Very pleasant day. After washing I went to the examination at the Academy. Things went off rather slowly, and not so well as when the <u>former preceptor</u> had charge of the school.

[Tuesday, November 18] Clar[a Walbridge] went to the examination this morning. I stayed at home & baked. In the afternoon Sarah [Walbridge Way] & her litle sis come.³¹ They are quite well. Mr. [Daniel] Bickford of Cabot come to hire Clara [Walbridge] to keep school. After much talk he agreed to give $10.00 per month if she did well.³² In the evening Mr [Humphrey] Bennett came & brought a letter from Alfred. Right glad was I to receive it. It bore the date

---

[30] The subject of Rev. Asaph Boutelle's sermon may have been either Joseph of the Old Testament, who became the governor of Egypt, or Joseph of the New Testament, the husband of Mary. David E. L. Brown, e-mail message to editor, November 30, 2008. I am indebted to David for his help in identifying biblical references in the journal.

[31] Chastina's sister Sarah Walbridge Way and her daughter, Martha, were visiting from Hardwick. First-born girls in New England families were often called "Sis."

[32] Ten dollars a month was much higher pay than most female teachers received. In 1847 Clara Walbridge had taken over the school in Peacham on Penny Street when the teacher could not handle the students, so she had a reputation as a good teacher. When she taught in Batavia, N.Y., and Littleton, N.H., she received $2 a week. Vermont teachers were hired and supervised by a local school clerk, such as Daniel Bickford from Cabot. According to Margaret K. Nelson, female teachers in Vermont earned less than $1.50 a week, whereas male teachers received about $3.25 a week. Nelson, "Vermont Female Schoolteachers," 13, 24–26; Bonfield and Morrison, *Roxana's Children*, 80–82.

of 21 of Oct., an account of their passage up the San Juan river, for particulars see his Journal No 4 They were tolerabe well at the time. Though I guess they see rather hard times

[Wednesday, November 19] Visiting of course— In the afternoon Sarah [Walbridge Way] & Clara [Walbridge] made calls. Invited Mrs. [Laura] Bennett & Mrs [Mary] Dana to make us a visit. Sis Way begins to talk every thing.

[Thursday, November 20] Warm this morning. In the afternoon came Mrs [Laura] Bennett & Mrs. [Mary] Dana with their two boys. So here were four girls formerly living in the East part of Peacham within two miles of each other who three years before were unmarried. Now all are married and have a baby apiece. Mrs. D. has beat us all in boys, for her's weighs 17½ pounds at nine weeks old. Had a very good visit.[33] In the evening came another letter from Alfred. He was yet on the [Nicaraguan] isthmus, but across, with the steamer in sight that will take them to San Fransesco. They have seen hard times surely, wet cold & hungry.

[Friday, November 21] Stormy day. I have had the blues a great part of the time. It is snowing & blowing a real storm—our shed is not fixed yet, every thing all over snow, and nobody to do a thing for me. I am almost discouraged & were it not for Alfred's hard lot I should be completely done up. Father [Watts] came over at night to carry us over home. Clara [Walbridge] concluded not to go so Sarah [Walbridge Way] & I packed off in the rain.

[Saturday, November 22] Had a very good visit. This is the second time I have been home since Alfred went away. I cannot enjoy myself so well as though I were not dependent upon other people. Others have their interests to care for, & what matter is it of theirs what becomes of others. Alvah Watts is getting desperate again

[Sunday, November 23] Came home this morning when they went to meeting. I have not been to church. George & Alma Currier called at noon[34]

CWR

---

[33] The four women were sisters Laura Blanchard Bennett and Mary S. Blanchard Dana and sisters Sarah and Chastina.
[34] Brother and sister George and Alma Currier lived in the East Part near the Watts farm. George went to California in 1854.

CWR   [Monday, November 24] Got up this morning about 5 o'clock, took my baby with & built my fire & went to washing. We got through about noon. I then made a chicken pie & by the time this was made Mother [Watts] John [S. Way] & Sarah [Walbridge Way] came here. They stayed a while in the evening— Then Johns folks bid us good bye for a time.

[Tuesday, November 25] Pleasant this morning— Sent of[f] some letters, one to the man that sent the dunning letter from Lancaster N.H. for Hale [Rix] & the other to Dalton to father Rix. We have heard a report that Hale [Rix] has got killed by the earth caving in where he was digging. I feel very anxious to know the truth of the story. Took cold so I feel rather unwell—Though Clara [Walbridge] & I have been visiting to Mr [David] Choate's Stayed in the evening.

[Wednesday, November 26] We awoke this morning & found it snowing hard, & there had during the night fallen a foot of snow. It looks dubious enough. The first thing I was oblige to sweep a path & go & get in my clothes. Rather a hard case for me to dig out through the snow. We have not had a road [path] shoveled down to the road to day— I do not [k]now but that I shall be obliged to burrow this winter

[Thursday, November 27] Clara [Walbridge] swept & shoveled a path down to the road, so that we might not be blocked in another day Nobody thinks of being so kind to us as to come and dig us out. Though we have plenty of neighbors, they are all Levites. Had another dun from the Lancaster man, about that debt of Hale [Rix]'s.

[Friday, November 28] Another snow storm; as many as six inches fell this time. This time it fell to my lot to clear out the snow. As yet we have done every bit of our diging in snow. Our Shed is not fixed yet. Wood all over snow. I am realy disheartened, when I see all around me heaps of snow & cold weather, with no one to look after me. It is some thing that I have not been obliged to do for years. Mrs Trustram Sanborn died this morning. She gave birth to a litle son last monday morning. Her death I believe was caused by taking cold before the child was born. This is their first Child & and they have been married eleven or twelve years. Thus she has been taken in the midst of their hopes[35]

[Saturday, November 29] I have cut a dress for Clara [Walbridge]. She is in a great hurry to get her things fixed. Strange how many little things some persons do for others & never themselves get one morsel of return If any thing is to be cut or fixed or patterns or any kind of under garments for patterns, Mrs. Rix has to run & bring hers & that is all the thanks I get from Jane M[arsh] & a good many others. I get almost out of patiense some times. [Ira] Miller called to read some of Alfred's letters. By the way he boards at our old home Mr [David] Choates. I swept our road again to day

[Sunday, November 30] Mrs Sanborn buried to day. I attended the funeral A solemn time. Mr [Asaph] Boutell preached well— Cold & blowing. Clara [Walbridge] gone home & I am left all alone I am going to writing Alfred. Bub eleven months & does not go alone yet. The wind commenced blowing this evening. Tis a dreary night. Grandfather [Oliver] Walbridge died some three or four weeks ago. He was about eighty five years of age.[36] He was a good old man, & I believe he has gone to Heaven if any one has. We saw him last summer he was bowed with age, but his countinance was smiling & cheerful. I never shall forget his good bye to us. The tears started in his eyes as he took us by the hand & bid us good bye & wished us well. His last farewell to us & no doubt he considered it as such.

[Monday, December 1] A cold stormy morning. I am alone. Had to take my baby & build my fire with him. It is so cold that water left upon the stove was frozen. However I have lived through the day & done my washing, but it is too hard for me. Mr. [David] Choate, & Way called on business of Alfred's. Mr [David] Currier called & paid up that note of $50.00. Had a letter from father Rix. They invite me to spend part of the winter at Dalton. The report concerning Hale [Rix]'s death they know no more about than we do. Pared

---

[35] Lucinda Clark Sanborn married Trustram Sanborn on December 8, 1840. She died at age thirty-three. The baby lived. *Caledonian*, December 6, 1851.
[36] Oliver Walbridge died in Wolcott, where he had moved from Cabot around 1800. Wallbridge, *Descendants of Henry Wallbridge*, 81.

CWR apples for pies. The wind blows furiously as ever. The house is no proof against such a wind.

[Tuesday, December 2] Rather warmer this morning—at least not so blustering Sent of[f] a letter to Alfred & one to Thomas S Hall of Lancaster, with eight dollars & forty one cents in it. A debt which he held against Hale [Rix]. Made pies & done house work all day

[Wednesday, December 3] Ironed & began a dress for myself. Made the skirt & sat up until eleven o'clock to get it done. By the way I sit up very late every night. I hate to go to bed in the cold.

[Thursday, December 4] This is our Thanksgiving day.[37] It is rather a pleasant morning. But lonely for me. I got up & made some buck wheat flapjack & coffe for my breakfast. The first time I ever eat a Thanksgiving breakfast alone. I am going home after meeting I suppose. I do not suppose it will seem any the less lonely to me there. We had a good supper but I could not enjoy it. Cynthia Brown there.

[Friday, December 5] Worked on my dress. Mrs. [Alma] Currier at father [Watts]s visiting. Received a recept of Mr. [Thomas S.] Hall of Lancaster for the money sent him. Uncle Simeon Brown came to our house.

[Saturday, December 6] In the afternoon we that is Clara [Walbridge] & I rigged of[f] & come to the Corner. Father [Watts] moved my bed down into the parlor It is rather hard to take bubby up stairs to sleep this cold weather. Justin Farr died about 9 o'clock this eve.[38] He has been sick about two weeks. We sat up till mid night.

[Sunday, December 7] Went to meeting in the forenoon. Snowing some—though not very cold

[Monday, December 8] Washed in the forenoon. Clara [Walbridge] went to Justin Farr's funeral. Rainy & cold, freezing cold. They do not want Clara to begin her school untill next week. Bub took his first step alone

[Tuesday, December 9] We have to stay in the house for it is a very cold & stormy day

---

[37]The date for Thanksgiving was set by each state's governor until President Abraham Lincoln made the day a national holiday in 1863, to be celebrated on the last Thursday of November.

[38]Justin Porter Farr (ca. 1829–51), the son of Dr. Asahel Farr, was buried in Peacham. He was listed as a student from St. Johnsbury in the 1849 and 1850 PAC.

[Wednesday, December 10] Very pleasant this morning, put out my clothes, & went to the store. Bought cloth for bub's clothes &c. Got a Harper of the reading circle.[39] In the evening we visited at Mr. [Ira] McClary's the first time I was ever in there to stop any. Before nine o'clock the wind arose & we had a real <u>whisker</u> to come home in. Fortunately for us it is but a short distance.

[Thursday, December 11] Finished my dress that I have been to work on so long. By the way Clara [Walbridge] & I sit up very late, that is till eleven or twelve almost every night. Bub has got so he can walk a little. Father [Watts] called to see if we were alive after the storm.

[Friday, December 12] Wrote a letter to father Rix. Clara [Walbridge] & I made bub a dress this afternoon. Clara reads & knits in the evening & I sew & tend baby.

[Saturday, December 13] Baking this forenoon. Clara [Walbridge] called to see Mr. [Trustram] Sanborns litle boy. poor little fellow he has no mother! Got an Eclectic of the reading circle

[Sunday, December 14] A bitter cold day. Went to church in the afternoon. Mr [Daniel] Bickford came after Clara [Walbridge]. I got supper for them & off they went leaving me all alone. I[t] seems as though we should nearly freeze it is so cold here, both out of doors & in

[Monday, December 15] Snowing again this morning. I have made out to get my washing done, but it was rather a hard one all alone. Bub is most sick teething & a hard cold. He has got so he can walk half across the room.

[Tuesday, December 16] Another <u>tremendous blow</u> last night. snow all drifted up. There was a gret pile of snow on the floor this morning, & plenty of it in the shed. Mr. [David] Choate called for the first time to dig me out. Said he felt guilty to think he had'nt fixed the shed. Bub cross & sick. I have fixed me a dress by sitting up till eleven o'clock.

[Wednesday, December 17] Pleasant but cold. Mr. [David] Choate came up this morning for me to go to their house & stay all day. So

CWR

---

[39] The November 1851 *Harper's* had a long article on Napoleon Bonaparte by John S. C. Abbott. Chastina shared Alfred's interest in biographies of famous men.

CWR of course I went. Had a good visit though Mrs. [Aurilla] C[hoate] had to work all the time as she has Mr. [Ira] Miller & Sister & another lady as boarders. Mr [David] Currier called & I let him have twenty dollars.

[Thursday, December 18] Very pleasant, but cold. Mrs. [Mary Elizabeth] McClary visited me this afternoon & in the evening Mr. [Ira] McClary & Jane [Marsh] came in.[40] Lyman [S. Watts] came up and stayed all night.

[Friday, December 19] The weather has moderated a good deal & it is pleasant. I have done quite a washing & my ironing & some baking & I feel some what tired. Got the Dec. No of the Knickerbocker.

[Saturday, December 20] Heard that Lyman [S. Watts] is sick again. Went visiting to Mr. [Ira] McClary's. Mrs. M. said she would not have it said that we have lived so close together almost a year & never visited, & she wanted me to go there before I went away, so I went. Called in to Dr [Asahel] Farr's. Dreadful snow & blow again could'nt hardly get home, though most of the way under cover.[41] Came home & wrote part of a letter to Alfred to send by Ashbel Martin.[42]

[Sunday, December 21] Have not been to church. very cold. Finished my letter to Alfred. Mr [David] Currier called to tell me that Lyman [S. Watts] is very sick. Another week has gone by. Time flies swifter with me than I should think it would, here all alone. If ever Alfred returns I think he will have hard work to get my consent to leave me alone again. No one know[s] how they will feel till they have experienced a separation.

[Monday, December 22] Pleasant. Get up befor light & got my washing done by noon. Finished off a letter to Alfred & sent it over to Ashbel Martin to Carry to Calafornia Mary Choate called

[Tuesday, December 23] Ephraim Clark called this morning to

---

[40] Mary Elizabeth Staples McClary (1822–91) and her husband, Ira McClary (1818–94), lived next door to Sarah Marsh, where Chastina rented. Ira ran a store in a small building next to his house from 1860 into the 1870s. *Walton's Vermont Register*, 1860–; Bogart, *Peacham*, 380–81.

[41] Thirty inches of snow had fallen in the area so far that winter. *Caledonian*, December 20, 1851.

[42] Ashbel Martin (1830–99) left for California on December 25, 1851, with a small group of Peacham boys, most of whom had attended the Peacham Academy under Alfred. Bonfield, "Ho for California," 29. See Long, "Yankee Argonaut," for the gold rush story of Ashbel Martin.

see if I wanted to send a letter to Alfred by him.[43] To day I have felt quite happy thinking that I should hear from Alfred as news of the arrival of a mail steamer has reached us. But alas we are subjects of disappointment. No letter[s] have come. We shall be obliged to wait another two or three weeks before there is a possibility of our hearing from them Got a Harper of the reading circle[44]

[Wednesday, December 24] Took dinner with Mrs. [Sarah] Marsh. She had tripe for dinner I do not love it. Made a dress for bubby. The litle fellow has got so he can run pretty well. Received a letter from Weltha Cory.

[Thursday, December 25] Another terrible blow. A snow drift half across the room when I got up. A long lonely day this has been to me. Why should it not be. Here I am shut up in a small room & no one thinks of calling to see me, so I sit all alone from morning till night. This evening is the "fair" at the town hall, the proceeds of which are to buy a chandelier for the meeting house. I might have gone I suppose, but I have no one to go with me & have no convey[ance] to go. As I have done nothing about the fair I shall see nothing of it

[Friday, December 26] Pleasant to day. It has been a very long day to me. I never scarcely experienced a more lonely day. I expected to go home last Wednesday, but on account of Lyman [S. Watts]'s sickness could not, & I have neither seen or heard any thing of them since the first of the week.

[Saturday, December 27] All day I have been alone again. In the evening Miss [Ann] Cameron called a few moments. And Mother [Watts] & Charles [Watts] came afterwards. They tell me I better go home tomorrow sat up till eleven. Showed Jane Marsh how to do sums

[Sunday, December 28] Snowing, hailing, & raining this morning. Do not know whether they will come after me or not. Went home in the afternoon found Lyman [S. Watts] pretty sick

---

[43] Ephraim W. Clark (1828–1900) went to California with Ashbel Martin. Bonfield, "Ho for California," 29–33.

[44] The December 1851 *Harper's* continued its series on Napoleon and added an article on Louis Kossuth (1802–94), who was traveling around the United States seeking support for Hungary's democratic government. Another article, "Gold—What It Is and Where It Comes From," mentioned gold sites all over the world, with only one sentence on California.

CWR   [Monday, December 29] Helped mother [Watts] about the house in the forenoon & sewed on her dress in the afternoon

[Tuesday, December 30] Bub's first Birth day! Go it, my lad! Worked for mother [Watts] all day & finished her dress.

[Wednesday, December 31] Very warm—rained almost all day— went down to Aunt [Sarah] Stevens The old lady smart as ever. Stayed all night. Saw John Martin & wife[45]

[Thursday, January 1, 1852] John Way & Lambert Watts stayed at our house all night[46] Lyman [S. Watts] got most well

[Friday, January 2] Mother [Watts] awoke me this morning with I have a letter for you I was on my feet very soon & dressed in short order to see what news Alfred has been sick all the way on the Pacific. He on landing became better & the 18th day of Nov. was going to start for the mines.

[Saturday, January 3] Mother [Watts] & I went to the corner. Took dinner with Mrs [Mary Blanchard] Dana. found all right at home— Got an "Eclectic" made a cap for mother

[Sunday, January 4] Nothing—only did'nt go to church. Sent a letter to A. R. [by] Dan Foster[47]

[Monday, January 5] Picked up my duds again & at about 9 o'clock father & mother [Watts] started with me for Dalton N.H. snowed during our whole ride of thirty miles—. We had rather a hard time though it was not very cold We arrived there about four o'clock P.M. Found father Rix' family all well

[Tuesday, January 6] Father & Mother [Watts] started for home— Pleasant— Bubby & I feel pretty lame to day— Bub is "tickled most to death" to find so many to take notice of him

[Wednesday, January 7] Bub almost sick with a cold— Another

---

[45] John Martin of Danville went to California with the group from Caledonia County, including John S. Way, who left in January 1850. Bonfield, "Ho for California," 11.

[46] Lambert Watts went to California, leaving a wife and four children, and returned in 1853. Russell Clark, Peacham, to his son Ephraim W. Clark, California, September 15, 1853, PHA-MS, Clark, Ephraim Wesson. There apparently was a reunion taking place of returned miners, who met with men planning to go.

[47] Dan Foster went to California and returned in late 1853. Elisabeth Clark Strobridge, Peacham, to her brother Ephraim Clark, California, December 31, 1853, ibid. Ephraim's location is not noted, but his letters from that time came from Placerville, California.

great snow storm. Ira, Morrill[,] Melvin[,] Charles & Alanson & Louisa [Rix] are at home—[48] All excepting Ira [Rix] go to school.

[Thursday and Friday, January 8 and 9] Bub quite sick— Visiting as hard as I can.

[Saturday, January 10] Wrote a letter to Weltha Cory— Bub better. I enjoyed myself pretty well— Mother Rix' health is not good this winter.

[Sunday, January 11] Went to meeting with Morrill [Rix]— Left bub at home. He was a good boy— Methodist preaching—about twenty or thirty composed the audiance

[Monday, January 12] Helped Louisa [Rix] wash— Cold day— Ira [Rix] & Morrill [Rix] read to us in the evening— By the way I think I have some pretty smart brothers— They are realy pretty young men & if I were not their sister I should be for speaking for them or their older brother

[Tuesday, January 13] Went down to Mr. Crain's. father Rix sisters & of course my uncles. Saw Miss Fisher Austins [Rix] girl there Had a very good visit, though she had a house full of boarders so I could'nt enjoy my visit so well.

[Wednesday, January 14] Mother [Rix] went away this morning & left Louisa [Rix] & I to do the work— Began to cut a dress for Louisa.

[Thursday, January 15] Sewed all day & evening on L[ouisa]'s dress

[Friday, January 16] Worked for myself some

[Saturday, January 17] Did the ironing— I always try to worke enough to pay the trouble of having me round Boys read to us in the evening from the Mexican War

[Sunday, January 18] Father [Rix] went down to the road & got me a letter from Alfred— It does my heart good to [hear] from him— This time he sent his journals—Six sheets of them. He is quite well now. Wrote to Alfred & to Peacham.

[Monday, January 19] Washing—that is Louisa [Rix] & I.

[Tuesday, January 20] So cold & stormy that father [Rix] could'nt

---

[48] Alfred's brothers and sisters mentioned here were still living at home in Dalton, N.H. Chastina called the tenth child Melvin, but the family genealogy lists him as Lewis Merwin. Rix, *History and Genealogy of the Rix Family*, 43.

CWR go to school with the children— Ira [Rix] is not at home now. Louisa [Rix] at home, so she works for herself. I am kind of a helper for every one. Do no particular kind of work but a little of all kinds. To day I have done house work some, made pies, helped Louisa &c. &c.

[Wednesday, January 21] Made bub a little shirt— In the evening I either read or listen to reading— Father [Rix] & I get <u>preached at</u> for reading politics. Mother [Rix] has some strange notions some times

[Thursday, January 22] This morning father & mother [Rix], bub & I started off for Moses Rixes— Before we got one mile I thought I should freeze & be squesed to death, for be it known that mother weighs over two hundred lbs. & of course we must make rather a full load in consequence— But after a long & cold draw, we arrived there— Distance about five miles. found cousin Louisa [Rix] at home but Moses absent at the time He came at last, & we were preparing for a good visit when Charles [Watts] came in & said that I was sent for. That my mother might not be alive when I got home. So we fixed ourselves as quick as possible & started for home through darkness & snow drifts My fear of riding added to my anxiety for mothers account well nigh over came me but I tried to keep up good courage Thus ended my visit there— We got home about nine o'clock— Found George Currier there waiting for me. Packed up my things & went to bed tired & weary enough.

[Friday, January 23] Cold & stormy— Started for Peacham at about eight in the morning The first ten miles was tedious enough Called & warmed & drove on as fast as possible. Stopped at Lower Waterford & got some dinner. Bub stood it better than I expected. We called again at Stevens village. The last part of the journey lagged— I never went any where before when there seemed such a dread to fall upon me It seemed as though I could hardly muster courage to approach the house for fear of sad news as we had not heard since George [Currier] came from there— But I found her [alive] & more comfortable than I expected, though she could not speak loud & was extremely low. After finding her I began to think of myself & bub. The little fellow got very tired and uneasy befor we got home for it was so cold I was obliged to keep him covered up. We were very tired.

[Saturday, January 24] Rather lame—but have worked all day at house work and washed into the bargain. Mother [Watts] on the gain a very little Found John [S. Way] & Sarah [Walbridge Way] & Augustus [Walbridge] here when I came home.

[Sunday, January 25] Sent a letter to Dalton. Worked again all day Bubby tired & almost sick— I found Lyman [S. Watts], & Jane Clark sick when I got home[49]

[Monday, January 26] Clara [Walbridge] & I have done the washing & work & took care of mother [Watts]. Father [Watts] gone to find a [hired] girl. John [S. Way] & Sarah [Walbridge Way] gone home

[Tuesday, January 27] Got a girl to help us— Mother [Watts] gains slowly I have a bad cold

[Wednesday, January 28] Bub sick. I have given him some medicine so he may not get clear down The family have all gone to bed & I am left to watch by mother [Watts]s bed side

[Thursday, January 29] About the same

[Friday, January 30] Bub sick—grew sick so fast that we sent for the doctor for him He gave him an emetic Threatened with a lung fever. Sat up with him all night— The litle dear how sick he was— O how much would I give could Alfred only be here. But that cannot be— If our litle boy should die how should I live alone, & he may die too![50]

[Saturday, January 31] Bub more comfortable, but still pretty sick. It is very hard work to take care of him he is so cross— Do'nt feel first rate, having sat up all night to take care of bubby

[Sunday, February 1] Bub some better, though he did'nt rest very well or let me. We are having another snow storm, just for a rarity. Clara [Walbridge] gone back to her school

[Monday, February 2] Worked hard & accomplished nothing, my business being to wait on the sick ones

[Tuesday, February 3] Got a letter from Alfred. Date Dec. 31— He writes he is well and hearty— How glad I am to hear from him. He

CWR

---

[49]Jane Watts Clark was one of Chastina's cousins.
[50]Children sometimes died while their fathers were gone to the gold mines. Such was the case for Susan Folger Gardner of Nantucket, Mass., whose only child died within a month of his father's departure for California in 1852. Rohrbough, *Days of Gold*, 232.

CWR says he shall stay two years & a half I will not think a word of his being gone so long Got the Dec No of Knickerbocker

[Wednesday, February 4] Bub better, but dreadful cross— It tires my patience a good deal to get along— Mother [Watts] gains—sits up considerable

[Thursday, February 5] Pleasant, too pleasant to stay in the house I have scarcely been out since I came home

[Friday, February 6] Real warm & spring like

[Saturday and Sunday, February 7 and 8] Nothing—only "nobody could'nt" go to meeting

[Monday, February 9] We have washed & done lots of other work— Sent a letter to Alfred

[Tuesday and Wednesday, February 10 and 11] Mother [Watts] is so she walks out in the kitchen— The school master—Mr. Fisher came here to board[51]

[Thursday, February 12] Another stormy day— We seldom witness such a stormy Winter. Miss Lyford took a notion to go home—so I am left alone with the work.[52]

[Friday, February 13] Clara [Walbridge] come home at night. But such a time as I have had to do the work & take care of the sick ones in the bargain. Bub screams after me every time I go throug a door & the tears run down his cheeks as though his heart would break.

[Saturday, February 14] Cold again— I have almost concluded to bring my things home and stay at home while Alfred is gone— Mother [Watts] wants me to help her some especially while she is so unwell, & I shall work for myself some— Got the Feb No of the Knickerbocker

[Sunday, February 15] Some of the family went to meeting I stayed at home & done the work— Jane Clarke come to help me

[Monday, February 16] Jane [Clark] & I done the washing & work— Charles [Watts] brought Ellen McLellan here to work for us for a time— Got a letter from Alfred. they are not in so good spirits as when he wrote before—the rain is down on them in abundance

---

[51] Schoolteachers in the East Part often boarded at the Watts farm through the 1850s. Bonfield, "A Constant Companion," 44.

[52] The work at the Watts farm must have been strenuous for a hired girl with the woman of the house ill and ten individuals to please, including four children ten years old and younger.

[Tuesday, February 17] Father [Watts] started after my things this morning— Lyman [S. Watts] & I went out about noon— Mrs. [Sarah] Marsh is full of wrath because I am going to leave her— A dreadful job it is to move. May I be so fortunate as some day to have a home of my own— Came home at night.

[Wednesday, February 18] Took bub out to the corner with me. Jane Clarke helped me clean up the house & all things ready for to quit— Took father [Watts] in with me to settle with the old lady. She claimed rent for the year. we have an agreement saying "Privilege to leave at any time" &c. She would not have a "final settlement" as she called it & promised to wait till Alfred come home & then trust to him for she "always had considered him an honest man." So I paid her six dollars & seventeen cents all that was due her up to that time. Sold my wood to [Ira] Miller—got $6.50 for it

[Thursday, February 19] Father [Watts] drew the wood to Mr. [Ira] Miller—& when he got through was going to take what few things remained—when Mrs. M[arsh] <u>forbid his touching another thing</u> untill a final settlement. Luckily I had over paid her for five or six days—of course he took all but the shed— She is dreadful mean— she talked very unchristian & very unbecoming indeed, so he left for a final trial— Mean while I have been regulating things at home It is a real hard job for me & one that I detest—that of moving. If Alfred was only here I would give almost any thing. But he is not and I must fight my battles alone— Though as yet Mrs M[arsh] & I have had no <u>words</u> that were unbecoming

[Friday, February 20] Got things picked up some, so I have had a little rest to day.

[Saturday, February 21] Father [Watts] went out to Mrs. M[arsh]'s in order to take the boards from a rough shed that Alfred made & paid for with his own money— But she an <u>old</u>! [blank] forbid his touching a single thing of it— She run on the longest rabble of stuff, twitted father of every thing imaginable. She guessed she had as much money to carry on a lawsuit as I How extravagant I was, "she could'nt have such nice things as I did." "Mr. Rix was owing her two dollars now for spoiling her drain" For occupying more land than belonged to him, &c. &c. I will not try to enumerate. But such a mess of

CWR   stuff was ill befitted to come from the mouth of a <u>church member</u>— much more a christian. My very blood boils at such treatment— So of course father left the boards for he could not lawfully take them away. So she has took her pay in part—I call it no better than stealing. May her conscience never be easy until she has confessed some of her hard saying & repented of what she has done. This needs no apology, more than to <u>know</u> the person mentioned above—

[Sunday, February 22] the family some of them went to church but I did not.

[Monday, February 23] Ellen [McLellan] & I washed— We have to work pretty hard Augustus [Walbridge] came home unwell— Sarah [Walbridge Way] has got a little boy. Born last Saturday—[53] Very tired— Have sat up late to bring up my journal during my absence. I hope to write some thing that will be better than what is on a few of the last pages.

[Tuesday, February 24] Have been baking— Have made pies, dough nuts wheat bread & brown bread, something that I have not done on so large a scale for a long time— father [Watts] came home sick— I have had to stop some where along on this page & go to the school house after Charles [Watts]. About 9 o clock P.M. Got a Harper for Feb.

[Wednesday, February 25] Sewing for mother [Watts]. I have done scarcely any work for myself, as yet. Mother has been sick so long that she has a great deal to do. Bub is real hard to take care of. I get almost tired sometimes, but there is no help for it

[Thursday, February 26] The above will answer for to day— I am going to writing this evening to Alfred. Sat up quite late.

[Friday, February 27] Finished and sent off a letter to Alfred. Sewing in the afternoon.

[Saturday, February 28] Sewing all day on a fine shirt for Augustus [Walbridge]. Last night I dreamed that Alfred came home. How distinctly I saw him in my dream— Got the March No. of Sartain's Magazine.[54]

[Sunday, February 29] I scarcely ever saw the wind blow or the snow fly worse than it has to day— It has been almost a hurricane,

---

[53] Sarah Walbridge Way gave birth to Edgar Stephen Way on February 21, 1852, at Hardwick.

[54] *Sartain's Union Magazine of Literature and Art* was founded in 1835 in Philadelphia.

& cold enough to freeze one Of course we have all been at home— I have read a good part of the time— These Sundays are long days to me. We used to enjoy ourselves so well when Alfred was at home

[Monday, March 1] "Comes in like a lamb it will go out like a lion" is a quaint saying. To day has been very pleasant & quite warm after our snow & blow. As for having any thing new to write it seems out of the question, but if it is all important to record what one does & how he feels—then I will just say that I am very tired, for I have helped do a large washing—for ten in the family & have done a good deal of other work besides— Bub burnt his little forehead quit[e] bad.

[Tuesday and Wednesday, March 2 and 3] Have sewed on fulled cloth what time I could get besides taking care of bub. Miss Underhill a tailoress is sewing here. Got Feb. No. of Sartain's Magazine.

[Thursday, March 4] Sewing again. Many received letters from Calafornia but I did not. John [S. Way] went home from here & took Augustus [Walbridge]— Mrs. Isaac Watts called here—[55] Poor woman she has not spoken loud for four week, & has a bad cough— To day I feel rather low spirited. No one knows how lonely I feel. Alfred! I would that you were here to be with me & our boy. Every day he needs you more & more—and I fear he will be spoiled My reading time is Sunday's & after I retire to rest

[Friday, March 5] All the same.

[Saturday, March 6] Making pies. We made nearly thirty— I had just got my hands into the dough when a man came & wanted me to go to Aunt [Sarah] Stevens & make a visit. I did'nt know who he was but after a long time he told me he was "father to Weltha Cory." So I went to see my new aunt & uncle—liked them very well. They are going west. He sold his farm for $2000.00 the rail-road is going through it so the value was increased from $600 to the above. George Clement came here from Dunham.[56] Henry Harriman & [Carlos] Sampson have got home, having been as far as the isthmus & returned[57]

---

[55] Martha J. Watts (1815–52) was the wife of Isaac Watts.
[56] George Clement was a cousin of Chastina's from East Canada.
[57] Henry Harriman (1826–1918) was married to Melvina Sampson (1828–91), sister of Carlos Sampson. In another attempt, Carlos Sampson arrived in California in 1853 and returned to Vermont in 1855. Alice Watts, Peacham, to her niece Augusta Gregory, unidentified location, August 15, 1855, Walbridge-Gregory Family Papers.

CWR [Sunday, March 7] Pleasant. All hands have been to church— I have not been before for two months— George [Clement] is a very pretty young man though his health is very poor, he has bled at the lungs several times.

[Monday, March 8] George [Clement] started with Lyman [S. Watts] for Cabot Helped wash. Lyman brought Clara [Walbridge] home— Ella [Watts] five years old. [Ira] Miller called

[Tuesday, March 9] Rainy. Uncle Simeon Brown & John [S. Way] came here & stayed all night. Bub cries after me so much I can scarcely do anything with him.

[Wednesday, March 10] Clara [Walbridge] gone to Hardwick with John [S. Way]. Each day I try to accomplish something but as often fail. I expect bub is teething, & in consequence of which he is extremely hard to take care of

[Thursday, March 11] Bub sick. We can hardly tell what does ail him, he is very feverish & extremely troublesome to take care of for he will let no one touch him but me. So I am obliged to confine myself close to him & tend him almost all of the time

[Friday, March 12] Bub no better. I have passed through another day like yesterday And now at bettween 10 & 11 o'clock P.M. I am writing or trying to write a few items in this journal— Dr. [Asahel] Farr's father died this morning.[58] This reminds me of a shocking affair which transpired in our village Mrs. F[enton] Hutchins was sick with the Erysipelas. she had been bathed pretty thoroughly in alcohol & wishing her attendants to look at the place upon her stomach where it had made its appearance, she said "let me see too" and drawing the candle nearer her—which a lady held in her hand—the heat came in contact with the gas which arose from her saturated garments & caught fire. the lady spoken of threw the bed clothes over her to smother the flames when Mrs. H. exclaimed "O! do'nt you will burn me down," & sprang out of bed. She was one sheet of flame. Her clothes were torn from her in a moment & she sank fainting in her husbands arms. She lived ten hours after this dreadful affair. She leaves a babe about two months old— She was scarcely

---

[58]Alpheus Farr (1784–1852) died in Peacham of erysipelas. *Caledonian*, April 24, 1852. Dr. Asahel Farr lost his son and his father within the space of three months.

twenty years of age. She was not considered very sick at the time of this horrible affair.⁵⁹

[Saturday, March 13] Bub is not quite so sick to day, though he is pretty unwell. I am obliged to tend him most of the time. it is such hard work for me, that some times it seems that I could not lift him up & dow[n] another time. O! Alfred *if* you were only! Bub is so fretty that he will let no one touch him but me. He has his little book & he begins to tell the pictures already, knows several— & begins to say a good many words. He weighs twenty four pounds.

[Sunday, March 14] Rainy. We have had a few days of warm weather— Old Winter has begun to relent of his severity, & has deigned to look pleasant & even shed a few tears now he reflects on his harshness. The days are quite long now & Sunday seems so particularly. Oh how pleasing it would be to Spend some sabbath as I used to. Now Alfred is gone I have no one to look to for comfort & kind words & little pleasing things— Every one at home is kind to me, but who can fill a husband's & fathers place in the heart of a wife— When I hear of the woes & sufferings of those bo[u]nd to the gold region, I am sick & wish & wish that <u>my friends</u> were at home. Now I am daily expecting to hear from him. Yet I dread to hear notwithstanding my anxiety to have news from there.

[Monday, March 15] Every body knows that washing comes on monday

[Tuesday, March 16] Ellen [McLellan] gone home. Mother [Watts] & I are going to try to get along alone for a time. Mrs. [Sarah Bailey] Watts & Mrs [Mary Elkins] Harriman visiting here

[Wednesday, March 17] Bub is so naughty that I hardly know how to get along with him. He will let no one else touch him to take care of him but me. Cousin Ellen Clement came here. She is a sweet little girl fifteen years old— She used to be my litle charge, when she was about nine months old— I went to her fathers in Dunham C[anada] E[ast] & stayed a year. I took almost the whole care of her during that time, & have never seen her since I left Uncles until now. How swiftly the years pass away. I was then fourteen years of age, & fourteen years have since passed away, can it be possible

---

⁵⁹The *Caledonian* of March 13, 1852, reported the tragic death of Mrs. Fenton F. Hutchins, wife of Peacham's deputy sheriff.

CWR [Thursday, March 18] A day of days to day, for I have heard from Alfred. His letter bears date of 1st & 6 of Feb. & post mark Feb. 14. Then he was quite well. How glad I am to hear this. If he can only live to return it is all I ask— He has heard not a word from me since he went there— Had a taste of new sugar[60]

[Friday, March 19] Mother [Watts] quite unwell to day— Bub has got to be quite a good boy—he does not cry after me but little & is realy growing pretty & cunning of course— Sewing some

[Saturday, March 20] Aunt [Sarah] Stevens called with a letter from sister Louisa [Rix]. they are all well— Chastina Brown came here visiting going to stay over Sunday.

[Sunday, March 21] Girls could'nt go to meeting because they had'nt their "Sunday go to meeting bonnets." Cousin Ellen [Clement] felt real bad because she could'nt go— Sunday is long lonesome day to me. I have been to church only twice since the middle of Dec.

[Monday, March 22] We have'nt washed—a remarkable thing in our history—not to wash monday—our folks would'nt let me do it alone, so I must wait for help— Got the American Journal of Science & Arts—from the reading circle.[61] Mother [Watts] better. Bub sings do. do. every time he hears Charles [Watts] sing— Sent a letter to Louisa Rix.

[Tuesday, March 23] Had a french woman to wash, baking & brewing &c. The snow has fell fifteen inches to day. It looks dreary enough.

[Wednesday, March 24] Pleasant after such a snow storm— Sewing some on a dress for myself. Got the March No of Knickerbocker.

[Thursday, March 25] Finished my dress & helped do the house work— My reading time is after I retire to bed. I place my candle upon a stand, where there is no danger of fire then I read about an hour.

[Friday, March 26] Began a letter to Alfred. Have done the ironing— Mary Johnsons beau died with the small pox at Mr Johnsons

---

[60] Warm days followed by cold nights are required in order for the sap to flow so that it can be boiled into sugar.

[61] The *American Journal of Science and Art* began publishing in 1818 and is the longest-running American science journal. In 1860 the title was shortened to *American Journal of Science*.

where he had come from down country with her to visit her friends. He is to be buried this evening. A sad thing for her. I pity her.

[Saturday, March 27] Today I have made twenty six pies, wheat & brown bread & a good deal of other work such as cleaning up after baking &c. I am real tired, but notwithstanding, it is now nearly eleven o'clock & I have been finishing my letter to Alfred. Have covered two sheets of paper all over, whether he ever receives it or no is a matter of uncertainty.

[Sunday, March 28] Pleasant. Have been to church— Mr. [Asaph] Boutell preached well— The subject of one discourse was Prayer— Sent off my letter to Alfred

[Monday, March 29] Jane Brown & I have done the washing. Got the April No of Sartains Magazine

[Tuesday, March 30] Cut two dresses for the girls. Went down to Aunt [Sarah] Stevens. Wrote a letter for her to send to Washington to the pension man.[62] Had the sick head ache all the evening. Bub awoke about ten & kept me awake till almost two. Rather a hard case for me to be sick & take care of baby too. It was all moonlight & he thought it was morning.

[Wednesday, March 31] Received a letter from Louisa Rix— Father [Watts] sugared off about fifty pounds this morning. About noon I got myself and bub ready & together with Lyman [S. Watts] started for Hardwick on a short visit to John [S. Way]'s. It stormed a good deal of the way and I was very tired when I got there. Found them tolerable well, though Sarah [Walbridge Way] & Clara [Walbridge] had bad colds. Sarah has a nice great boy.

[Thursday, April 1] There fell about ten inches of snow during the night. We had not got the work done up before there came in five or six ladies from the village to a "sugar party," which by the way was an April fool [affair] got up by part of the girls to fool the rest. This flustered Sarah [Walbridge Way] a good deal, however she mustered round melted some sugar over & had a very good time

CWR

---

[62] Sarah Stevens had applied for an army pension, claiming that her husband, Joshua Stevens (b. 1761), had died in the War of 1812. Sarah and Joshua were among the early settlers of Danville and had four boys, born between 1790 and 1797. After her husband's disappearance around 1804, Sarah moved to Peacham so that her sons could attend the Academy there. No trace was ever found of their father. Trefousse, *Thaddeus Stevens*, 2.

CWR   [Friday, April 2] Uncle Guyer & wife came to John [S. Way]'s so I had a visit with them. Augustus [Walbridge] got the mumps so Bub & I have been exposed to them. Clara [Walbridge] took the School at Stevens village.[63] Started to come home about noon. Had a very pleasant time to come home in. But I could not enjoy my ride At each place noticeable I could recall the conversation and remarks passed between Alfred & I when we passed over the road last summer. The thought that "I may never enjoy another ride with him" made me gloomy all the way. I hoped to find a letter from him when I arrived home, but in this was disappointed. Alfred! You endure hardships & suffrings I only suspense & sorrow. How can I wait & wait & then for augh I may know you are suffering in that land of hope & misery.

[Saturday, April 3] To day I find it certainly that there is no letter for me. Got the March No. of Harper— very cold weather it looks dreary enough. The snow is deep as in mid winter. I have sewed for mother [Watts] all day— Read in the evening, and untill eleven o'clock.

[Sunday, April 4] Have'nt been to church. Sundays are lonely days. How happy I should be could Alfred only come home he has now been gone six months from home, this very day of the month. Can it be that another six months will pass before I can again be with you! Alfred. Our little Julian needs you every day.

[Monday, April 5] After washing I went to the corner with Lyman [S. Watts]. Made some few little purchases & called at Mr [Humphrey] Bennett's. Laura's boy is rather small beside ours.

[Tuesday, April 6] Sewing for myself— And commencing a job which I detest—that is fixing drawers for little boys. last night I read one of Bayard Taylor's letter from New York to Nineveh & to night I shall read one of [Lajos] Kosuth's[64] speeches. I do not consider myself literary by any means, but I read considerably.

[Wednesday, April 7] Sick with the head ache all day. We had company—Mrs. [Louisa Martin] Parker & Riley Farr, Dr. [Asahel]

---

[63] Stevens Village, one of five residential centers in Barnet, was located at the falls of the Stevens River and was once the site of considerable manufacturing. Wells, *History of Barnet*, 3. It is unclear when Clara planned to teach at Stevens Village, because on May 27 she goes to Hardwick to teach.

[64] Hungarian patriot Lajos Kossuth (1802–94) toured the United States from December 1851 to July 1852.

Farr's brother. He told me how he used to go to school to Alfred, when he taught at Waterford. This was his first school, he was about seventeen. Farr said "he never learned so much in a season as he did at that time." Said he "we all feared him & yet we all loved him. he was so kind & pleasant & took so much interest in our studies & advancement." Uncle Simeon [Brown] came & carried Grandmother [Olive Brown] away. she has been here for a few days. To day completes Alfred's thirtieth year, & of course commences his thirty first. How quickly time passes away thirty that begins to sound as though age was coming on fast. now & a few years to come is considered the prime of life. May he not spend but a short time of these precious years in Calafornia.

[Thursday, April 8] Better to day than I was yesterday. I have been trying to sew some but have done house work most of the time so of course failed in sewing. It has been pleasant, but rather cold. I have tried to sit down up stairs where I used to spend so many hours before I was married, but the cold drove me back to a warmer room. I love to go off alone and sit by myself, this is a privilege denied me of late. I must take care of my little boy. I am not alone when he is with me. To day I have been thinking over my troubles. When I look on the dark side every thing seems gloomy and sad therefore I am sad too. If Alfred could only be at home He has been absent six months his birthday, the longes[t] time but what I have seen him since I first became acquainted with him. If it is hard for lovers to be separated how much harder is it for a husband & father to be away from his wife & child. I do not complain. But it is certanly my right to think of what I am loosing by being deprived of the society of one very dear to me. Then on our little Julian's account, it is a great sorrow to me. He is a smart little fellow—notwithstanding a mother says it—and fear that I shall not do by him as I ought, & that he will not be so good a boy & we shall be glad to have him. May I be directed from on High to do as I ought & do my duty to this our child[65]

---

[65] This was one of the few times that Chastina referred to her religious faith in the journal. She was raised by a Christian mother who often used phrases from the Bible. Although going to Sunday meeting was important to Chastina, maybe for the social contact, she never became a member of the Congregational church.

CWR [Friday, April 9] Fast day.[66] Father & mother [Watts] went out to meeting very good sleighing & a great deal of snow; the snow drifts as high as they are in the midst of winter. Leonard Brown & wife visited here— I did not fast much but worked all day.

[Saturday, April 10] All things about as usual—Bub grows cunning every day. He is all taken up with pictures teases for a "dogeh" as he calls a book—all the time. He calls it "dogeh" because the first picture he learned was a dog.

[Sunday, April 11] Have been to church. Went in a sleigh though it is very bad going. In the afternoon the funeral of Mrs Farnum & child was attended.[67] Mrs. F. before her marriage was Mary Ann Ewell an old mate of mine and about my age. She has been married about three years. And now she is gone & left a husband to mourn her loss. She & her little infan[t] sleep side by side in the same coffin. It was a sad and mournful sight that young mother stricken down so young; with her first and only child. But our father in heaven is just & "doeth all things well" & for some wise purpose

[Monday, April 12] Washing. Jane [Brown] & I make out together to manage our washing though it makes me rather tired.

[Tuesday, April 13] Snow storm again last night. The boys sugared off one hundred and fifty pounds of sugar. making some little drawers for bub. He is getting to be quite a chap

[Wednesday, April 14] Mother [Watts] & Jane [Brown] went down to the Hollow in a sleigh. it is bad sleiging but there is plenty of snow if it was in the right places. Baking— To show that we are not sick here the present time I will just say that I have made eight loaves of bread, six of wheat & two of brown, &c.

[Thursday, April 15] It commenced snowing last night some time & has snowed steady all day. There must have fallen ten or twelve inches [She added the numeral 12 above "ten" and 16 above "twelve"— possibly referring to the snowfall dates.] Sewing for myself. Do not get along with it very bravely Do'nt feel very well & bub takes a good deal of my time

---

[66] The Friday before Easter, called Good Friday, was designated as a day of prayer and fasting by the Vermont governor.

[67] The *Caledonian* of May 22, 1852, announced the death from erysipelas of Mary Ann Ewell Farnum (1825–52), wife of Alvin B. Farnum (1818–90).

[Friday, April 16] It looks gloomy enough this morning. The snow fell during the night so now it is considerable over a foot in depth. There is not a bare spot of ground in sight. Door ways are all filled in just like mid winter. It has been thawing some but not enough to settle the snow but little. Have made Bub an apron— Received a letter from brother Ira [Rix]— All well at Dalton. Abot these days I am & have been reading Bayard Taylor's letters from "New York to Ninevah." He's now in Nubia. I never read any letters so interesting. Except Horace Greely's. Taylor is a very pleasing writer. He always thinks of things that will interest others and convey to ones mind an exact ideal of realities. Some would think the world would call them vulgar & narrow minded to speak of small things, as he does. But these are what makes interesting, his other descriptions, which are of graver nature.

[Saturday, April 17] Not well. Had company! Clara [Walbridge] came home. John [S. Way] came with her. I am sadly disappointed at not hearing from Alfred to day. it is passed the time in the month for letters to come. I feel just as though I should get one this time.

[Sunday, April 18] Clara [Walbridge] & the boys went to meeting in a sleigh. Mrs Ralph Blanchard is dead.[68] It is and has been very sickly in our town The erysipelas is the prevailing disease. No letter. Got "Harper" for April the first I have had for some time[69]

[Monday, April 19] Helped do the washing. Mrs. Simon Blanchard had an apoplectic fit. They do not expect her to live but a short time.

[Tuesday, April 20] The snow is leaving us pretty fast. Though people go with sleighs. Sewing— Read at night in Harper. I admire John S. C. Abbott's life of Napoleon. If anything, I should think him prejudiced in his favor. But his style is easy and graceful. I cannot but admire Napoleon's character. He seemed to be far above all that surrounded him. Such a mind, he had to foresee and provide & plan for future seems astonishing.

[Wednesday, April 21] Had the sick head ache when I awoke this morning. Have been unwell all day so I have'nt [done] much of any

---

[68] Maria Kellogg Blanchard (1802–52) died at age forty-nine after an illness of only three days. *Caledonian*, May 15, 1852. Watts and Choate, *People of Peacham*, 36, gives an incorrect death year.

[69] The April 1852 issue of *Harper's* continued the biography of Napoleon and began its serialization of *Bleak House*, the first time this classic by Charles Dickens (1812–70) was published.

CWR work. George & Moses & Alma Currier spent the evening here. Jane Brown has gone to Gid' Clarke's to watch with his wife & Jane who are both sick[70]

[Thursday, April 22] I have resolved that I would begin to wean Bub, though it is hard to resist the little fellow's pleadings. I shall have to give my time to him. Read one of Charles Dickens storys in the evening. I cannot say that I admire Dickens' writings.

[Friday, April 23] Bub does pretty well so far. I pity the little dear. He is a good boy, though he teases me dreadfully to go out door's I am almost discouraged about hearing from Alfred. Though my hope is in—[that] when the mails do come I shall have a letter— The spring rains and snow have prevented communication to the cities for several days.

[Saturday, April 24] This morning I had two letters brought to me from Alfred How glad I am to hear from him & that he is well. But how much would I give were he only at home. Every day I feell more and more as though we ought to be together spending our time as profitably & as happily as possible. Life is short. I see & think of it more every day, when so many are sick and dying around us. Accompanying Alfred's letter was a song for Bubs first birth day & a plan of a house for us when we get so we can have a home of our own— Calafornia is not all gold. They see some hard times there as well as in Vermont. The streams there are inundating the country for miles around. Sacramento & other cities are flooded.[71] this makes a scarcity in the mines and consequently much suffering among the miners. Though I hope our friend[s] are not among the sufferers.

[Sunday, April 25] Jane Brown went home yesterday in a sleigh & cousin Ellen Clement came down here She and Clara [Walbridge] went to meeting Pleasant day. Mrs. Simon Blanchard died this morning in consequence of the apoplectic fit of a week ago.[72]

---

[70]Gideon Clark (1804–93) married Jane Watts (1815–35) in 1833; after her death he married her sister Harriet (b. 1823) in 1839.

[71]Sacramento and the surrounding area experienced major flooding in January 1850, called the "Great Inundation," and again in spring 1852.

[72]The *Caledonian* of May 1, 1852, announced the death of Betsey Spencer Blanchard (1796–1852). She left a husband, Simon Blanchard, and eleven children, the youngest being fourteen. Hers was the first death in the family house in the East Part where they had lived for sixty-five years.

[Monday, April 26] Clara [Walbridge] & I washed in the forenoon & in the afternoon attended Mrs. [Betsey] Blanchard's funeral. The going was extremely bad, but all made out to get through with wagons without any trouble. Mr. [Simon] Blanchard's eleven children were all at home & this is the first death that has ever been in the family. Left Bub at home with mother [Watts]. He was a good boy only full of mischief as ever a little chap was.

[Tuesday, April 27] To day I am so lame from my ride yesterday I can scarcely take care of myself

[Wednesday, April 28] Sewing a little. I have been rather unwell for some time. Have the head ache a good deal. Bub is pretty troublesome these days.

[Thursday, April 29] About the same as yesterday. Father [Watts] sugared off one hundred pounds of sugar— Began to write a letter to brother Ira Rix

[Friday, April 30] Sick. Been taking medicine for a bilious complaint. The girls, that is Clara [Walbridge] & Ellen Clement, are preparing for a may [day] party. Received a letter from Alfred sent by Josiah Shedd, written April first & received the last.[73] He is now in San Francisco, he could not tell what he was going to do for he had been there but a short time.

[Saturday, May 1] Dark and lowery in the morning. Commenced raining about 10 o'clock & rained till the middle of the afternoon. We did not expect any would come it was so rainy & bad, but towards night about twenty came. We had tables set & things went off pretty well. Though there was not a may flower to be found & scarcely a green leaf— I am quite well now. Josiah Shedd came in from N.Y. this evening.

[Sunday, May 2] Clara [Walbridge] & Ellen [Clement] went to meeting. Commenced a letter to Alfred.

[Monday, May 3] Mother [Watts] and I washed— In the evening wrote again untill eleven o'clock.

[Tuesday, May 4] Clara [Walbridge] & Ellen [Clement] walked over to the corner & home again. Took my letter to Alfred to the

---

[73]Josiah Shedd (1830–97) was in New York on his way to Peacham from California. He was the grand-nephew of Dr. Josiah Shedd of Peacham, who had raised young Josiah after his father died in 1842. Shedd, *Daniel Shedd Genealogy*, 308, 532.

CWR P[ost] O[ffice] Got the May No. of the "Eclectic." Father [Watts] brought me home a letter from Alfred. Date Apr. 4. I do not hear so favorable an account as I could wish. He is well. But they are seeing sorry times there as it regards money matters. Thousands upon thousands are there, to catch at every opportunity of making any thing— I live in hope—

[Wednesday, May 5] Mother [Watts]'s birth day—50 years of age. Girls visiting at Mr. [David] Currier's. Mother at Mr Gilfillan's so I am mistress of the house this afternoon. Got along very well. This evening for the first time I ventured to take a walk on <u>bare ground</u>. The ways are now quite dry— My steps led me direct to one of our "trysting places," and where we used to deposit our bilets. My thoughts wondered far away in the past. Years have gone by since we used to steal an interview now & then. Shy and afraid some one would know we used to "think of each other." Those were happy days. My thoughts did not have to go <u>thousands of miles across the trackless ocean to rest on</u> him upon whom my affections were bestowed— 'Tis not that I wedded makes me unhappy now— But how can I be so lighthearted as of yore. I will say no more. This is not a fitting place to speak further

[Thursday, May 6] Very warm. Summer has at last begun— We that is Clara [Walbridge] & Ellen [Clement] and myself went over to Cap. Simon Blanchard's. We had a nice walk across the woods. We went over some snowdrifts & found a very few May flowers. Mr. Blanchard's family feel their loss in loosing their mother. Margaret [Blanchard] & Abba [Blanchard] are both at home.

[Friday, May 7] Cut a dress for Alice [Watts]— Bub real troublesome now days— He wants to run out, but does not like to go without me. Mrs. I[saac] Watts, after being married twelve years, had a baby. It is not living.

[Saturday, May 8] Sick again to day. Last night had the head ache all night & one of my breasts very painful— I am about weaning Bub is the cause— Have not set up all day. Have taken some more blue pills. Cousin Ellen [Clement] gone back to Cabot

[Sunday, May 9] Feel some better— Lived on gruel so am rather week. But my head does not ache 'so' hard, nor feel so dull.

[Monday, May 10] I am quite well again— Helped do the washing— Trimmed Bub's hat that his father got in New York.

[Tuesday, May 11] Cut a dress for Eleanor [Ella Watts] & did some house work— Every day it seems that I feel more and more sad, and wish for the return of Alfred. Spring with all its beauties is making glad & merry the song of the birds; & the music of thousands of frogs is now on my ear— But what are all these to me. Spring has less charms for me than there was wont to be, though, though I Enjoy it some what.

[Wednesday, May 12] Fixing a dress for myself. Bub real hard for me to take care of. He cries after me whenever I leave him. He is greatly attached to me. Wants "Ma Ma" to do every thing for him. He is learning to talk quite fast. This morning when I awoke it almost seemed a reality— So distinctly did [I] dream of seeing Alfred. Would, it were "not all a dream."

[Thursday, May 13] Sewing and taking care of baby.

[Friday, May 14] Washed some in the forenoon & in afternoon went to the Hollow with mother [Watts]. Called to see Mrs. Isaac Watts. She is in a very bad state. Such a cough—and has not spoken loud for six months. We visited to L[eonard] W. Brown's & called to see Mrs Gid' Clarke who is also quite sick. The way Bub cut round & flourished the yard stick in the store, shows he is [into mischief] some yet. I was real ashamed of him. Hope he will improve for he has not been out much yet

[Saturday, May 15] Have been baking bread & pies most of the day— Have'nt any thing to read now days except newspapers. Do not get books regular from the "corner." It is a busy time for farmers now

[Sunday, May 16] Stayed at home as usual— Got a Knickerbocker for Apr. from the Reading Circle

[Monday, May 17] Washed as usual. Sarah Ann Goodnough came here to board. She is the School marm.

[Tuesday, May 18] Cleaned house almost all day. Made a call to Mr. Sargeants, came home and found a letter from Alfred. The date Apr. 14. He is now in San Francisco. Well and doing pretty well. Glad to hear of his good health. But it makes me feel so sad every time I

CWR

CWR think of how long he wishes to stay there. O! I can never have him stay two years. He Sent me two, 2½ dollar gold pieces in the letter.

[Wednesday, May 19] Sewing to day— Clara [Walbridge] & I went to the Corner after tea. Traded some, at least spent some money. Saw Mrs. Gilfillan. She that was Helen Patridge— Got Sartains Magazine for May.

[Thursday, May 20] Sarah Chamberlain came to cut Clara [Walbridge]'s silk dress. Sewed for Clara.

[Friday, May 21] Miss [Sarah] C[hamberlain] here to day. Sewed again for Clara [Walbridge]. Miss C. fitted a dress for me, the third dress that has been fitted by other's besides myself since I was fifteen years old.

[Saturday, May 22] Have lined & trimed my bonnet. A description of which is as follows. Bonnet Straw diamond braid—One that I have had over three years, but has been dressed over so it looks quite well. Lined with white crape, gathered in very full, with white strings to fix up in puffs under the chin. The outside trimed with blue & white ribbon. Frill of ribbon cut cross wise & about an eighth of a yard in width— A little of the ribbon upon each side of the bonnet but none over the top So much for my bonnet. Bub grows nicely now, in mischieveousness, as well as in sprightliness. He learns some new words every day now. He teams oxen & horses in his way, & cuts up all manner of shines He is more than commonly attached to me. Nobody can do like "ma me."

[Sunday, May 23] Went to church. Got terribly frightened coming home— I was driving & the horse acted bad. But fortunately overtook Lyman [S. Watts], who took the reins himself. I have done teaming that horse at any rate. I am a real coward, when riding unless I am sure the reins are in safe hands.

[Monday, May 24] Washing of course, though my work has been more house work than washing. Have been unwell. The going to meeting, hearing a long sermon from Mr. [John] Dudly of Danville & getting frightened coming home, gave me the sick head ache— I have the head ache a great deal this spring— Got Harper for May. "Bleak House" one of Dickens stories, together with Abbotts Napoleon makes up a pretty good book

[Tuesday, May 25] Sewed on Clara [Walbridge]'s silk dress. Read Harper in the evening.

[Wednesday, May 26] Mother [Watts] and Clara [Walbridge] went to the corner & left me to keep house. Mr [Ira] Miller called over here & was here to tea. Clara laughed at me well when came home about Miller. She loves to hector me. "She thought it very strange that Miller should know she & mother were away from home."

[Thursday, May 27] Clara [Walbridge] gone to Hardwick to her school. Bub & I went to Mr. Harriman's on a visit. Bub fell upon the stove & burned his little hand badly. Poor little fellow he took on for a hour, in a dreadful manner. Mr. [John M.] Martin sent me the Knickerbocker for May.

[Friday, May 28] Made Bub a dress. Mother [Watts] gone visiting to Mr [Asa] Sargeants Bub took a ride with her when they carried her down & when the[y] brought her home. The little fellow is so delighted to ride, it does me good to have him go. How much would I give if his father was only here to ride with him. If wishing would bring him, he would soon be here

[Saturday, May 29] Helped mother [Watts] bake. Sewed some & done some of the forty unnamable things which belong to house hold affairs.

[Sunday, May 30] Stayed at home & wrote a letter to Alfred Mr. Lyman Patridge was buried. Died of cancers in his eyes.[74]

[Monday, May 31] Washed or helped wash & cleaned my room

[Tuesday, June 1] To day we have had a regular New England house cleaning. Consequently I am very tired to night. I feel disappointed & uneasy because I cannot know whether there is a letter for me or not from Alfred. One thing I regret living away from the Corner for is because I can't get to the P[ost] O[ffice] when I wish to without troubling any one.

[Wednesday, June 2] Sewing for myself. Getting ready to go to the corner to make a visit.

[Thursday, June 3] I thought I would begin Ma [Watts]'s Journal

---

[74]Lyman Partridge (ca. 1792–1852) was named in Rev. Asaph Boutelle's list of recent deaths in Peacham. *Caledonian*, June 12, 1852. Helen Partridge Gilfillan may have been back in Peacham on May 17, 1852 because of her father's illness.

CWR for her to day.[75] We got ourselves ready this morning & started for the corner did some shopping. Made Miss [Abigail] Chamberlain a call. Saw Josiah Shedd a few moments & went down to Mr [Humphrey] Bennetts. Found Laura [Bennett] & her little boy all alone. Bennett gone to Danville as one of the Jurors. Had a very good visit. Made a call to Col. Blanchard's

[Friday, June 4] After dinner called on Mrs. [Mary] Weeks. Glad to see her with a baby. She was <u>so smart</u> when <u>Laura</u> & <u>I</u> had ours. Went to Dr [Asahel] Farr's. Stayed the afternoon. Bub had a great time with the little dog he found there. Had a very good visit. Settled my doctors bill which was 1.75 a very high charge for services done when bub was sick as he made only one visit for him. Went down to Mr Ephraim Morse's to stay all night. Found Elder Currier there, a very pleasant man for a minister.

[Saturday, June 5] Stayed at Mr. [Ephraim] Morse's till after dinner Called a few moments on Mrs. [Sarah] Marsh. I ca'nt feel right towards her my heart is not forgiving enough to overlook all her meanness. The people at the corner are a strange people. They do not know how to treat any one decent. Especially their teachers. Poor [Ira] Miller has been treated shamefully there. People & scholars have abused him. I hope they will get their pay. Went back to [Humphrey] Bennetts & stayed till night, when our folks came after me. Bub has behaved himself well. But I am heartily glad that I do not live in the [corner], or a village, for he would want to be in the street as well as others. Received a letter from Alfred. How glad I am to hear from him. The news this time seems the most favorable that it has been. For this I am glad. Because it seems as though he was so much nearrer his return. He says his weight "is 189 lbs. gross weight." His usual weight being 180. He sends me five dollars more in gold it being he says what he earned Saturday afternoon May 1. The letter being written May 2. He thinks he shall stay two years from this month. I do not know about that. He has the offer of a school there at $150.00 per month. Wants me there. I wish I was there with him. But I can never go that journey without him

---

[75] No diaries kept by Roxana Walbridge Watts have been located.

[Sunday, June 6] Stayed at home. Bub rather cross. His visit has not affect him favorably, for he has been sreming around me half of the time while I have written [in this journal the entries since] last Thursday. The writing looks like it

[Monday, June 7] Bub sick. Was taken vomiting this morning early. He has been so he has scarcely been out of my care to day. Josiah Shedd called to see us. Bub was so sick & we were in such a hubbub that I could'nt think of scarcely anything to say or ask of our friends in Calafornia.

[Tuesday, June 8] Bub quite well to day, so he has played round the house a good part of the time though he is rather wee. We have had a fine rain this afternoon & is still raining this evening. Our season of Spring has been without its showers. The earth is so dry it takes this as a grateful drought.

[Wednesday, June 9] Sewed on my dress. Took care of Bub & finished a letter to Sister Adeline [Rix Bierstadt].

[Thursday, June 10] Sewing on my dress again. We are having rathe[r] dull weather of late. Began a letter to Alfred.

[Friday, June 11] Nothing worth recording. Bub is yet rather unwell

[Saturday, June 12] Finished my dress, and in the evening finished a letter to Alfred.

[Sunday, June 13] Went to meeting. Very pleasant and warm. We had a deacon's meeting. Some good sermons read. Sent my letter. Bub better to day than he has been for a week.

[Monday, June 14] After washing, I received a letter from Alfred. He is now teaching school in Calafornia. About three miles from San Francisco at the Mission Dolores, one of the first settlements of the country. He says his school is situated among the richest gardens & farms in the country. His Salary to be $150.00 per month. On the whole I feel well pleased with his situation. For now I can know something what his daily business will be. How I wish I was there. We might live as comfortable as we chose & stay as long as we pleased. But perhap[s] it is all for the best as it is. Yet it is hard to live so widely separated as we are. He sends me the five dollars & some engravings of San Francisco. The rest of the boys are well.

CWR

CWR [Tuesday, June 15] This morning Julian & I started for Danville to get our daguereotype taken. It is an extremely warm day but we did not mind the heat if we could only get our pictures to send to papa. But the fates would have us disappointed for Mr [E.] Perry was away from home to be gone all day. Too bad! Well after cousining a little while at Mr H[iram] Brainard's, we came home tired and disappointed To be sure I can go again But I have no one to go with me who cares to go, only for accommodations sake. But I must have it some way[76]

[Wednesday, June 16] Very warm again— Have been ironing, & have done something I never did before, to cover a parasol.

[Thursday, June 17] This morning Lyman [S. Watts] carried me up to Harvey Blanchard's Stayed all day— Esther [Blanchard] manages pretty well for a new woman[77]

[Friday, June 18] Came to Mr [David] Curriers from Harve Blanchard's stayed all night and came home this evening. Had a good visit. Alma [Currier] going to be married soon.[78] Bub is a pretty good boy but is not at all affraid of his "bear" & makes a good deal of sport. He loves to be played with. If he had a father to take notice of him he would be tickled most to death

[Saturday, June 19] Father and mother [Watts] started for Hardwick bright and early. Mother intends to stay a week— This evening I am all alone. The children have retired to their Saturday eve's rest. The boys have gone to meeting or any other place where inclination leads them.[79] I hardly know what to do with myself I am so lonely— Saturday evening is always a hard & dreary evening for me. We used

---

[76] E. Perry of Danville, a well-known daguerreotypist, won first premium for daguerreotypes at the 1854 Caledonia County Fair, September 17–18. *Caledonian*, September 30, 1854. This was the first time Chastina used the term "cousining," meaning visiting her cousins, who unfortunately are not identified.

[77] Esther Harvey of Coventry married Harvey Blanchard of Peacham on March 3, 1852. *Caledonian*, March 27, 1852.

[78] Alma Currier and William Gilfillan (1826–1911) of Danville married on March 10, 1853. *Caledonian*, March 26, 1853.

[79] Lyman and Roxana traveled to Hardwick to see John S. and Sarah Walbridge Way and their children, especially the new baby boy. Both Clara and Augustus Walbridge were living with the Ways, working nearby. At the Watts farm, Chastina looked after her young siblings Isaac, Alice, and Ella Watts and her son, Julian. The older boys, Lyman S. and Charles Watts, could come and go at will.

to be so happy— In our courting days it was not always spent alone. Could Alfred only come to us now and then it seems as though we need not be so lonesome

CWR

[Sunday, June 20] Have not been to church. To day is the Presbyterian Sacrament.[80] A great many attend out of curiosity— Read a story & Sequel to it, called Judith Bensaddie & Seclusival— I must have something to divert my attention even if it be of the story kind.[81]

[Monday, June 21] I have worked very hard to day, a large washing & other work which has taken Ellen [McLellan] & I almost all day— Bub has been cross, & caused me a great deal of trouble, & now after 9 o'clock he is crying bitterly while I write for this day— I ought to spank him & make him behave, I suppose. But this time I thought I would not mind him & let him cry it out.[82]

[Tuesday, June 22] Nothing very particular only I have baked pies & salted a churning of butter.

[Wednesday, June 23] Lewis Morrill our uncle called on me. Ellen [McLellan] gone to a sewing circle. So I had to get tea alone, & had company too.

[Thursday, June 24] Baked bread and ironed— After tea went out with bub to find some strawberries. Found only enough "dawby's" for bub. The little rouge eats them just as though he knew what was good. Have read the firs[t] vol. of "Uncle Tom's Cabin" by Mrs. Harriet Beecher Stowe.[83] Tis extremely interesting. I hate slavery & always did— This work although a fiction is calculated well to touch the feelings & enlist ones sympathics for this unfortunate race. A curse upon our country will surely come if men will persist in keeping these poor creatures in such a degraded condition aye & hold there own children in bondage too! It makes my blood burn when I think on it— Sat up till midnight writing to Alfred.

---

[80]The Presbyterian church has two sacraments, Baptism and the Lord's Supper; the latter took place that day.

[81]"Judith Bensadi, a Romance" and a sequel, "Seclusiville," were stories written in 1840 by antislavery preacher Dr. Henry Ruffner (1789–1861) in Virginia.

[82]Since Roxana was not at home, Chastina felt free to let Julian cry. Her mothering was indicative of the new national view of child rearing, emphasizing affection and gentle persuasion instead of parental authority. Bonfield and Morrison, *Roxana's Children*, 98–99; Evans, *Born for Liberty*, 74, 92, 95; Cott, *Bonds of Womanhood*, 58, 84.

[83]*Uncle Tom's Cabin*, a novel by Harriet Beecher Stowe (1811–96), was published in 1852.

CWR [Friday, June 25] Finished off my letter & after tea Lyman [S. Watts] & Bub & I rode out to the Corner & put them,—my letter, one to Dustan & Ashbel Martin—into the [Post] Office— Cold to night.

[Saturday, June 26] Expected mother [Watts] home. But she probably has concluded she will have to stay more than a week to get her visit out— George Currier Called on us— Took a run in the fields with bub—rather tiresome business for me, when I have to carry him in my arms— Another Saturday has almost gone, week after week passes by—some pleasantly, and others O! how lonely— What would I give to be placed in a quiet home that I could call mine with a kind husband & dear boy such as I already have— But perhaps this is too much of happiness for a poor soul like me.

[Sunday, June 27] I need hardly mention that I have staid at home from church, for I think I have only been twice as yet this summer— Sundays are long days to me—and lonely I wonder what Alfred is doing thousands of miles away from us— Would he were only with us— I have read an address by [Lajos] Kosuth in N.Y. before a large audience— The proceeds of which are to help his poor mother & thre[e] sisters now on their way to this country, after sufferings & imprisonments and all manner of ill treatment by the wicked Austrians Kosuth had he lived in olden time would have been a prophet he is no less so now.

[Monday, June 28] Ellen [McLellan] & I have got through with another Monday's washing & work. Mother [Watts] and Augustus [Walbridge] came home— Augustus is unwell & somewhat nervous I should think. Mother talks of going to Dunham with him to see the Doctor.[84]

[Tuesday, June 29] Again I have tried my luck at Danville to get our Daguerotypes. We found Mr [E.] Perry at home this time. But just on the point of going to a Whig convention. Of course he was in a hurry, & cross, but made out to make him wait a few moments— Bub would'nt keep still long enough to get a good one. But we got a kind of thing—Bub is all up in a heap & looks like a little monkey— Mr Perry was so cross & unaccommodating, that I would not

---

[84]Roxana's older brother, Leonard Brown, lived and practiced medicine in Canada.

have had any thing done, had not Alfred requested me to—I am real provoked about it— Would'nt do a thing as I wanted to have it done If I had waited till to morrow Bub would have been just a year and a half old

[Wednesday, June 30] Cut a dress to day for mother [Watts]— fixed a cap & colar for her also Am not a bit well— My days work Monday & ride Tuesday in the heat of the day was too hard for me— Received a letter from Alfred— He is well & happy or would be completely so were Julian and I only there. He wishes me to go there to him. He does not say I must come—But "invites me to come." "Were I only there." How many, many, times this passes through my mind— I would give almost any thing to be there. But how can I ever think of going there without Alfred— I was scarcely ever out of my own town & how can I go so far when there is so much to go through. Still I want to go & be with my husband— I am alone— as it were—here. How pleasant to be in each others society. Two almost boundless oceans separate us. One of us must cross them ere we are blest with choisest of God's blessings O May this mighty sea not always roll between us— Dustan [Walbridge] is in the mines at Little Fork.

[Thursday, July 1] Mother [Watts] started again with Augustus [Walbridge] for Canada, or Dunham. My mind is ill at ease in regard to going to California— We are at this moment having a delightful shower.

[Friday, July 2] Have been baking again. Had first rate luck in making bread. Received a letter from Cousin Emily Taylor Jesseph of Cattaraugus N.Y. Got the Knickerbocker for June.

[Saturday, July 3] This morning tis rainy. This spoils the fun of the young folks who are to have Picnic's. The boys & girls intended to have one "over in Aunt [Sarah] Stevens sugar place," but could'nt for the rain, so they adjourned here. thirteen couple's & we had to set the tables for them & have a real "tear up" & then a real "clean up" all in the same day. So take it all round I have had a pretty hard time— The young folks had a pretty merry time

[Sunday, July 4] Stayed at home again— Had a letter from Mr [E.] Perry that my Daguerreotype is spoilt, & I must go again in

CWR

CWR order to have a picture— A plague upon the old fellow to be so Crabbed in the first place & then to have things turn out so— Finished Uncle Tom's Cabin. It makes my heart bleed to think of the horrors attendant upon the abominable system of Slavery— Poor Uncle Tom! There are ma[n]y such Martyrs as thou wast.

[Monday, July 5] Margaret Spencer & I have accomplished another Monday's work & a pretty hard days work it is too.[85] I wish washing did'nt come so often. Nothing of note. O yes. Lyman [S. Watts] started for the salt water this morning—for his health.[86]

[Tuesday, July 6] Nothing especial has happened— Very warm weather.

[Wednesday, July 7] Making bub a dress—&c. Writing to Alfred.

[Thursday, July 8] Went visiting to Mr Gilfillans' Dreadful hot day— Sent my letter to Alfred.

[Friday, July 9] Baking— Extremely warm. Thundershower

[Saturday, July 10] Sewing for myself— Margaret [Spencer] gone home. Mother [Watts] came home after dark. Folks all well to Canada. Dreadful warm weather.

[Sunday, July 11] Went to church notwithstanding it is so warm. I suppose I am wicked because I could not attend to the sermon & keep myself comfortable too & chose the latter rather than the sermon.

[Monday, July 12] Mother [Watts] & I have done the work and a very large washing— I am some tired.

[Tuesday, July 13] Cleaned the boys chamber in the fore noon. Mother [Watts] gone to see Grandmother [Olive] Brown—[87] Sewing some. Though not very well for I have had company— Wrote part of a letter to Cousin Emily [Taylor] Jesseph.

[Wednesday, July 14] Have been almost sick to day. Have had the blues a good deal. Been thinking over old times as compared with

---

[85]Margaret Spencer (1832–63) was the hired girl. Her family were neighbors of the Wattses.

[86]Many people at the time believed that ocean air could restore good health, so Lyman gave the ocean cure a try, but as he wrote in a letter to an old friend who was in California, he went "just long enough to find out how good it felt to be sea-sick." Lyman S. Watts, St. George, Maine, to Ashbel Martin, White Rock, Calif., December 25, 1852, private collection; Bonfield and Morrison, *Roxana's Children*, 146.

[87]Roxana went to Cabot to report to her mother, Olive Brown, and her brother, Simeon Brown, on their family in Canada.

the present. I hoped to hear from Alfred, sat up late waiting & went to bed & left my candle burning so I might read— No letter came— One cannot but shed tears when their minds are fairly made up to see or hear from a dear friend, when after waiting & watching for hours they are at last disappointed. Sent a letter to Cousin Emily Jesseph, that was Emily Taylor. She lives in West Yorkshire, Cattaraugus Co N.Y.

[Thursday, July 15] Feel some better than yesterday— Have been sewing some Went Strawberrying with Bub— He bawled most all the time. No letter yet I am so impatient to hear.

[Friday, July 16] This morning I expected to go & get our daguerotype's, got my mind all made up to go when Mother [Watts] was taken unwell & I could not go. I[t] does seem as though it was fated that I cannot have our likeness, & therefore I cannot fulfill Alfred's wish. The only thing I can do for him now, & perhaps it may be the last. I have cried most all the forenoon about it. Tears will not avail. They only relieve a poor lone heart like mine— Nothing but disappointment for me— No letter from Alfred yet. How my heart yearns to hear from him. It is all my life, to hear from him. Were it not my hope to hear often from him I could not stand it. I have as much as I can bear now. A letter from Brother Morrill Rix

[Saturday, July 17] I am almost sick with a cold on my lungs. Head ache. O dear me! To night at ten. I am sick with sick head ache. I have sat up waiting patiently & anxiously for a letter— I cannot go my self to the [post] office. I am dependent. But hoped they would be so kind as to send me one if it came to night. I feel confident there is one for me at the corner. But no sympathizing heart has seen fit to take pity on me, nay. My poor heart is almost breaking, for I had set it on hearing from Alfred to night. Alfred, O Alfred. You know not half I suffer. I cannot here record all my though[t]s & sorrows.

[Sunday, July 18] Sick both in mind and body. How impatiently I waited till after meeting was done to know whether I have a letter or not. There is no pleasure in suspense— I blame no one, & yet methinks things would be different if all could feel alike interested in absent friend— My letters come at last—three of them, all from Alfred. God bless him. He is well & happy or would be if Bub &

CWR   I were only there I wish I was there, and perhaps my wish may be gratified some time. Alfred still wants me to come. Hale [Rix] has been sick. The rest are well. Dustan [Walbridge] in the mines at Little Fork. Alfred taking lessons in Spanish. He likes his school. Sent me a little song of "He's among them," refering to Bub. Also a report of the schools in San Francisco by the Superintendent.

[Monday, July 19] Some better so I have helped wash &c. Wrote part of a letter to Morrill [Rix], in the evening— Began haying— our folks did

[Tuesday, July 20] Finished up Morrill [Rix]s letter & one to Clara [Walbridge] and sent them off Have been spinning some. The first I have spun for about three years. I make rather bad work to what I used to, & it makes me rather tired. Have spun little more than half a days work— Bub learns to talk very fast now trys to say almost every thing. He has some queer words. Calls the old cat Tickaldy. Teapot Teatop— Water Moger— Da pa & Da ma he says. O he is a smart boy shurely.

[Wednesday, July 21] Spinning again—& sewing some. Very warm. Coughed so I did not sleep much last night

[Thursday, July 22] Mrs. [Alma] Currier & [her daughter] Alma here visiting. At work on my mantilla. Began to write a letter to Alfred

[Friday, July 23] Finished my mantilla, & sewed on other sewing. [Ira] Miller made us a call He finishes up his school for Peacham next Tuesday. Poor man. He has reason to feel rather hard towards some of the people in Peacham.

[Saturday, July 24] We have been baking & brewing &c to day— Saw Laura Harvey & her man go by to night— I should have said Mrs. Frost Esq— She is or was one of our old neighbors— Was married last spring—[88] Bub weighed 25 pounds to day— He weight almost as much six months ago.

[Sunday, July 25] Went to church— A Mr Shaw, a very aged man preached in the forenoon— Mr [Asaph] Boutell in the P.M. Saw lots of my old friends Marrela Clarke, Laura Harvey, alias, Mrs.

---

[88]Laura Harvey married Henry H. Frost in Coventry on March 3, 1852. *Caledonian*, March 27, 1852.

Frost. Esther, Margaret, & lots more of them.[89] We had quite a chat together notwithstanding it was Sunday. Sent my letter to Alfred.

[Monday, July 26] Raining beautifully this morning, & has combined to rain most of the time to day— We have washed. And besides the weeks washing I have washed three bed quilts— Had a call from Mr. & Mrs. [Henry] Frost of Coventry Vt. I like the appearance of Mr. F. very much. He looks just like brother Ira Rix & not much older— Laura [Harvey Frost] looks younger than she used to.

[Tuesday, July 27] Pleasant day. Priscella Marsh came over to see me.[90] Made Aunt [Sarah] Stevens a call. Got some cherries to eat. Had some letters come from California— One from Dustin [Walbridge] and from Ashbel Martin. Again I am disappointed in not getting a letter— Where is my letter? I know there is one come from California for me. I will have a cry now for I cant help it. My heart aches it is so full— I live almost on my letters, at any rate I should not stand it long if I did not hear often.

[Wednesday, July 28] I have lived in hopes that I should hear from Alfred to night. But alas I am doomed to another disappointment What is the matter? He said he should write, I fear some trouble.

[Thursday, July 29] To day the 29 July is our third anniversary. Rather a lonely holiday to me. I have wrote another and sent another letter to Alfred, but with little hopes that it will go from N.Y. untill the next mail. No one knows what anxiety the absence of a friend causes. Especially when they are so far away from home as Alfred is— Many very many lonely & bitter hours I have spent all alone thinking of him.

[Friday, July 30] I have done a variety of work. Such as doing house work, taking care of baby, Spinning & twisting stocking yarn, Sewing, & writing— It has been a fine day. Neither too hot or to[o] cold for comfort & withall showery. Mother [Watts] & I get along with our work as yet, But Mother is very lame with rheumatism, or something of the kind

[Saturday, July 31] Baking and washing some. Have worked real

---
[89]The period after morning meeting, between services, was often a social time for parishioners.
[90]Priscella Marsh of Peacham (1840–1916) was listed as a student in the 1851 and 1852 PAC.

CWR hard for me. Morrill [Rix] came over this evening.[91] He never was in Peacham before.

[Sunday, August 1] Have not been to church. Stayed and let the rest of the family go. It has been a long and lonesome day to me. Though I do not feel quite so low spirited as I did a few days ago. But I almost always have something to make me down hearted after being more cheerful.

[Monday, August 2] Got up this morning and went to the washtub, and finished washing before noon. Morrill [Rix] went to Danville with me in the afternoon, and strange to tell have got a daguereotype—a very good likeness too. Came home & picked up my duds to go to Dalton. I am a tired child. My head aches severely— Bub behaved well out to Danville.

[Tuesday, August 3] Started for Dalton early this morning. Got there about two o'clock P.M. Had a very pleasant ride. Bub enjoyed it first rate. Found the folks all well at father Rix. Three years ago now at this very time Alfred & I visited there together. How differently are we situated now. He in California & I here alone as it seems to me. How much would I have given could I only have had him to go round with me to visit our old haunts.

[No entries August 4–21 while in Dalton, N.H.]

[Sunday, August 22] Yesterday I arrived at my home again in Peacham. I must give a kind of abstract on the past 20 days as I have kept no journal during this time. In the first place—Though it may seem strange at first—I have not enjoyed my visit so well as I had hoped to. I was hardly ever so home sick— This was no fault of any one but myself. How could I, when every thing around seemed to be lacking of one feature that was the most attractive in my former visit. My friends were all very kind to me but yet I wished many a time during my stay that [I] had never gone there. Visited at Mr. Whites a neighbor & to Cousin Moses Rix. Saw Mrs Underwood from Boston & her daughter Caroline & little son Walter. Mrs Underwood is Alfreds cousin Uncle Nat. Rix daughter. Also made short visit at

---

[91]Alfred's brother Morrill was probably in from Dalton, N.H., visiting his great-aunt Sarah Stevens and checking out the Peacham Academy, where he is listed as a student in the 1852 PAC. He took Chastina back to Dalton, N.H., for a brief visit.

Mr Tenny's a neighbor. Did not see the girls. Ira [Rix] is going to California so made a pair of Shirts for him, & did some other sewing and fixing for the family Bub enjoyed himself pretty well, only he was constantly getting <u>bit</u> or bruised some way. The little rogue learns to talk very fast. When I ask him where papa is. He says "Fannyforny." "Horse & wagon" are the two first words he attempted to put together— Received a letter from Alfred while at Dalton— He is urging me hard to go to California. I want to be there But it does seem to me that I never can go the journey all alone, or with any one but Alfred. I may go. Time will tell, I cannot now. The time comes for me to go home to Peacham. Ira carries me to Uncle Crains where I stay all night and take the stage at about six o clock in the morning. After being jolted almost to death, and sick too, I arrived at Barnet the stopping place of the stage, at 11 A.M. Stayed at Mr Norrises untill almost night & Charles [Watts] came down after me. I felt my old stomach complaint this afternoon the first time for two years and a half— Weighed at the Depot 113½ pounds. Bub 25½. Never weighed less than 122 or 3 before when I was weighed— I mean since I got my growth. Bub was very much afraid of the cars.

Chastina Walbridge Rix and her son Julian,
Vermont, August 2, 1852

Daguerreotype made in Danville, Vermont, to send to Alfred in California. Julian, at twenty months, wears a dress with a vertically pleated bodice and pleated skirt. Little boys dressed very similarly to girls until they were potty trained, after which they were put in pants. Chastina wears her hair in the typical style at mid-century, parted in the center and pulled back in loops over the ears. Her dress sleeves have scalloped caps, and the collar is fairly small, a fashion common early in the decade. Her white cotton undersleeves appear around her lower arms, below the beginnings of the narrow bell sleeve. *Private collection.*

CHAPTER NINE

Chastina Prepares for California
August 22–November 16, 1852

> *Began packing my box . . . I must bid Adieu to this our journal . . .*
> *But if . . . I meet again with this [journal] and*
> *my other friend [Alfred] there will be joy.*
> CHASTINA

NOT GETTING ANY POSITIVE RESPONSE TO HIS INVITATION TO Chastina to join him in California, Alfred wrote again to her mother, this time more insistent:

> You express the hope that I shall not take Chastina away so far from her old home and friends as California. I tell you plainly it is my wish to do so. I am as confident that it is for the best as I was that it was best for me to come, and now I cannot look back to the time when Hale [Rix] came in my stead without a regret that it was not I that took the pack, and when I think that there was a time when I was in doubt I almost tremble at the possibility that the decision might have gone the other way. If it were not for the journey here I should give you a real lecture but there is some danger and almost always sickness of one sort or another and a good deal of care & toil on the road here—so I'll pardon all you have done or can do to keep Chastina away—but I shall have her here—put that down as pretty certain.[1]

By the time this letter arrived at the Watts farm, Chastina's resolve to stay put in Peacham had crumbled and her mind was "more settled": she was going to try to make the trip. "No day passes without my thinking over and over again about going to California," she wrote. "My only desire and wish is to be there with him."

If Chastina was going to make the long journey to California without the protection of her husband, she would need to find a traveling

---

[1]Alfred, San Francisco, to Roxana Walbridge Watts, Peacham, September 11, 1852, private collection.

281

companion.[2] In hopes of finding someone to accompany her, she went to New Hampshire to see Alice Locke, who had attended her wedding with Alfred's brother Hale. Alice's brothers were already in California, and she was hoping to join them at some point, but they had yet to send her any money, so she had no means to finance the trip. This discouraging news caused Chastina to hesitate again about joining Alfred. But her mind was made up. On October 28 she announced that she would definitely be going to California.

Now nothing could stop her from making the trip, and she quickly put her plans in motion. She began sewing clothes for Julian, commenting, "it will take me a long time to rig alone." She ordered a box from a man in Boston (with the unlikely name of Mr. Coffin) to use in sending her personal things around Cape Horn, having been advised by Alfred that it would be expensive to take baggage with her as she traveled across the Isthmus of Panama. Noting in the journal the anniversary of Alfred's departure on October 4 and her twenty-eighth birthday on November 6, the second she had spent without her husband, she reflected on how much had changed in her life, and how quickly that life was passing by. She needed to be with her husband, and Julian needed to be with his father.

Alfred had invited Clara to come to California with Chastina, but Chastina made no mention of whether the sisters discussed this possibility, maybe because Clara was in Hardwick teaching for the summer. But Chastina may also have had concerns about whether the two would make good traveling companions. The sisters were both scholars and thus had both gone into teaching, one of the best ways at the time for educated women to earn money away from the farm. But they were six years apart in age, and one was married with a child while the other was independent, enjoying a social life with her peers and evaluating her many choices in life.

Clara's decision to join Chastina may have been linked to Enoch Blanchard's plans. A recent Dartmouth graduate, he and Clara may have

---

[2] At the time, families were concerned about daughters traveling long distances alone. In 1849, when Clara returned home from upstate New York, where she had gone to school and was teaching, Chastina wrote of their mother's anxiety: "for it seems rather a long journey for one to go alone without some friend to look to for protection." Chastina Walbridge, Peacham, to Clara Walbridge, Oakfield, N.Y., July 13, 1849, private collection. Likewise, when Augusta Merrill (1829–87) was returning home from Bradford Female Seminary in Massachusetts, her father wrote that he was "worried about your getting here" alone and requested that she leave early in the morning so as to "arrive the same day" in Peacham. Hazen Merrill, Peacham, to Augusta Merrill, Bradford, Mass., July 26, 1849, private collection.

been courting, or maybe Clara thought they were courting. On September 2, when Enoch came to call on her at the Watts farm, he announced that he was going "west to teach." Chastina wrote nothing of this matter. She probably knew that Clara and Enoch were courting, or at least she wrote that he had stopped by to see Clara, but she added no word of explanation. Clara may have had dreams of marrying Enoch, or even his cousin Ebenezer, whom she had gone riding with in July 1851. Both men attended Dartmouth and probably appeared to have promising futures to a smart woman such as Clara, who must have recognized that if she was going to marry a Peacham man, she would do better with a college graduate than a farmer. She had only to look at her mother's long working days to know that the life of a farmer's wife was a hard one.

With no prospects for marriage in Peacham, at least no prospects for marrying an educated man, Clara now had to consider her choices. She could continue teaching in the district schools in New England, or she could leave the area and start a new life in California. A single woman with no marriage plans might find San Francisco the perfect place to seek new opportunities. She could take on women's work such as laundry and sewing, or she might find a teaching job or become a governess. She probably felt that she was well prepared to make a living in the developing city, plus she would have the security of living with her sister and Alfred. The reasons why Clara agreed to leave Peacham are unknown, but she definitely knew that moving away from New England would have its advantages.[3] Chastina seems not to have wondered why Clara had suddenly agreed to join her. Preoccupied with her own plans, she may not have given a second thought to her sister's.

On November 16, Chastina added one last entry to the journal before she placed it in the box for the trip. "I must bid Adieu to this journal," she wrote. "It is especially dear to me." She was already mourning her separation from this "everyday friend" that had kept her such good company during her time alone. But she was on her way to California at last, looking forward to the time when she, the journal, and Alfred would "meet again."

---

[3] In 1855, Clara wrote her mother that her reason for coming to California was "to see if new and strange people would not cause me to forget my past troubles; and thank Heaven I am no longer feel obliged to feign gayety and cheerfulness when I do not really feel cheerful and gay." She added that she had "forgotten all old troubles, and intend in future to keep clear of them." Clara Walbridge, San Francisco, to Roxana Walbridge Watts, Peacham, February 14, 1855, private collection. This may explain Alfred's comment in a January 1854 letter to the Ways that Clara "wont be courted."

[*CWR*] [Sunday, August 22, 1852] Have not been to church. have read a letter which came from Alfred three or four days ago. He urges me to go to California Everything he says is pleasant and inviting there. If I was only there. I would give almost any thing, I possess. But wishing will never take me there. I wish to do that which is for the best, and I cannot tell whether to go or stay. During my absence a few things have happened. Mrs. Isaac Watts is dead.[4] Our Cousin Elizabeth Sizer is also dead. Young she is, only about twenty two year of age, just married, with every prospect of a happy future. But she is gone to her long home and angels are her companions How short is our life. Young as well as old are called to pass the dark valley, and how important it seems to be prepared, as was our Cousin to meet the call of him who made us. Yet how neglectful we are to look to these things. Tis so with me, ever waiting for a better time

[Monday, August 23] Mother [Watts] and I have done our work and washing— I am pretty tired yet not having got over my journey home— My mind is in a constant state of agitation, about what to do. May I be enabled to do that which is right.

[Tuesday, August 24] Jane Brown came down after mother [Watts] to go up and see Uncle S[imeon] Brown who is very sick— Accordingly she went & father [Watts] went up in the evening, so I am chief cook now.

[Wednesday, August 25] John [S. Way] and Sarah [Walbridge Way] with her two little ones came Sarah is looking rather pale and slim. Her children are pretty. A good solid rain has been pouring down a good part of the day— Father [&] mother [Watts] did not come till night— Ester Blanchard called and spent the evening. I am tired enough

[Thursday, August 26] Mother [Watts] real sick with the Summer complaint— Sarah [Walbridge Way] & I have a pretty hard time to get along—with the work and babies

---

[4]Martha J. Watts, age thirty-six, the wife of Isaac Watts, had died on August 7 of consumption. *Caledonian*, August 28, 1852.

[Friday, August 27] Mother [Watts] little better but not so she can *CWR* do much Began to cut a dress for Sarah [Walbridge Way].

[Saturday, August 28] Mother [Watts] better— I have scarcely looked up from my sewing to day. Sarah [Walbridge Way] must have her dress done for Sunday So I have been trying to see if we could not complete it.

[Sunday, August 29] Went to church. Sarah [Walbridge Way] & John [S. Way] went half a day. Saw Marilla Clarke all the noon time in burying yard.[5]

[Monday, August 30] Mother [Watts] and I have done our washing— John [S. Way]s folks went away before 9 o'clock A.M. Before we got through washing Ira [Rix] and Morrill [Rix] came here— Alfreds brothers. Ira to go to Cal. and Morrill to go here to school.

[Tuesday, August 31] Ira [Rix] & Isaac [N. Watts] took the teams and went to Danville and found Clara [Walbridge] & Augustus [Walbridge] there from Hardwick Ira rather unwell— Went to the Corner but found no letters there from Alfred— Sent a letter to Alfred

[Wednesday, September 1] Ira [Rix] unwell. Rather doubtful whether he is able to start for California. Got a letter from Alfred a good long one of three sheets. He will be so disappointed if I do not start to go to California— My only desire and wish is to be there with him. Every thing is so delightful there—and he is there too. Would I were with him.

[Thursday, September 2] Nothing very especial happened. Only I have sent off a letter post haste to Alfred that Ira [Rix] is sick and will not start at the time he expected. Ene Blanchard call on us or Clara [Walbridge]— He graduated with honor at Dartmouth this fall, and is about starting west to teach for a time[6]

---

[5]Marilla Clark (b. 1820) was a neighbor from the East Part. The Peacham cemetery is located up the hill west of the Congregational church. People who attended meeting on Sunday often walked up to the cemetery during the period between services.

[6]Enoch Blanchard (1830–89) called on Clara at the Watts farm. He was listed as a student in the 1843, 1845–46, 1846–47, 1848, and 1849 PAC. According to his Dartmouth College records, he graduated in the class of 1852 and was selected by his peers to present a lecture at commencement, which may be the honor that Chastina refers to. He completed his M.D. at Dartmouth in 1857 and married the daughter of a physician in 1862. Sarah Hartwell, Reading Room Supervisor, Rauner Special Collections Library, Dartmouth, e-mail message to editor, January 6, 2009.

CWR [Friday, September 3] I do nothing [s]carcely now a days. Since I went to Dalton four weeks ago, I am almost tired working for <u>every body</u>. I have almost come to the conclusion that I shall not go visiting any more I do not like to I have to fuss to get ready—Go—and be miserable through my visit— Come home and it [is] all of a week before I am settled again. There is no profit in it.

[Saturday, September 4] Work, work. Ira [Rix] not so well. Sent for the doctor for him. He has bled and blistered him. His complaint is in his stomach and bowels.

[Sunday, September 5] Sick folks about the same I am getting somewhat tired. I feel very sorry for Ira [Rix] he feels bad to think he has been so disappointed in his intended journey.

[Monday, September 6] Clara [Walbridge] and I had a very large washing. Took us most all day to do it. Bub's face is getting well— Ira [Rix] about the same— About tea time Mr [David] Currier came along to go to Cabot and watch Uncle Simeon Brown He asked some of us to go up with him. So I went, & left bub at home. Found uncle very sick The girls feel very bad Cynthia [Brown] is oblige[d] to put off her wedding day— Stayed all night and came home

[Tuesday, September 7] At about 9 o'clock A.M. Ira [Rix] about the same. Bub made some fuss in the night. I never slept without him before. Mother [Watts] had to put him in the cradle and rock him in the night. I am almost sick, but when others are sicker I must not complain. Some days I have the blues so I am just on the point of starteen for California No day passes without my thinking over and over again about going to California

[Wednesday, September 8] After helping mother [Watts] do up the work and seeing to babies & sick folks went to spinning— Spun three skeins.

[Thursday, September 9] Ironing. Have done up six fine Shirts and lots of other fixings. Alice Locke & Mrs. Henry Walker called to see me Alice to see about going to California this fall. Extremely warm— Ira [Rix] gaining slowly.

[Friday, September 10] Spinning some though I cannot make a business of it. Wrote a letter to Weltha Cory in Wisconsin Some ladies called & Clara [Walbridge] & I run, with our old spinning dresses on.

[Saturday, September 11] I have made out two days of work spinning this week. Ira [Rix] is about the same— Rainy day.

[Sunday, September 12] Have not been to church— Not very well. Bub comes on bravely now days. He grows worse and worse in mischief. This morning he wanted something to eat. I got him some wheat bread & butter. He tasted it and laid it down in a chair— "Sour-Puke" says he Little rogue— Some corn bread & butter would not make him <u>puke</u> he loves it better than the best cake that can be made.

[Monday, September 13] Clara [Walbridge] and I have done one more large washing. We have'nt but twelve to wash for. Father and mother [Watts] gone to Cabot

[Tuesday, September 14] Mother [Watts] gone. So We baked all manner of things for eating. We I say but Tine did all the baking. Got a letter from Alfred He still wants me to come to him. I am almost crazy about it. I do not know what to do. He is doing well there & seems to enjoy himself well, but only wishes for bub & I to be there.

[Wednesday, September 15] Sent off a letter to Alfred & one to Alice Locke to see about going to California— I have spun a day's work to day besides doing other work. Weighed 110 pounds. I am [not] growing very fast now [a] days. Weighed 113½ a short time ago. I shall get to be a mere shadow if I do not have my mind more settled than it has been for the few past months

[Thursday, September 16] Spun a days work to day— Have almost made up my mind to go to California—

[Friday, September 17] Prepareing for company— News come of Uncle Simeons Brown death.[7] Preparing for the funeral.

[Saturday, September 18] Father [&] Mother [Watts], Augustus [Walbridge] & I, Clara [Walbridge] & Charles [Watts] went to Cabot to attend Uncles funeral. His corpse was brought to Peacham to be buried by his wife— The family are now all broken up.

---

[7] Simeon Brown, Chastina's mother's brother, died at age fifty-eight. Of Roxana's three siblings, Simeon was the only one who lived near Peacham, and his children and hers were close cousins. Simeon's wife, Clarissa Blanchard Brown, had died on September 15, 1851, at age fifty-six. They were both buried in the Peacham Cemetery. Obituaries, *Caledonian*, October 4, 1851, and October 2, 1852.

CWR [Sunday, September 19] Went to church. Listened to the Rev Mr [John] Mattock both in the forenoon & afternoon. quite cold.

[Monday, September 20] Clara [Walbridge] and I have washed again. This evening the boys & Clara have gone to Mr E[lijah] Sargeants to spend the evening— I expected to go but was disappointed.

[Tuesday, September 21] Ira [Rix] and I started about eight o'clock for Lyman N.H. to see Alice Locke. We had to climb a mountain to get there. I walked all the way up it. Arrived at Mr [David] Lockes. Alice was off to school. Ira went and brought her home. She is a sweet girl, and wants to go to California with me but her brothers have not yet sent her the money and so she cannot go now. This throws my plans all aside. I had made up my mind to go to California if she could go. Now I must give it up for I do not feel right to go without some female to accompany me. Had a very pleasant time at Mr Locks. And returned home to night.

[Wednesday, September 22] Had the blues the hardest kind— Somehow everything goes against me. My mind is in such a constant state of agitation that I cannot take a moment peace. I do hope and pray that at no distant day I may be permitted to have some quiet nook which I may call home. O! that is an enderaing name to me. I long & look forward with anxiety to the future. But I know not what is in store for me. Happiness or misery certainly—Suspense is little better than misery— Some Ladies from Brunswick visited here. Relatives of Mr. Sargeants.

[Thursday, September 23] Have ironed— Have not yet got my mind settled I do not [grow] fat much under such excitement as had agitated me for the past summer

[Friday, September 24] Clara [Walbridge] and I have finished spinning our web. We sat up till about 11 o'clock to read "Uncle Toms Cabin" and father scolded because we disturbed him—notwithstanding we were still as possible

[Saturday, September 25] Have been fussing about and playing with bub a good part of to day. Bub is getting to be so funny. He talks so cunning and sad to say he is beginning to say many naughty things, which he learns from the children. I feel sorry for this but cannot help it now

[Sunday, September 26] Have not been to church. Sunday passes drearily away.

[Monday, September 27] Washed. In the evening all hands of us went dow[n] to Cap. Simon Blanchard's. Bub cried and screamed when I went away. First time I have been out in the evening since Alfred went away. Had a very good visit.

[Tuesday, September 28] Cold and rainy. Doing a little of every thing.

[Wednesday, September 29] Fixing and fussing. Spinning a little and so on.

[Thursday, September 30] Fixing Ira [Rix]'s things to start for California— Wrote a letter to send with my daguereotype to Alfred.

[Friday, October 1] got up about two o'clock this morning and started Ira [Rix] off for California. Though it was with a good deal of hesitation that he started for he is so unwell but he was bound to try it if he had to come home after he got to N.Y. All day I thought of him and worried about him fearing he would be sick and die on his journey. About 11 o'clock at night I was awakened by some one Saying "Chastine I have come back." I sprang up & there he stood alive but sick enough & tired almost to death. Having gone as far as Springfield Mass. and returned before resting. I was glad he had come while he could.

[Saturday, October 2] Ira [Rix] does not feel as bad as he did last night but is very unwell. His disease is liver complaint. We have been trying to comfort him & devise some means for his future course. He thinks he would like to study medicine & I have encouraged him in the notion of doing so, after he is properly fitted for such a course— The Hon. Thaddeus Stevens arrived in town this morning—[8] I have lined and trimmed a bonnet for Mother [Watts]

[Sunday, October 3] Have not been to church— I do not have a chance to go very often Wrote a letter to Adeline [Rix] Bierstadt— Warm and pleasant.

[Monday, October 4] We finished our washing sooner than usual this week for we expected a visit from the Hon. T[haddeus] Stevens.

---

[8] Thaddeus Stevens traveled from Pennsylvania at least once a year to visit his mother in Peacham. *Caledonian*, October 9, 1852.

CWR He only called a moment when on his way to St Johnsbury. I did not see him to speak with him. Clara [Walbridge] and I went to the corner after supper. Did not get a letter from Alfred. Strange why the Steamer does not come. It has been due now one week. Ira [Rix] went home to Dalton last Saturday although he was extremely unwell and not fit to go. One year to day since Alfred left home.

[Tuesday, October 5] Began to make over a dress for myself— It seems real odd to be doing such a thing for it is so long since I have made one for myself— Received a letter from cousin Emily Taylor Jesseph.

[Wednesday, October 6] Work on my dress & helping mother [Watts] some— Rainy— We are rather hard up for material for writing now a days

[Thursday, October 7] Sewing.

[Friday, October 8] Got a letter from Alfred. He is more than ever urgent for me to go out there. He is well and doing very well. How I wish I were there. Clara [Walbridge] and I have spun stocking yarn all day began in the morning and spun till half past eight in the eve Wrote a letter to Ira [Rix].

[Saturday, October 9] Spinning & ironing & working very hard all day. Clara [Walbridge] went to the Corner and got Misses Bruce & McDuffe, some of her Cabot scholars to make a visit. Will Brown come, & John [S. Way] came down after me. all are here to stay all night. John paid me $45.00 & interest since last Nov.[9] Cold and rainy.

[Sunday, October 10] Rained steady until 4 o'clock in P.M. when I started with John [S. Way] for Hardwick. got there safe though covered with mud

[No entries October 11–17 while in Hardwick]

[Thursday, October 28] From the 10 to this time I have been in Hardwick. I have worked most of the time either for myself or Sarah [Walbridge Way]. Sarah has rather a hard time Her children are small & she has quite a large family keeping her <u>constantly</u> doing her work and taking care of her children— I went to Church one half day. Saw our old friend Charles [S.] Smith in the pulpit— I

---

[9]John S. Way, Chastina's brother-in-law, had borrowed money from the Rixes and was paying his debt, as he realized that Chastina was about to leave Vermont.

hoped to hear him preach but was disappointed. He made a very good prayer—one from the heart— I went to visit my poor unfortunate aunt Cynthia Stevens. She is nearer in her right mind than I expected to find her. Though she is not what she was once— John [S. Way] and Sarah [Walbridge Way] went to Wolcott & I kept house for them while they were gone. Friends all well as usual there— Bub & Sis [Martha Way] did not agree very well, they did not hurt or strike each other but could not bear to be touched by one another— Received one letter from Alfred while there. I have made up my mind to go to California as soon as I can go. Came home from Hardwick with a Mr Cade who was coming to Peacham. Had not been to home more than a half hour before Josiah Shedd called and told me he was going to California I was fairly struck by surprise. But it was so— How I wish we had been ready to have gone in company with them I cannot help feeling very bad about it. Somehow things seem to work against me. Found a letter from brother [Edward] Bierstadts folks. They have a little daughter added to their family. All well. Daniel Webster died Oct 24 1852.[10]

[Friday, October 29] I am so lame after my ride I can do but little. Though I have began to fix some.

[Saturday, October 30] Sewing— Wrote a letter to California. Have had the blues a good deal— How much, Oh! how much I would give if Alfred was only here to help and encourage me—about going.

[Sunday, October 31] Been to church. Sent off my letter.

[Monday, November 1] Washing. I went to a "pareing-bee" down to Capt Simon Blanchard's.[11] Did not seem to me much like old times

[Tuesday, November 2] Had two long letters from Alfred. He gave me particular directions about going myself to Cal. & sending a box round the cape. Accordingly I wrote to Galen Coffin of Boston to see what he could do for us, in the matter of sending the box.[12]

---

[10] The noted lawyer and politician Daniel Webster was born in New Hampshire and toured Vermont several times during his career, including a visit to St. Johnsbury in 1830. At his death, the flags in Montpelier were lowered to half-mast. *Caledonian*, October 30, 1852.

[11] A paring bee was a popular fall activity. Young people could enjoy a social time while making themselves useful—paring apples for women preparing food for the long winter.

[12] Alfred had met Galen Coffin at Oscar Rix's shop when he traveled to Boston in May 1850.

CWR   [Wednesday, November 3] Charles [Watts] went to the Corner with me to see if we could make a raise of a box to send my things in, but failed as yet in doing so. Peacham cant afford boards enough of the right kind to make a box after my directions

[Thursday, November 4] Making bub's clothes. It will take me a long time to rig alone. There are a great many stiches to take in these little clothes

[Friday, November 5] Made Aunt [Sarah] Stevens a visit The old lady about as usual so she can do her work

[Saturday, November 6] My birth day— Cold and stormy— I have not witnessed quite so sad a day as last year. Yet these two birth days will long <u>be</u> remembered by me. As will the events of the past year. How various and changeful are the scenes and events of this life— We pass away year after year. How short—as every year adds one more to our number, before we think we are old I can hardly persuade my self that twenty eight years have rooled over my head; but it is even so. a good part of my life is passed even if I should live to the common age— There have been many happy scenes in my life as well as many sad ones. On the whole I have been and still am one of those whose fortune is to be "tossed about," which is a reverse of my nature.

[Sunday, November 7] I do not feel remarkably smart, for I had <u>company</u> yesterday and Bub kept me awake untill after midnight. The little rascal—I spanked him to pay for it. This is the third time he has served me the same trick. To get waked up about bed time and then keep me awake half the night. He has got so he talks pretty smart.

[Monday, November 8] Washing all day— Clara [Walbridge] and I called at Mr. Harriman's. Saw Mrs David Sanborn.[13] Mr. S. was one of Alfred's olld Scholar's

[Tuesday, November 9] Mother [Watts] & the little girls went up to see Grandmother [Olive] Brown. Sewing for bub. I progress slowly.

[Wednesday, November 10] Began a sack for Bub. it is pretty I

---

[13] This was probably Kate Spear Sanborn, who married David Sanborn, Jr., in 1849.

think— His papa wanted me to get something pretty for him— Cap. Blanchard's young people here in evening.

[Thursday, November 11] It is not much use for me to write daily. For every day does not seem to "bring something new" for me I wish I could get along and not think so much about California for it really disturbs me. My mind does not go from this subject scarcely at all.

[Friday, November 12] Had a letter from Mr [Galen] Coffin— He says he will attend to my box. Snowy & cold.

[Saturday, November 13] Went to the Corner to get Bub vaccinated—[14] The doctor had no infection so I have got to go again. Had a letter from Cousin Weltha Cory. Her mother died about four weeks ago.

[Sunday, November 14] Wrote letters to Alfred, Mr. [Galen] Coffin & sent a dunning letter to Dr Fayette Jewett.[15] Hope I shall succeed in getting a few dollars from him.

[Monday, November 15] Snow's and blows. Clara [Walbridge] gone to her school. She has almost concluded to go to California with me— I began this afternoon about packing my box.

[Tuesday, November 16] Began packing my box again for California. I feel many doubts about my ever seeing it again, and it is with feelings of regret that I put in <u>my all</u> that has cost me so many hard days labor—to first <u>earn</u> & then make. Many an hour & day & week I have labored for them & should they all be lost this testimony of my regrets will also be lost. I must bid Adieu to this our journal. In itself there is no merits—only it is especially dear to me. For I have turned to this in my husbands abscense as the only place where I could unburthen my thoughts. Even here I have been oblige to suppress much for many reasons. But this journal is very dear to me, because it is an <u>every day</u> friend & such are few in this wide world— How I

CWR

---

[14] By 1852 the smallpox vaccination was widely available. As early as 1848, Chastina's mother had advised her daughter Sarah, who was working in the Lowell mills, to get vaccinated. Roxana Walbridge Watts, Peacham, to Sarah Walbridge, Lowell, Mass., January 2, 1848, private collection.

[15] Dr. Fayette Jewett (1824–62) and Alfred were classmates at the St. Johnsbury Academy and the University of Vermont, class of 1848. In 1853 Jewett sailed to Turkey as a medical missionary. St. Johnsbury Athenaeum, Manuscript Box 2, Jewett Family Genealogy; Fairbanks, *Town of St. Johnsbury*, 367.

CWR shall regret & even mourn to loose so good a friend— But it must go, as I shall be compelled to part with all my friends here— But if on the contrary I meet again with this and my other friend there will be joy at meeting coresponding with my sorrow at parting— And O! how much more happy shall I be to meet <u>this</u> old friend in company with one other one for whom I sacrifise all old friends to meet.

Adieu adieux for a long time. Peacham Nov 16, 1852. Vermont. Chastina W. Rix

CHAPTER TEN

Travels to California
Recounting Events of October 1851 to February 1853

*Each of us have a tale to tell of our suffering or
our pleasures in finding this land of gold.*
CHASTINA

"WE ARE THERE." SO WROTE CHASTINA IN HER POCKET JOURNAL as the steamer *Golden Gate* approached San Francisco on February 19, 1853. She and Julian had reached their destination after thirty-four days of travel. In a letter to Peacham the next week, Alfred joyously announced the arrival of his wife and son:

> Last Saturday, Feb. 19, a friend tapped me on the shoulder and suggested that the Golden Gate had got into port and had a passenger or two who would be pleased to see me . . . Now and then Chance, Providence, or Fortune has shown me an acceptable favor, and I have felt thankful for it and happy in its enjoyment, but this safe transfer of my little family from the Eastern to the Western border of the continent is the "kindest hit of all" and gives me more satisfaction than anything else I could ask for.[1]

The newly reunited family boarded at the house near Mission Dolores where Alfred had been teaching since May. Within a few weeks, they had rented rooms in a house in the center of San Francisco, on Kearny Street.

After almost five months at sea traveling around Cape Horn, Chastina's box of personal household items finally arrived as well, catching up with her in San Francisco on May 1. After unpacking their "old friend," the Rixes resumed their habit of alternating entries. They left some pages blank, to be filled in later with their individual summaries of their separate

---
[1] Alfred Rix, San Francisco, to "Dear Friends," Peacham, February 27, 1853, Edward A. Rix Collection.

trips to California, but they did not find the time to write at such length until July 10, more than five months after Chastina's departure from Peacham and twenty-one months after Alfred had set off for California.

Chastina wrote first. She described her trip in detail, starting with the sadness she had felt when parting with "father, mother, brothers, and sisters, acquaintances, old and familiar places, haunts dear to memory." She recalled her fears and the difficult situations she had encountered without her husband there to protect her and Julian. She wrote of cold and wind, of rough waves and seasickness, of frightening events and inferior rooms on steamships on both the Atlantic and the Pacific. She wrote of an outbreak of yellow fever and the resulting burials at sea.[2] But she also wrote about the "enchanting" landscape in Panama and the kindness of the people who had helped her along the way.

This reminiscence was her third account of the trip. During the journey itself, she had kept a pocket journal that she called "Journal of My Journey to California," in which she noted her location and brief details of her activities and emotions.[3] She also wrote two letters to her mother in Peacham, one as the steamer approached the Isthmus of Panama and the second upon arriving in San Francisco. Those letters were primarily intended to assure her family that she, Julian, and Clara were safe and in good spirits.[4] This third version, in the journal she kept with Alfred, was specifically for his eyes, and it was there she felt free to recount the trials, dangers, and insults she had endured in order to join him.

There were many women traveling to California in the 1850s, on their way to join husbands, fathers, or brothers who had decided to settle in the Golden State and wanted their families with them.[5] However, it was a trip that only families with money could afford to make: the cost of Chastina's sea voyage and crossing at Panama, according to her carefully

---

[2] In a letter home after her arrival in San Francisco, Clara reported that "from forty to fifty deaths occurred while on the [steamer] Golden Gate—Most of them died with the Yellow Fever." Clara Walbridge, San Francisco, to "Dear Friends," Peacham, February 27, 1853, ibid.

[3] Chastina, "Journal of My Journey to California," 1853, Rix Family Papers. Excerpts from this journal—often called her pocket journal—and the financial account that Chastina kept on the trip were published in Bonfield, "When Money Was Necessary."

[4] Chastina, Steamship *Ohio*, to "Dear Friends," Peacham, January 29, 1853; and Chastina, San Francisco, to Peacham, February 27, 1853, Edward A. Rix Collection. "Friends" at that time often meant family, but these letters were most certainly for her mother. Chastina gave details of their stark conditions on the steamer but ended with "I have not wished a thousand times that I had never started . . . Do not give yourselves any uneasiness on our account."

[5] See Bonfield, "When Money Was Necessary," 135–36, 138–42, for stories of women traveling to California.

kept account of expenses, totaled $408.64, equivalent in 2009 dollars to $11,746.52.[6] Women who were traveling alone or with only one child tended to choose the Panama route, as Chastina did. Mothers with several children usually chose to take the longer sea route around Cape Horn, as disembarking from the steamer on the Atlantic side, crossing the Isthmus of Panama, and re-boarding on the Pacific side was difficult even under the best of circumstances. After a railroad line had been completed in early 1855, the trip across the isthmus was almost as comfortable as taking a train ride at home. But in 1853, it was not yet possible to take a train all the way across; Chastina had to travel partway by train, partway in a boat rowed by natives, and the final twenty-four miles riding sidesaddle on a mule, separated from Julian, who was being carried across the hills by a "dusky & almost naked" native.

In contrast to Chastina's lengthy narrative in the journal, Alfred's gave only the briefest sketch of his trip. He had already written letters to her and others in Vermont, so perhaps he felt that there were few new facts to add. He did not dwell in his narrative on his troubles or hardships. With his dreams for a life in California with Chastina and Julian now a reality, his trip a year and a half earlier was in the past. His focus now was on settling the family in the bustle and excitement of San Francisco.

[CWR] [Sunday, May 1, 1853] San Francisco. Thrice welcome friend Journal! You and I have at last met on this side of the Atlantic. Each of us have a tale to tell of our suffering or our pleasures in finding this land of gold. I would most gladly hear your story— Mine I shall give you as well as I can though you can bear witness that it is in poor way. If I am not mistaken you Sailed from Boston Nov. 25, 1852 on board the Fleetwood—Arrived in San Francisco Cal. about the middle of Apr. making our separation about four months— During that, much has transpired.

After getting you started I set about getting myself ready to go too— Worked very hard in prepareing for the journey— Sold the reminder of my furniture & fixings at low prices, and got two hundred and fifty dollars from Alfred, so I had plenty to go with. Clara

---
[6]This figure is based on the Consumer Price Index found at http://www.measuringworth.com.

CWR [Walbridge] prepares herself to come with me so we bid adieu to our friends in Peacham on Monday morning Jan. 16, 1853. The last was hard! I parted with you, with many regrets and even tears—but to bid adieu to father, mother, brothers, and sisters, acquaintances, old and familiar places, haunts dear to memory—is almost heart rending— Never Shall I forget those two partings for this distant land— the one when my husband left me—the other when I left my friends to seek him. Little Julian was impatient to start when he was ready. I see him & the others just as they were that morning— I will dwell no longer on those scenes for they trouble me.

Father Watts carried us to Barnet where we said good Bye to every body we knew. For a time our party were Clara Ira Rix & Bub & myself. The day was extremely cold, and we suffered from cold— Nothing occurred on [the way] except we like to have got run into by a baggage train as we were nearing Hartford. We stopped at Hartford over night—and arrived in New York about ten next morning—[7] Put up at the Eastern Pearl Street House. Found [Barron] Moulton waiting for us.[8] New York in Jan. looks dismal enough—we did'nt go out at all so we can not say much against it; but it looked uninviting to me. In P.M. Moulton purchased our tickets on board the Steamer Ohio—Paid $305 for each.[9] Thursday we got ourselves on board and at about two o'clock we were going down north river—and now—

[7] The sisters boarded the train at Barnet, the nearest railroad station to Peacham. According to the pocket journal Chastina kept on her trip, they stopped overnight at Springfield, Mass., not Hartford, as she wrote here. Chastina, "Journal of My Journey," January 17, 1852.

[8] Chastina had arranged a meeting in New York with an acquaintance who had agreed to look out for them on the trip. Ibid., January 18, 1852. Barron C. Moulton was a well-respected man in Waterford, serving as a bank director and frequent estate commissioner. *Caledonian*, June 22 and August 31, 1850, March 13, 1852.

[9] The price of $305 for the steamship trip was the going rate according to newspaper accounts, down from $350 in 1851. *Caledonian*, February 8, 1851. Lewis, *Sea Routes*, 238, put the ticket price at between $200 and $400. For a lower price one could share steerage with between six hundred and seven hundred people, including Alfred's brother Ira. Chastina, Steamship *Ohio*, to "Dear Friends," Peacham, January 29, 1853. Two-year-old Julian apparently did not need a ticket. The *Ohio*, built in New York by Bishop and Simonson for the U.S. Mail Steamship Company, was a wooden side-wheel steamer of 2,432 tons, with three decks and four masts. Launched in August 1848, it began operating in September 1849 between New York and Chagres, Panama (renamed Aspinwall in 1853), with "stateroom accommodations for 250 first-cabin and permanent berths for eighty in steerage." Kemble, *The Panama Route*, 239. Kemble provides an excellent overview of the trip from New York to San Francisco via the isthmus.

> "O'er the glad waters of the dark blue sea.
> Our hearts as boundless and our souls as free."[10]

This sentiment I cannot appreciate; as our voyage was not one of pleasure— The first and second day we came near freezing—never suffered so much from the cold in my life— We paid for first class tickets, & were oblige to be put in the meanest place possible—down stairs along a dark passage and beyond the machinery. The Ship had not been out for Six months—consequently every thing was damp & mouldy— I felt as though we were badly used, but as we had no one to stand up for our rights we had to make the best of it— The sea was very calm for two days, and had Alfred been with me I might have enjoyed it. How grand, how Sublime to contemplate the sea, when borne upon its waves by the art and ingenuity of man.

Jan. 22, the third day out from N.Y. began to be stormy—the wind rose gradually & continued to increase through the night. I lay in my berth all night listening to the roaring of the wind—the creaking & jar of the machinery with the constant roll of the ship—made night hideous, to me. I never was so frightened in my life. The dear boy sleeping beside me so calm, while every sound was so horrid to me, made it seem so much more dismal to me— Morning came at last and with it the bustle and noise of a crowded ship— I was not so sea sick but I could sit up and take care of Julian. Clara was very sick Mrs [Elizabeth] Varney was frightened almost to death—[11] Julian sick enough to make him quiet and vomit a little. The storm commenced Saturday night and lasted till Tuesday night. Such a time as we had. I sat up two nights in the ladies cabin holding Julian in my lap all the time. The vessel rocked from side to side, every joint in the inside creaking most dismaly. Never shall I forget that time on the Atlantic, and I shall curse the old Ohio as being a most miserabe affair and altogether to blame for making a pretence that she was something. After the storm was over we passed the time away tolerably. We came along side of Cuba, for a long distance. It looked

---

[10] These are the opening lines of "The Corsair," written in 1814 by English poet Lord Byron (1788–1824).

[11] Elizabeth Varney of Danville was traveling with her young son, Henry, to meet her husband in San Francisco.

CWR beautifully to see land once more, and covered too with luxuriant foliage. We had no more frights until we got into the bay of Aspinwal where we came near running aground, and were oblige to go out to sea again during the night. This was Sunday

Jan. 31. Monday we came within a mile of Aspinwal and there the old Ship lay all day rocking from side to side most fearfully. There had never been such a rough sea in the bay before. They began taking off the baggage in the forenoon, & in the afternoon passengers began to go ashore— They were let down in a chair at the stern of the ship—and away they went "o're the dancing waves." This was rather a slow process to land a thousand passengers, so some staid on board another night Clara and I & Mrs [Elizabeth] Varney were among that number. We had a good time; supper and breakfast, and a good place to sleep.

Tuesday morning the sea was very calm, & the old boat came up very near the wharf, but not <u>so</u> near, but we had to go ashore in a small boat— But we had a good time & in a few moments we were once more on land. We went on board the cars immediately & soon were going over the Isthmus by the aid of steam.[12] I never shall forget the pleasing sensation which took possession of me after taking my seat in the cars. I felt as though I had awoke from a fearful dream, where every moment I was in danger of my life, & now I could rest, was perfectly safe. I do not know as I ever enjoyed a few hours—and could appreciate the enjoyment at the time—as I did in going from Aspinwall to Gorgona a distance of twenty miles. The trees, the foliage, the birds, the flowers, everything was enchanting. I must not forget to mention some gentlemen that kindly assisted us on our way— Cap. Chadwick & Cap. Mathews two sea Captains from New Bedford. They were whole souled men & we owe them much for their kindness to us. We might have perished for aught I know had it not been for these kind friends— I must also mention Mr Nye & Mr Woods as among those who kindly assisted us.[13] Our ride on the rail road terminated all too soon— We rested

---

[12] A railroad had been completed from Aspinwall to Gorgona. In January 1855 it crossed the isthmus.

[13] The listing of arriving passengers on February 19 included H. B. Wood, but no further information was found on the captains from New Bedford. *Alta California*, February 20, 1853.

awhile at Gorgona— I am mistaken about Gorgona being the present terminus of the rail road— We got on board a little boat, some twenty five of us— rowed by five or six hardy natives, and away we went up the Chagres river— Stayed at Gorgona over night, had most miserable fare and had to pay very dear for it— Started early in the morning for Cruses got there about noon— Had a very good time going up the river—Though Julian was very cross & tired out it was so warm— He was not willing any one should touch him but me. I consequently was very tired. We had a very comfortable place to stay but the victuals! a dog in the States would turn up his nose and leave it.

Thursday morning Feb 4. We mounted our mules—for which we had to pay $25.00 apiece—I had a Side Saddle & Clara rode on a Spanish one.[14] I paid a native $14.00 for carrying Julian across the final hills of the Isthmus. The dear little fellow I pitied him so, to send him away from me. But as it proved he and little Henry Varney enjoyed it very much—and became attached to the natives—so much so, that they would put out their little arms to go from us to their dusky & almost naked friends. We saw the children every now and then; but the natives have their foot paths round in the woods. Once or twice we came up with them where the boys had stoped at a ranch & were giving them drink & something to eat— We had a very good time crossing. Such roads can be found nowhere else I am sure— There was no part of my journey that I enjoyed so much as my mule ride on the Isthmus— and had it not been for Julian being with a native away from [me] I should have enjoyed my ride excedingly.

We did not arrive in Panama untill nearly nine o'clock in the evening, our ride haveing been about twenty four miles— The hotels were all filled to the overflowing, and through the kindness of some gentlemen we got a room which they had engaged for themselves. Bub had gone to sleep a long time before he got there— Mr Nye

---

[14]The difference in temperament between the sisters is obvious here, with Chastina riding sidesaddle, "as ladies do," and Clara riding "astride with my bloomer dress." Twenty-nine-year-old Chastina, a married woman with a child, was conscious of her status, while twenty-three-year-old Clara, unencumbered by family responsibility, still sought new adventures. Clara Walbridge, San Francisco, to "Dear Friends," Peacham, February 27, 1853.

CWR carried him a while to rest him— We went out to a restaurant & got some supper. Had some good eggs & bread. I was so tired I could eat but little. <u>Such</u> a room & <u>such</u> beds. We took off the sheets for fear of disease— We went to bed and presently we heard such groans & cursing & swearing, that it made ones blood chill— It proceeded from an adjoining room with only loose board partition— We tried to sleep but in vain. We spoke to a man through the partition & found a man was sick & dying close to our heads— He called it the Panama fever. There was no window in our room & but one door, a stone floor & dark dismal walls. This was the first time I ever felt as though I was really imprisoned. Twas an awful night to us. Before dawn the poor creature had breathed his last. He was a young man from New York on his way to California & had falen a victim to that pestilence the <u>Yellow fever</u>—and we were in the midst of it!

 We got away from this place as soon as we could in the morning. Went out of town to what is called Cocoa Grove, a beautiful place. There were all kinds of tropical fruit all about the house— Our accomodations were very good, but the fare like all other places on the Isthmus was miserable— We Stayed at this place one night, and Saturday 6 of Feb. we packed up our duds & Started for the beach on the Pacific— Our party at this time was Cap. Chadwick, Mr. Nye, Mr. Woods, Mr Moulton, & Ira Rix—Mrs. Varney, Mrs. Erwin, Clara & myself, little Henry & Julian. We walked to the beach, Where there were plenty of natives with their boats to take us out to the "Golden Gate—"[15] The gentlemen procured a boat got in our luggage, & first we knew each of us were caught up in the arms of a brawny & almost naked native & set into the boat. Then twas "<u>Two reals Senorita</u>" from the half dozen mouths in such confusion that we hardly knew whether we were taken actually and carried of[f] by the natives, or what the Dickens they wanted making gestures over our heads—

---

[15] The *Golden Gate*, built in New York by William H. Webb for the Pacific Mail Steamship Company, was a wooden side-wheel steamer of 2,067 tons with three decks and three masts. Launched in January 1851, it entered the San Francisco–Panama service in November 1852. Kemble, *Panama Route*, 228.

We shoved off at last, and once more we were launched upon the boundless ocean, But thank heaven it was the <u>Pacific</u> and this gave us some consolation— We had a very pleasant time going out to the vessel but were frightened most to death before we got on board. There were such a crowd of small boats all jaming & smashing to get up first that it frightened us very much—But we got on board— Such a contrast between the Golden Gate & Ohio—Every thing looked so nice and pleasant that I began to feel quite happy. But in the evening came a sad reverse. Bubby had gone to bed in a berth in a state room which I had vainly considered to belong to me in part at least—When I was informed by the Cap. that the berth belonged to another lady & I must turn out. Our tickets were the same then, but hers had been changed— She had a husband to look out for her, I had no one to stand up for me. So I had to give in, & take my berth on a matross in the ladies saloon. Julian by this time had got all tired out & was very difficult to take care of. He would'nt let any on[e] touch him but me without screaming— We had plenty of good victuals to eat & every thing was so much cleaner & neater that we felt better even with poor accommodation— There were over a thousand passengers & consequently it must be very crowded— Soon the yellow fever broke out on board & more than fifty persons fell victims to this awful disease. We were none of us sick, and it is surprising with what indifference one can look upon such melancholy scenes— when out to sea. Every one is filled with their own troubles, and they hardly have time to think of others. It is <u>well</u> it is so, for much excitement together with change of climate is almost sure to bring on disease. But it was awful to think of our situation. We could'nt tell whose turn next to be plunged in the deeep blue sea, for our last resting place.

We had a rough sea in crossing the gulf of Tuhuantepec, so lots of them were sea sick. We stoped at Acapulco, but no one was allowed to go ashore. We touched at San Diego & Monterey, & Saturday morning Feb. 19 at about Six o'clock in the morning I hurried on deck for we were then passing through the "Golden Gate"—a most beautiful sight The sea was calm, the sun shining on the green hills the

CWR

CWR morning mist, & all looked so refreshing— Soon Came the booming of the cannon.[16] Every where was bustle & preparation—beating & anxious hearts there were—as we neared the wharf of San Francisco. We are there. Friend meet friends. Husbands & wives meet. friends hear sad tales— Let all pass. We went to the Rassette house—where some friend went to the Mission & got Alfred to come over to the City & See who was there.[17] Here friend journal ends my story, & I give you an invitation to relate yours, at your leisure.
[The above was written on July 10 in space left blank as the couple returned to daily entry writing]

[*ASR*] [Tuesday, May 10] Again we open our old Journal & proceed as before with our daily reckoning. After being boxed up some four months & taking a fine passage around the Horn in the Clipper Ship Fleetwood this book turns up in the State of California in the City & County of San Francisco—on Kearny St. in a large two story white house—at our new Secretary. In the Same place to be found Alfred Rix, Chastina W. Rix, Clara B. Walbridge & Julian W. Rix. We are all in pretty good health except Chastina who has been unwell for a month. After some delay & a good deal of care & toil and some suffering we are all on the Pacific coast and in circumstances, to say the least, fair & promising. For the particulars of the Girls' voyage see Chastina's Small Journal & her further account herein.

[Wednesday, May 11] Perhaps it will be well for me to give an abstract of my doings since leaving home in Sept. 1851, though reference has already been made to letters & small Journals for particulars.[18] The company of forty Peachamites left in good spirits on the fourth day of September & reached New York the same evening—All put up at the Eastern Pearl Street House. Remained there with various adventures till Tuesday 7 when we went aboard

---

[16] A cannon was fired at the top of Russian Hill to announce the arrival of a steamship in the San Francisco Bay.

[17] The Rassette House, a first-class San Francisco hotel, was located at the corner of Bush and Sansome streets. It burned to the ground in May 1853 and was rebuilt. Soulé, Gihon, and Nisbet, *Annals of San Francisco*, 448–49; this book is the classic contemporary account of San Francisco in the 1850s.

[18] Alfred's memory was poor; he left Peacham on October 4, 1851, not in September. No small journals kept by him have been located.

the Steam Ship Prometheus, Capt. Churchill, & sailed for San Juan Del Norte where we arrived in ten days through storm & stink.[19]

Immediately embarked on board the small river Steamers and after running aground a few times landed at Castillo Rapids on the San Juan River some 40 miles from its outlet from lake Nicaragua. Here we delayed 3 or 4 days & at last took the lake Steamer and went to Virgin Bay—beautiful scenery as ever met the eye. A mountain with a cataract of hundreds of feet fall is seen on an island of the lake. From V.B. we walked some 15 miles thro' mud & rain to San Juan Del Sur on the Pacific. Here we lingered again and had a mess with the agent of Vanderbilt.

Finally got aboard the Independence & sailed for San Francisco where we arrived Nov. 16.[20] During the whole passage on the Pacific I was sick a-bed and neither knew or cared what happened. After remaining a few days at San Francisco we went to Oregon Bar on the North Fork of the American River where we remained with rather poor luck till Feb. 1852.[21] Then came to Auburn & stopped a week or two, then I came to San Francisco, and after a few weeks got my present business of School-teaching at the Mission. For Daily Particulars see my small Memorandums for 1852 & 3.[22]

---

[19] The *Prometheus* was Vanderbilt's fastest steamer at the time. Lewis, *Sea Routes*, 210. It was a wooden side-wheel steamer of 1,500 tons with three decks and three masts; built for service between New York and San Juan de Nicaragua, it was launched in December 1850. Kemble, *Panama Route*, 243. Many men chose the Nicaragua route to California, which shortened the distance of the sea voyage on each side, although the distance on the isthmus crossing was longer with few accommodations.

[20] The steamer *Independence*, built for Vanderbilt, was a wooden side-wheel steamer of 613 tons with two decks and two masts. It was launched in December 1850 from New York but was in service from San Juan del Sur to San Francisco beginning in September 1851. Kemble, *Panama Route*, 231.

[21] This is the only description of Alfred's mining days given in the journal. None of his letters written from the mines have been located.

[22] No memoranda kept by Alfred have been located.

CHAPTER ELEVEN

The San Francisco Years
May 12, 1853–April 23, 1854

Bub's business is to laugh, play in the sand [and] run after his parents . . . The old man is Justice of the Peace & spends nearly every hour of the day at his office . . . Chastina does the house-work, sews & tinkers.
ALFRED

In all this week I have ironed sixty shirts. 35 starched one[s] & 25 plain besides hosts of other clothes & I have made twelve dollars by my labor. . . . Hard work this—but in this "land of gold" you must work or starve.
CHASTINA

So much to do I cant find time [to] journalize.
ALFRED

There is but little that is interesting in the common routine of family affairs.
CHASTINA

IN THE FALL OF 1851, WHEN ALFRED FIRST ARRIVED IN SAN Francisco, he found a city bursting with men either returning from gold country and heading home or taking off for the mines, as were he and Dustan. In a letter to Chastina's parents, he told the story of the gambling dens he and Dustan had found in the city:

> On the last arrival of the Golden Gate we walked down towards her along long warf—the new comers were scattered along the streets "sucking" the various baits set for them. We noticed an usual crowd about one of the gambling tables—we went into the Saloon and looked over their shoulders. The victims were "<u>in</u>" & thick at it. It was what is called the A.B.C. game—we noticed one poor fool—as fresh & innocent as a basket of garden sauce—putting

307

down his tens & twenties—losing at every shake—& expecting, yes <u>absolutely knowing</u> that he must win . . . I knew full well the rules of the house, viz, that there must not be even the wink of an interference . . . but I could'nt stand by & see what I did and do nothing—I pulled the booby gentle by the coat-tail—he took the hint & was fool enough to follow me out . . . we were stopped by 6 of them who were ready for a brush, but after a short tongue fight both parties backed off . . . the influence of gamblers though still great in this city is on the decline. On my return one night from my Spanish recitations I was stopped by some scoundrel in a dark street, but I was too soon for him—I had been warned to keep all persons at a distance at such times & in such places—a man had been knocked down & robbed a few paces from our door, but a few days previous.[1]

Like others who came first and foremost to try their luck in the mines, Alfred did not speculate on the future of the city, or, for that matter, his part in it.

That changed in March 1852 when he returned to San Francisco having gained no "pile" in the mines. No longer blinded by the goal of easy fortune, he looked around and evaluated the city, noting the great changes he had seen in only a few months, many of which were to his liking. He saw the urban infrastructure changing with increased necessary services such as food, water, and mail. San Francisco had been "raised from a hamlet to a bustling city," as Herbert Howe Bancroft put it.[2]

Before the discovery of gold in January 1848, fewer than 100 people lived in the town, but by the end of 1849 the population was more than 25,000. By 1852, when Alfred took a close second look at the city, the census was more than 34,000 and growing by the day. As he wrote Chastina's parents, the churches were "very well attended," and "good men and good reputations are rapidly gaining the ascendancy—men are bringing their families & accumulating their property here & they <u>must</u> have their things in a <u>safe</u> place."[3]

Educated and business-savvy men found the economic opportunities in the city promising, as San Francisco was the coastal hub, not only for the gold fields, but also for the increasing export of local goods, especially agricultural products. Commercial and financial interests thrived as well, and with them the necessities that lured families to the city, including lodging,

---

[1]Alfred, San Francisco, to Lyman and Roxana Walbridge Watts, Peacham, June 26, 1852, private collection.
[2]Bancroft, *Chronicles*, 1:289. The full quote is "raised from a hamlet to a bustling city, from a local town to the metropolis of the coast."
[3]Alfred, San Francisco, to Lyman and Roxana Walbridge Watts, Peacham, June 26, 1852.

public safety, and, of special interest to Alfred, education. The first public school opened in April 1850, and by the middle of 1851 more than three hundred students were enrolled, showing the increase in the number of families residing there. Seven school districts were organized, and the one near Mission Dolores was offered to Alfred.[4] His years as a teacher and school principal came to his rescue when he needed a way of making a living in the city. Fortunately, many of the men involved in establishing the school system were from New England colleges, including his alma mater, the University of Vermont, and many must have known of the fine reputation of the Peacham Academy. The advantage to Alfred of being assigned to the school on the outskirts of the city was that he could live where he could maintain a small garden, growing some of his food.

Chastina, Julian, and Clara arrived on this scene in February 1853. After living "at the Mission" for a few weeks, they moved to rented rooms—a parlor, dining room, kitchen, and bedroom—in a newly built house for four separate families—two up and two down—on Geary Street near Kearny at the cost of $60 a month. Through the spring, Alfred taught his classes, and Chastina worked in the home and cared for Julian. Clara assisted Chastina some, but being young and single, she also enjoyed a busy social life. During the early years of the Gold Rush, American women were scarce in San Francisco; in 1853 they accounted for only 8,000 out of the city's total population of 50,000. Few of the women there were single and well educated with close family ties. Clara was courted by many men, as Chastina's journal entries reported callers almost every evening.

The gold miners had been forced to do women's work, but with the arrival of each vessel at the Golden Gate, women arrived and took up these jobs, often making good money. "The girls," as Alfred called Chastina and Clara, put their New England industriousness and farm skills to good use, taking in laundry and sewing and then adding boarders at $8 per week. "Women's work" was highly valued, as the city's male population still far outnumbered the female.

In a letter to her mother, Chastina admitted that she missed home, but in their journal she wrote that she had "so much to do that I cannot stop to be homesick." The twice-a-month mails from the East Coast were anticipated with great excitement, and when the steamer arrived without a letter from home, Chastina expressed disappointment. Letters were "visits from our friends," as were the copies of the *Caledonian* that she called "old friends." Even Alfred felt "mean & disappointed" if he went to the post

---

[4] Soulé, Gihon, and Nisbet, *Annals of San Francisco*, 679–86; Lotchin, *San Francisco*, 312.

office and had to "go away empty."[5] With postage on letters costing only six cents prepaid, the couple corresponded regularly with family from home. And when Alfred's great-aunt Sarah Stevens, now eighty-eight years old, sent them a lock of her hair, they so cherished it that they preserved it among the pages of the journal. In November Chastina wrote that "every letter from home brings news of changes there deaths, marriages, absences & the like." Letters came from Sarah and John S. Way, too, first from their farm in Hardwick, and after spring 1855 from Minnesota, where they had moved with a handful of other families—men who had gone to California with John in 1850. The bonds forged on that adventure, both on the ocean and in the mines, remained strong.[6]

Daily life for the Rixes in San Francisco differed from their schedule in Vermont. Alfred was gone from the house all day—first as a teacher "at the Mission" and later as a lawyer and justice of the peace, a position he was elected to in the fall of 1853. He described his work in a letter to John in September:

> I am practicing law & politics a little. I have just been elected one of the Justices of the City—there are three besides me—our jurisdiction includes ordinary Criminal Justice matters & all civil cases where the value in disputes is $200 & under—this gives the Justices very constant employment aided by a clerk & constable. The ordinary profit is about 700$ per annum—not very much like the shilling justices in Vermont. I shall enter on my duties next month.[7]

Chastina stayed at home with "the work," meaning washing, cleaning, preparing meals, sewing, taking care of Julian, and providing for the boarders. Some weeks she rarely left the house. Occasionally she accompanied Alfred for a walk in "the sand hills" or down to "Tobin's and Duncan's," a local store where she purchased cloth. At the beginning of 1854, he filled in Sarah and John on the rest of the family. Chastina, he reported, was "as plump & red-cheeked as a Miss of 16 & is up every morning before daylight & it is perfectly refreshing to see with what a zest she dips into

---

[5] Alfred, San Francisco, to John S. and Sarah Walbridge Way, Hardwick, January 15, 1854, private collection. Stories of long post office lines in San Francisco in the early years of the gold rush are abundant in contemporary accounts. By 1853, the congestion was not so great, but the eagerness for news from home continued. Henkin, *Postal Age*, 131–33.

[6] Bonfield, "Ho for California," 18. Among those moving to Minnesota after returning from California at the same time as the Ways were Bill Whittle and brothers Chester and John Martin.

[7] Alfred, San Francisco, to John S. Way, Hardwick, September 15, 1853, private collection. Alfred's salary as a teacher was $150 a month; women teachers received $100. *Alta California*, November 6, 1852.

the 'accomplishments.' She now dont hesitate to say she made a decided hit in coming to California—she's glad she came."[8] In the same letter, he wrote of Clara:

> But what, the devil Clara thinks about it I dont know any more than you did till she started. She's one of the inexplicable enigmas. She takes the bus every day for her school and comes back every night—sews—helps Tina—smiles on this young man & frowns on that—gets a hundred a month—wont be courted—eats ice cream & oysters—attends alternately church & the Theatre—teaches day & Sunday school—attends evening parties with us and laughs & giggles till the corners of her eyes pucker up like an old work bag.

Alfred did not forget to report on their three-year-old son: "Bub grows fat & frolicksome every day—we must send him over to you in a year or two for this is no good place to bring up boys—the streets of a city play the devil with their morals & manners." He finished the letter with a few words about himself:

> As to myself I am in Statu quo. Every morning at 8 A.M. I walk down to my office, Corner to Bush & Montgomery Streets, & find my clerk has got me a good coal fire & is reading papers. I join him. At 9 comes on John Doe vs. Richard Roe & then the next & the next till night. Sometimes, I get time to go home & get a lunch about noon. At 5 P.M. I retire in disgust & take home some law material. At six—supper & all hand[s] together again— The evening at anything everything or nothing. This is a birds eye view of my daily life.

The Vermont "boys" stopped by on their way to and from the gold mines, allowing the Rixes to catch up on news from home as well as activities in the mines. They were happy to see some old neighbors from Peacham's East Part, but when a group of men from Vermont came in April 1854 on their way to the mines, Chastina wrote, "Rather hard for those who come to this country now," for she knew that their chance of fortune was slim.

When the Walbridge sisters first arrived in San Francisco, Clara worked alongside Chastina in the house. This arrangement proved unsatisfactory to Chastina, who was particular about how the work was done. Clara, six years younger, simply did not meet Chastina's high standards and was not committed to the domestic business that Chastina was running out of the house. Finally, near the end of July, Chastina announced that she would criticize no more and that Clara "may rise when you please & do as pleases you."

---

[8] Alfred, San Francisco, to John S. and Sarah Walbridge Way, Hardwick, January 15,1854. *LeCount & Strong's San Francisco City Directory for the Year 1854* [hereafter cited as *San Francisco Directory 1854*] places Alfred's office at the corner of Bush and Montgomery.

CLARA WALBRIDGE,
SAN FRANCISCO, 1854
Ambrotype taken in San Francisco of Chastina's sister Clara Walbridge, dressed for the Pickwick Assembly. She wears her hair in ringlets, a popular hairstyle for young women from the 1840s to at least the mid-1850s. Her evening dress, denoted by the exposed shoulders and short sleeves, appears to have a velvet bodice, trimmed with black lace, with tiered ruffles on her skirt. She wears elegant jewelry—gold necklace, drop earrings, and bracelets fashionably worn on both wrists. *Private collection.*

Fortunately, about this time, Alfred decided to leave teaching and devote full time to law. He recommended Clara for his replacement as teacher at the Mission, and she was appointed. When school started in the fall of 1853, Clara commuted by "omnibus" or "stage"—both modes of transportation are noted—from the Rix home, where she paid $8 a week for board, the same as the non-family boarders.[9] In the rainy season she lived out at the Mission, but once the new plank road was completed along Market Street, she returned to the comfort of the house on Geary and commuted daily.

One of the special social events that both Chastina and Clara enjoyed was the Pickwick Assemblies, dances that were open to the public. The sisters made new dresses and learned to dance, and in general they had a splendid time at these events. There were also parties at the Mission with music and dancing, hosted by their Spanish friends.[10] Like Alfred, Clara

---

[9] In 1850 a plank road from Kearny Street to Mission Dolores was built, and on June 1, 1851, an omnibus line was started. It ran on city streets with stops for boarding and offloading. Trimble and Echeverria, "San Francisco's Omnibuses," 37–38. The public school at the Mission was located on the north side of the street, east of the Catholic chapel. *San Francisco Directory for the Year 1852–53.*

[10] San Francisco enjoyed a reputation for all-night public balls, an indication of the increased social life in the city. Lotchin, *San Francisco,* 286–87; Berglund, *Making (continued, next page)*

DUSTAN WALBRIDGE AND IRA RIX, SAN FRANCISCO, CA. 1854
Ambrotype of two failed miners who roomed together at the Rix home while they tried their luck in San Francisco. Chastina's brother Dustan Walbridge, on the left, with fashionable bushy sideburns and his watch chain peeking out of his vest, worked at his trade as a wheelwright. Alfred's brother Ira Rix, on the right, with a "trencher" beard, worked at a sawmill. Both men wear turn-down collars with cravats with large bows and horizontal ends, popular at the time. *Private collection.*

took Spanish lessons, but no mention was made in the journal or in letters home of the success that either of them achieved. As she had been in Vermont, Clara was well loved by her pupils and regularly received gifts of flowers from them. She earned a salary of $100 a month, a third of what male teachers in San Francisco were paid.

The Rixes reported in their journal on family members. Alfred's brothers Oscar, Hale, Austin, and Ira came in and out of their lives. None struck it rich in the mines, and all had a hard time finding and keeping work in San Francisco as newly arriving tradesmen undercut their wages. Sidney Rix, a cousin of Alfred's and a former student at the Peacham Academy, had come with Alfred to California. Unfortunately, he contracted typhoid fever in the gold country; Alfred and Chastina rushed to his sickbed, and after his death they settled his debts. Chastina's brother Dustan also had no luck in the mines, trying off and on for more than a year to get his "pile." Two months after arriving, Chastina wrote home to her parents:

San Francisco American, 58. The Anglo Rixes' close relationship to the Spanish-speaking residents near Mission Dolores was unusual. There are few other known social relationships between the two communities. Robert W. Cherny, co-author of *San Francisco, 1865–1932: Politics, Power, and Urban Development*, conversation with editor, spring 2008.

We were waiting this time to have Dustin come down as he wrote to us he should come the first of Apr. But he did not come . . . If he was here now he could go into a shop close by where we board, where they repair old waggons & make some new—no nice waggons, but milk waggons, some for two horses & some for one . . . the man who is in now will hire him when he needs help & he may have his own bench & make new work for himself the rest of the time.[11]

Dustan finally took up permanent residence in San Francisco and found work at his previous trade as a wheelwright, earning $4.50 a day. Like his sister Clara, he paid $8 a week to board with the Rixes.

In the early 1850s, San Francisco was as exciting as Peacham had been quiet and routine. Clara and her suitors often went to the theater, and even Chastina and Alfred saw *Hamlet* at the Metropolitan. Alfred attended meetings on the proposed cross-country railroad, and he recorded in the journal the first telegraph service from San Francisco to San Jose. They went to an agricultural fair and described vegetables "large as a mans leg." Only apples were "inferior to the fruit in any part of the atlantic states. they sell here at 25 cts pr pound."[12] Alfred paid $50 a month for his law office and seems to have done well. He did not record any information about his cases in the journal as he had in Vermont, where Chastina knew most of the men involved personally. An indication of his financial success was his continued practice of loaning money, "either on stocks or real estate," which he claimed was "just as safe as in a Bank's vault."[13] Both he and Chastina had a keen business sense. She was particularly enterprising; she captured the order from a local church to cover eighteen dozen buttons on pew pillows and fretted when her boarder count did not reach eight.[14]

Their Vermont pattern of attending Sunday meeting did not continue in California. Chastina wrote that one had to be rich to go to church, for the congregation was full of women in expensive, fashionable clothes. She missed church but was put off by the snobbery of the wealthy churchgoers. She and Alfred tried to practice the day of rest on Sundays and noted regretfully in their journal the fun they missed by not breaking the Sabbath. They picked up their old habit of reading aloud in the evening. Dickens's *Bleak House* amused them for weeks.

Their life in San Francisco took on a regular pattern, in their traditional

---

[11]Chastina, San Francisco, to "Dear Friends," Peacham, April 20, 1853, private collection.
[12]Dustan S. Walbridge, San Francisco, to Lyman S. Watts, Peacham, September 13, 1853, private collection.
[13]Alfred, San Francisco, to "Dear Friends," Peacham, May 10, 1853, Edward A. Rix Collection.
[14]Chastina, San Francisco, to John S. and Sarah Walbridge Way, Hardwick, June 26, 1853, private collection. "It will not be much more work to take care of eight boarders than it is four."

roles of husband working in the office and wife working in the home. In early 1854, Chastina wrote in the journal that "each member of the family has his or her labor to perform." They were again in harmony with each other, settled comfortably in their roles. The journal entries became shorter, and often consisted only of the simple phrase "the same" or "the same round as usual." Chastina complained that she had little new to write about because she was at home all day working, and Alfred complained that he was tired of writing because that was what he did all day at his desk in the law office. Days were missed, and then weeks; finally, Chastina wrote the last entry in the journal on April 23, 1854.

[*ASR*] [Thursday, May 12, 1853] Clear weather and rain over. Chastina is feeling some better of late, though far from being completely well. We have got a very pleasant situation and all of us seem to be very well contented. This week is vacation and I am about out of business. Dr [N. P.] Taplin, Mr Murray & Mr [Wm] Muir are now boarding with us.[15] Went down town and saw Hale [Rix] & Austin [Rix] sitting on the wharf in a dead quandary as to the future. Took Hale aside and talked to him like a father—left him to call on us & let us know what he had concluded upon. Austin is out of business & out of money. Our folks wash & bake beef. Pretty smart folks.

[Friday, May 13] Walked to the Mission with Hale [Rix] and Austin [Rix] to see about renting Lockwood's ranch, cows &c.[16] Called at Lockes with Chastina & on Mrs. [Elizabeth] Varney.[17] Chastina is a good deal better.

---

[15] Beginning May 1, 1853, the Rixes rented rooms on Geary Street, three doors above Kearny Street. Chastina took in boarders, including Dr. N. P. Taplin, whom the Rixes knew from Peacham, where he had opened his practice as a "Botanic Physician" at Peacham Hollow in October 1848. He left for California in January 1850. *Caledonian*, October 7, 1848, and January 19, 1850. "Wm. Muir" was listed as a carriage maker at the corner of Kearny and Post streets in the *San Francisco Directory 1854*. For information on taking in borders in San Francisco, see Eliassen, "Our Intangible Home," 34; Sparks, *Capital Intentions*, 121–22.

[16] Alfred's brothers Hale and Austin were not listed in the city directory. Mr. Lockwood, on whose property near Mission Dolores Alfred lived and where the whole family lived before moving to Geary Street, was listed in the *San Francisco Directory 1854* as "Lockwood & Lewis, Never Sweat Ranch, 22 Clay."

[17] Silas Merrill Locke (1826–1903) sailed for California in 1849, where he met David Merrill Locke (b. 1824) and a few months later Josiah Hannibal Locke (1831–1904), all brothers to Alice P. Locke. Eysenbach, "Staying Behind," 97–98. Elizabeth Varney lived in town and boarded for a short time at the Rassette House with her husband and son. Chastina, San Francisco, to Roxana Walbridge Watts, Peacham, February 27, 1853, Edward A. Rix Collection.

ASR [Saturday, May 14] Carried water—[18] Saw [Chester] Brown— Call from Silas Locke, Alice [Locke] & Mr Webster.[19]

[Sunday, May 15] Dustan [Walbridge] with us—[20] All at home.

[Monday, May 16] Alf began school again—& to hear Ruffino Girls. Was pd 75$ by Syl [Courter].[21] Primary Election. Was pd bill by [T.J.] Nevins.[22] [Chester] Brown Began boarding. Girls begin to assume the Responsibility in Boardinghouse.

[Tuesday, May 17] Girls did their first washing for others— Besides other work they did some 5 dollars worth of washing. All else as usual. Hale [Rix] rejects our milk offer. Looked up more furniture— bought Damask.

[Wednesday, May 18] Very warm. Dustan [Walbridge] came in out of work. All as usual. Chastina went over town with me to look up furniture.

[Thursday, May 19] All as usual. Bought & moved home more furniture & fixins.

[Friday, May 20] Rode home with [Alonzo] Farr.[23] Austin [Rix] begs a little money 2½$.

[Saturday, May 21] Got a place for Dustan [Walbridge]. Painted floor & put up curtains &c Call from Locke as to Hale [Rix] & Alice [Locke]. Called on Hale. Call in Evening from [W.H.] O'Grady.[24]

---

[18]Alfred carried water either from artisan wells located east of Montgomery Street or from wagons on the street that brought water from Sausalito. Lotchin, *San Francisco*, 181–82. When he carried water, Chastina wrote in a letter to her mother that he had to "go some distance and up a steep sand bank"; otherwise they had to buy water at "one dollar per cask, which holds about two common barrels." Chastina, San Francisco, to "Dear Friends," Peacham, May 10, 1853.

[19]Chester Brown came to California from Peacham with Alfred. This is the first indication that Alice Locke had arrived in California from New Hampshire.

[20]In May, when Dustan Walbridge came to San Francisco from the mines, he stayed with the Rixes. Chastina wrote, "Dustin looks healthy and precisely as he used to. He says he has 'tried as hard as he could to raise some whiskers, but he ca'nt raise one.'" Chastina to "Dear Friends," Peacham, May 10, 1853.

[21]Alfred was teaching English to the Ruffino girls "at the Mission," where he taught at the public school. Sylvester Courter was the proprietor of the National Hall at Mission Dolores. *San Francisco Directory for the Year 1852–53*. "Syl" must have borrowed money from Alfred.

[22]Thomas J. Nevins (1875–1861), born in Hanover, N.H., the San Francisco agent of the American Tract Society, was appointed the first superintendent of common schools in 1850 to organize the education system. Lotchin, *San Francisco*, 312; *San Francisco Directory for the Year 1852–53*; *Alta California*, January 19, 1862.

[23]Alonzo Farr was with the firm of Smith & Farr, Centre Street, Mission Dolores. *San Francisco Directory 1854*.

[Sunday, May 22] Letters from John [S. Way], Sarah [Walbridge Way], Mother Watts & James M. Dickson of Hanover.[25] Flies are eating me up. ASR

[Monday, May 23] At school as usual.

[Tuesday, May 24] Paid Elaria Sanchez 30$ for rent.[26] Recd 20 of Syl [Courter] as interest on Note paid.

[Wednesday, May 25] All as usual. Dustan [Walbridge] out of work. Bought a cord of wood. Clara [Walbridge] & Morris Went to Teatre.

[Thursday, May 26] Forgot what happened.

[Friday, May 27] Chastina & I went to the Teacher's Monthly Convention. [W. H.] O'Grady delivered his Essay.

[Saturday, May 28] Call from Mrs. Lockwood and girls. Dustan [Walbridge] into business again.[27]

[Sunday, May 29] Nothing unusual.

[Monday, May 30] Went to P[ost] M[aster] to see about getting up a penny post. Dr. [N. P.] T[aplin] pd 16.00! Syl [Courter] &c mad because we dont attend their balls. Tina sick a-bed.

[Tuesday, May 31] Fine day. Tina sick yet.

[Wednesday, June 1] Chastina very sick—called in Mrs. Henley & Mrs. Plummer & Dr [Samuel] George.[28] Clara [Walbridge] does the work alone. Trying to start a Penny Post. Last night hard fire corner of Kearny & California Sts. Evening Call from Mr Perkins & Mr [James] Denman.[29]

---

[24] William Henry O'Grady (1823–58), born in Middlebury, was a former classmate of Alfred's at the University of Vermont. He went to California in 1849 and later succeeded T. J. Nevins as superintendent of public schools in San Francisco, serving from 1854 to 1856. Ibid.; *Alta California*, January 19, 1862.

[25] James M. Dickson (1831–1913), after attending the Peacham Academy, graduated from Dartmouth and the Union Theological Seminary.

[26] It is unclear what this payment was for. Perhaps Alfred was paying half a month's rent for the house on Geary. Elaria Sanchez does not appear in the city directory. She may have been collecting for the owners.

[27] Dustan Walbridge was listed as "carriage maker, Kearny, near Post." *San Francisco Directory 1854*.

[28] Mrs. Henley and Mrs. Plummer were neighbors of the Rixes. Dr. Samuel G. George was listed at "corner Dolores and Centre, Mission Dolores." Ibid. George W. and Margaret Blen Plummer had a son, George E., who was born in 1850, just the right age to play with Julian. Anne T. Protopopoff, Oakland, Calif., July 8, 1997.

[29] James Denman (1829–1909), born in New York, came to San Francisco in September 1851, and was listed in 1854 as "teacher, boards at 160 Mission." He was the *(continued, next page)*

ASR [Thursday, June 2] Chastina some better, though still quite ill. Fine morning. Sent Dr. [Samuel] George to C[hastina]. Call from Oscar [Rix].[30]

[Friday, June 3] Chastina no better— Took bread & milk with Mrs. Lockwood. Call from Sidney M. Marsh on his way to O[regon] T[erritory]. Morris & [Wm] Muir had a blow up. In the Evening we were pleasantly surprised with an "No it roba!" All passed off pleasantly. The following was the text on the occasion of the late lamented "hijo de sus padres!" "No man knoweth the day nor the hour when the son of man cometh.["]

[Saturday, June 4] At home.

[Sunday, June 5] Nothing new.

[Monday, June 6] Call from [W.H.] O'Grady & Sidney H. Marsh.[31]

[Tuesday, June 7] OO

[Wednesday, June 8] Lo Mismo. Called on [Thomas J.] Henley —P.M.[32]

[Thursday, June 9] Duel between Bowie [Bovee?] & Green prevented.[33] Windy as ever.

[Friday, June 10] Hays & Nugent fought with rifles & latter shot in the arm.

[Saturday, June 11] Went round a little on Penny Post affairs. Chastina sewed some five dollars worth.

[Sunday, June 12] Clara [Walbridge] & Dust [Walbridge] wrote to Peacham. Chastina & I took a walk to Cal[ifornia] St[reet] Wharf & Long Wharf Saw fine Clippers & Gambling Dens & men fighting.

---

principal of the first San Francisco public school and later served as superintendent of common schools. Upon his retirement, the school where he had first taught was named for him, and it continues to carry his name into the twenty-first century. Several sources credit Denman and John C. Pelton with founding the San Francisco public school system. *San Francisco Directory 1854*; Phelps, *Contemporary Biography*, 412–16; Schellens Papers, no. 389; Bancroft, *Chronicles*, 8:299–300; Lotchin, *San Francisco*, 312.

[30]Alfred's brother Oscar was listed as "carpenter, Washington Mills" in *San Francisco Directory 1854*.

[31]Sidney H. Marsh, identified above as Sidney M. Marsh, was not listed in the city directories.

[32]Alfred needed the cooperation of the postmaster, Thomas J. Henley, for the penny post delivery he planned to start. *San Francisco Directory 1854*.

[33]Changes were taking place in San Francisco by the mid-1850s, but before then, dueling happened frequently. Lotchin, *San Francisco*, 294.

[Monday, June 13] Girls Sewing. Duel—Capt Patterson & another. ASR

[Tuesday, June 14] Chastina tried to wash with Excelsior Soap and dirtied her clothes most horribly.[34] Clara [Walbridge] rides out with Mr Morris & has'nt got home yet. Finished our Pig-Pen.

[Wednesday, June 15] Excessively Warm.

[Thursday, June 16] Warm again. Lost a place for Dustan [Walbridge].

[Friday, June 17] Not so warm— This Journal shows of late that the records are all made a day after the [af]fair.

[Saturday, June 18] Did an inordinate amount of Running about. Visit from Ruffinos folks.[35] Called on P.M. Austin [Rix] came to us sick and hungry and we took him not in. Clara [Walbridge] & girls called with me at Tobin's and Duncan's. Dr [N. P.] Taplin comes back.

[Sunday, June 19] Nothing worth noting up to 12 o'clock [P]M

[Monday, June 20] Morris & [Wm] Muir had a bloody fight—& Muir Left.

[Tuesday, June 21] Girls Washed &c

[Wednesday, June 22] Mr Taplin Senior called for counsel— Made an appointment to see [Enoch] Smith.

[Thursday, June 23] Saw the P[ost] O[ffice] Clerk Mr [John] Ferguson. Saw [Enoch] Smith the new Lawyer.

[Friday, June 24] Saw P[ost] M[aster] Again. Saw [Enoch] Smith again. Case from Taplin.

[Saturday, June 25] Formed Partnership with Enoch W. Smith for the Practice of the Law—name of firm—Smith & Rix.[36] Run about for Calder, Taplin &c &c.

[Sunday, June 26] All as usual. Wrote to Weltha [Cory] at Pierceville, Wis.

---

[34]Chastina complained about the hard water in San Francisco and wrote: "Give one a plenty of soft water & soap such as we have in Vermont." She tried to buy soap "for using in hard water." Chastina, San Francisco, to John S. and Sarah Walbridge Way, June 26, 1853.

[35]The Rixes' friends Francesco and Petrona Ruffino had three daughters at the time, all under the age of seven. The elder Ruffinos are both buried in the Mission Dolores Cemetery, #156, section #7. Translated from the Italian, the inscription on their gravestone reads: "Francesco Ruffino 1809–74 adored husband of Petrona Ruffino 1816–79." I thank historian Robert M. Senkewicz for the translation. They were not listed in the city directory, but they do appear in the early census records; in the 1860 census their name is misspelled as "Raphena."

[36]Alfred's new law partner, Enoch W. Smith, came from Baltimore. Chastina, San Francisco, to John S. and Sarah Walbridge Way, June 26, 1853.

ASR

The Miner's Progress—

A Pilgrim from the Eastern Shore[37]
  Stood on Nevada's strand;
A tear was in his hither eye
  A Pickaxe in his hand.
A Tear was in his hither eye
  And in his left, to match,
There would have been another tear
  But for a healing patch.

(The above is one of the few California literary Novelties which I <u>appreciate</u> on the first leaf of the same—others follow. It is from Sacramento and altogether worthy of the times and the locality. More follows.)

The Pilgrim Deploreth his habits.

And other patches, too, he wore,
  About his garments hung,
And two were on that ill-starred spot
  Where mothers smite their young
His hat a shining "Ca star" once
  Was broken; now & dim,
And wild his bearded features gleamed
  Beneath the tattered rim.

The Pilgrim deserteth his friends—

The Pilgrim Stood; and, looking down,
  As one who is in doubt,
He sighed to see how fast <u>that</u> pair
  Of Boots was wearing out.
And while he filled an ancient pipe
  His wretchedness to cheer
He stopped, with hurried hand, to pick
  A flea from out his ear.

---

[37]Alfred drew "The Miner's Progress" in the journal, a take-off on the drawings and text/poetry of *The Miner's Progress; or, Scenes in the Life of a California Miner. Being a* (*continued, next page*)

The Pilgrim Drowneth his sorrow.

Then spoke this Pilgrim from the East,
   "I am a wretched man,
For lust of gold hath lured me to
   The shovel and the pan.
I saw, in dreams, a pile of gold
   Its dazzling radiance pour:
No more my visions are of gold,
   Alas! My hopes are <u>ore</u>!["]

The Pilgrim thinketh of his latter end.

"Thrice have I left this cursed spot,
   But mine it was to learn,
The fatal truth, that "dust we are—
   To dust we shall return."
So, here condemned, by Fates unkind,
   I rock illusive sand,
And dream of wailing babes at home
   Unrocked—an orphan band."

The Pilgrim seeketh for Rocks.

The Pilgrim paused, for now he heard
   His distant comrades shout,
He drew a last whiff from his pipe,
   Then knocked the ashes out.
And stooping as he gathered up
   His shovel and his pan,
The breeze his latest accents bore
   "I am a ruined man."

Series of Humorous Illustrations of the "Ups and Downs" of a Gold Digger in Pursuit of His "Pile" (1853), with verse written by Alonzo Delano (1806–74) and illustrations by Charles Nahl (1828–78), based on William Hogarth's *Rake's Progress* (1735). Hogarth (1697–1764), a leading British illustrator and satirist of the times, was often imitated in the U.S., as seen here in Alfred's rendition, one of many based on the popular Hogarth's works. See Kurutz, *California Gold Rush Bibliography*, item 179.

ASR *The Pilgrim's Stomach Yearneth for "Grub."*

> Once more returned, at close of day
>   To a cheerless, dismal home,
> He vows, if he was back in Maine
>   He never more would roam.
> Now hunger makes "his bowels yearn,"
>   For yams or "Irish roots"
> But these he tries in vain to find
>   Then tries to fry his boots.

The Pilgrim Dreameth of Home.

> The night is passed in happy dreams
>   Of youth & childhood's joys:
> Of times when he got flogged at school
>   For pinching smaller boys.
> His wife, whose smiles hath cheered him oft,
>   And rendered light his care,
> He sees in far New England's clime,
>   Enjoying better fare.

The Pilgrim Rejoiceth over his "Pile!"

> But morn dispels these fairy scenes,
>   And want arouses pluck;
> He shoulders pick & pan once more,
>   Again to try his luck.
> He digs in dark, secluded depths,
>   The spots where slugs abound.
> And oh, what rapture fills his breast—
>   His pile at last is found.

The Pilgrim Vamoseth the Diggings.

He drops his pick, his pan is left,
   He e'en neglects his pipe,
He leaves the diggings & his purse
   He holds with Iron gripe.
Resolved to dig & toil no more,
   Nor more in dreams to trust
His well filled bag upon his back
   Of pure & shining dust.

The Pilgrim in the Bosom of his Family —

His wardrobe changed, behold him now,
   In affluence & pride,
Surrounded by the forms he loves,
   With joy on every side.
Pressed closely to his heart he holds
   His wife & children dear,
The latter shouting madly, while
   The former drops a tear.

[Monday, June 27] Nothing of importance.

[Tuesday, June 28] The Girls washed as usual. Mr. Burkee begins to board.

[Wednesday, June 29] Syl [Courter] paid us $100.00

[Thursday, June 30] All as usual.

[Friday, July 1] Made writings for Mrs. Valencia. Got a Water Yoke.

[Saturday, July 2] Chastina's old female Acquaintance made her appearance for the first time in this country.[38] Attended Recorders court— Saw Smith[,] Lockwood &c. Letters from John [S. Way], Margaret B. Bierstadt, Mary A. B. Rix.

---

[38] Chastina's menstruation indicated that she was not pregnant.

ASR [Sunday, July 3] All at home all day— Call from Russ Rogers.[39]

[Monday, July 4] Of course this is celebration day. We all turned out & saw what we could—Saw the Military and a big fire and eat a horrible big dinner— Witnessed the fireworks in the Evening. Clara [Walbridge] & Morris went to the Theatre. [CWR] Russel Rodgers called here

[ASR] [Tuesday, July 5] At school as usual— Call from Ira [Rix] & Mrs Pierce & [Russell] Rodgers

[CWR] [Wednesday, July 6] Washing and baking. Had a call from Mark Blanchard. in the evening Mr. [John] Co[u]rter & his brother were here.[40] The brother played the accordeon & <u>we</u> danced!

[Thursday, July 7] Clara went to ride with Mr Courter in the forenoon Clara came home about two o'clock. After that we did our ironing. Mark Blanchard called again. Ira [Rix] here also.

[Friday, July 8] Sewing and doing our work. Russel Rodgers called on us in the afternoon. In the evening Mr. [David] Locke & Alice [Locke] & Miss [Mary Jane] Jamison made us a short visit. We made up a fire in the kitchen & had a real sociable time.[41]

[Saturday, July 9] We had an invitation by father [T. J.] Nivens, or by some of his friends to take a trip over the bay to the new town of Alameda. So we dressed ourselves & got down to California Street Wharf, where we found all the teachers father Nevins & lots of people waiting for the boat. We were to go at ten. We waited till nearly noon, when <u>we teachers</u> adjourned to Wins & got some oysters ice cream & strawberr[ies.][42] We went into Tobins & Duncans & saw some of the articles in the great raffle, among the rest the in got of

---

[39]Russell Rogers (1827–86), a Vermont native, stopped at the Rixes' six times in July. Before going to California in 1852, he had clerked in Isaac Watts's store in Peacham Hollow, where the Walbridge sisters were well acquainted with him. Chastina often spelled his name "Rodgers."

[40]Sylvester's brother John P. Courter, a carpenter, lived "at the National Hall, Mission Dolores." *San Francisco Directory 1854.*

[41]A fire in the kitchen would have been welcomed because the weather in San Francisco during the summer months is foggy, damp, and cool much of the time as the high temperatures from the inland meet the cool air from the Pacific Ocean.

[42]Winn's was a confectionery and ice cream saloon at the corner of Montgomery and Washington streets; the proprietor was M. L. Winn. *San Francisco Directory 1854.*

Gold, looked in form like a bar of soap. I could make out to lift it with one hand—so thus ended our excursion over the bay.

[Sunday, July 10] A beautiful day. We none of us go to church now days. I hope we shall one of these days— I have to day tried to write a description of my journey here to California. I have succeeded but poorly— Alfred writes to Father Rix & [Edward] Bierstadts folks.

[Monday, July 11] Sewing, making shirts at $3.00 apiece. Mr. [Enoch] Smith—Alfred's partner in law—called in the evening

[Tuesday, July 12] Washing & baking. Russel Rodgers called in the afternoon. In the evening we had visits from the public school teachers—namely—[W. H.] O'Grady, [James] Denman, Cole, Holmes, first & second, two brothers, Tracy, Miss [Helen] Allen, Miss [Anna] Sanford, Miss [Marian] Bain, Miss [Harriet] Hancke, & Mr. [T. J.] Nevins the superintendent of the schools.[43] We had a very pleasant visit indeed. They are very pleasant gentlemen and ladies.

[Wednesday, July 13] A Mr Wilson came here to board— We do not have boarders enough to make anything. I get most discouraged about our boarding business. We are sewing what time we can get. We work early & late but do not accomplish much. A Mr Collins called in the evening.

[Thursday, July 14] Ironing— Bub not very well. He is a great boy; he talks everything, and is full of his fun.

[*ASR*] [Friday, July 15] Wrote to Mary Ann [Rix]—to the little girls [Alice and Ella Watts]—to Father Rix—& to [Edward] Bierstadt.

[Saturday, July 16] Engaged Mr. [Thomas] Tennent at 20$ to make wheel— got a bookcase for [Enoch] Smith— & other articles and visited Papy & Reynolds—[44] Call from Smith in the evening.

---

[43] Helen M. Allyne was a teacher at District No. 4, at the corner of Broadway and Montgomery streets; Anna E. Sanford was a teacher at District No. 2, at Bush Street between Montgomery and Sansome streets; Marian Bain was a teacher at District No. 1, at Rincon Point; Harriet A. Hancke was a teacher at District 3, at Washington Street below Stockton Street. Ibid. The *San Francisco Directory* is confusing with regard to the teachers named Holmes: it lists Dr. Stillman Holmes as a teacher at District No. 1, at Rincon Point; Ahira Holmes at District No. 4, at the corner of Broadway and Montgomery streets; and Mrs. E. H. Holmes at District No. 3, at Washington Street. Female teachers were in the majority.

[44] Thomas Tennen was listed as "surveying and naval warehouse, 29 Commercial, cor. Front." J. J. Papy was listed as "Deputy United S. Marshall." Ibid.

ASR [Sunday, July 17] Nothing noteworthy up to 5 o'clock.

[*CWR*] [Monday, July 18] Morris left us this morning. Sewing. Got a letter from Aunt [Sarah] Stevens. She is now about 88 years of age. she sent us a lock of her hair, as it is now and here it is. [Chastina attached a long braided lock of hair with ribbon to the journal page.]

[Tuesday, July 19] Clara [Walbridge] has done the washing and I have done the work. Had a boiled dish for dinner, & baked bread as usual on washing day We are getting on about as usual. Three boarders besides our selves.

[Wednesday, July 20] Sewing doing the work & ironing seems to be the order of the day. Sidney Rix, a cousin of Alfred's came down from Sacramento to see us.

[Thursday, July 21] Went out to the Mission with Alfred. This is the first time since I came from there Found Mr Lockwoods people all well. Mrs. L made me a present of a dress, a lawn one.[45] Had a very good visit. Julian enjoyed himself highly with the chickens ducks & pigs.

[Friday, July 22] Clara [Walbridge] kept school for Alfred to day. I stayed & done the work, while Alfred attended his first case in California, a petty case, which he knew they would loose before they undertook it. William Hooker, Mark & Harvey Varnum called on us. Mark & Harvey are on their way home with their "piles."[46]

[Saturday, July 23] Alfred writing an essay to read at the teachers meeting. I am not very well. Had a job of covering buttons for church cushions, covered eighteen dozen. Alfreds old acquaintances Colins & Birch called in the evening.[47]

[Sunday, July 24] Pleasant day at home all day. Mark [Varnum] & Harvey [Varnum] & Russel Rodgers called here also Oscar [Rix]. Mark coming here to board while he stops in San Francisco.

---

[45]Lawn is a fine, sheer cotton fabric.

[46]William Hooker (b. 1831) and Harvey Varnum (b. 1826) left Peacham in October 1851 with Alfred. Hooker was a student listed in the 1849 and 1850 PAC; Mark Varnum is listed in the 1839, 1840, and 1841 PAC. Harvey Varnum is not listed as a student in the PAC.

[47]G. Collins and W. H. Birch were listed as machinists at the Vulcan Iron Works. *San Francisco Directory 1854*.

[Monday, July 25] Nothing of importance. We have very damp CWR chilly mornings now. almost like rain. Mark Varnum came here to board.

[Tuesday, July 26] We had a large washing to day, boiled victuals & baked bread. We have to work prety hard.

[Wednesday, July 27] I am not very well. Have a breaking out upon my face neck & arms. I do not know what it is. Cut out half a dozen Shirts. made a call on Mrs. [Theodore] Smith.

[Thursday, July 28] Very damp and foggy. Of course such a morning will not call out ones cheerful spirits especially in California. Therefore, I have had the dumps. Clara [Walbridge] tells me she does not take any comfort living with me, I find so much fault with her. If I am all wrong I am sorry for it. I own that I have talked pretty plain, but I have said to her this morning "here is an end to these things. You may rise when you please & do as pleases you. I will say no more." It is a shame for me to record any such misunderstanding, and only those acquainted would in any degree pardon us for thus disagreeing; and I only record this here to help me keep my vow that I have made.[48]

[ASR] [Friday, July 29] Finished the Summer term of my school and looked still further after the Post Office affair. Accompanied by Clara [Walbridge] to Teacher's Monthly Convention. Read an essay on Our Public School System. It was well recd & voted to be printed.

[Saturday, July 30] Harvey Varnum unwell. Chastina & Clara [Walbridge] went out shopping for Presents to send home by the Varnums. Clara applies for a school.

[Sunday, July 31] All the family rode out to Mission & round the city in one of the nice carriages on the invitation of Mr Morris. Morris & Willey at tea with us.

[Monday, August 1] Vacation in our schools. Trying to effect an arrangement as to Post office. Girls sewing on Morris' shirts. Mark

---

[48]Sisters Chastina and Clara, six years apart, were in different phases of life: Chastina married and a mother, Clara single and busy with a social life, probably not helping around the house as much as Chastina thought she should.

ASR & Harvey Varnum obliged to delay their departure for home on account of Harvey's illness.

[Tuesday, August 2] Girls Washing & Mrs. [Elizabeth] Varney called & spent the day. Evening Call from Messers Nye & Smith & Morris.

[Wednesday, August 3] Went into our Post Office arrangement.[49] Got a few subscribers. Girls as usual.

[Thursday, August 4] Alf continued looking for Subs[cribers for Penny Post]. Girls Ironing.

[Friday, August 5] More Ironing— The Girls have this week done a good week's work. Clara [Walbridge] has done the house work an[d] cooking & Chastina has baked, sewed & washed—made 1 shirt, washed 18 & other things accordingly & took care of the family—thus earning a little extra bill of $15 dollars.

[Saturday, August 6] Alf. carried his first mail through the city— Good luck. Met Dr. [N.P.] Taplin & cursed him at his face & dried him up.[50] Got an engagement for Clara [Walbridge] at the Mission.

[Sunday, August 7] All at home. Cold day. All of us a little unwell.

[Monday, August 8] Clara [Walbridge] went to the Mission as teacher in my old place—Good luck. Alf. looking up subscribers.

[Tuesday, August 9] Chastina washed out her clothes last night and finished up to day & baked & took entire care of the family & Sewed some. The rest as usual. A day or two ago Dr [N.P.] Taplin blew me up and I blew him down.

[*CWR*] [Wednesday, August 10] Sewing on a shirt bosom for Mrs. Henly. Heard that Ira [Rix] is sick over to San Jose.

---

[49]Alfred's may have been the first penny post in San Francisco, a system whereby mail was delivered personally so that individuals did not have to stand in line at the post office. Letters were enclosed in a prepaid envelope and transmitted by messenger. By 1855, the Penny Post Company was a booming business among interior California towns, with the envelope costing five cents. Schellens Papers, no. 582, newspaper clipping from the *Daily Placer Times and Transcript*, June 29, 1865.

[50]Dr. N. P. Tapin left the Rixes' before paying for four weeks' board. Chastina to John S. and Sarah Walbridge Way, June 26, 1853.

[Thursday, August 11] Did my ironing—Began a Shirt for Morris. Alfred in his Penny post business. Call from Jarvis Jewette.[51]

[Friday, August 12] Nothing of importance. <u>Had company</u>[52]

[Saturday, August 13] Baking & sewing—finished the shirt we began— Morris & Mr Smith here in the evening.

[Sunday, August 14] Took a walk on telegraph hill. We have a grand view of the bay & city from its top. From here they give the signal of a ships arrival as it comes through the "golden Gate["]— Wrote letters home & fixed up the little bundle to send home.

[Monday, August 15] Ira [Rix] came this morning before breakfast; he looks pretty slim. has had rather a hard run of fever. Clara [Walbridge] gone to her school again this morning. I am trudging about the house as usual. Bub unwell this morning.

[Tuesday, August 16] Mark and Harvey Varnum started for home. Sailed on board the Steamer Sierra Nevada.[53] I wanted to go and see them start off but was washing and could not. I have done a large washing and baked bread and pies. Have to keep pretty busy with six in the family, & sewing &c.

[Wednesday, August 17] Alfred at his Penny post business. Clara [Walbridge] teaching & I doing house work and sewing. We are at work on the eighth shirt for Morris.

[Thursday, August 18] Had letters from home, our people all as well as usual. Ironing. I have done about seven dollars worth of washing this week.

[Friday, August 19] Went to Mr [Robert] Varneys visiting. They live now up on a high hill, and have a beautiful view of the bay. Met Mr & Mrs. Howland there. Mr H is the first officer of the steamer Golden Gate. Had a very good visit. I go out but very little & it is pleasing to me whenever I do go.

CWR

---

[51] Jarvis Jewett left Ryegate for California in the early 1850s, settled in San Francisco, and married there. Miller and Wells, *History of Ryegate*, 285.

[52] Chastina's menstruation indicated that she was not pregnant.

[53] The Varnum brothers left San Francisco on the Steamer *Sierra Nevada*, owned by the Nicaragua Steamship Company at Sacramento and Leidesdorff streets. One of the company's four steamers left on the 1st and 16th of every month for San Juan del Sud. *San Francisco Directory 1854*.

CWR [Saturday, August 20] Clara [Walbridge] at home, baking and sewing— Sewed very hard all day to oblige a <u>lady</u> who wanted to go visiting, and when it was carried home she "was very much obliged" for making her dress. My back will not be bent again for a "much obliged" from <u>such a lady</u>— Had a treat from a big water melon.

[Sunday, August 21] Sunday passes always the same doing our work reading writing in Journal—talking over home affairs &c. Alfred's friend [H. P.] Carlton came here last evening.[54]

[Monday, August 22] Mr [H. P.] Carlton came here to board. Sewing what time I can get Two gentlemen from the Mission called and told Alfred they were going to nominate him for Justice of the Peace in the Eight ward— Washed out my clothes in the evening— Mr. [W. H.] O'Grady called.

[Tuesday, August 23] Washed and baked and brewed and every thing else to day. tired enough. Nothing of account happened.

[Wednesday, August 24] Have done my work and a large ironing— Ira [Rix] is washing some here.

[Thursday, August 25] Ironing fine shirts all day. Alfred went to the Mission

[Friday, August 26] Ironing again— In all this week I have ironed sixty shirts. 35 starched one[s] & 25 plain besides hosts of other clothes & I have made twelve dollars by my labor. Went to a temperance discussion this evening, at Mr [M. C.] Briggs church. They are discussing the Maine law here.[55] this requires considerable courage with their hundreds of rum selling places open in their faces. The rum seller was on the ground to defennd his side

[Saturday, August 27] Baking &c. Calls from Mr. Smith and Morris.

[Sunday, August 28] At home as usual— Wrote letters home— I

---

[54]Henry P. Carlton (1821–1909) was a teacher at District No. 5, North Beach. Ibid.

[55]The Methodist Episcopal church was located on Powell Street, near Washington; Rev. M. C. (Martin Clark) Briggs (1830–1902) was the pastor. Ibid. The Maine Law, passed in June 1851, prohibited the sale of alcoholic beverages. The term "Maine Law" came to designate prohibition laws passed throughout the northern and western states during the 1850s. It ranked with the Fugitive Slave Act of 1850 as one of the most controversial political issues of that decade and helping in the rise of the Republican Party. Feintuch and Watters, *Encyclopedia of New England*, 929.

do not like to stay at home from meeting so much. But it costs so much, that poor folks can hardly afford to go.

[Monday, August 29] Sewing for Mrs Haskal a lady who is going home. Nothing particular hapened.

[Tuesday, August 30] Washing Washed all day very tired. Alfred practicing law & attending to his post office.

[Wednesday, August 31] Alfred is the nominee for justice of the peace in the eighth ward—

Clara [Walbridge] has got her appointment from the "board of Education," to the Mission school—at $100. per month.[56]

[Thursday, September 1] Ironing. I have to work pretty hard have seven in the family most of the time. I hope I shall not always have to work so hard.

[Friday, September 2] Sewing on Morris Shirts— Mr Smith here in the evening. Alfred lawing it considerable now days.

[Saturday, September 3] Baking— Had a boiled dish for dinner— I know but very little that is going on here. Stay at home very close. Alfred attended a great rail road meeting Heard a splendid Speech on the subject of the great Pacific rail way. People are getting pretty much waked up on the subject.

[Sunday, September 4] Very pleasant day. at home as usual— Jim Dorland & Russel Rodgers called here We have just heard the report of a cannon. The Mail Steamer I suppose is in. Hope we shall have news from home

[Monday, September 5] I declare, the old song says "every day brings something new," but it does not exactly apply in my case & in my family. It has been extremely warm to day for San Francisco. People are out with summer clothing on, a thing which I have hardly seen all this summer Have sewed as usual— Callers in the evening— Alfred attending his law.

---

[56]The certificate for teachers of the free common schools in San Francisco, dated August 8, 1853, was signed by T. J. Nevins, John Wilson, and R. H. Waller. I thank Janice Rix Manjoras, Clara's great-granddaughter, for providing me with a copy of it. Nevins and Royal Hiram Waller (b. 1802 in Royalton) were New Englanders, probably aware of the good reputation of the Peacham Academy. John Wilson may have been an attorney in the Montgomery Block. *San Francisco Directory 1854*.

CWR [Tuesday, September 6] Washing—have done my own & enough for other folks to amount to seven dollars. Hard work this—but in this "land of gold" you must work or starve. I choose the former. The Democrats held a meeting at which Alfred & Mr [M. P.] O'Conner were the chief speakers—both being candidates for justice of peace.[57]

[Wednesday, September 7] Election day. Such an excitement such a running of horses I never saw & I doubt whether any other place than Cal[ifornia] could produce it. It is not known yet who are elected to fill the various places— Mr Smith, Oscar [Rix], Mr Morris, Mr. Perkins & Miss Fowler all called in the evening.

[Thursday, September 8] Ironing day with me. A letter from home Father & Mother [Watts']s health was quite poor when they wrote us. Aunt [Clarissa] Brown was hardly expected to be alive having had a third shock of the numb palsy— The rest of our folks were well as usual

[ASR] [Friday, September 9] Mail Arrived. No it did'nt—it was last Wednesday. Carrying as usual & Nothing more Chastina Sewing as hard as ever.

[Saturday, September 10] Attended to the trial of a case. Carried papers &c. In the Evening went with Chastina & Clara [Walbridge] to Mr [David] Locke's. Learned that he was married—to Miss Mary Jane Jamison. It was done on the sly a week ago—but we were bound

---

[57] M. P. O'Connor, an attorney, is listed in the *San Francisco Directory 1854* as "Justice of the Peace, Mission Dolores." He served in 1853 and lost to Alfred for the 1854 term. Alfred described nothing in the journal about the election, but his brother-in-law Dustan wrote to his same-age stepbrother: "It is the fashion here for every candidate for office to do his own electioneering and besides going around and verry modestly setting fourth their good qualities and capabilities for the particular office that they are seeking, and asking your vote, they are expected to stand <u>treat</u> for at least a weake before election—they also get out large <u>posters</u> and stick up to let the people know who is <u>the</u> man to vote for and now on any of the principle streets you look and as far as the eye can reach you can see these same <u>posters</u> entirely covering every place that they could possibly be stuck on." Dustan was quite a storyteller in his letters, but this one rings true and is confirmed in other sources, including Lotchin, *San Francisco*, 214–15. In addition, Dustan included in his letter some drawings of the posters on display. Dustan Walbridge, San Francisco, to Lyman S. Watts, unidentified place, September 13, 1853, private collection. The drawings and letter are reproduced in Bonfield and Morrison, *Roxana's Children*, 124–25.

to have a scrape out of it & so made Locke shell out a ten spot & we got up a fine show of Fruits & nuts & drinks & cakes—& had a good natured time & came home at 10½

[Sunday, September 11] Chastina unwell—oldoldoldold. Call from Dowling an Ass. Call from Ira [Rix]. Looking up Statutes a little.

[CWR] As we live in Cal[ifornia] this land of adventures we ought to relate occasionally some of the adventures & horrible deeds done in our own city— Let me speak of what happened two weeks ago to day. There was to be a balloon ascension at Contra Costa, but instead of the man who intended to go up, a lad—after the car was detached—got upon a board placed upon the hoop— The balloon became unmanageable & unfastened, & up, up, & away he went— He got away some sixty miles from San Francisco—he came in contact with a counter current of air, this collapsed the balloon, & he by some means let off some of the gas & he came safely down to earth, & arrived in San Francisco after an absence of about 48 hours. There was great joy at his return—much sympathy was felt for this young adventurer, & none thought he would ever return being wholly unacquainted with his aerial carriage. Some gentlemen of the press printed an account of his adventure & the boy sold them next day—the little fellow made over a thousand dollars out of it. Good Strike for him as it proved.[58]

[Monday, September 12] Nothing more than common occurred in our family— Alfred is tending to his law and Po[st] office business, & I am as usual.

[Tuesday, September 13] Mr Courtier called. Have done a very large washing & am tired enough.

[Wednesday, September 14] Sewing— Gentlemen Smith, Morris, [Russell] Rodgers & [Oscar] Rix called on us in the evening. A most Shocking affair took place on Clay Street a man had become jealous

---

[58] Joseph "Ready" Gates, a sixteen-year-old fruit peddler, took this unexpected balloon ride on August 28, 1853, from Oakland. Upon his return by steamer to San Francisco, he made $300 to $400 telling his story to the press and an audience at the San Francisco Theater. Kurutz, "Informal History of Ballooning," 38–40. For a fictionalized account for young adults, see Dorothy Kupcha Leland, *The Balloon Boy of San Francisco* (Davis, Calif.: Tomato Enterprises, 2005).

CWR of a certain M.D. The doctor was walking along the street in the evening, some one be-hind said ["]Doctor look here," where upon the Doc. looked round & the man drew a pistol & shot him through the head. At last accounts he was alive. Such things are so common that they are performed and forgot almost the same day— [W. H.] O'Grady here in Evening.

[Thursday, September 15] Ironing— I average eight or ten fine shirts that I do up every week besides my other ironing Alfred <u>is elected</u> Justice of the peace for the eighth ward & fourth township of San Francisco. San Francisco has four townships & a justice for each. He does not enter upon his duties untill the first of October— We awoke this morning with a fine rain. The beginning of the rainy season

[Friday, September 16] Today is Steamer day. Sent letters home. Mrs & Mr Haskall started for home this morning on board the John S. Stevens. Smith here in evening. We have the fragrance of some of the sweetest of boquets in our parlour. Clara [Walbridge]'s scholars keep her supplied.[59]

[Saturday, September 17] baking & making tomato preserves. Smith called in the evening. Had a game of Whist— Another rain this morning but it clears away delightful.

[Sunday, September 18] A beautiful day— The same round as usual—

[ASR] [Monday, September 19] I hardly know what occurred for I am now recording the week's events after the time— I think to-day Bub was taken sick with the Dysentry.

[Tuesday, September 20] Bub much worse— Chastina not able to wash as usual— I am preparing for my year's labor.

[Wednesday, September 21] Bub so much worse that we called Dr [J. P.] Bush—and active remedies are applied.[60]

[Thursday, September 22] Bub as usual. The Girls wash &c. I am trying to dispose of my P[ost] O[ffice] business.

---

[59] The *Alta California* of October 21, 1853, announced Clara B. Walbridge as the teacher at "School District No. 7, at Mission Dolores" with forty-one pupils.

[60] Dr. J. P. Bush had an office at Tehama House, at the corner of California and Sansome streets. *San Francisco Directory 1854*.

[Friday, September 23] Bub a little better. Brown Called.   ASR

[Saturday, September 24] Looking about for a Court Room. Bub better. Chastina finished a large ironing. Mrs [Theodore] Smith has been unwell for a few days past.

[Sunday, September 25] Bub better. At work on forms. [CWR] Poor little Julian has been very sick & is sick yet. He does not sit up yet. We are hoping he will get along well. The Doctor has called twice a day to see him. Had no letters from home this mail but received three "Caledonians"—they seem like old friends to us here. This week has been marked as being the time when the first Telegraph was put in operation in California From San Francisco to San Jose. [Illegible] years ago who thought a telegraph would communicate its lightning speed through the vales of California— Such is progress

[Monday, September 26] Julian about as usual. I am all alone with him. Alfred is very busy prepareing for entering on his duties as Justice of the peace—

[ASR] [Tuesday, September 27] All things as usual. Looking up a Court Room. Found one at the Corner of Montgomery & Bush Streets. Bub is decidely better.

[Wednesday, September 28] Agreed to take the Room at 50 dollars a month. Miller angry at it. Talk of making me associate Judge of Co. Court. Disposed of all my Interest in the Letter Delivery—to Mr Reed of Adams & Co's House.[61] Tina Washed.

[Thursday, September 29] Gave my official Bonds—Stuart & Burkes sureties. Got some new clothes &c. Bub is slowly improving.

[Friday, September 30] Lo Mismo.

[Saturday, October 1] Went to the Mission for notes & Records of Dr Corbett—found a carpet bag and—an owner. Very pleasant weather.

[Sunday, October 2] Reading a story called Agatha's Husband.[62] Enjoyed a dish of mush & milk & a Sherry Cobbler. Chastina a little unwell.

---

[61]Reed's City Dispatch Post was located at Adams & Co.'s Express in Parriott's Granite Building on Montgomery Street. The proprietor was Henry Reed; J. B. Brown was the superintendent. Ibid.

[62]English novelist and poet Dinah Maria Mulock Craik (1826–87) wrote *Agatha's Husband* in 1853. It appeared first in *Colburn's New Monthly Magazine*.

ASR [Monday, October 3] This day An Election of Associate Judges of the Court of Sessions took place. Alfred Rix was chosen the 1st unanimously. Entered immediately on my duties & also on those of Justice.

[Tuesday, October 4] In c[our]t of Sessions & my own—case or two brought in. [M. P.] O'Connor making a little muss.

[Wednesday, October 5] Idem

[Thursday, October 6] The Same

[Friday, October 7] Chastina sick

[Saturday, October 8] So much that we cant record it. [*CWR*] Call from Mr. Locks people

[*ASR*] [Sunday, October 9] Had a wedding. Married John Moon & Catherine Brown— Fee 20.00—presented to Tina. [*CWR*] Call from Hale [Rix] & R[ussell] K Rodgers

[Monday, October 10] Alfred married another couple to day. Fees this time ten dollars. doing pretty good business in the marrying line— For me I have been cleaning house. Bub is getting along very slowly— Alfred came home feeling so nicely, what does he do but go & sell our pig—a beauty of his kind—for thirty dollars, about twenty less than his worth— Of course I felt bad seeing twas all done before I knew our pet had any notion of leaving us.

[Tuesday, October 11] Washing. I have a real hard time to do my washings. Julian so unwell, he cant walk any yet, and it takes me a long time to do his waiting. Mr Morris made me a call—paid the ballance for making his twelve shirts—which makes $48.00. quite a little sum— or would be at home.

[Wednesday, October 12] For my own part I have nothing new to record. Unless it be to say it is nearly six week since I have been in the street, and I dont get time to read the papers, so we are likely to have rather a dry Journal. Opposite is a specimen of Alfreds journalizing now days [The left-hand page contains Alfred's short entries.]

[Thursday, October 13] I have forgotten if there was any thing worth telling.

[Friday, October 14] Ironinging. Have done up twelve fine shirts among other things Alfred is very busy now days.

[Saturday, October 15] Baking— Traded some with a peddler— Clara [Walbridge] at home rather unwell— Dustan [Walbridge] out of a job— Had letters from [Edward] Bierstadt & Oscar [Rix]s wife—all well Got two Caledonians from home

[Sunday, October 16] Sent letters home— All hands at home as usual.

[Monday, October 17] Alfred acted as attorney for the defendants in a suit. Clara [Walbridge] very unwell with the dysentery, but has gone to school. Mr. Berkis our landlord took $325.00 of us $210.00 belongs to me, a good part of it my own hard earnings— Got letters from home. All quite well. better than when they last wrote— Augustus [Walbridge] has returned from his three month fishing voyage improved in health.

[Tuesday, October 18] Washing— Clara [Walbridge] not able to go to school, very bad with the dysentery— Alfred very busy. Gone this evening to the court of Sessions. Dr [J. P.] Bush came to See Clara. Poor man! Three of his children are dead of the Yellow fever, in Natchez— Never has there been such a sweeping disease in our country as the fever this year. Thousands have died. None are exempt—children as well as grown people are swept off by this terrible pestilence. Poor man, how I pity him. Yet I know not by experience how to sympathize with him. Doctor thinks Clara will get along.

[ASR] [Wednesday, October 19] Clara [Walbridge] no better. The weather very fine. Alf attending the court of Sessions as Judge & Chastina Taking care of Clara & doing all her work alone. Dustan [Walbridge] out of work.

[Thursday, October 20] Nothing new.

[Friday, October 21] Nothing new.

[Saturday, October 22] Chastina indignant at a certain call by the <u>Ladies</u> of San Francisco for a meeting to reduce servants' wages. Was in my Justice office & Had lots of business.

[Sunday, October 23] Read Marcus Warland—[63] Pretty good. Bub very much better now-a-days. Notwithstanding she has us all

CWR

---

[63]Caroline Lee Hentz (1800–56), *Marcus Warland; or, The Long Moss Spring* (1852).

ASR to take care of & extra work to do—Chastina is as smart as a streak of lightning and looks a little prettier than ever before— [CWR] (ie. when she gets her fixins on)] [ASR] Clara [Walbridge] seems to be a little better.

[CWR] [Monday, October 24] I shall be oblige to write my Journal like Alfred's, for there is nothing remarkable happening now a days. Clara [Walbridge] about the same There is a vacation in the schools this week.

[Tuesday, October 25] We are having some delightful weather now a days, very warm & pleasant. Much pleasanter than during the summer. The winds blow but little & the evenings are delightful really. Today I have done a large washing, & all my other work besides. Alfred at the court of Sessions.

[Wednesday, October 26] Clara [Walbridge] some better— I have picked a chicken & made her some broth— I get but little time to do any thing beside about the house. I am called upon so constantly for something I am almost tired out.

[Thursday, October 27] Ironing. Ironed thirteen fine Shirts & other things. Clara [Walbridge] getting better. Fine weather yet.

[Friday, October 28] Had part of the day to sit down and rest me. Julian got to be quite well now. Hungry all the time—and it puzzles me to know *what* to get for him. Continues pleasant yet, & it is very warm now. Alfred in his office now.

[Saturday, October 29] Clara [Walbridge] had her clothes on for the first time Baking &c. Walked out in evening, the first for months.

[Sunday, October 30] Alfred & Clara [Walbridge] making out school report.

[Monday, October 31] Got up, prepared breakfast & bustled about till after seven. Then got ready & went to the Mission to keep Clara [Walbridge]'s school. Had some fifteen scholars. Seemed some like old times with this exception Most of them were Spanish & I could [not] understand them much— Went down to Mrs. Lockwoods at noon— Had a very good time. Clara stayed at home & took care of Julian

[Tuesday, November 1] Clara [Walbridge] went to her school. I have been washing, had a large wash— Clara got along very well though it was rather hard for her to ride out & back from the Mission.

[Wednesday, November 2] [W. H.] O'Grady called—He is superintendent in the schools. We, that is Clara [Walbridge] & Alfred & myself went to the "Agriculteral Fair" in the evening— Saw some large vegetables, beets three feet long & large as a mans leg. Squashes over two feet in diameter. Corn fourteen feet high—ten feet up to the ears, oats almost as high, onions over six inches in diameter, big apples from Oregon & other places. Lots of needle work, specimens of all kinds of vegetables &c &c.

[Thursday, November 3] I have been ironing— Mrs. Lockwood called with her sick boy— Alfred very busy now a days.

[Friday, November 4] Clara [Walbridge] at home, had some trouble about her school house Mrs [Mary Jane] Locke & Alice Locke called. [James] Denman called also. Mrs Henly called. Baking some

[Saturday, November 5] Baking again— Dustan [Walbridge] went out a riding with Morris— brought home four ducks. We began about 9 o'clock to pick them and we did not get through till one o'clock.

[Sunday, November 6] Had a great time cooking ducks. My birth day. Alfred presented me with a beautiful ring & Shell hair comb The ring is large & Solid & very pretty. Morris & Smith here to supper. This birthday has been very different from my birth day two years ago— How many changes have taken place in these two years. I have just tiped the candle over in my lap & spilled the tallow all over me so I will stop.

[Monday, November 7] Cut a dress for Clara [Walbridge]. Alfred has resigned his place in the court of Sessions because he has so much business to attend to in his own office.

[Tuesday, November 8] Nothing of any account happened—only I must say that Julian is getting well and growing fat every day— We had a letter from John [S. Way]s folks all well—and also one from Mother [Watts] and Alice [Watts], all well at home. They say Laura Harvey Frost is dead—one of my old mates & friends. Every letter

CWR from home brings news of changes there deaths marriages absences & the like are changing every day [among] our old friends & associates so that in a few years at least we shall hardly recognize what was once our home.

[Wednesday, November 9] Washing. Alfred brought home Dickens "Bleak House." We have commenced it to read aloud.

[Thursday, November 10] Sewing, rained at night.

[Friday, November 11] Ironing. Smith called

[Saturday, November 12] Baking. Dan Foster took dinner with us he is going home

[Sunday, November 13] Cloudy & rainy. Alfred married a couple got a "ten." Russel Rodgers called.

[Monday, November 14] Rained almost all day— I suppose I have seen a specimen of the rainy season. seems some as it does at home— only we have no sheds &c to keep things dry.

[Tuesday, November 15] Pleasant out doors— I have been cleaning house for my comfort. Dan Foster called to bid us good bye before going home to the States.

[Wednesday, November 16] Washing and cleaning house. Been very rainy all day so I have had <u>foging</u> times, in the rain We are reading Dickens Bleak House evenings and are very much interested in it.

[Thursday, November 17] Got a very bad cold by being out in the rain and am about sick. Julian is sick with a cold also—

[Friday, November 18] Ironing & baking pies—& sewing some. Julian better of his cold. "I do'nt know nothink" now a days as "Jo" says in Bleak House.

[Saturday, November 19] Baking &c as usual.

[Sunday, November 20] Pleasant day— Took a <u>little</u> walk out round— Saw a big tame Grisly, a <u>hedious</u> looking animal. I should dislike to meet one of them in their natural state in the mountains

[Monday, November 21] Sewing—&c.

[Tuesday, November 22] Washing, very pleasant day.

[Wednesday, November 23] Baking mince pies for thanksgiving.

Our preparations for thanksgiving are rather small to what they are at home—and we have not much heart to do anything about it.

[Thursday, November 24] Thanksgiving day in California— Got breakfast—done up the work; then Alfred & I & Julian got our selves ready & started for the Mission— We went down street & called on Mr Locke's people—then went to the Mission on the new plank road. Very pleasant way indeed— Called at Messers. Moses, Rufino, [Syl] Courter, [Jim] Dorland & Brown— Made our calls short & polite of course— Came home & got our supper—Roast pork pudding, quince & pumkpin.

[Friday, November 25] Ironing— Very rainy— O[n] yesterday evening Alfred went out and joined a pair in the holy bonds of matrimony.

[Saturday, November 26] Baking, & rainy again rather gloomy weather now days— Alfred very busy now days.

[Sunday, November 27] Just as usual Sundays. Reading writing talking as usual on sundays— We are reading Bleak house & are very much interested in it

[Monday, November 28] Sick all day with the Sick headache.

[Tuesday, November 29] Washing— For me to merely write the doings of myself seems all foolishness, for one week might do for every other week, save now an[d] then something that happens, so I will sum the week up in one lump and say—That we sent letters home the first of Dec. have had some of the pleasantist weather for a whole week—that one can imagine—so sunny so mild so delightful—That Julian has walked out on the street alone several times to the great discomfuture of his mother.[64] By the way he is getting to be "some pumpkin" as the saying is.

---

[64]Clara Walbridge, San Francisco, to Sarah Walbridge Way, Hardwick, November 29, 1853, private collection. Clara told the story about Julian slipping out of the house. When Chastina noticed, she "ran up to Kearny street which is a short distance from here and went on a while untill she saw his light dress away some distance from her . . . She would not have been so worried about him but Kearny street is constantly thronged with Carriages[,] drays &c of every kind and there is no sidewalk in this part of the City. She went with an old wash-dress on bare headed and bare armed—and this is the first time she has ever been out in the City so far alone. She will not go out at all unless some one goes with her."

CWR   For the first time I have been out shoping alone & bought me a silk dress. Clara [Walbridge] got one too & we have set up two nights most all night to get it done, & now it is done—on this day.

[Sunday, December 4] We feel rather sleepy for sewing late nights. [ASR] There was this night at the White House, on the Mission Road one very fine dance according to all accounts— We all had a pressing invitation, but did not go but sat in proud & solitary & I may add pious state, thinking of the event & suffering a holy martyrdom for the Lord's sake—no doubt. Went to bed all round 11 p.m.

[Monday, December 5] Rainy as to the weather & Dry as to incident.

[Tuesday, December 6] This is Chastina's Weekly Washing Day. We have just Finished Dickens Bleak House & are all abundantly pleased with it.

[Wednesday, December 7] Not a red incident worth recording.

[Thursday, December 8] OOOOOOOOOOO

[Friday, December 9] Rainy—muddy—melancholy and murderous.

[Saturday, December 10] Made a deposit of $500. in Page Bacon & Co's for the purpose of making a Bank Acct.[65] About these times the Judge is doing a brisk business in his way—he tries on an average 6 cases per day & has more business than any other office in town. We are all in excellent health and spirits & happy. The girls are perfectly contented. Bub is a[s] fat as a pig but for particulars see New Year's day. [CWR] Oscar [Rix] called & brought our Caledonians.

[ASR] [Sunday, December 11] All hands took a walk to Rincon Point & saw the State Marine Hospital & an army of old hulks. Rincon Pt is a decided locality.[66] We had a chicken pie for supper & a nice one it was too. We are now going to have some oranges & grapes which causes my present bad chirography.

---

[65]The banking house of Page, Bacon & Co. was located at the corner of California and Montgomery streets. This was the first time Alfred reported opening a bank account for savings instead of investing. Lotchin, *San Francisco*, 58; *San Francisco Directory 1854*.

[66]The United States Marine Hospital, at the corner of Harrison and Spear streets in Rincon Point, was completed December 12, 1853. *San Francisco Directory 1854*.

[Monday, December 12] All hands at our usual work. ASR
[Tuesday, December 13] Girls are learning to dance a little.
[Wednesday, December 14] Dustan [Walbridge] receives a letter from Augustus [Walbridge] who is a[t] Lyndon & very well contented.
[Thursday, December 15] A call from Mrs [Elizabeth] Varney P.M.
[Friday, December 16] Another call from [Robert] Varney & wife. Chastina & Bub called on the old man at his office & all went a shopping & purchased a work stand for Clara [Walbridge]'s Room.
[Saturday, December 17] Wrote letters to OOO. Baking & fine weather.
[Sunday, December 18] Took a walk ou[t] to a sand hill. Russ Rodgers called & two Morrises.[67] Wrote a few law documents.
[Monday, December 19] Cold—rainy.
[Tuesday, December 20] New Stove in my office.
[Wednesday, December 21] Lots of Business now a-days.
[Thursday, December 22] So much to do I cant find time [to] journalize
[Friday, December 23] Locke & I conclude not to buy a law-suit.
[Saturday, December 24] Locke pays me $200 on Ira [Rix]'s account. Send to White $50, to Burkes $300 & pay out 400 due customers.
[Sunday, December 25] This is Christmas day. We awoke & to our utter astonishment found a large bag in the corner full of all manner of funny presents some to one & some to another. Dustan [Walbridge] found a beautiful Cravat—Gunter's Rule & Protractor & gold pen & Silver stock & a cork & small tinkey [trinket?]. Clara [Walbridge] found a beautiful silver Sewing Bird—pair of tongs— Embroidered Handkerchief Pencil &c. Bub found a wagon & whip & socks &c. Chastina found a silken bead purse, Embroidered Handkerchief, Shovel, ivory comb, elastics & a roll of tape. Writing paper, pens &c &c. Alf found a pair of Slippers—a memorandum,

---

[67] George and Abram Morris ran a dry goods establishment at the corner of Jackson and Dupont streets. *San Francisco Directory 1854*. It is not clear which Morris boarded with the Rixes and courted Clara. The shirts Chastina made for Morris may have been to sell in his store.

ASR a jack knife & glass globe to hold down papers &c. Warent we a Happy family? [*CWR*] Calls from Jno Courtier & Jim Dorland & the [George and Abram] Morrises.

[Monday, December 26] Clara [Walbridge] has a vacation during the holydays. Sewing—as usual.

[Tuesday, December 27] Washing. Mrs. Dagget sick so I did part of hers and together with mine it made enough to nearly tire me out.

[Wednesday, December 28] Began to fix over my silk dress that I had at the time I was married— Bub is so fat now days we hardly know what to do with him. He is perfectly healthy.

[Thursday, December 29] Sewing the same as usual—

[Friday, December 30] Ironing & sewing like "all natur" to day— Alfred & I went to the Metropolitan Theater for the first time—that is we have never been to any theater before in San Francisco. Saw Hamlet played by Mr Murdock.[68] The play was very interesting, but Mr M. was not so pleasing to us, as his reputation as an actor lead us to hope to find him. [*ASR*] The Building is new and beautifully finished & decorated.[69]

[Saturday, December 31] Chastina Baking & Alf Settling up & off.

[Sunday, January 1, 1854] Awoke at Midnight by a horrible deluge of fire crackers, squibs, pistols, & Bell-ringing, but concluded to turn over & snore a-while. Tina's old Female Friend called early.[70] After Breakfast Russ Rodgers & Milton Blanchard called on us— Milton & his brother Phin have just arrived. They report all well in Peacham when they left a month ago. Phin has the Measles.

---

[68] James E. Murdock (1812–93), a well-known reader and actor, played Hamlet at the Metropolitan Theatre, which was located on Montgomery Street between Washington and Jackson. *San Francisco Directory 1854*; Lotchin, *San Francisco*, 289. For the program, see Theater Scrapbook, 1853.

[69] The Metropolitan Theatre, "one of the finest theatres in America," opened December 24, 1853. It was "distinguished by the beautiful and chaste appearance of the interior . . . The prices of admission were—for the orchestra and private boxes, $3, for the dress circle and parquette, $2, and for the second and third circles, $1." Soulé, Gihon, and Nisbet, *Annals of San Francisco*, 481–82.

[70] Chastina's menstruation indicated that she was not pregnant.

It will no doubt be expected that at this point in time we shall ASR make a short Summary of our positions—as usual. We are now in the City of San Francisco Cal. on Geary Street 3 Doors above Kearny. Our house a good one—described hereinbefore. We have lived here since the 1st of May last. We pay $60 per month rent. Our Family consists of Alfred & Chastina W. Rix & son Julian W. Rix, & Dustan S. & Clara B. Walbridge. The two last pay $8.00 a week each for board. Descriptions of persons will be omitted. Bub's business is to laugh, play in the sand run after his parents & bawl & eat victuals. The old man is Justice of the Peace & spends nearly every hour of the day at his office on the Corner of Montgomery & Bush Streets, for which he pays $50. a month. He tries on an average about 4 cases per day, & receives as per cash book on file. Chastina does the house-work, sews & tinkers so as to make by herself some $30. a month— She is up & has breakfast every morning before daylight and is perfectly healthy & full of contentment & fun. Clara teaches school at the Mission at $100 per month & rides back & forth every day. Dustan works at Wheelwrighty at $4.50 per day. We are all as happy as crickets and as healthy as pigs. We await the revolution of another 12 mos. to see what will turn up.

[CWR] [Monday, January 2] It is the <u>fashion</u> in San Francisco on new years day for the ladies to stay at home & receive callers from the gentlemen and treat them on cake and wine.[71] So as I happen to be among the Romans, I of course must do as the Romans do, so I made some cake &c, had some wine & we entertained Messrs. Gay, [Charles S.] Smith, Sarles, [Enoch] Smith & Theodore Smith, Courter[,] Williams, [James] Denman & the two brothers [George and Abram] Morris. Alfred & I and Julian took a ride to the Mission also. We had one of the pleasantest days I ever knew. Warm & so calm and delightful it was almost enchanting—

[Tuesday, January 3] This evening we are invited to a ball at the mission. Donna [Doña] Carmel gives the ball in honor of her new

---

[71]New Year's social visiting was an "old New York custom" according to which "the ladies held open house for their gentlemen friends." Lotchin, *San Francisco*, 287.

CWR house She is a rich Spanish lady. So at Seven P.M. Alfred Clara [Walbridge] & I put on our <u>fix up</u> & went out in the <u>Buss</u>. We had a perfect jam most of the ladies spanish. Clara [Walbridge] & I got upon the floor twice each as for our dancing that remains for the spectators to relate. Suffice it to say "we didnt get home till mornin." I did not go to bed at all—

[Wednesday, January 4] Did my washing—& felt slack enough. cold to day.

[Thursday, January 5] Ironed cold and windy almost as cold as winter at home.

[Friday, January 6] Sewing— Went to the teachers meeting in evening consider it no great affair.

[Saturday, January 7] Baking as usual— Clara [Walbridge] & Alfred made Mrs [Elizabeth] Varney a call—we had a call from [Charles S.] Smith our old friend.

[Sunday, January 8] At home as usual. Julian had the croup very bad last night—the medicine which I used was salaratus & molasses.

[Monday, January 9] Sewing on Julian some clothes Rather a dark and gloomy day although we have had no rain yet. I get rather lonesome sometimes here alon[e] day times, but I have so much to do that I cannot stop to be homesick—

[Tuesday, January 10] Washing— Have washed a very large number of clothes, & consequently am very tired.

[Wednesday, January 11] Nothing of importance Alfred is very busy now days—

[Thursday, January 12] Rainy day—have had no rain before for some time. ironing—done up sixteen shirts.

[Friday, January 13] and ——————————

[Saturday, January 14] Doing my work as usual. The mail has got in and we are very anxious to hear from home. Letters from home are welcome here. They are like visits from our friends.

[Sunday, January 15] Had a call from Phineas Blanchard. [Charles S.] Smith called also, & took supper with us— Had Oysters for supper. Wrote letters to Peacham, sent one to John[S. Way]'s folks,

Mary A. Rix, Cousin Emily Taylor Jessuph, Harriet Guyer, Daniel Taylor & one or two more.

[Monday, January 16] Steamer sailed to day— Do not feel very well.

[Tuesday, January 17] Got a letter from Mother [Watts] folks all well at home

[Wednesday, January 18] Washing. Cold & rainy & windy, like Nov. weather at home.

[Thursday, January 19] I think it the coldest morning I have seen in Cal[ifornia]. Ice quite thick in the yard. I hung out some clothes about eight o'clock and they froze stiff while out. It makes me think of old Vermont. I like such sharp weather once in a while for a change. About nine in the evening a pair came in to be married, so we sent out for some wine. Alfred joined them we drank their health & they went home happy no doubt—

[Friday, January 20] Tremendous cold. The coldest ever known here since Americans lived here. Ice froze two inches in thickness in our yard. Boys had fine times skating upon the ice The same as one year to day since we saild from N.Y. for this place—

[Saturday, January 21] The cold weather continues. baking some. Went out with Alfred & got some trimmings for my dress— Oscar [Rix] took supper with us. Had another wedding here this evening, the parties were German & could not speak English. Morris came in & spent the evening.

[Sunday, January 22] Cold as usual. nothing happened of account

[Monday, January 23] Weather moderated commenced raining. Began a dress for myself. The Steamer Golden Gate is aground & expected to be lost. Every thing safe.

[Tuesday, January 24] Warm & rainy— Had a letter from home— all well as usual Hubbell Gregory—The husband of my sister—and his little girl are at our fathers to stay the winter.

[Wednesday, January 25] Cleared off pleasant—quite warm.

[Thursday, January 26] Nothing of importance—indeed there is but little that is interesting in the common routine of family affairs.

CWR Our life is one of quiet Each member of the family has his or her labor to perform. We have no time to make calls, therefore we have few callers.

[Friday, January 27] Sewing on my dress, nearly completed it.

[Saturday, January 28] Baking and ironing.

[Sunday, January 29] A most splendid morning Bub & I took a walk with Alfred to his office— Did some copying for Alfred. About sundown Alfred and I took a walk up on top of one of the hills in San Francisco.[72]

[Monday, January 30] After doing up my work sat down & wrote a letter to Mother [Watts]. Sent five dollars to Augusta Gregory.

[Tuesday, January 31] Have done a very large washing—and am very tired. We send letters this time to Johns [S. Way], Augustus [Walbridge], Mother [Watts], Amanda Morrills husband, Mr. Mighell.

[Wednesday, February 1] Commenced another dress for myself. It is rather discouraging for me to begin such a piece of work for it takes me a long time besides the botheration of it.

[Thursday, February 2] News from the States. Fires & shipwreck & wars & treaties is the Cry in the Streets to day. The great Republic the greatest ship upon the waters was burned in the harbor at N.Y. Have done my ironing—Ironed thirteen shirts besides all the others.

[Friday, February 3] At home all alone. Alfred & Clara [Walbridge] have gone to a teachers meeting Dustin [Walbridge] to the theater. I have written part of a letter to Ira Rix. Been sewing to day, & kind of lonesome or sick of home or home sick—

[Sunday, March 5] A whole month has passed by and not a word has been written in this book. The truth is Alfred wont write, and I have nothing to say worth recording— We go on from day to day with the same round, each and all of us engaged in our several occupations— It has been rainy for the most part of the past

---

[72]From the city's hills, Alfred and Chastina saw "the remarkable achievement of their instant city," an urban setting unlike their rural town in Vermont. Ibid., 281.

month— Clara [Walbridge] has been obliged to Stop at the Mission on account of the road being shut up. We attended a ball on the eve of Washington's birth day at the Mission; had a very good time. "Did'nt come home 'till mornin" as we were obliged to stay all night. Had letters from home. Folks all well— Visited Mrs. [Elizabeth] Varney & Mrs. Hendly—and attended one of the Pickwick Assemblies, which is no more or less than a social ball—where some of a doubtful character are admitted & w[h]ere each can dress as he or she pleases without being subject of remark. We had a very good time and mean to go again. Today Sunday, Alfred has been out and joined one couple in the holy bonds of matrimony. It is a fine day and we have improved it by taking a walk over the hills. The sand is a great objection to walking here.   *CWR*

[*ASR*] Chastina has handed me the Journal, pen & ink & asks me to continue her essay—Poor me! Have to write all day & then at night or Sunday have to write it all over again in an old Copy Book. But for the sake of future reference and generations I suppose I must submit to it. So here goes for a few lines. In the first place our City is in a precious pinch for money. Hundreds of Lots & Houses to lease & sell. Hundreds moving out of good into poor buildings to avoid the Excessive rents. And those who have money can invest it at a fine rate of interest & at good advantage in real estate etc. About these times we are all having very good luck in our several occupations. Dustan S. Walbridge who still continues with us, is at work by the day at the Wheel wright business—has $4.50 per day— keeps steady at his work & is gaining slowly away on his pile. Clara is at her school yet & makes about fifty dollars a month clear of all expenses. She is well contented & so is Dustan. Julian W. Rix, the son of his parents—presents some <u>striking</u> features occasionally— also some strikable ones—at any rate—they get struck. He is as fat & hearty as a pig. Chastina is the same old coon. Alfred 'lo mismo' [*CWR*] Dry up!

[Monday, March 6] and so on through the week— Every thing goes on about as usual. Clara [Walbridge] boarding at the mission.

CWR [Saturday, March 11] Work. Work. all the week—and be glad enough when Saturday night comes— Alice Locke made me quite a visit this week— Got a letter from W[eltha] A. Cory

[Sunday, March 12] Undertook to take a walk to the mission but had to come back the wind blew so hard. R[ussell] K Rodgers called in the evening

[Monday, March 13] Very rainy. Clara [Walbridge] did'nt go to school on account of the rain— Washed in the afternoon— Clara went out and bought a pink Tibet dress to wear to Pickwick Club.

[Tuesday, March 14] At work on Clara [Walbridge]'s dress. Had letters from Charles Watts, Augustus [Walbridge], Louisa Rix. All well.

[Wednesday, March 15] At work on C[lara Walbridge]s dress. Sent letter home.

[Thursday, March 16] Getting ready to attend the Pickwick Club.

[Friday, March 17] Feel rather sleepy to day did'nt get home till three this morning— Had a very good time. We have a splendid ball good musick and a very pleasant company numbering one hundred or more in all— The persons who attend are respectable all of them & who like occasionally to go some where of an evening with out so much expense as is attendant upon going to fashionable balls in this city. The ladies all dress well, but not in ball costume— We have refreshments and every thing in good order, and all enjoy themselves exceedingly well—of course I tried to dance.

[Saturday, March 18] Baking as usual—

[Sunday, March 19] rainy again— Had a chicken pie for supper— It goes first rate here. Seems some like home—

[Friday, March 31] A long time has passed by since a word has been written here. I have teased Alfred to write until I am tired of it & now in my poor way I shall endeavor to do a little—during this time no change has taken place in our situations. We hear from home, go through the same routine each day as for some time past. Attended another Pickwick assembly, had a good time. It is really laughable to see Mrs Rix try to dance—but she hopes to learn.

[Saturday, April 1] We are having our kitchen painted—makes a bad piece of work— By the way—we had a first rate April fool performance. Alfred came home at noon for lunch—very soberly he went and called in three of our neighbors, viz. Mrs Daggett, Mrs [Margaret] Plummer & Mrs [Theodore] Smith—& asked them all to step in as quick as possible with their camphor bottles—in they came with their highbottles, frightened enough, when lo and behold, it was Apr 1. Women love to revenge themselves for any such sell— so we put ourselves to work & planned to see him sold if possible. So in the evening a perfect stranger to him came & requested him to go out and marry a couple— Meanwhile all the <u>sold</u> parties had gone to a certain Mr Martins—a Scotch man—and sent him here after a Justice. Of course he went off through the sand pondering upon the happiness of the happy pair—But to his <u>great delight</u> the wedding party were no other than our good neighbors— Did'nt they have a nice time! & did'nt they all come back here & have a nice time too! We considered [it] a first rate thing.

[Sunday, April 2] More of the Peacham boys come. Among them George Currier & William Gilfillon. People all well at home—boys took supper with us & stayed in evening. It seems good to see those with whom we have been acquainted before we came here— Had a real wedding.

[Monday, April 3] Sewing— a very warm day.

[Tuesday, April 4] Washing. George [Currier] and W[illiam] Gilfillon called on us they start this afternoon for the mines. Rather hard for those who come to this country now—

[Wednesday, April 5] Did my ironing— Mrs [Elizabeth] Varney visited me. Mr. [Robert] Varney took supper with us— Had a very good visit[73]

[Thursday, April 6] Sewing— Warm now days.

[Friday, April 7] Sewing again— It is the same with me each day I rise at about 15 minutes before six every morning get breakfast the family get up and eat, & go to their work. I get my work done up

CWR

---

[73] Robert Varney is listed in the *San Francisco Directory 1854* as "clerk, 102 Commercial."

and get ready for sewing about ten o'clock A.M. so [sew] what I can besides looking after Bub, get a lunch, then sew, get supper then sew again & so passes my time— I go out on the street very seldom. Alfreds thirty second birth day

[Saturday, April 8] Baking— Went out with Alfred in the evening to make a few purchases— Raining a little.

[Sunday, April 9] Rather cold to day— We stay at home sabbath after sabbath—& I get most tired of it although I have to work very hard through the week & need rest one day.

[Monday, April 10] Washed a lar[g]e number of clothes—am very tired. Wrote part of a letter to cousin Chastina Brown of Cabot Vt.

[Tuesday, April 11] Got my work done in good season, and went up in the afternoon to see Mrs Hendly.

[Wednesday, April 12] Mrs [Elizabeth] Varney called this morning— In the evening we went to the Musical Hall to hear a lecture from Mr Winslow on "The preparation of the earth for the intelectual races." It was a very scientific lecture, therefore good & interesting But it was hardly suited to the people of San Francisco.

[Thursday, April 13] Sewing and baking some— This evening was the Pickwick assembly— We did not go for we had so much to do we could not very well.

[Friday, April 14] Mrs Hendly & the boys visiting here all day. Mr H[endly] here to tea & stayed a short time in evening. Steamer in. We get no letters. Wrote to Augustus [Walbridge], C[hastina] Brown, John[S. Way']s folks & Ella [Watts]. Sent papers also. It is a very warm day—a hot day too.

[Saturday, April 15] Steamer sailed— Very warm again Baking some and sewing—

[Sunday, April 16] Not quite so warm to day. Alfred & Julian & I took a walk away down in one of the vallies— The vallies among the sand hills are very fine grass growing & what with art [withal?]— Some lovely reminisces are made.

[Monday, April 17] Sewing on Julians dress[74]

---

[74] Chastina, San Francisco, to Sarah Walbridge Way, Hardwick, February 28, 1854, private collection. "Julian wears petticoats yet & will some time longer—They wear them in cities until they are much older than they do in the country."

[Tuesday, April 18] Washing got my clothes all ready to iron Had a present of a nice little pig

[Wednesday, April 19] Ironing and baking.

[Thursday, April 20] Sewing very busy—rained in the night

[Friday, April 21] Had a fine shower this afternoon sewing Alice Locke & her brother Silas [Locke] spent the evening

[Saturday, April 22] Baking Bub went to the mission with Clara [Walbridge].

[Sunday, April 23] Had a ride out in the country about seven miles to the "Abbey." The country is fine lovely you may say— Had a very good time. J[im] Dorland & J[ohn P.] Courter called

The Rix Family Home,
Market Street, San Francisco, August 1855

Unusual whole-plate outdoor scene daguerreotype made by Robert H. Vance. At the front door are Alfred and Chastina Walbridge Rix with their sons on the sidewalk, Edward in the baby carriage and Julian standing with his dog. On the right side of the porch sits Alfred's older brother, Oscar Rix. Dustan Walbridge and his sister Clara stand on the balcony, and to the right of Clara are Alfred's brother Hale Rix, seated, and his wife, Alice Locke Rix. The wooden sidewalk was the only one between Kearny and Montgomery. *Oakland Museum of California.*

CHAPTER TWELVE

Alfred's Afterword
May 21, 1857

*Great changes have taken place . . . I must now . . . supply
the deficiencies of this Record . . . in obedience to the wishes of Chastina.*

IN LATE MAY 1857, THREE YEARS AFTER CHASTINA'S FINAL ENTRY, Alfred wrote in the journal one last time.

[Thursday, May 21, 1857] Since the last page was written in this Journal great changes have taken place. She who wrote the last words is now dead and lies buried in Lone Mountain Cemetery.[1] How far was it from my thoughts when she and myself commenced these Records, that she so soon would be unable to continue them. We have both blamed ourselves again & again for not having kept up the old record—day by day, as we commenced, and especially because the events of the last 2 or more years have proved to be the most important to us as a family & to each personally that could possibly occur.

In that time we have made and lost a little fortune of some $20 000. and saved out of it a homestead—built our house moved into it and

---
[1] Chastina died unexpectedly on February 3, 1857. She was thirty-three years old.
[2] In early 1855, they had moved to a new house on Market Street, near where they had boarded on Geary. In a letter to Chastina's family in Peacham, Alfred described the new house as "a very nice & comfortable place for us . . . It is <u>all</u> paid for & finished . . . land and all cost five thousand dollars more or less." Chastina added: "our house is much better than I ever expected to have in California and indeed it is good enough for any place." Later that year, San Francisco suffered through the Panic of 1855, and Alfred lost what (*continued, next page*)

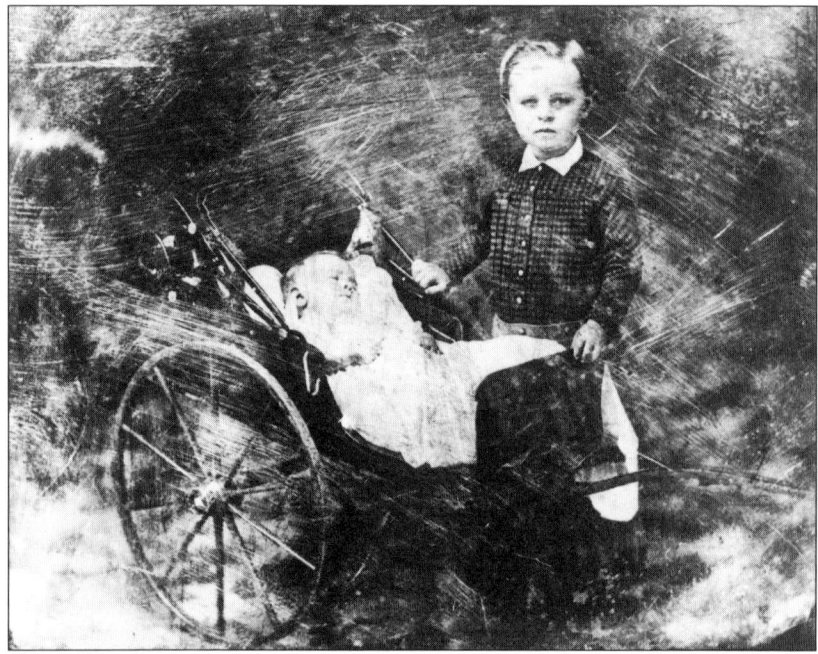

BROTHERS JULIAN AND EDWARD RIX, SAN FRANCISCO, AUGUST 1855
Daguerreotype made by Robert H. Vance of Julian Walbridge Rix and Edward Austin Rix. Wearing pants that button to his jacket and a shirt with white collar under his plaid jacket, five-year-old Julian stands next to seven-month-old Edward, who is in the baby carriage that his Uncle Dustan made for him. *Private collection.*

enjoyed two years of uninterrupted happiness & then been ruined.[2] Eddie has been born—& Chastina has died.[3] I must now look over my pocket memorandas for the dates & look to my memory for the facts of this long period and do what can be done to supply the deficiencies of this Record. I do it not so much on my own account as in obedience to the wishes of Chastina, though there is a melancholy pleasure in dwelling upon & recording the happy history of the past, so strongly in contrast with the gloom now promised for the future.

---

he termed "a little fortune." Page, Bacon & Co., the bank where he had opened an account in December 1853, failed, and the money he lost was probably related to his speculative and real estate investments. He was able to hold on to their new "homestead."

[3] A second son, Edward Austin Rix, called Eddie, had been born on January 29, 1855.

Epilogue

Despite Chastina's history of illness, her sudden death came as a shock. She had seemed to be feeling fine after Eddie's birth. Two weeks after he was born, she wrote to her mother: "I am quite well now. Have been out doors, & work some besides taking care of the baby. I am obliged to <u>cook</u> some for I am not so fortunate ever as to get any one that knows how to cook Yankee fashion if they know how at all. Our little boy—he wouldnt be a girl—is fine healthy child."[1] But her health began to deteriorate over the following year. In March 1856, looking for a healthy retreat away from the city, she had gone to "Knights Ferry," north of Stockton, where a mill operated by the Locke brothers was located and where Ira Rix worked.[2] Her mother described her condition to Sarah:

> I feel bad about Chastine she has never been well since her babe was born and she is verry slim this winter she was going up Country as they call it to see if a change of air would not help her how I wish I could have her with me next summer.[3]

Chastina spent three weeks away, during which time her condition improved; she even gained twelve pounds. But any improvement was only temporary. Eleven months later, she was dead.[4] The only letter preserved with any details of her final days was written by her mother a year later:

---

[1] Chastina, San Francisco, to "Dear Friends," Peacham, February 15, 1855, Edward A. Rix Collection.
[2] Knights Ferry was the first mail landing for boats to the Gold Country, a place that Alfred knew from his mining days. Chastina took the boys with her, and Clara kept house for Alfred.
[3] Roxana Walbridge Watts, Peacham, to Sarah Walbridge Way, Northfield, Minn., March 7, 1856, PC private collection.
[4] Undated death notice in unidentified San Francisco newspaper, from the files of Elizabeth Rix De Wolf Fairfax: "RIX—In this city, on the 3d inst., Chastina W., wife of Alfred Rix, aged thirty-two years." A card in this Fairfax collection reads (*continued next page*):

[Chastina] was taken sick January 21 1857 her complaint was such as frequently happens to married women, she felt rather delicate about making it known, and I suppose she took cold and did not have the proper treatment that she should have had in the proper time, and her old billious complaint set in and she suffered very much from her stomach and Liver, but her Physician thought she would soon get up and they did not apprehend any danger untill the morning before she died, when there was a change came over her and the mortification set in and she died at half past 11 oclock that night on February 3. She had her senses untill a few hours before she died. She talked with her husband. She told him she was not afraid to die, but she wanted to live yet. Poor dear girl. She had a great deal to attach her to with a kind husband two lovely boys and everything around her for her comfort so far as the good things of this life are concerned, but Oh it all could not stay the hand of death.[5]

Not thinking that Chastina was in danger, Alfred had continued working during her illness, but when the end was inevitable, he stayed by his wife's bedside through the last day and night. Clara, who had married her suitor from Vermont, Russell Rogers, the previous summer and moved to a new house on Pine Street, watched after Julian and Eddie during this time. She and her husband continued to care for the boys through the spring. Their own first child, Nellie, was born a month after Chastina's death. Alfred later moved in with them at their home on Pine Street and threw himself into his work.

Alfred had always had concerns about the schools in San Francisco. As far back as January 1855, he had written to Roxana that "there is one consideration which alone would compel us to move to the East as soon as we well can, that is the unfitness of this place for educating our boy."[6] So when Dustan announced that he was returning to Vermont, Alfred decided that Julian, now six years old, should go with him to be educated

---

                    RIX, MRS CHASTINA Born in Vermont AGE 32
                    Died in San Francisco of Pherperal Peritimitis
                    Buried Feb. 3 1857

Most likely this means she died of peritonitis, an inflammation of the membrane lining the abdominal cavity. She died the evening of February 3 but probably was not buried on the same day. Chastina's grave is in the Lone Mountain Cemetery, "a beautiful tract of land lying between the presidio and the mission," according to Soulé, Gihon, and Nisbet, *Annals of San Francisco*, 596–97. "The grounds embrace one hundred and sixty acres, inclosed with a handsome fence . . . twenty miles of avenues have been laid out," each given the name of one of the cemeteries in the eastern states, such as Laurel Hill. The cemetery records at the Society of California Pioneers give the following information: "Place of Internment: Vault. Feb. 7 Removed & buried in Private Lot—Lot 61. Sec. 11—Laurel Path."

[5]Roxana Walbridge Watts, Peacham, to Augusta Gregory, Michigan, February 18, 1858, Walbridge-Gregory Family Papers.

[6]Alfred and Chastina to "Dear Friends," Peacham, January 14, 1855.

in the good New England schools under the supervision of Chastina's mother, Roxana, in Peacham. Dustan delayed leaving San Francisco for a few weeks, trying to get his final wages for his work and also to complete the sale of some of the nine buggies that his brother Augustus had built in Vermont and shipped around the Cape to San Francisco.[7] In late May, Julian traveled east via the Panama Isthmus with his Uncle Dustan. They stopped in New York for some new clothes before taking the train to Barnet, Vermont, where Lyman Watts picked them up for the wagon ride to the farm in Peacham's East Part.

On November 28, 1858, a little more than a year and a half after Chastina's passing, Alfred remarried at the age of thirty-six. With Annie Margaret Tuite, the twenty-nine-year-old daughter of an Irish immigrant, he had four more children: twin girls who died at birth, and two boys, William A., born in 1863, and Alfred Shirley, born in 1866. Clara and Russell Rogers moved to Petaluma in 1858 and sold their house on Pine Street to Alfred, who listed this as his address for the rest of his life. In 1866 he was appointed judge of police courts to fill a vacancy and thereafter used the honorific title of "Judge."

Russell Rogers struggled to support his family. He kept cows and delivered milk on the streets of San Francisco. They tried ranching in Petaluma, but Clara disliked being isolated with small children, and they soon returned to the city, first living "at the Mission" and eventually building a home on 14th Street, above Castro. They had five children, two of whom died young. Although no formal agreement was ever reached between them and Alfred, Eddie continued to live with his Aunt Clara, making short visits to his father. Clara and Alfred's second wife never met. Clara harbored a deep resentment toward her and the financial benefits Alfred bestowed upon her; she felt he was ignoring his sons with Chastina, and he provided little financial help toward raising Eddie. During the Civil War, Clara also kept an eye on Chastina's and her brother Augustus Walbridge, who had left Vermont because of mental illness and moved to California to avoid the Union Army draft. After the war, he returned to Vermont.[8] In the summer of 1871, Clara and Russell, with their three children and Eddie, took the Transcontinental Railroad, stopping along the way to visit

---

[7]Dustan Walbridge, San Francisco, to Roxana Walbridge Watts, Peacham, May 2, 1857, private collection. The buggies were finally sold, mainly by Alfred's doing, after Dustan had returned to Vermont and gone off to Minnesota for work. Roxana Walbridge Watts, Peacham, to D. Augustus and Dustan Walbridge, Northfield, Minn., January 4, 1858, private collection. Roxana wrote that mail had come "from Cal[ifornia] stating how Dust[an's] Carriages were disposed of and also that the Check was answered at the Bank here."

[8]Bonfield and Morrison, *Roxana's Children*, 137–39.

Clara's sister Sarah and her family in Northfield, Minnesota, and Clara's niece Augusta Gregory Mills and her family in Wisconsin. They spent several weeks in Vermont at the Watts farm and visited Russell's mother in Boltonville, later part of Ryegate. Both Russell and Clara died in California, Russell in 1886 and Clara in 1917.[9]

Once back in Vermont after returning with his Uncle Dustan, Julian lived on the Watts farm. Alfred had agreed to pay Lyman Watts $100 per year for his room and board. Julian stayed in Peacham until he was eighteen. He went to the district school across the road from the farm, as had his mother. From 1863 to 1868 he attended the Peacham Academy, where both his parents had attended and later taught, and where his father had been principal. A good student, he served as editor for the student publication at the Academy.

Dustan had married a local Peacham girl and was the father of a daughter. He was serving as a soldier in the Union Army when Roxana, his mother and Julian's grandmother, died in 1862 during an influenza epidemic. Even from his army camp, he expressed concern for Julian in a letter to his sister Alice: "I can't satisfy myself with any plan that I can conjure up for him. I dont think his Father wants him—and I know it is not the right place for him their, but as you say I think he is better off [in Peacham] than to be left to himself in a City like San Francisco . . . if I was at home I would see to him."[10] But in June 1864, Dustan was wounded at the Battle of Cold Harbor; he died two weeks later in a Washington hospital and was buried in Peacham. By the age of thirteen, Julian had lost three people—his mother, grandmother, and uncle—who had cared for him. He stayed on the farm in Peacham and worked alongside his Uncle Ike, who was only eight years older. He enjoyed a teasing relationship with his aunts Alice and Ella, who were just a few years older than he.

Upon graduation from the Peacham Academy in the spring of 1868, at the urging of his Aunt Clara, who sent him money for the trip, eighteen-year-old Julian left Vermont for California on his own, crossing Panama—this time alone—for the third time in his young life. Once settled in San Francisco at his father and stepmother's, he went to his mother's gravesite at Lone Mountain Cemetery on the outskirts of the city. He wrote his aunt back in Peacham: "Father has never put up a Stone or done anything

---

[9]Ibid., 88–95; Edward A. Rix, "A Trip East," summer 1871, Edward A. Rix Collection. In the introduction to his travel journal, Eddie wrote: "Was gone 6 months—travelled on 11 different railroads, travelled 7520 miles on railroad, 360 towns, 12 different capitals. Managed to cost about $700."

[10]Dustan S. Walbridge, Fort Totten, Washington, D.C., to Alice Watts, Peacham, November 5, 1863, private collection.

except put a rough Board fence around it . . . When I get money enough I hope with Russel to make that one of the best in the Cemetary, not for the show but it seems almost to wicked to think that my Father never has paid what the poorest are willing to pay—respect for their <u>dead</u>." He went on to say that Alfred was making him and Eddie work on Sundays, and he "had to get over all such silly notions" of going to Sunday school. And "the Step Mother," he wrote, "is always finding fault with Ned [Eddie] & I."[11]

After arriving in San Francisco, Julian worked in Alfred's law office. He did not do well at copying documents, so Alfred apprenticed him to a local sign and decorative painting company. Shortly afterward, he began his art career with etchings, but soon expanded to oil, watercolor, and pastel. By 1882, Julian had become a well-recognized painter, exhibiting in San Francisco galleries and creating illustrations for magazines, including *Harper's*. In the 1880s he shared a studio with Jules Tavernier on Montgomery Street, and the two were founders of the Bohemian Club. Unable to make a living in California when the second generation of local art patrons turned their fancy to European art, Julian accepted a patronage from businessman William T. Ryle of Paterson, New Jersey, where he maintained a studio and a close relationship with the Ryle family. He opened a second studio in New York City, where he died in 1903 at age fifty-two, a year before his father. Julian Walbridge Rix is considered among the noted nineteenth-century painters of California scenes. His paintings are held by many major American museums, from the Oakland Museum of California to the Corcoran Art Gallery in Washington, D.C. According to family legend, Julian had been discouraged by his father from being an artist. In his will, he noted that only his brother Edward had helped him, and to Edward he left several of his large canvases.[12]

Alfred and Chastina's youngest son, Edward, attended the Mission Dolores and Lincoln Grammar schools and San Francisco Boys' High. In 1873 he entered the University of California, where in 1877 he was a member of the first class to graduate from the Berkeley campus. He studied in the School of Engineering, then called the College of Mechanics. He became a successful San Francisco businessman, founding the Rix Compressed Air and Drill Company, which he ran until his death in 1930. He had five children, including a daughter named Chastina, called Christine.[13]

---

[11]Julian, San Francisco, to Ella Watts, Peacham, November 14, 1868, private collection.
[12]Bonfield and Morrison, *Roxana's Children*, 104–14.
[13]DeWolf, "Biography of Edward Austin Rix"; interviews with Edward's youngest child, Elizabeth Rix De Wolf Fairfax (1914–2007), 1976–96. Edward's daughter Christine Sterling (1881–1963) was the founding force behind Los Angeles's historic Olvera Street.

By 1860, Alfred's brothers Oscar, Austin, Ira, and Charles had all died in California. His brother Hale had become a prominent San Francisco lawyer and judge. In 1855, Hale married Alice Locke after a long courtship in New Hampshire and California.[14]

Alfred lived another forty-seven years after Chastina's death. In a letter to one of his granddaughters, Genevieve, in 1901, he referred to the journal that he and Chastina had kept:

> If you read that old record of your grandparents' early life you will learn that it was a happy one, and just here I desire to impress on you that it was mainly due to the simple fact that we knew each other thoroughly—not only each others excellencies but also their defects and this had the means of meeting the mutual demands. Till now I have never had the opportunity to say what I have always wished to say to my progeny, to wit: that from the beginning to the end of our mutual life there never occurred between your angel grandmother and myself one single word or look or act not wholly harmonious and affectionate.

In the letter he added a few words about Chastina: "She was a genuine lady—in the highest sense of that term and I am certain I appreciated her accordingly." Then he ended with this advice:

> This leads me to encourage you strongly to maintain your position to secure for your husband a man among men or live an old maid. A girl who is so weak & cowardly as to be frightened into marrying a stick for fear of old maidism deserves what she gets. Stand by your colors and have a good one or none.[15]

With the passing of years, Alfred's recollections of the relationship that he and Chastina shared grew more romanticized, but he never lost perspective on the deep respect and love that was the bedrock of their marriage. Tragically, Chastina did not live to raise her boys or to share in the success that came to Alfred, but she believed that good and noteworthy things would happen.

When Alfred died in 1904, the *San Francisco Bulletin* printed a three-paragraph obituary under the headline "Former Judge Alfred Rix Dies at His Home After a Distinguished Career Before the Bar." It said that he had died at 743 Pine Street "after a brief illness." The *San Francisco Call* of

---

[14] Chastina to "Dear Friends," January 14, 1855. "We had our house christened by a wedding. Saturday evening the 6 of Jan. Who do you think were married? Hale & Alice were the victims & Alfred performed the ceremony."

[15] Alfred to Genevieve Rix, San Mateo, Calif., November 2, 1901, Rix Family Papers.

Epilogue 363

HALE AND ALICE LOCKE RIX, SAN FRANCISCO, CA. 1855
When her brothers in San Francisco sent her the money for passage in spring 1853, Alice Locke left New Hampshire and came to California, where her husband-to-be was working after failing in the gold mines. On January 6, 1855, Alice and Hale were married by Alfred at the new Rix family home on Market Street. Hale wears a fashionable plaid vest under his wool coat with buttons high in style at the time. His goatee with moustache is common for the time. Alice wears her hair pulled behind the ears and wrapped into a chignon, fashionable in the 1860s. Her dress has coat sleeves that are wide at the elbow, then taper to the wrist. The collar is smaller in the 1860s with a ribbon bow at neck. *Private collection.*

May 2, 1904, went into detail about his career, from which he had retired fifteen years before his death. It described him as

> a man of practical mind, and this trait led him into patent law as his favorite vocation. Among the famous cases with which he was connected was the litigation over the Nobel dynamite patent. He had drawn the original patent on which Nobel built up his vast industry, that now has its factories in nearly every European country and under which high explosives were manufactured in the United States. The litigation over this patent occupied Judge Rix for years, in the courts both of the United States and Europe. He was also general counsel for the Atlantic Dynamite and Giant Powder Company, as

well as for many other corporations. His practical bent led him to interest himself in the problem of cable railways in San Francisco, and the solution of this question was worked out with his professional aid.[16]

In his will, Alfred summarized his life, including these words on his days in the gold fields:

> In the autumn of '51 I came to this state and played tenderfoot miner on the North Fork of the American River till the next spring when I came to San Francisco and served as teacher in its public schools and then opened a law office.[17]

More than two hundred men left the Peacham area to try their luck in the California gold fields. Some were successful and returned to Vermont with their "pile," using their bounty to buy farms. Others remained in California and contributed to its spectacular growth. Alfred was one of the latter. He became an upstanding, well-respected, and successful San Francisco resident. His accomplishments were due in no small part to his considerable skills, his commitment to a new and challenging future, and his persistence in insisting that Chastina join him in his endeavors. Their Gold Rush adventure as recorded in a journal for "future generations" took form and survived mainly because of the diligence of the journalists. This journal, which was born in a tiny hill town in northern Vermont, traveled to California around the Horn, endured the flurry of activity as the Rixes moved to and fro in San Francisco, and survived the great earthquake and fire of 1906, now goes from handwriting to print.

---

[16] I am grateful to Kevin Mullen for sending this obituary. Family lore emphasizes Alfred's role in creating the San Francisco cable car system. His granddaughter Genevieve Rix Burrows wrote of this on June 3, 1948, when she donated the Rix journal to the California Historical Society: "Grandfather and I discussed many times his part in the birth of the Cable Cars of San Francisco. He was counsel for A. S. Hallidie of the California Wire Works, both in a legal and engineering capacity. More than once he told me the whole idea of propelling cars up and down the steep hills of the city was his own. That the idea was not original. That he had taken it from a similar mode of transportation in an Eastern town where they had to haul cars up steep inclines. Mr. Hallidie was not an inventor, but had a keen adaptive mind. He was in the wire rope, or cable business. Together they produced the famous San Francisco Cable Cars. Mr. and Mrs. Andrew Hallidie were social friends of our family as well. They owned a 'ranch' near ours in the Portola Valley, San Mateo County, called 'The Eagle's Lair,' high up on the mountainside. Leading to it was a dirt road and also a wire tramway." A lengthy obituary appeared in the July 27, 1904, *Caledonian*, announcing that "at his request his remains were cremated." A card in the personal collection of Elizabeth Rix De Wolf Fairfax reads:

> RIX, ALFRED BORN IN CANADA AGE 83
> DIED DIABETES
> BURIED MAY 10 1904 CREMATED

[17] Alfred Rix will, undated, Edward A. Rix Collection.

APPENDIX ONE

Alfred's Rix Family Noted in the Rix Journal

Father	Hale Rix (1798–1878), married 1819 Adeline Morrill
Mother	Adeline Morrill Rix (1798–1879)
Siblings	Oscar Rix (1820–58), married 1846 Mary Ann Burton (1823–82)
	Alfred (Alf) S. Rix (1822–1904), married 1849 Chastina Walbridge (1824–57)
	Lavina Rix (1824–36)
	Adeline Rix (b. 1826), married 1850 Edward Bierstadt (1824–1906)
	Hale Rix (1828–1901), married 1855 Alice P. Locke (1828–1915)
	Austin Rix (1829–54)
	Ira Osmer Rix (1831–60)
	Jonathan Morrill Rix (b. 1833)
	Louisa Farr Rix (1836–93)
	Lewis Merwyn Rix (1838–1902)
	Charles Carrol Rix (1839–60)
	Alanson Stephen Rix (b. 1841)
Sons	Julian (Bub, Bubby, Jule, July) Walbridge Rix (1850–1903)
	Edward (Eddie, Ned) Austin Rix (1855–1930)
Nephews	Eugene Rix (b. 1845), son of Oscar
	Oscar Bierstadt (b. 1850), son of Adeline
	Charles Rix (1851–77), son of Oscar
Nieces	Mary Adeline Bierstadt (b. 1852), daughter of Adeline
	Emma Rix (b. 1847), daughter of Oscar
Great Aunt	Sarah Morrill Stevens (1766–1854)

Aunts	Margaret Rix Crane (1799–1872)
	Lucretia Rix Eastman (1804–74)
	Amanda Morrill, married to Mr. Mighell
	Narcissa Rix Underwood (d. 1883)
Uncles	George Clark
	Thomas Crane, married to Margaret Rix
	Joel Eastman, married to Lucretia Rix
	Lewis Morrill
	Nathan Underwood, married to Narcissa Rix
Cousins	Weltha Ann and Sophia Cory
	Moses Crane (b. 1835)
	Alfred Eastman
	Melvina Gile (1827–54), married 1851 Stephen H. Sanford
	Perris Eastman Gile (1809–89)
	Clark Rix, married to Becky Rix
	Eliza Rix
	George Rix (1789–1843), son of Alfred's father's brother George
	Moses Rix, married to Louisa Rix
	Sidney Redfield Rix (1830–54), son of Alfred's father's brother George
	Susan E. Rix
	Alanson Stevens (1797–1847), son of Sarah Morrill Stevens
	Alanson Stevens (d. 1863), son of Thaddeus' brother, Abner Morrill Stevens
	Thaddeus Stevens (1792–1868), son of Sarah Morrill Stevens
	Caroline Underwood
	Walter Underwood

APPENDIX TWO

Chastina's Walbridge/Watts Family Noted in the Rix Journal

IN THIS FAMILY OF STEPCHILDREN AND HALF-SISTERS AND HALF-brothers, each referred to the other as simply "sister" or "brother," and called Roxana "mother" and Lyman "father." For clarity in this chart the "step" and "half" are used.

Mother   Roxana Brown Walbridge Watts (1802–62)
         married 1821 Daniel A. Walbridge
         married 1840 Lyman Watts
Father   Daniel A. Walbridge (1796–1835)
Stepfather   Lyman Watts (1801–75)
         married 1830 Esther Sargeant (1803–36)
         married 1840 Roxana Walbridge
Grandmother   Olive Lamb Brown (ca 1769–1862), mother of Chastina's mother
Grandfathers   David Brown (d. 1844), father of Chastina's mother
         Oliver Walbridge (1767–1851), father of Chastina's father
Siblings   Martha Walbridge (1822–46)
         married 1840 Hubbell S. Gregory (1820–79)
         Chastina (Chastine, Tina, Tine) Walbridge (1824–57)
            married 1849 Alfred (Alf) S. Rix (1822–1904)
         Sarah (Sally) B. Walbridge (1827–1909)
            married 1849 John S. Way (1822–1909)
         Clarissa (Clara) B. Walbridge (1830–1917)
            married 1856 Russell K. Rogers (1827–86)
         Lyman S. Watts (1838–72)

	D. S. (Dustan, Dustin, Dust) Walbridge (1832–64)
	Charles Watts (1835–75)
	D. Augustus (Guck) Walbridge (1835–81)
	Isaac N. Watts (1842–81)
	Alice Watts (1845–82)
	Ella (Elly, Eleanor) Lucy Watts (1847–1915)
Sons	Julian (Bub, Bubby, Jule, July) Walbridge Rix (1850–1903)
	Edward (Eddie, Ned) Austin Rix (1855–1930)
Nieces	Augusta Gregory (1843–1903)
	Martha (Sis) Way (1850–77)
Nephew	Edgar Stephen Way (1852–1925)
Uncles	Leonard Brown, brother of Chastina's mother
	Simeon Brown, brother of Chastina's mother
	Chauncey Clement, husband of Chastina's mother's sister Sarah
	Thomas Parker (1803–81), husband of Chastina's stepfather's sister Ruth
	Elijah Sargeant (1805–75), brother of Chastina's stepfather's first wife Esther
	Asa Sargeant (1807–89), brother of Chastina's stepfather's first wife Esther
	Ira Walbridge (1799–1877), brother of Chastina's father married 1827 Martha Morrill
	Thomas Watts (1787–1872), brother of Chastina's stepfather married 1830 Sarah Bailey Sampson
Aunts	Clarissa Blanchard Brown (d. 1851), wife of Chastina's mother's brother Simeon
	Sarah (Sally) Brown Clement, sister of Chastina's mother
	Hannah Walbridge Davis, sister of Chastina's father
	Martha Walbridge Guyer, sister of Chastina's father married Hezekiah (Hiah) Guyer (d. 1851)
	Ruth Watts Parker (1806–73), sister of Chastina's stepfather
	Cynthia Walbridge Stevens, sister of Chastina's father
	Phoebe Walbridge Taylor, sister of Chastina's father married Morehouse Taylor
	Sarah Bailey Watts (1805–84), wife of Chastina's stepfather's brother Thomas

Chastina's Walbridge/Watts Family Noted in the Rix Journal 369

Cousins Chastina Brown (d. 1881), daughter of Chastina's mother's brother Simeon
Cynthia Brown, daughter of Chastina's mother's brother Simeon
Jane Brown (1831–56), daughter of Chastina's mother's brother Simeon
Leonard Brown (ca. 1817–63), son of Chastina's mother's brother Simeon
Willard (Will) Brown, son of Chastina's mother's brother Simeon
Jane Watts Clark (1834–90), daughter of Chastina's stepfather's brother Thomas
Ellen Clement (b. ca. 1837), daughter of Chastina's mother's sister Sarah
George Clement, son of Chastina's mother's sister Sarah
Earl Guyer (d. 1891), son of Chastina's father's sister Martha
Harriet Guyer (d. 1909), daughter of Chastina's father's sister Martha
Hezekiah Guyer, daughter of Chastina's father's sister Martha
Daniel Taylor, son of Chastina's father's sister Phoebe
Elizabeth Taylor, daughter of Chastina's father's sister Phoebe
Emily Taylor, daughter of Chastina's father's sister married Mr. Jessup
Elizabeth Sizer (d. 1852)
Elizabeth Walbridge (d. 1850)
Alvah Watts (1822–77), son of Chastina's stepfather's brother Thomas
John Watts (1818–87), son of Chastina's stepfather's brother Thomas
Lambert Watts (1820–1913), son of Chastina's stepfather's brother Thomas
Isaac (Ike) Watts (1812–86), son Chastina's stepfather's brother Thomas

APPENDIX THREE

The 25 Men Who Left for California with Alfred Rix, October 1851

NAME	TOWN	BIRTH YEAR	OUTCOME WITH GAIN OR NOT
A. S. Allen	Danville	Unknown	Unaccounted for
Chandler Blanchard	Peacham	1829	Returned 1856 with $1,006
John C. Blanchard	Peacham	1827	Returned 1856; purchased farm valued at $1,150
Mark Blanchard	Peacham	1821	Returned 1854; no gain
Chester Brown	Peacham	Unknown	Returned 1853 with $300
Timothy Cowles, Jr.	Peacham	1814	Returned 1855; purchased real estate valued at $925
George C. Dana	Peacham	1824	Returned 1853; purchased real estate valued at $1200 plus $304
John Ewell	Peacham	1827	Returned 1867 with $305
Benj H. Fuller	Ryegate	Unknown	Returned 1854; gain unknown
John Gracy	Peacham	1815 (Ireland)	Returned 1853; purchased real estate valued at $250

372 *Appendix 3*

Sprague Harriman	Peacham	1826	Returned 1854; purchased real estate valued at $1,997
Robert M. Harvey	Barnet	Unknown	Unaccounted for
William D. Hooker	Peacham	1831	Returned 1857 with $908
Henry M. Howe	Danville	Unknown	Unaccounted for
Michael Kavanagh	Peacham	1805 (Ireland)	Went to Australia; unaccounted for
Ambrose Knight	Ryegate	1827	Settled in California
Henry T. Knight	Ryegate	1828	Settled in California
John S. Ladd	Danville	Unknown	Unaccounted for
Erastus S. Libby	Danville	Unknown	Unaccounted for
Asa Livingston	Peacham	1826	Returned 1854 with $403
Alfred S. Rix	Peacham	1822	Settled in California
Oscar Rix	Boston	1820	Died in California 1858
Sidney Rix	Peacham	1830	Died in California 1854
Harvey Varnum	Peacham	1828	Returned 1853 with $741
Dustan S. Walbridge	Peacham	1832	Returned 1857 with little gain

Birth years are from the town office's vital statistics or Watts and Choate, *People of Peacham*. The return years are from family letters or newspaper accounts. The amount of gain for the men from Peacham is from the town grand lists, which give property values and money in bank or stocks; unfortunately these records are missing from Barnet, Danville, and Ryegate. Not included in gain is the cost of the return trip.

Of the twenty-five men, two died in California before 1860, three settled in California, fourteen returned to Vermont, and six are unaccounted for. Ten of the fourteen men who returned brought back $300 or more.

Bibliography

Primary Sources

Brown, Beatrice Rogers. "Following the Frontier: An Attempted History of the Peregrinations of an American Family." Master's thesis, Black Hills State College, 1970.

Caledonia County. Probate Records, Peacham, 1790s–ca. 1910. County Courthouse, St. Johnsbury, Vt.

DeWolf, Elizabeth Rix. "Biography of Edward Austin Rix." 7 typed pages. Oakland Museum of California, Oakland, Calif.

Long, Harold M. "Early Schools of Peacham." Paper read at Peacham Historical Association, August 29, 1971. Transcript, 22 pages. Peacham Historical Association.

Long, Maxine Marin. "A Yankee Argonaut." Paper read at Peacham Historical Association, August 8, 1996. Transcript, not paginated. Peacham Historical Association.

Peacham Historical Association. Manuscripts (PHA-MS), Peacham Academy [Student] Card File, and Photograph File. Individual collections are listed by name.

Peacham Town Office. Peacham Cemetery Card File.

———. Peacham Grand List, 1849–57 and scattered.

———. Peacham Land Records, scattered.

———. Peacham School Records, scattered.

———. Peacham Town Meeting Records, 1845–65.

———. Peacham Vital Statistics Card File.

Plimpton, John H. "The North Fork of the American River." Interoffice Publication of the California State Department of Parks and Recreation, n.d.

Rix, Edward A. Collection. The Bancroft Library, University of California, Berkeley.

Rix Family Papers. MS 1797, including "Daily Journal of Alfred and Chastina W. Rix," 1849–54; and Chastina W. Rix, "Journal of my Journey to California," 1853. California Historical Society, San Francisco.

"San Francisco Streets." News clipping by E. G. Fitzhamon. Vol. 2, p. 3, Rix House. California Historical Society, San Francisco.

Schellens Papers. Reference Collection, California Historical Society, San Francisco.

373

St. Johnsbury Athenaeum. Manuscript boxes. St. Johnsbury, Vt.
Stevens, Thaddeus. Papers. Library of Congress.
Theater Scrapbook, 1853, 1854. San Francisco Performing Arts Library and Museum, San Francisco.
Walbridge-Gregory Family Papers. California Historical Society, San Francisco.

NEWSPAPERS

Alta California (San Francisco). Scattered 1851–54.
Caledonian (St. Johnsbury Vt.). August 8, 1837–65.
North Star (Danville, Vt.). Scattered 1848–54.

PUBLISHED PRIMARY SOURCES

Bonfield, Lynn A., ed. "'A Constant Companion': The 1860 School Diary of a Vermont Farm Girl." *Vermont History* 78, no. 1 (Winter/Spring 2010): 43–87.
———. "The Work Journal of Albert Bickford, Mid-Nineteenth-Century Vermont Farmer, Cooper, and Carpenter." *Vermont History* 72 (Summer/Fall 2004): 113–59.
Boutelle, Rev. A. *Sermon Occasioned by the Death of Newell Marsh.* Concord, N.H.: McFarland & Jenks, n.d.
[Caledonia County Grammar School]. *Catalogue of the Officers and Students of Caledonia County Grammar School, for the Academical Year 1839, 1841, 1842, 1843, 1844, 1846–7, 1848, 1849, 1850, 1851, 1852, 1853, 1854.* Publication information varies.
———. *100th Anniversary of the Caledonia County Grammar School, Peacham, Vermont. Report of the Commemorative Exercises, August 11–12, 1897.* Peacham, Vt.: Alumni Association, 1900.
Kaufman, Polly Welts, ed. *Apron Full of Gold: The Letters of Mary Jane Megquier from San Francisco, 1849–1856.* Albuquerque: University of New Mexico Press, 1949.
McCullough, Eliza Hall Park. *Within One's Memory: Recollections of My Family & My Early Days.* North Bennington, Vt.: Park-McCullough House, 1923; rev. ed., 1944.
Middlebury College. *Catalogue of the Officers and Students, 1800 to 1900.* Compiled by Walter E. Howard and Charles E. Prentiss. Middlebury, Vt.: Middlebury College, 1901.
Myres, Sandra L. *Ho for California! Women's Overland Diaries from the Huntington Library.* San Marino, Calif.: Huntington Library, 1980.
Palmer, Beverly Wilson, and Holly Byers Ochoa, eds. *The Thaddeus Stevens Papers.* Wilmington, Del.: Scholarly Resources, 1994.
Peacham Academy. Catalogue. *See* [Caledonia County Grammar School], *Catalogue of the Officers and Students of Caledonia County Grammar School.*
[Peacham Congregational Church]. *Anniversary Exercises of the Congregational Church, Peacham, Vt., April 14, 1894.* St. Johnsbury, Vt.: I. W. Rowell, 1894.

———. *Manual of the Congregational Church, in Peacham, Vermont.* Jericho, Vt.: Roscoe Publishing House, 1890.
Pearson, Thomas Scott. *Sermons, of the Late Rev. David Merrill, Peacham, Vt., with A Sketch of His Life.* Windsor: Vermont Chronicle Press, 1855.
Roberts, Andrew. "Letters to Mathilda Roberts, Walden." *Vermont Quarterly* 20 (April, July, October 1952) and 21 (January, February 1953).
St. Johnsbury Academy. *Catalogues,* 1845–46, 1846–47, 1849, 1850. Newbury, Vt.: L. J. McIndoe, 1846, 1847, 1849, 1850.

SECONDARY SOURCES

Amory, Cleveland. "Dr. Parkman Takes a Walk." In *The Harvard Book: Selections from Three Centuries,* edited by William Bentinck-Smith, 119–34. Cambridge, Mass.: Harvard University Press, 1959.
Bancroft, Herbert Howe. *Chronicles of the Builders of the Commonwealth.* 2 vols. San Francisco: History Company, 1891.
Bassett, T. D. Seymour. *The Gods of the Hills: Piety and Society in Nineteenth-Century Vermont.* Montpelier: Vermont Historical Society, 2000.
———. *The Growing Edge: Vermont Villages, 1840–1880.* Montpelier: Vermont Historical Society, 1992.
Beck, Richard. *A Proud Tradition, a Bright Future; A Sesquicentennial History of St. Johnsbury Academy.* St. Johnsbury, Vt.: St. Johnsbury Academy, 1976.
Belding, Patricia W. *Where the Books Are: History and Architecture of Vermont's Public Libraries.* Barre, Vt.: Potash Book Publishing, 1996.
Beneman, William, ed. *A Year of Mud and Gold: San Francisco in Letters and Diaries, 1849–1850.* Lincoln: University of Nebraska Press, 1999.
Berglund, Barbara. *Making San Francisco American: Cultured Frontiers in the Urban West, 1846–1900.* Lawrence: University Press of Kansas, 2007.
Bernard, Jean-Paul. "Vermonters and the Lower Canadian Rebellions of 1837–1838." *Vermont History* 58, no. 4 (Fall 1990): 250–63.
Blaisdell, Katharine. *Over the River and Through the Years.* Book Six. North Haverhill, N.H.: K. Blaisdell, 1985.
Bogart, Ernest L. *Peacham, the Story of a Vermont Hill Town.* Montpelier: Vermont Historical Society, 1948.
Bonfield, Lynn A. "Four Generations of Quilters in One Nineteenth-Century Rural New England Family." In *Proceedings of a Symposium at Old Sturbridge Village, June 13, 1998: "What's New England about New England Quilts?"* edited by Lynne A. Bassett, 34–47. Sturbridge, Mass.: Old Sturbridge Village, 1999.
———. "Ho for California! Caledonia County Gold Miners." *Vermont History* 74 (Winter/Spring 2006): 5–47.

———. "Two Families of Teachers: Personal Stories and Family Histories in Manuscript Collections." *California History* 75 (Spring 1996): 63–67.

———. "When Money Was Necessary to Make Dreams Come True: The Cost of the Trip from Vermont to California via Panama." *Vermont History* 76, no. 2 (Summer/Fall 2008): 130–48.

Bonfield, Lynn A., and Mary C. Morrison. *Roxana's Children: The Biography of a Nineteenth-Century Vermont Family.* Amherst: University of Massachusetts Press, 1995.

Bonfield, Lynn A., with Mary C. Morrison. "'Tell Us All the News': Letters from Peacham Vermont at Mid-Nineteenth Century." *Vermont History* 68 (Summer/Fall 2000): 162–84.

Brown, Dona. *Inventing New England: Regional Tourism in the Nineteenth Century.* Washington, D.C.: Smithsonian Institution Press, 1995.

Brumberg, Joan Jacobs. *The Body Project: An Intimate History of American Girls.* New York: Vintage Books, 1997.

Clifford, Susannah. *Village in the Hills: A History of Danville, Vermont, 1796–1995.* West Kennebunk, Maine: Phoenix Publishing, 1995.

Comstock, John M. *The Congregational Churches of Vermont and Their Ministry, 1762–1942.* St. Johnsbury, Vt.: Cowles Press, 1942.

Coontz, Stephanie. *Marriage, a History: How Love Conquered Marriage.* New York: Viking Penguin, 2005.

Cott, Nancy F. *The Bonds of Womanhood: Woman's Sphere in New England, 1780–1835.* New Haven, Conn.: Yale University Press, 1977.

Delaney, Janice, Mary Jane Lupton, and Emily Toth. *The Curse: A Cultural History of Menstruation.* Rev. ed. Urbana: University of Illinois Press, 1988.

Doan, Ruth Alden. *The Miller Heresy, Millennialism, and American Culture.* Philadelphia: Temple University Press, 1988.

Dreyfus, Philip J. *Our Better Nature: Environment and the Making of San Francisco.* Norman: University of Oklahoma Press, 2008.

Dye, Nancy Schrom. "History of Childbirth in America." *Signs: Journal of Women in Culture and Society* 6, no. 1 (1980): 97–108.

Eliassen, Meredith. "Our Intangible Home." *The Argonaut* 16, no. 1 (Summer 2005): 26–53.

Ethington, Philip J. *The Public City: The Political Construction of Urban Life in San Francisco, 1850–1900.* Cambridge: Cambridge University Press, 1994.

Evans, Sara M. *Born for Liberty: A History of Women in America.* New York: Free Press, 1989.

Eysenbach, Mary Locke. "Staying Behind: A Lyman, N.H., Notebook of Florinda Locke." *New Hampshire Genealogical Record* 25 (July 2008): 97–103.

Fairbanks, Edward T. *The Town of St. Johnsbury, Vt.* St. Johnsbury, Vt.: Cowles Press, 1914.

Feintuch, Burt, and David H. Watters. *The Encyclopedia of New England: The Culture and History of an American Region.* New Haven, Conn.: Yale University Press, 2005.

Flaherty, Jeremy. "A Multivariate Look at Migration from Vermont." *Vermont History* 74 (Summer/Fall 2006): 127–55.

Fracchia, Charles A. *When the Water Came up to Montgomery Street: San Francisco during the Gold Rush.* Virginia Beach, Va.: Donning Co., 2009.

Fussell, Clyde G. "The Emergence of Public Education as a Function of the State of Vermont." *Vermont History* 9, no. 1 (January 1961): 13–47.

Gilmore, William J. *Reading Becomes a Necessity of Life: Material and Cultural Life in Rural New England, 1780–1835.* Knoxville: University of Tennessee Press, 1989.

Goodrich, John E., comp. *General Catalogue of the University of Vermont and State Agricultural College Burlington, Vermont, 1791–1900.* Burlington, Vt.: Free Press Association, 1901.

Guy, Tirzah, comp. *Souvenir: Caledonia County Grammar School, 1797–1897.* Peacham, Vt., [1897].

Henkin, David M. *The Postal Age: The Emergence of Modern Communications in Nineteenth-Century America.* Chicago: University of Chicago Press, 2006.

Holliday, J. S. *Rush for Riches: Gold Fever and the Making of California.* Berkeley: University of California Press, 1999.

———. *The World Rushed In: The California Gold Rush Experience.* New York: Simon and Schuster, 1981.

Howard, Vicki. *Brides, Inc.: American Weddings and the Business of Tradition.* Philadelphia: University of Pennsylvania Press, 2006.

Huden, John C. *Development of State School Administration in Vermont.* Burlington, Vt.: Free Press Printing Co. for Vermont Historical Society, 1944.

Issel, William, and Robert W. Cherny. *San Francisco, 1865–1932: Politics, Power, and Urban Development.* Berkeley: University of California Press, 1986.

Jackson, James R., ed. *History of Littleton, New Hampshire.* Genealogy compiled by George C. Furber, revised and enlarged by Ezra S. Stearns. Vol. 3. Cambridge, Mass.: University Press, 1905.

Kemble, John Haskell. *The Panama Route, 1848–1869.* Berkeley: University of California Press, 1943.

Kurutz, Gary F. *The California Gold Rush: A Descriptive Bibliography of Books and Pamphlets Covering the Years 1848–1853.* San Francisco: Book Club of California, 1997.

———. "An Informal History of Ballooning in California." *The Californians,* July/August 1988, 38–45.

Leavitt, Judith Walzer. *Brought to Bed: Childbearing in America, 1750 to 1950.* New York: Oxford University Press, 1986.

LeCount & Strong's San Francisco City Directory for the Year 1854. San Francisco: San Francisco Herald Office, 1854.

Levy, Jo Ann. *They Saw the Elephant: Women in the California Gold Rush.* Norman: University of Oklahoma Press, 1992.

Lewis, Oscar. *Sea Routes to the Gold Fields: The Migration by Water to California in 1849–1852.* New York: Knopf, 1949.

Lotchin, Roger W. *San Francisco, 1846–1856: From Hamlet to City.* New York: Oxford University Press, 1974.

Ludlum, David M. *Social Ferment in Vermont, 1791–1850.* New York: AMS Press, 1966.

———. *The Vermont Weather Book.* Montpelier: Vermont Historical Society, 1985.

Lystra, Karen. *Searching the Heart: Women, Men, and Romantic Love in Nineteenth-Century America.* New York: Oxford University Press, 1989.

Miller, Edward, and Frederick P. Wells. *History of Ryegate.* St. Johnsbury, Vt.: Caledonian Company, 1913.

Nelson, Margaret K. "Vermont Female Schoolteachers in the Nineteenth Century." *Vermont History* 49, no. 1 (Winter 1981): 5–30.

Nissenbaum, Stephen. *The Battle for Christmas.* New York: Vintage Books, 1997.

O'Meara, James. *The Vigilance Committee of '56.* San Francisco: James H Barry, 1887.

Peavy, Linda, and Ursula Smith. *Women in Waiting in the Westward Movement: Life on the Home Frontier.* Norman: University of Oklahoma Press, 1994.

Phelps, Alonza. *Contemporary Biography of California's Representative Men.* San Francisco: A. L. Bancroft, 1881–82.

Preston, Jo Anne. "Female Aspiration and Male Ideology: School-Teaching in Nineteenth-Century New England." In *Current Issues in Women's History*, edited by Arina Angerman et al., 171–82. New York: Routledge, 1989.

Quimby, Daphne Craig. "*People of Peacham* Addendum." Pamphlet. Privately printed, 1971.

Quimby, Lorna Field. *Peacham Academy, 1795–1971.* Peacham, Vt.: Peacham Academy Alumni Association, 2005.

Richards, Rand. *Mud, Blood, and Gold: San Francisco in 1849.* San Francisco: Heritage House, 2009.

Rix, Guy S., comp. *History and Genealogy of the Rix Family of America.* New York: Grafton Press, 1906.

Roberts, Brian. *American Alchemy: The California Gold Rush and Middle-Class Culture.* Chapel Hill: University of North Carolina Press, 2000.

Rohrbough, Malcolm J. *Days of Gold: The California Gold Rush and the American Nation.* Berkeley: University of California Press, 1997.

Roth, Randolph A. *The Democratic Dilemma: Religion, Reform, and the Social Order in the Connecticut River Valley of Vermont, 1791–1850.* Cambridge: Cambridge University Press, 1987.

Rothman, Ellen K. *Hands and Hearts: A History of Courtship in America.* Cambridge, Mass.: Harvard University Press, 1987.

Rozwenc, Edwin Charles. *Cooperatives Come to America: The History of the Protective Union Store Movement, 1845–1867*. Philadelphia: Porcupine Press, 1975.

The San Francisco Directory for the Year 1852–53. San Francisco, Calif.: James M. Parker, 1852.

San Francisco Directory 1854. See *LeCount & Strong's San Francisco City Directory for the Year 1854*.

Scott, Jutta, comp. *A Pictorial History of 18th and 19th Century Homes and Buildings in Peacham, Vermont*. Peacham, Vt.: Peacham Historical Association, 2007.

Searls, Paul M. *Two Vermonts: Geography and Identity, 1865–1910*. Lebanon: University of New Hampshire Press, 2006.

Sears, Daniel Scott, and Michael S. Hindus. "Premarital Pregnancy in America, 1640–1971: An Overview and Interpretation." *Journal of Interdisciplinary History* 5, no. 4 (Spring 1975): 537–70.

Shedd, Frank E. *Daniel Shedd Genealogy: Ancestry and Descendants of Daniel Shed of Braintree, Massachusetts, 1327–1920*. Boston: Published for the Shedd Family Association, 1921.

Sherman, Michael, Gene Sessions, and P. Jeffrey Potash. *Freedom and Unity: A History of Vermont*. Barre: Vermont Historical Society, 2004.

Smith, Anne Kendall, and Stuart E. Smith, comps. *Vital Statistics from St. Johnsbury Caledonian, 1837–1919*. Privately printed, n.d.

Soulé, Frank, John H. Gihon, and James Nisbet. *The Annals of San Francisco*. Facsimile edition of original published in 1855 by D. Appleton & Co. Berkeley, Calif.: Berkeley Hills Books, 1998.

Sparks, Edith. *Capital Intentions: Female Proprietors in San Francisco, 1850–1920*. Chapel Hill: University of North Carolina Press, 2006.

Stilwell, Lewis D. *Migration from Vermont*. Montpelier: Vermont Historical Society, 1948.

Strasser, Susan. *Never Done: History of American Housework*. New York: Pantheon, 1982.

Suitor, J. Jill. "Husbands' Participation in Childbirth: A Nineteenth-Century Phenomenon." *Journal of Family History* 6, no. 3 (Fall 1981): 278–93.

Swift, Eleanor Munroe, and Mona Beach. *Brattleboro Retreat, 1834–1984: 150 Years of Caring*. Brattleboro, Vt.: Book Press, 1984.

Taylor, Bayard. *Eldorado: Adventures in the Path of Empire*. Berkeley, Calif.: Heyday Books, 2000.

Trefousse, Hans L. *Thaddeus Stevens: Nineteenth-Century Egalitarian*. Chapel Hill: University of North Carolina Press, 1997.

Trimble, Paul C., and Emiliano Echeverria. "San Francisco's Omnibuses: Muni's Forerunners." *The Argonaut* 20, no. 1 (Spring 2009): 36–37.

Ulrich, Laurel Thatcher. "Women's Travail, Men's Labor: Birth Stories from Eighteenth-Century New England Diaries." In *Women's Work in New England: 2001 Proceedings of the Dublin Seminar for New England Folklife,* edited by Peter Benes, 170–83. Boston: Boston University, 2003.

University of Vermont, Committee of the Associate Alumni. *University of Vermont Obituary Record.* Burlington, Vt., 1895.

Vermont Legislative Directory. Prepared by the Secretary of State. Montpelier: Vermont Watchman Co., 1902.

Wallbridge, William Gedney, comp. *Descendants of Henry Wallbridge Who Married Anna Amos December 25th, 1688, at Preston, Conn.* Litchfield, Conn.: William Gedney Wallbridge, 1898.

Walton's Vermont Register. Montpelier, Vt.: E. P. Walton & Sons, 1818–1900.

Watts, Jennie Chamberlain, and Elsie A. Choate, comps. *People of Peacham.* Montpelier: Vermont Historical Society, 1965.

Wells, Frederick P. *History of Barnet, Vermont.* Burlington, Vt.: Free Press Printing Co., 1923.

Welter, Barbara. "The Cult of True Womanhood, 1820–1960." *American Quarterly* 18 (1966): 151–74.

Wertz, Richard W., and Dorothy C. Wertz. *Lying-In: A History of Childbirth in America.* Expanded ed. New Haven, Conn.: Yale University Press, 1989.

Woody, Thomas. *A History of Women's Education in the United States.* Vol. 1, New York: Octagon Books, 1914. Vol. 2, New York: Science Press, 1929.

Wortley, Lady Emmeline Stuart. *Travels in the United States, etc. in 1849 and 1850.* London: Richard Bentley, 1851.

Yale, Allen R., Jr. *While the Sun Shines: Making Hay in Vermont, 1789–1990.* Montpelier: Vermont Historical Society, 1991.

Yalom, Marilyn. *A History of the Wife.* New York: HarperCollins, 2001.

Index

Page numbers in italics refer to illustrations.

ASR = Alfred S. Rix; CWR = Chastina W. Rix

Abbott, Rev. Jacob Jackson, 168 & n, 212
Abolition, 12, 96–97, 126, 129n, 142; anti-slavery, 30n, 70, 96, 97, 116, 147n, 202n; reading of *Uncle Tom's Cabin*, 271 & n, 274, 288. *See also* Compromise of 1850; Free-soilers; Fugitive Slave Act; Stevens, Thaddeus
Accordion (accordeon), 324
Aiken, Daniel, 177 & n
Allen, A. S., 223, 371
Allyne (Allen), Helen, 325 & n
American Bible Society, 102 & n
Auction, 164, 167
Ayer, Laura W., 61 & n, 67, 80, 112

Bailey (Baley), Sarah T., 34 & n, 53, 75, 81, 209n, 255, 368
Bain, Marian, 325 & n
Baker, Permelia Blanchard, 73
Balch, John, 89
Balch, Louisa C. S., 54, 64, 85, 88, 89
Balloon ascension, 333
Ballou, Otis, 82
Barnet, Vt., 66, 91n, 169, 175, 177 & n, 182, 188, 190, 192, 193, 198, 211, 219, 222, 279, 298
Bear, grizzly, 340
Beattie, Rev. James M., 169 & n

Benedict, Bob, 211
Bennett, Humphrey H., 53 & n, 73, 91, 92, 107, 133, 159, 173, 195 & n, 201, 203, 213, 220, 238, 258, 268
Bennett, Laura M. Blanchard (Mrs. Humphrey Bennett), 73 & n, 91, 92, 94, 105, 107, 109, 133, 164, 165, 173, 185, 191, 195, 196 & n, 204, 220 & n, 222, 239 & n, 258, 268
Bennett, Judge Milo L., 154 & n
Bickford, Daniel, 170 & n, 172–73, 238 & n, 243
Bierstadt, Albert, 113n, 210n, 221n
Bierstadt, Adeline Rix (Mrs. Edward Bierstadt) (ASR's sister), 113 & n, 128, 159 & n, 210, 221n, 269, 289, 365
Bierstadt, Charles, 210 & n
Bierstadt, Edward, 113n, 128, 159n, 210 & n, 221 & n, 291, 325, 337, 365
Bierstadt, Margaret, 323
Bierstadt, Mary Adeline (ASR's niece), 365
Bierstadt, Oscar (ASR's nephew), 365
Birch, W. H., 326 & n
Blake, Abigail, 55 & n
Blake, Ira Green, 55n
Blanchard, Abigail (Abba) Spencer, 88 & n, 119 & n, 231 & n, 264

381

Blanchard, Rev. Amos, 38, 39 & n
Blanchard, Betsey, 88 & n
Blanchard, Betsey Spencer (Mrs. Simon Blanchard), 261, 262 & n, 263
Blanchard, Chandler, 179 & n, 188 & n, 219 & n, 223, 371, 371
Blanchard, Ebenezer S., 88 & n, 179, 186, 206 & n
Blanchard, Enoch, 282, 283, 285 & n
Blanchard, Esther Harvey (Mrs. Harvey Blanchard), 118, 230, 270 & n, 284
Blanchard, Harriet Partridge (Mrs. Mark Blanchard), 229 & n
Blanchard, Harvey, 81 & n, 230 & n, 270 & n
Blanchard, John C., 160, 223, 371
Blanchard, Laura M. *See* Bennett, Laura M. Blanchard
Blanchard, Margaret, 39, 55, 108, 168, 264
Blanchard, Maria, 118
Blanchard, Maria Kellogg (Mrs. Ralph Blanchard), 261 & n
Blanchard, Mark, 219 & n, 223, 229n, 324, 371
Blanchard, Mary S. *See* Dana, Mary S. Blanchard
Blanchard, Milton, 344
Blanchard, Permelia. *See* Baker, Permelia Blanchard
Blanchard, Phineas (Phin), 231 & n, 344, 346
Blanchard, Simon, 97, 262n, 263, 264, 289, 291, 293
Blanchard, Theodore (Thad), 121 & n
Bloomers, 208 & n, 209, 301n
Boardman, Chauncey, 206
Bond, William, 233 & n
Bonnet(s), 37, 64, 66, 67, 84, 88, 89, 118, 119, 129, 233, 234, 256, 266, 289
Boston, Mass., 55 & n, 56, 65, 79, 81, 110, 123, 124, 127–30, 133, 173–74, 188n, 206–209
Boutelle, Rev. Asaph, 195n, 198 & n, 213 & n, 215, 221n, 237, 238 & n, 241, 257, 267n, 276
Bovee, Elizabeth, 180 & n, 189
Bowker, Charles, 73 & n
Boynton, Moody, 30 & n
Bradlee, Louisa P., 54 & n, 57, 92, 105, 108, 127, 129n, 154, 160, 192; as drawing teacher, 110, 115, 118, 121, 127n, 147n, 233n
Bradley (Bradlee), Elizabeth Chamberlain (Mrs. Nehemiah Bradley), 54 & n
Bradley (Bradlee), Nehemiah, 54 & n, 57, 89, 121–22, 129n, 173
Bradley (Bradlee), William Chamberlain, 129 & n, 173 & n
Brainard, Amos H., 174
Brainard (Brainerd), Asa, 108, 165, 166n
Brainard (Brainerd), E. P., 179, 185 & n, 186, 189, 192, 200, 205
Brainard, Hiram, 270
Brattleboro Retreat, 63 & n, 199n, 232
Breast-feeding, 183, 196 & n; weaning, 262, 264
Breast infection (broken breast, painful breast), 139 & n, 186, 264
Brewer, Dr. Francis B., 57 & n, 58, 62, 91
Brewing (brewed), 156, 177, 256, 276, 330
Brewster, Rev. Loring, 229 & n
Briggs, Rev. Martin Clark, 330 & n
"Bristol Bill" (William Warburton), 110 & n, 112, 136–37, 154. *See also* Counterfeiting
Brock, Phebe, 61 & n, 75
Brooks, Murray, 42
Brooks, Oliver, 42
Brown, Andrew J., 94 & n
Brown, Betsey Weeks (Mrs. Ephraim C. Brown), 57 & n, 63, 92, 100, 118 & n, 157, 169, 170, 177, 195
Brown, Charles, 84
Brown, Chastina (CWR's cousin), 39, 159, 196n, 204, 256, 352, 369
Brown, Chester, 223, 316 & n, 371

Brown, Clarissa Blanchard (Mrs. Simeon Brown) (CWR's aunt), 196n, 287n, 332, 368
Brown, Cynthia (CWR's cousin), 39, 159, 167, 196n, 201, 231 & n, 242, 286, 369
Brown, David (CWR's grandfather), 33 & n, 367
Brown, Ephraim C., 57n, 63 & n, 67, 81, 97, 98, 100 & n, 104, 136, 152, 159 & n, 160, 162, 163, 165, 166, 195n
Brown, Jane (CWR's cousin), 231, 257, 262, 284, 369
Brown, Dr. Leonard (CWR's uncle), 272 & n, 368
Brown, Leonard Wheeler (CWR's cousin), 195 & n, 260, 265, 369; death of child 195 & n
Brown, Maria Kittredge (Mrs. Leonard W. Brown), 195n, 260
Brown, Olive Lamb (CWR's grandmother), 33 & n, 70, 120, 204, 231, 259, 274 & n, 292, 367
Brown, Simeon (CWR's uncle), 34 & n, 196 & n, 242, 254, 259, 274n, 284, 286, 287 & n, 368
Brown, Willard (Will) (CWR's cousin), 290, 369
Brown & Weeks (store), 81, 108, 120, 159n, 179
Bruce, Samuel, 39 & n
Burbank, G. A., 188
Burbank, Moses A., 62 & n, 79 & n
Burke, Vt., 169
Burnham, Charles G., 190
Burrows, Genevieve Rix. *See* Rix, Genevieve
Bush, Dr. J. P., 334 & n, 337
Butler, Beauman, 108 & n
Butter, salting a churning of, 271
Button, Rev. Amasa G., 55 & n, 63, 85, 94 & n, 107, 114, 119 & n, 131, 138, 141, 143, 197, 213n; school superintendent, 119, 169, 173, 176, 177, 189, 195n

Button, Lucinda Johnson (Mrs. Amasa G. Button), 55 & n, 74, 114, 131

Cabot, Vt., 84, 103, 120, 160n, 170, 196n, 238, 241n, 254, 264, 274, 286, 287
Calder, Margaret, 58 & n, 115, 186
Calder, Mary, 59 & n, 64, 65, 66, 67, 73, 89, 105, 107, 233
Caledonia County Conference of Churches, 165 & n
Caledonia County Grammar School. *See* Peacham Academy
California: admitted as free state, 97, 102n, 109n, 126, 135, 140, 166; cost of trip to California, 297, 298 & n; women going to California, 12, 281, 282, 283 & n, 286, 287, 293, 296 & n, 316n
California Gold Rush: Alfred as miner, 305, 364; Alfred's decision to go, 157, 217, 219; Alfred's letters from California, 226, 227, 228 & n, 230 & n, 235, 238, 239, 246, 247, 249, 250, 256, 262, 263, 264, 265, 268, 269, 273, 275, 279, 281, 284, 285, 287, 290, 291, 295, 307–308, 310, 311; carpetbag, 96, 188; company contract, 81n, 95, 96; cost of trip, 188n, 217, 218 & n, 230 & n; death on voyage to or in California, 157n, 192n, 195n, 210 & n, 302, 313, 372; discovery of gold, 11, 139n; dollar gold piece, 157, 266; gold fever (California fever), 9, 11, 149, 168, 222; gold in a trunk sent from California, 163 & n; gold samples sent from California, 126, 132; life insurance, 177 & n, 182, 187, 188 & n, 189, 232 & n; men leaving for California, 11, 24, 43 & n, 52, 95, 99, 102 & n, 111n, 212n, 217, 222, 231n, 234 & n, 235, 239n, 244 & n, 245n, 246 & n, 253n, 289, 291, 315 & n, 317n, 364; miners doing women's work, 309; miners moving from Vermont to Minnesota, 310 & n; North Fork of the American River, 305, 364; outfitting for

California Gold Rush (*continued*)
  mining, 217, 218n, 220 & n; planning for trip, 150, 172, 174, 181, 182, 188 & n, 217, 220, 279, 285, 289; trip to California, 11, 99, 191n, 220 & n; return to Vermont, 68, 149, 157n, 163, 177 & n, 181, 188n, 246 & n; Vermont miners stopping at Rixes in San Francisco, 311, 326 & n, 340, 344, 351; women's response, 25, 43, 152, 168, 219 & n, 221, 225 & n, 226, 235n, 249 & n. *See also* Aiken, Daniel; Allen, A. S.; Blanchard, Chandler; Blanchard, John C.; Blanchard, Mark; Blanchard, Milton; Blanchard, Phineas; Brown, Chester; Clark, Ephraim W.; Cowles, Timothy, J. Jr.; Currier, George; Dana, George C.; Ewell, John; Foster, Daniel; Fuller, Benj H.; Gilfillan, Robert W.; Gracy, John; Harriman, Sprague; Harvey, Robert M.; Hooker, William D.; Howe, Henry M.; Isthmus of Nicaragua; Isthmus of Panama; Jewett, Jarvis; Kavanagh, Michael; Knight, Ambrose; Knight, Henry T.; Ladd, John S.; Libby, Erastus S.; Livingston, Asa; Locke, David Merrill; Locke, Josiah Hannibal; Locke, Silas Merrill; MacLeran, Alex; Marsh, Newell; Martin, Ashbel; Martin, Chester; Martin, John; O'Grady, William Henry; Parker, Addison F.; Rix, Austin; Rix, Hale; Rix, Ira O.; Rix, Oscar; Rix, Sidney R.; Rogers, Russell K.; Sampson, Carlos; Shedd, Josiah; Stuart, Seth; Taplin, Dr. N. P.; Varney, Robert; Varnum, Charles; Varnum, Harvey; Varnum, Mark; Walbridge, Dustan S.; Walbridge, James M.; Watts, Lambert; Way, John S.; Whittle, Bill
California widow, 225n
Cameron, Ann, 57 & n, 90, 170, 245

Camphor bottles, 351
Camp meeting (Christian), 160 & n, 161 & n, 164n
Candle(s), 254, 256, 275, 339; candle making, 232; candlesticks, 128, 130
Carlton, Henry P., 330 & n
Carpenter, Byron, 111 & n
Carpenter, Mary, 111 & n
Carter, Olando, 90 & n
Carter, Thad, 196
Case, Rev. Rufus, 115 & n, 121, 142
Chadwick, Albert G., 40n
Chamberlain, Abigail (Aunt Nabby), 121 & n, 123, 124, 130, 131, 132, 136, 139, 159n, 165, 176, 189 & n, 192, 195n, 196, 199, 235 & n, 268
Chamberlain, Catherine M. (Katy), 80 & n, 119 & n, 192
Chamberlain, Deborah Shedd (Mrs. Ezra Carter Chamberlain), 147
Chamberlain, Ezra Carter, 80n, 118 & n, 148 & n
Chamberlain, Jane, 80n, 119 & n, 164 & n
Chamberlain, Martin C., 202
Chamberlain, Sarah Ellen, 80n, 148 & n, 192, 266
Chamberlain, Sarah Little Gilman, 80n
Chamberlain, William (father), 45
Chamberlain, William (son), 80n
Chandler, George, 66
Chandler, John W., 109 & n
Chandler, Laura, 67n, 138, 140
Chandler, Samuel A., 67 & n, 92, 106 & n, 120, 121, 122, 124, 131, 148, 152, 159, 172, 212, 213, 234
Chandler, Sophia Wilkins (Mrs. Samuel A. Chandler), 67 & n, 144, 186
Chandler, Susan, 67 & n, 73, 79 & n
Chandler, Susannah (Mrs. John W. Chandler), 109 & n, 110
Chapin, Emeline, 72
Chase, Charles C., 32 & n, 34
Cherokee (Atlantic steamship), 191 & n

Chess, 103, 104, 105, 106, 109, 166
Child, Ann Maria, 160
Childbirth, 10, 12, 24, 118n, 119n, 124, 152, 180 & n, 181, 240, 252& n, 357, 359
Choate, Aurilla Ingraham (Mrs. David Choate), 46, 53n, 64, 73, 90, 92, 94, 102, 104, 106, 114, 115, 130, 137, 197, 233, 244; assisted at Julian's birth, 180 & n
Choate, Charles A., 53n
Choate, David W., 46, 51, 53 & n, 59n, 62 & n, 66, 73, 80, 92, 94, 100, 102, 104, 108, 110, 120, 121, 137, 140, 141, 143, 152, 159, 170 & n, 189, 200, 212, 230, 234, 235, 240, 241, 243; director in New England Protective Union Protective Union, 97, 103, 106, 107 & n, 109, 119, 134 & n, 140, 159, 214–15; overseer of the poor, 63n, 202 & n; property on Cow Hill, 121, 170n, 172; Rixes boarding with, 100, 101, 107, 108, 123, 124, 130, 131, 143
Choate, Elsie (Elsey, Elsa), 53n, 114, 138
Choate, Mary B., 53n, 62, 75, 92, 101, 102, 106, 107, 118, 244
Choate, Schuyler, 53n
Christmas, 93 & n, 343; fair, 245
Church service (meeting), 24, 41, 42, 53, 54, 55, 57, 59, 65, 69, 72, 73, 80, 89, 91, 94, 102, 104, 106, 107, 109, 111, 112, 113, 114, 116, 117, 118, 132, 134, 137, 139, 141, 147, 153, 158, 163, 164, 167, 168, 170, 172, 183, 189, 192, 193, 197, 198, 201, 202, 203, 208, 209, 212, 213, 215, 221, 229, 233, 234, 236, 237, 238, 242, 243, 247, 250, 252, 254, 256, 257, 259n, 260, 261, 262, 263, 266, 269, 274, 276, 285, 288, 290, 291, 311, 331; church funeral, 125, 142; church wedding (Rix), 38; deacon's meeting, 51, 118, 142, 221 & n, 269. *See also* Congregational Church; Donation party; Methodist Church
Clark, Clara B., 82 & n
Clark, Ephraim W., 244, 245 & n
Clark, George W. (ASR's uncle), 156, 185, 366
Clark, George W., Jr. (ASR's cousin), 103 & n, 117, 178, 366
Clark, Gideon, 262 & n; Mrs. Gideon Clark, 265
Clark, Harvey, 91, 113 & n
Clark, Jane Watts, 214, 249, 250, 251, 369
Clark, Marietta Blanchard (Mrs. Thomas Clark), 187, 229 & n
Clark (Clarke), Marilla (Marrela), 276, 285 & n
Clark, Morris & newton H., 138 & n
Clarke, Dan, 113 & n, 120, 140
Clement, Chancey (CWR's uncle), 29 & n, 368
Clement, Ellen (CWR's cousin), 29, 255, 256, 262, 263, 264, 369
Clement, George (CWR's cousin), 253 & n, 254, 369
Clement, Sarah (Sally) Brown (CWR's aunt), 29 & n, 368
Cleveland, Rev. Edward, 203 & n
Clothes stick, 231n
Clothes whirl, 200
Clothing: baby clothes, 81, 152; barage (berege) dress, 128 & n; bloomer dress, 301n; boy's cap, 232; boy's drawers, 258, 260; boy's hat, 265; calico dress, 113, 128 & n; child's apron, 237 & n, 261; child's cloak, 232; children's clothes (dresses for Julian), 208, 243, 245, 267, 274, 280, 292, 352 & n; clothes patterns, 169, 170, 241; flannel garments (for babies), 163, 164; flannels (for Alfred), 222, 228n; fulled cloth, 253; hoods, 167; lawn dress, 326 & n; loose dress (maternity), 168; Lyonese dress, 88; mantilla, 276; muslin dress, 37, 70, 128 & n; shawl, 37, 128; sheer cotton dress, 128; shirt, 248, 252, 279, 329; shirt bosom, 328; silk dress, 266, 267, 342, 344; skirt of a dress, 203, 242; spinning dress, 286; Tibet dress, 350; washing apparel (wash dress), 192, 341; wedding: men's, 38, 70, women's,

Clothing (*continued*)
37, 55, 70, 142n; white dress, 58, 141, women's cap, 178, 273. *See also* Bloomers; Bonnet(s); Fashions; Knit; Shawl pin; Tailoress; Walbridge, Clarissa; Women's work for wages in San Francisco

Cobb, Dr. Gardner, 33 & n

Coffin, Galen, 128, 282, 291 & n, 293

Colby, George, 163

Colby, James K., 57, 58 & n, 82 & n, 142, 143 & n, 178n

Colby, Martha, 42

Collamer, Judge Jacob, 154n

Collins, G., 325, 326 & n

Compromise of 1850, 70n, 109n, 110, 111, 112 & n, 140n, 168n. *See also* Fugitive Slave Act

Congregational Church (Bell-House), 37n, 39, 54n, 103n; carpeting, 91, 99, 105, 134; chandelier, 245; fair (at Christmas), 245; Rix wedding, 38–39; youth joining, 200. *See also* Boutelle, Rev. Asaph; Church service; Merrill, Rev. David; Worcester, Rev. Leonard

Convention of Superintendents for the County [of Caledonian], 169, 199 & n

Cooking stove, 124, 130, 131, 134n

Cory, Sophia (ASR's cousin), 89, 92, 100, 107, 110, 117, 118, 366

Cory, Weltha A. (ASR's cousin), 64 & n, 89, 92, 93, 100, 105, 107, 109, 113, 115, 117, 118, 141, 187, 245, 247, 253, 286, 293, 319, 350, 366

Counterfeiting, 110 & n, 112, 124. *See also* Bristol Bill; Meadows, Christian

Courter, John P., 324 & n, 344, 353

Courter, Sylvester, 316 & n, 317, 323, 341

Courtship and courting, 10, 24, 32, 37, 172, 206n, 225, 271, 283, 362

Cowles, Cynthia Shaw (Mrs. Timothy Cowles, Jr.) 66 & n

Cowles, John O., 200, 201 & n

Cowles, Timothy, 55 & n, 161

Cowles (Cowls), Timothy, Jr., 66 & n, 70, 223, 371

Cradle (for babies), 196, 238, 286

Craig, Janette, 66

Crane, Margaret Rix (Mrs. Thomas Crane) (ASR's aunt), 41, 366

Crane, Moses (ASR's cousin), 41, 42, 248, 278, 366

Crane, Thomas (ASR's uncle), 41, 279, 366

Cricket (footstool), 82 & n

Currier, Alma (daughter), 39, 87 & n, 239 & n, 262, 270 & n, 276

Currier, Alma (mother), 195, 204, 242, 276

Currier, David, 31 & n, 82, 94, 127, 147, 179, 197, 221, 230 & n, 241, 244, 264, 270, 286

Currier, George, 81 & n, 147, 163, 195, 209, 239 & n, 248, 262, 272, 351

Currier, Moses, 39, 235, 262

Cutler, T. A., 170 & n, 177

Daguerreotype, 2, 127, 141, 142 & n, *155*, 270, 272, 273, 275, 278, *280*, 289, *354*, *356*

Daguerreotypist, 76, 226, 270n

Dalton, N.H., 24, 39n, 40, 41, 42, 229, 246, 278, 290

Dana, Ann Eliza Muncey (Mrs. William Varnum Dana), 93 & n

Dana, George C., 219, 223, 371

Dana, George Gleason, 91, 92

Dana, I. P., 106

Dana, Mary S. Blanchard (Mrs. George G. Dana), 91, 92, 235 & n, 239 & n, 246

Dana, William Varnum, 93 & n

Dance, 312, 324, 342, 343, 346, 350. *See also* Pickwick Assembly

Danville, Vt., 33, 82, 124, 127, 132, 142, 154, 176, 190, 191, 193, 194, 201 & n, 203, 270, 272, 278, 285; courthouse and court proceedings, 136, 137, 154 & n, 155n, 175, 191, 202, 203, 204, 268. *See also* Phillips Academy

Darling, Brock, 33

Dartmouth graduates, 32n, 33, 35n, 37n, 47, 96, 103n, 125, 282, 283, 285n, 317n
Dartmouth press, 66, 69
Davenport, Rufus C., 186
Davis, Bliss N., 137 & n, 154, 197 & n, 201
Davis, Hannah Walbridge (CWR's aunt), 75, 368
Death, caused by: apoplectic fit, 261; cancers in his eyes, 267; at childbirth, 240, 241n; consumption, 284n; diabetes, 364n; erysipelas, 142, 254 & n, 260n, 261; fire, 254; influenza, 360; peritonitis, 358n; smallpox, 256; wounded in Civil War, 360; Yellow fever, 296
Delano, Rev. Samuel, 103 & n
Denman, James, 317 & n, 325, 339, 345
Dickson, James M., 54 & n, 56, 82, 317 & n
Diseases: apoplectic fit, 261; bilious fever (complaint), 33, 263, 279, 358; bowel complaint, 232; chicken pox, 183, 205; dysentery, 334, 337; liver complaint, 289; measles, 344; mumps, 258; spring complaint, 109; summer complaint, 214; stomach complaint, 279; typhoid fever, 313; typhus fever, 173n. *See also* Death, caused by; Vaccination, smallpox; Yellow fever
Donation party (visit), 94 & n, 103
Donna Carmel, 345–46
Dorland, Jim, 331, 341, 344, 353
Dow, Thomas B., 66 & n
Dudley (Dudly), John, 201 & n, 266
Dumb-watch, 93
Duncan, T. W., 170 & n, 172
Dunham, Canada East, 29 & n, 71, 75, 255, 272, 273

Eastman, Alfred (ASR's cousin), 43, 44, 366
Eastman, F. J., 213
Eastman, Frank, 180
Eastman, Joel (Joe) (ASR's uncle), 43, 44, 366

Eastman, John, 58n
Eastman, Lucretia Rix (Mrs. Joel Eastman) (ASR's aunt), 43, 366
Eastman, Lucy, 58 & n
Eastman, Miriam, 58 & n
Eaton, Horace, 115n, 151
Evans, Carter W., 127 & n, 159n
Ewell, John, 223, 371
Ewell, Mary Ann. *See* Farnum, Mary Ann Ewell

Fairbanks, J. P., 178n
Farmers and Mechanics Mercantile Company of Peacham, 97 & n
Farnum, Alvin B., 260n
Farnum, Mary Ann Ewell (Mrs. Alvin B. Farnum), 260 & n
Farr, Alonzo, 316 & n
Farr, Alpheus, 254
Farr, Dr. Asahel, 56 & n, 63, 91n, 111n, 139, 147n, 157, 168, 177, 180, 222, 235, 242n, 244, 254 & n, 258–59, 268; assisted at Julian's birth, 180; doctor bill, 268
Farr, Justin Porter, 242 & n
Farr, Martha Wheeler (Mrs. Asahel Farr), 65, 111 & n, 157, 180, 235 & n
Farr, Riley, 258–59
Fashions: child's clothing, 280, 356; facial hair, 68, 125, 313, 363; hairstyle, *frontispiece*, 68, 280, 312, 363; jewelry, 155, 312, 310; men's clothing, *frontispiece*, 125, 313, 363; women's clothing, *frontispiece*, 68, 125, 155, 280, 312, 363. *See also* Clothing; Women's work for wages in San Francisco
Ferguson, John, 319
Ferrington, Lewis, 63
Fire at Peacham Corner, 192, 193, 194 & n
Fire at San Francisco, 317
Fireworks: at St. Johnsbury, 205n, 206; at San Francisco, 324
Fishing, 140, 161, 204, 206, 337
Fisk, Rev. Wilbur, 101 & n

Fixing (for marriage), 35 & n, 62n
Flies, in San Francisco, 317
Folsome, Abby, 129
Food: beef, 315; biscuit and butter, 70; boiled victuals (boiled dinner, boiled dish), 136, 160, 172, 214, 326, 327, 331; bread, 42, 130, 140n, 226, 234, 236, 252, 257, 260, 265, 271, 273, 287, 302, 318, 326, 327, 329; cake(s), 71, 200, 202, 333, 345; chicken, 338; chicken pie, 180, 240, 342, 340, 342, 350; cookies, 70; cooking ducks, 339; doughnuts, 130, 226, 252; green apple pie, 214; flapjack, 242; green beans and corn, 53; green corn and string beans, 153; greens for dinner, 131; mince pies, 172, 177, 234, 340; nut-cakes, 179, 180; pickerel, 204; pies, 197, 200, 226, 236, 242, 248, 252, 257, 265, 271, 329, 340; roast pork pudding, 341; pumpkin, 341; quince, 341; Sherry Cobbler, 335; stewed beans, 137; tarts, 200; tomato preserves, 334; tripe, 245; trout, 131; wedding cake, 24, 40, 69, 75; short cake, 40. *See also* Brewing; Butter; Isthmus of Panama; Maple sugar; Thanksgiving
Football, 164
Foster, Daniel (Dan), *47*, 111 & n, 134 & n, 135, 139, 169, 176, 194 & n, 246 & n, 340
Fowler, Anne and Sarah, 61 & n
Freeman, Laura H., 54 & n, 55, 57, 59, 63, 66, 67, 71, 72, 73, 74, 75, 77, 79, 80, 90, 91
Free-soilers, 135 & n, 156n, 159, 168n
Frost, Henry H., 276n, 277
Frost, Laura Harvey. *See* Harvey, Laura
Fugitive Slave Act, 112n, 129n, 168n, 197, 214, 330n
Fuller, Benj H., 223, 371
Fuller, Elizabeth A. (Lizzie), 35n, 58, 59n, 82, 109
Funeral, 55n, 103, 109 & n, 110, 121, 125, 142, 195, 213 & n, 241, 242, 260, 263, 287

Garden and gardening: in Peacham, 46, 137, 138, 164n, 201, 231 & n; in San Francisco, 228, 309
Gates, Joseph "Ready," 333 & n
George, Dr. Samuel G., 317 & n, 318
Gifford, Jesse, 210. *See also* Walbridge, James M.
Gile, Melvina (Malvina) (ASR's cousin), 43, 44, 84 & n, 366
Gile, Perris Eastman (ASR's cousin), 366
Gilfillan, Daniel (Dan) William, 142 & n, 144, 155
Gilfillan, Helen Partridge (Mrs. Daniel W. Gilfillan), 135, 142n, 155, 266, 267n
Gilfillan, Mary, 159, 180 & n
Gilfillan, Robert W., 179 & n
Gilfillan (Gilfillon), William, 270n, 351
Gill, George, 84, 201 & n
Golden Gate (Pacific steamship), 295, 296n, 302 & n, 303, 307, 329, 347
Gold Rush (California). *See* California Gold Rush
Goodenough, John C., 185 & n
Goodenough, Mary Jane C. *See* Weeks, Mary Jane C. Goodenough
Goodenough (Goodenoug, Goodnough), Sarah Ann, 113 & n, 265
Goodenough, T. C., 190
Goodman, Edward, 211
Goodwillie, Rev. Thomas, 169 & n
Gould, Emily, 138 & n
Gracy, John, 219, 223, 371
Graham, Charles (Charley), 105 & n, 107n, 115, 116
Graham, John M., 178, 179
Graham, William, 107 & n
Gregory, Augusta (CWR's niece), 76 & n, 347, 348, 360, 368
Gregory, Hubbell S., 35, 76 & n, 91, 347, 367, 368
Gregory, Martha Walbridge (Mrs. Hubbell S. Gregory) (CWR's sister), 28, 35, 76 & n, 367

Groton counterfeiters. *See* "Bristol Bill"; Meadows, Christian
Guy, Chester, 54 & n, 74
Guy, Oscar, 94 & n
Guyer, Earl (CWR's cousin), 101 & n, 369
Guyer, Harriet (CWR's cousin), 101 & n, 108, 111 & n, 115, 120, 211, 238, 347, 369
Guyer, Hezekiah (Hiah) (CWR's uncle), 211, 258, 369
Guyer, Martha Walbridge (Mrs. Hiah Guyer) (CWR's aunt), 258, 368

Hale, Geo. H., 179
Hale, Rob, 190, 191
Hadgsdor, A. B., 102
Hall, Thomas S., 237, 242
Hallidie, Andrew S., 364n
Hancke, Harriet A., 325 & n
Hardwick, Vt., 176, 190n, 195n, 203, 206 & n, 211, 212, 254, 257, 258, 267, 270n, 282, 285, 290, 291, 310
Harlow, Reuben, 61 & n, 66, 70, 71, 73, 79
Harlow court case, 104, 105, 106
Harriman, Henry, 253 & n
Harriman, Mary Elkins, 255
Harriman, Sprague, 223, 372
Harriman, William (Wm), 177, 178, 196, 198
Harvey, Cloud, Jr., 84, 94 & n
Harvey, Elizabeth, 214
Harvey, Esther. *See* Blanchard, Esther Harvey
Harvey, Laura, 61 & n, 64, 168, 276 & n, 277, 339
Harvey, Margaret Jane, 214 & n, 230
Harvey, Nathan, 188
Harvey, Robert M., 223, 372
Hay and haying, 41, 117, 141, 147, 156n, 209, 210, 276; hay cart, 208
Hendry, John, 105
Henley, Thomas J., 318 & n
Henley (Henly), Mrs. Thomas J., 317 & n, 328, 339

Hidden, Elvira (Mrs. George Gill), 201 & n
Hidden, Esther (Mrs. John Watts), 129n
Hired girl(s), 175, 180 & n, 181, 185, 208n, 249, 250 & n, 274; French woman, 256. *See also* Bovee, Elizabeth; Brown, Jane; Gilfillan, Mary; McLellan, Ellen; Ricker, Yuba; Sampson, Perley; Sheppard, Mary; Spencer, Margaret
Hitchcock, Rev. Harvey, 213 & n
Hitchcock, Mahala (Mrs. Harvey Hitchcock), 230 & n
Hodgeden, Amanda, 153, 167
Holmes, Ahira, 325n
Holmes, Mrs. E. H., 325n
Holmes, Dr. Stillman, 325n
Hooker, Hartwell, 160n, 164 & n
Hooker, Orman, 161 & n
Hooker, William D., 223, 326 & n, 372
Hopkins, Elizabeth H., 66 & n
Howard, Erastus, 212
Howe, Henry M., 223, 372
Hubbard, Rev. Anson, 185 & n
Hubbard, Rev. Austin O., 163; school superintendent, 79 & n, 80n, 169 & n, 173
Hunting, 81 & n
Husking, 164 & n
Hutchins, Fenton (Fent) F., 189n, 200, 255n
Hutchins, Mrs. Fenton F., 77, 91, 189 & n, 237, 254, 255 & n

Independence (Pacific steamship), 305 & n
Ink, 72, 73, 82, 92, 99, 116, 117, 178, 190, 349
Insanity. *See* Mental illness
Isthmus of Nicaragua, 218, 226, 235, 239, 305
Isthmus of Panama, 99, 111, 163n, 191n, 192n, 210, 218, 282, 296, 297 298n, 301, 302n, 359, 360; mule ride, 197, 301

Jamison, Mary Jane, 324, 332, 339

Jesseph (Jessuph), Emily Taylor (CWR's cousin), 101 & n, 108, 111 & n, 117, 273, 274, 275, 290, 347, 369

Jews-harp, 93

Jewett, Dr. Fayette, 293 & n

Jewett (Jewette), Jarvis, 329 & n

Johnson, Alix, 118, 120

Johnson, Mrs. Blake, 74

Johnson, Mary, 256

Johnson, Sarah, 61

Johnston (Johnson), Alexander J., 66 & n, 70, 213

Jones, Alger, 211

Journal and journal writing, 9, 10, 11, 12, 13, 23, 94, 99, 116, 117, 118, 126, 132, 134, 152, 153, 171, 181, 183, 185n, 190, 204n, 206 & n, 218, 219, 222, 225, 234, 236, 238, 252, 253, 282, 283, 293–94, 295–96, 297, 304, 313, 315, 319, 330, 336, 338, 343, 348, 349, 355, 362, 364; Chastina's pocket journal (1853), 207, 295, 296 & n, 298, 304; Edward Rix's travel journal (1871), 360n; lock of hair attached, 234, 310, 326

Juvenile Society, 213 & n, 214

Kaulback, John G., 119 & n, 128 & n, 134

Kavanaugh, E. G., 102

Kavanagh, Elizabeth (Lib) L., 107 & n

Kavanagh, Michel, 223, 372

Kellogg, Judge Daniel, 154n

Kelsey, Hiram, 178, 191

Kilburn (Kilbourn), Edward, 108, 114, 119, 143

Kilburn, Emily (Emma), 113n, 119, 137 & n, 138

Kinerson, Jim, 192

Knight, Ambrose, 219, 223, 372

Knight, Henry T., 219, 223, 372

Knight, Thomas S., 89 & n

Knit (knitting), 110, 236, 237, 243

Kossuth (Kosuth), Lajos, 258 & n, 272

Ladd, John S., 223, 372

Lang, Jane, 134 & n

Laughlin, Julia Ann, 230 & n

Law books and reading law, 41, 56, 57 & n, 59, 62, 63, 65 & n, 84, 85, 88, 112 & n, 116–17, 136, 138, 139, 140, 141 & n, 144, 153, 158, 163 & n, 164, 165 & n, 168, 179, 188; law study, 10, 46, 51, 56, , 57n, 98, 100, 102, 103, 110, 124, 139, 150

Law practice in California, 12, 310, 311, 314, 315, 319, 326, 331, 333, 336, 342, 343, 345, 363, 364; office rent, 314, 345; partnership with Enoch Smith, 319 & n, 325

Law practice in Vermont, 59, 151, 160, 161, 178, 179, 181, 182, 183, 184, 186, 187, 188, 191, 192, 193, 196 & n, 197, 198, 201, 213; apprenticeship with William Mattocks, 115, 152; partnership with William Mattocks, 181, 185, 217, 220n; passed Vermont law exam, 152, 175

Leavitt, Sophia A. *See* Leverett, Sophia A.

Lee, Daniel, 103

Lee, Edward E., 72 & n, 115 & n, 116

Lee, Helen Irene, 72 & n

Lee, J. P. 54, 64

Lee, Leonard, 72 & n

Leverett (Leavitt, Leverette), Sophia A., 89 & n, 90, 92, 94, 111, 113, 119, 121, 127 & n, 160

Libby, Erastus S., 223, 372

Liquor license law, 96, 110n, 134 & n. *See also* Maine Law

Livingston, Amanda, 117n

Livingston, Asa, 223, 372

Livingston, Lafayette, 117 & n

Locke (Lock), Alice Parsons, 39, 40 & n, 41, 282, 286, 287, 288, 315n, 316 & n, 324, 339, 350, 353, *354*, 362 & n, *362*, 365

Locke (Lock), David (father), 40n, 41, 288

Locke, David Merrill (son), 315n, 324, 332, 333, 341

Locke (Lock), Florinda (Mrs. David Locke), 40n, 41

Locke, Josiah Hannibal, 315 & n
Locke, Mary Jane Jamison. *See* Jamison, Mary Jane
Locke, Silas Merrill, 315 & n, 316, 353, 357
Lockwood, Mrs., 317, 318, 326, 338, 339
Lockwood & Lewis, Never Sweat Ranch, 315 & n, 323, 326
Lowell, Mass. (mills), 118, 184, 293n
Lyceum, 66 & n
Lyndon, Vt., 169, 343

MacLeran, Alex, 163
Magic lantern, 74 & n
Maine Law, 188, 330 & n
Mandeville's Series of Readers, 151, 168 & n, 169 & n, 172, 176, 177, 178 & n
Maple sugar, 114, 115n, 197, 198, 220, 256 & n, 257; sugared off, 257, 260, 263; sugar place, 273
Marriage banns, 69 & n
Marsh, Benjamin, 57n
Marsh, Jane, 57n, 140, 199, 232, 233, 236, 241, 244, 245
Marsh, Jonathan, 57n, 182n
Marsh, Newell, 57n, 120, 195n
Marsh, Priscilla, 57n, 277 & n
Marsh, Sarah K. (Mrs. Benjamin Marsh), 57 & n, 68–69, 105, 108, 110 & n, 111, 114, 193; quit renting, 251, 252; rent from, 182 & n, 195 & n, 197, 199, 202 & n, 204, 206, 215n, 220 & n, 229, 230n, 244n, 245, 268
Marsh, Sidney, 318 & n
Marsh, William (Wm.), 143
Marshfield, Vt., 166, 167n, 208
Martin, Ashbel, 244 & n, 245n, 272, 277
Martin, Chester, 163, 188 & n, 310n
Martin, E. C. G., 102
Martin, Elizabeth, 70 & n
Martin, Eunice, 79 & n
Martin, Henry N., 140 & n
Martin, John (49er), 163 & n, 188 & n, 246 & n; 310n
Martin, John M. (merchant), 64n, 71 & n, 79n, 84 & n, 137, 159n, 189 & n, 220 & n, 232n, 267
Martin, Louisa, 70 & n, 134 & n, 258
Martin, Martha Sprague (Mrs. John M. Martin), 64 & n, 79n
Martin, Sarah, 185
Mattocks, Eliza Brock (Mrs. William Mattocks), 73 & n, 105, 167, 200
Mattocks, Governor John, 55n, 72n
Mattocks, Rev. John, 72 & n, 236, 288
Mattocks, William, 55 & n, 56 & n, 57 & n, 62, 73n, 105, 115, 152, 157, 160, 163, 164, 172, 179, 200, 214, 215; law practice, 160, 168, 170, 176, 179; Peacham representative to state legislature, 159 & n, 166, 167n, 173, 179; partnership with Alfred, 181, 185 & n, 186, 191, 197, 198, 201, 206, 211, 220 & n
McArthur, J., 169 & n
McClary, Abigail (Abba), 202
McClary, Ira, 182, 243, 244 & n
McClary, Jane, 66 & n
McClary, Mary Elizabeth Staples (Mrs. Ira McClary), 117 & n, 244 & n
McIndoe, S. J., 61, 62
McKeen, Phebe, 233 & n
McLary, Miss A., 65
McLellan, Ellen, 250, 252, 255, 271, 272
McLeran (McLaran), Owen, 74 & n, 75, 108, 114, 119
Meadows, Christian, 110n, 112, 137 & n. *See also* Counterfeiting
Medicine(s) (medical treatment), 63, 207, 249, 263, 346; alcohol as medicine, 254; "gal-vanic trial," 63
Meeting. *See* Church service; Congregational Church; Methodist Church
Menstruation, 10, 63, 72 & n, 81 & n, 91 & n, 102 & n, 114 & n, 119 & n, 261, 271, 274, 292, 323 & n, 329 & n, 344 & n
Mental illness (insanity, "crazy"), 63 & n, 115, 199n, 232, 239

Merrill, Cynthia, 61 & n
Merrill, Rev. David, 37 & n, 56 & n, 59, 65, 68, 71, 73, 94, 96, 101n, 103, 109n, 116 & n, 118 & n, 120, 125, 134 & n, 151, 169n, 198n, 214n; died, 125, 142 & n
Merrill, Hazen, 97, 121, 125
Merrill, James, 73 & n, 75, 79 & n, 115, 160
Merrill, Mary P., 58 & n, 214 & n
Merrill, Mary Hunt (Mrs. David Merrill), 56 & n
Merrill, Schuyler, 106 & n, 107
Merrill, Sophia, 61
Methodist Church (Chapel), 54n, 85, 143; wedding, 142n. *See also* Church service; Button, Rev. Amasa G.; Hitchcock, Rev. Harvey
Mighell, Amanda. *See* Morrill, Amanda
Miller, E. H., 140
Miller, Ira O., attended teachers' convention, 167n; Hinesburgh Academy principal, 81, 82 & n, 150, 168n; living in Peacham, 157 & n, 158, 159, 160, 161, 164, 167, 168, 170, 173, 197, 198, 200, 204, 206, 214, 221, 241, 244, 251, 254, 267, 276; offer of Peacham Academy principal, 98, 108, 110, 111, 112, 113, 114, 115, 116, 133, 134, 137, 139, 140, 143 & n; Peacham Academy principal, 147n, 148n, 151, 154, 155, 167n, 168n, 172, 179, 187, 220 & n, 233 & n, 268
Miller, Mary, 157n, 160, 235 & n, 244
Miller, Stearns Robert, 157n
Miller, William, 29 & n
Mills, Augusta Gregory. *See* Gregory, Augusta
Mills at Lowell. *See* Lowell, Mass.
Miner, Francis, 138 & n
Miner, Sarah Morrill, 117 & n
Miner, Uriah W., 109 & n, 114, 120, 215
"The Miner's Progress" (Alfred's drawing), 320 & n, 320–23
Mission Dolores (area of San Francisco), 227, 228, 269, 295, 304, 305, 309, 310, 312, 313n, 315 & n, 316n, 317n, 319n, 324, 326, 327, 328, 330, 331, 332, 334n, 335, 338, 339, 341, 342, 345, 349, 350, 353 358n, 359, 361
Montpelier, Vt., 76, 108, 119, 120, 158, 166, 167 & n, 173. *See also* New England Protective Union
Moreau, Francis, 187
Morrill, Amanda (ASR's aunt), 31, 32, 118, 196, 348, 366
Morrill, Carlton J., 143, 155, 156
Morrill, Lewis (ASR's uncle), 271, 366
Morrill, Martha, 368
Morrill, Stephen S., 79 & n
Morris, George & Abram, 343 & n, 344, 345
Morse, Abel, 194
Morse, Cynthia Blanchard (Mrs. Thomas Morse), 180 & n
Morse, Ellen, 65 & n, 170, 194
Morse, Ephraim, 268
Morse, Frank, 211
Morse, James, 39, 108
Moulton, Barron C., 298 & n, 302
Moulton, Stillman, 30
Mount Holyoke Seminary, 70n, 164n
Muir, William (Wm.), 315 & n, 318, 319

Nevins, Thomas J., 316 & n, 317n, 324, 325, 331n
New England house cleaning, 267
New England Protective Union, 97, 98n, 103, 104, 105, 106, 107, 108, 109, 110, 112, 113, 119 & n, 120, 122, 123, 128–29, 133, 134, 152, 163, 179, 182, 188 & n, 190, 194, 196, 200, 201, 202n, 205, 215; Montpelier division, 167n. *See also* Choate, David W.; Kaulback, John G.
Newbury, Vt., 34
Nicaragua. *See* Isthmus of Nicaragua
Norris, Amos, 135 & n, 137
Norris, Mary B., 135 & n

O'Conner (O'Connor), M. P., 332 & n, 336

O'Grady, William Henry, 316, 317n, 318, 325, 330, 334, 339
Ohio (Atlantic steamship), 296n, 298 & n, 299, 303
"Old maid," 57, 74, 77, 362
Old Man of the Mountain, N.H., 43 & n
"The Oracle," 74 & n
Orcutt, John G., 66 & n
Oregon (Pacific steamship), 111
Overseer of the Poor. *See* Choate, David W.

Page, Bacon & Co., 342 & n, 356n
Panama. *See* Isthmus of Panama
Pangborn, Zebina Kellogg, 111 & n
Panic of 1855, 355n
Papy, J. J., 325 & n
Parasol, 270
Paring-bee (pareing-bee), 32, 174, 291 & n
Parker, Addison F., 137 & n
Parker, Dr. Luther Fletcher, 91 & n, 134 & n, 137n, 177
Parker (Mrs. Thomas Parker), Ruth Watts, 71, 88, 368
Parker, Rev. Theodore, 129 & n, 174, 208
Parker, Thomas, 82, 368
Parkman, Dr. George, 113 & n, 114, 139n
Party (parties), 92, 93, 100, 167, 173, 175, 189, 200, 233, 257, 263, 311. *See also* Donation party
Partridge, Helen. *See* Gilfillan, Helen Partridge
Pattridge (Partridge), Lyman, 104, 267 & n
Paul, John, Jr., 35 & n
Paul, Mary, 187
Peacham Academy, 9, 10, 24, 32 & n, 34 & n, 37 & n, 39, 40n, 45, 46, 47, 74n, 75, 81, 84n, 91 & n, 93, 95, 96, 98, 100, 117, 121, 123, 124, 125, 136, 137n, 143 & n, 147 & n, 148 & n, 150, 152, 154, 159, 162, 167n, 170, 182, 195n, 213n, 219, 220n, 222n, 227, 233n, 236, 257, 278, 313, 360; courses, 48; female teachers, 48, 233n; Julian W. Rix attended, 360; music, 55, 106 & n, 147n, 163; reputation, 309, 311n; residents board students, 46n, 124; salary of principal, 100 & n, 148, 227; tuition, 49; trustee(s), 48, 54n, 56n, 57 & n, 67n, 98, 106n, 140, 148n, 169n, 183, 197n, 198n, 203n. *See also* Bailey, Sarah T.; Bradlee, Louise P.; Chase, Charles C.; Freeman, Laura; Leverett, Sophia; Lyceum; McKeen, Phebe; Miller, Ira O.; Paul, John, Jr.; Shedd, Dr. Josiah; Stoddard, Josephine M.; White, Mary W.
Peacham Temperance Society, 33n, 96
Pelton, John C., 318n
Penny post (letter delivery), 317, 318 & n, 327, 328 & n, 329, 331, 333, 334, 335
Perry, E., 270 & n, 272, 273
Phillips Academy, Danville, Vt., 82 & n, 166n
Pickwick Assembly (Club), 312, & n, 349, 350, 352
Pierpoint, Judge Robert, 154n
Pig, 46, 62 & n, 178, 336, 353, 326, 336, 353; pig-pen, 319
Plainfield, Vt., 166
Plummer, George W., 317n
Plummer, Margaret Blen (Mrs. George W. Plummer), 317 & n, 351
Poland, Judge Luke P., 154 & n
Poor, Erastus, 109 & n
Potts, Joseph, 154 & n
Pregnant (family way), 12, 43n, 84n, 100, 119 & n, 124, 142, 133, 151, 159, 184. *See also* Bierstadt, Adeline Rix; Gile, Melvina; Way, Sarah Walbridge
Prometheus (Pacific steamship), 226, 230, 233, 235, 305 & n
Protective Union. *See* New England Protective Union
Purchases, 67, 69, 98, 118, 123, 124, 128, 134n, 167, 197, 232, 243, 258, 266, 310, 342, 343, 347, 352; peddler, 337

Quilt(s) (quilting), 10, 30 & n, 32, 52, 54, 62 & n, 85; quilting bee, 30n; washing quilts, 213n, 277

Railroad and railroad cars, 92n, 127n, 222n, 279, 298; railroad across Isthmus of Panama, 297, 300 & n; railroad meeting in San Francisco, 314, 331; sold land to, 253; Transcontinental Railroad, 359, 360n
Rassette House, 304 & n, 315n
Reading Circle, 232 & n, 243, 245, 256, 265
Reading Club (Peacham men), 200
Redford, Judge Isaac F., 154 & n
Reed's City Dispatch Post, Adams & Co., 335 & n
Report of the State Superintendent for Common Schools, 1849, 85 & n
Richardson, Edgar, 79 & n
Ricker, Yuba, 222
Rix, Adeline. *See* Bierstadt, Adeline Rix
Rix, Adeline Morrill (Mrs. Hale Rix) (ASR's mother), 40, 41, 42, 67, 247, 248, 365
Rix, Alanson Stephen (ASR's brother), 247, 365
Rix, Alfred Shirley, 359
Rix, Austin (ASR's brother), 42, 120, 188, 212 & n, 247, 313, 315 & n, 316, 319, 362, 365
Rix, Becky, 41, 366
Rix, Charles (ASR's nephew), 365
Rix, Charles Carrol (ASR's brother), 247, 362, 365
Rix, Clark (ASR's cousin), 41, 366
Rix, Edward Austin (Eddie, Ned) (ASR & CWR's son), 13, 356 & n, 357, 359, 360n, 361 & n, 365, 368; attended University of California, 361; children, 361 & n. *See also* Rix, Genevieve; Walbridge, Clarissa
Rix, Eliza (ASR's cousin), 43, 366
Rix, Emma (ASR's niece), 365
Rix, Eugene (ASR's nephew), 365
Rix, Frank, 211
Rix, Genevieve, 13, 362, 364
Rix, George (ASR's cousin), 203, 366
Rix, Hale (ASR's father), 36, 40, 111, 154, 187, 190, 196, 203, 240, 241, 243, 246, 247, 248, 278, 325, 365
Rix, Hale (ASR's brother), 24, 39 & n, 40 & n, 41, 54, 109, 150, 170, 176, 178, 179, 234, 237, 240, 282, 365; life insurance, 177n, 189; living in California, 203, 208 & n, 209, 215, 241, 276, 313, 315 & n, 316, 336, 362 & n; planning trip to California, 175, 177n, 182, 187, 188; trip to California, 191n
Rix, Ira Osmer (ASR's brother), 41, 220 & n, 221, 247, 248, 261, 263, 277, 279, 285, 286, 287, 288, 289, 290, 365; died, 362; living in California, *313*, 324, 328, 329, 330, 333, 348, 357; trip to California, 298, 302
Rix, Julian Walbridge (Bub, Bubby, Jule, Julee, July) (ASR & CWR's son), 181, 182, 183, 193, 195, 198, 204, 205, 207, 218, 220n, 225, 226, 227, 237, 243, 254, 255, 256, 258, 259, 260, 265, 266, 269, 271 & n, 287, 365; accidents as child, 253, 267, 279; birth, 152, 180 & n; daguerreotype of, 270, *280, 354, 356*; died, 361; doctor saw, 201, 249, 334, 335; learns to talk, 260, 276, 279, 288, 292; learns to walk, 243; living in San Francisco, 304, 309, 310, 311, 317n, 325, 326, 334, 335, 339, 340, 341, 345, 346, 352, 358; lock of hair attached to journal, 234; missed by Alfred, 227, 228, 229, 273; painter, 361; returns to San Francisco (1868), 360, 361; returns to Vermont (1857), 358, 359, 360; trip to California (1853), 295, 296, 297, 298 & n, 299, 301, 302, 303; weaned, 262, 264. *See also* Clothing; Farr, Dr. Asahel; Walbridge, Clarissa; Walbridge, Dustan S.

Rix, Lavina (ASR's sister), 365
Rix, Louisa (Mrs. Moses Rix), 42, 248, 366
Rix, Louisa Farr (ASR's sister), 41, 247, 248, 256, 257, 350, 365
Rix, Mary Ann Burton (Mrs. Oscar Rix), 128, 174, 202, 203, 204, 205, 221n, 323, 325, 337, 347, 365
Rix, Melvin (Lewis Merwin Rix) (ASR's brother), 247 & n, 365
Rix, Morrill S. (ASR's brother), 193, 196, 247, 275, 276, 278 & n, 285, 365
Rix, Moses (ASR's cousin), 41, 42, 248, 278, 366
Rix, Oscar (ASR's brother), 40, 100, 102, 113, 198, 202, 203, 206, 211, 230 & n, 365, 372; Alfred received Boston papers from, 105, 135, 136, 177; Alfred received letter from, 63, 94, 103, 105, 136, 140, 159, 189, 190, 193, 199, 221 & n; Alfred visited in Boston, 123, 128, 174, 182, 207 & n, 208, 291; Alfred wrote letters to, 57, 73, 91, 94, 103, 104, 110, 112, 116, 134, 153, 163, 166, 172, 178, 179, 189, 196; died, 221n, 362, 372; family visited Peacham, 202 & n, 203, 204, 205; helped pay Alfred's college expenses, 112; life insurance, 177; living in San Francisco, 313, 318 & n, 326, 332, 333, 337, 342, 347; planning trip to California, 174, 182, 207n, 221, 223; trip to California, 219, 223, 230 & n. *See also* New England Protective Union
Rix, Sidney Redfield (ASR's cousin), 114 & n, 203, 219, 222 & n, 223, 313, 326, 366, 372
Rix, Susan E. (ASR's cousin), 43, 44, 67, 84, 366
Rix, William A., 359
Rochester Knockings, 166 & n
Rogers, Clara Walbridge. *See* Walbridge, Clarissa
Rogers (Rodgers), Russell K., 324 & n, 325, 326, 331, 333, 336, 340, 343, 344, 350, 358, 359, 361, 367; died, 360

Rowell, S. H., 82
Royce, Judge Stephen, 154 & n
Ruffino, Francesco & Petrona, 316 & n, 319 & n, 341
Rug making, 46, 52, 53, 56, 58, 59, 64, 98, 104
Ryder, Widow N. P., 208
Ryegate, Vt., 169, 204
Ryle, William T., 361

Sacramento, Calif., 228n, 262 & n, 320, 326
Salt water cure, 274 & n
Sampson, Carlos, 209 & n, 253 & n
Sampson, Melvina, 253n
Sampson, Perley, 180 & n
Samuel, Robert, 61 & n, 79
Sanborn, David, Jr., 292n
Sanborn, Kate Spear (Mrs. David Sanborn, Jr.), 292 & n
Sanborn, Lucinda Clark (Mrs. Trustram Sanborn), 34 & n, 89; died, 240, 241 & n
Sanborn, Mrs. Polly, 194
Sanborn, Trustram, 34 & n, 74, 89, 137, 158, 160, 212, 241, 243
Sanchez, Elaria, 317 & n
Sanford, Anna E., 325 & n
Sanford, Stephen H., 84, 366
San Francisco: agricultural fair, 339; Bohemian Club, 361; cable cars, 364 & n; Court of Sessions, 336, 337, 338; dueling, 318 & n, 319; earthquake & fire (1906), 13, 364; gambling dens, 307, 318; Lone Mountain Cemetery, 355, 358n, 360; Judge of Police Court, 359; Justice of the Peace, 13, 310, 330, 331, 332, 334, 335, 336, 345; meeting to reduce servants' wages, 337; Metropolitan (Metriopitan) Theater, 344; Musical Hall, 252; omnibus (buss), 312 & n, 346; plank road, 312 & n, 341; public schools, 12, 227, 228, 309, 317 & n, 318n, 364; Teachers Monthly Convention,

San Francisco (*continued*) 317, 327, 346, 348; theater (teatre, theatre), 311, 314, 317, 324, 344, 348; Tobin's and Duncan's, 310, 319, 324; U.S. Marine Hospital, 342 & n; water, 316 & n; Winn's 324 & n; women in, 309. *See also* Balloon ascension; Fire at San Francisco; Mission Dolores; Pickwick Assembly; Penny post; Teachers; Rassette House; Women's work in San Francisco
Sargeant, Asa, 39, 267, 368
Sargeant, Elijah, 288, 368
Sargeant, Esther (Mrs. Lyman Watts), 367
Sargeant, Mary Elisa, 39
Seasick, 99, 296, 299, 303
Seward, William H., 112 & n, 140 & n
Sewing bird, 343
Sewing circle, 271
Sexual relations, 10, 58 & n, 59, 63, 187 & n
Shaw, Albert John, 85 & n
Shaw, Daniel G., 169 & n
Shawl pin, 93
Shedd, Dr. Josiah, 54 & n, 56n, 57, 79, 80, 81, 93, 98, 102 & n, 105, 106 & n, 107, 153, 161, 167, 178, 189, 190, 197, 200, 212, 263n; died, 183, 213 & n, 214; trustee for Peacham Academy, 110, 112, 113 & n, 114, 119, 148 & n, 172
Shedd, Josiah (grandnephew of Dr. Shedd), 263 & n, 268, 269, 291
Shedd, Lydia Chamberlain (Mrs. Josiah Shedd), 56 & n, 102n, 176, 192
Sheppard, Mary, 180
Sierra Nevada (Pacific steamship), 329 & n
Singing school, 113
Sizer, Elizabeth, 284, 369
Skeeles, Asa, 143
Slavery. *See* Abolition
Smith, Charles Strong, 69 & n, 92, 108, 116, 117, 160, 161, 290, 345, 346
Smith, Ebenz, 30
Smith, Enoch W., 319 & n, 323, 325, 345

Smith, Theodore (Mrs. Enoch Smith), 327, 335, 345, 351
Soap, Excelsior, 319; making, 196; new, 197; shaved-up soap, 231n; soft soap, 198
Spanish classes (lessons, recitations), 228, 276, 308, 313
Spanish friends (Spanish-speaking community), 12, 312, 313, 338, 346
Spencer, Ebenezer, 193n
Spencer, Hannah M., 193 & n
Spencer, Margaret, 274 & n
Spencer, Sarah Robinson (Mrs. Ebenezer Spencer), 193n
Spinning, 55, 276, 277, 286, 287, 288, 289, 290; spun stocking yard, 290
Spruce gum, 93
Squirrels, 204, 212
Stage (transportation), 127 & n, 169, 220, 279, 312
Stevens, Alanson (ASR's cousin, Sarah Stevens' grandson), 24, 39 & n, 55, 366
Stevens, Alanson (ASR's cousin, Sarah Stevens' son), 97, 120n, 132n, 366
Stevens, Cynthia Walbridge (CWR's aunt), 291, 368
Stevens, Enos, 71 & n
Stevens, Henry, 120 & n
Stevens, Joshua, 257n
Stevens, Sarah Morrill (ASR's great-aunt), 9, 24, 30 & n, 37, 39, 46, 53, 55, 68, 69, 84, 88, 94, 96, 97, 108, 120n, 136, 147, 163, 167, 182, 189, 198, 204, 205, 222 & n, 231 & n, 246, 253, 256, 257 & n, 273, 277, 278n, 292, 326, 365; lock of hair attached to the journal, 310, 326; Thaddeus (son) visited, 97, 182, 206n
Stevens, Thaddeus (ASR's cousin, Sarah Stevens's son), 9, 10, 30n, 46, 96, 97, 102 & n, 109 & n, 111, 112 & n, 133, 120, 140, 366; contributed to Peacham library, 213n; visited Peacham, 182, 206 & n, 289 & n
St. Johnsbury, Vt., 24, 33, 35 & n, 37n, 39,

40 & n, 58 & n, 74, 167, 169, 205 & n, 206; St. Johnsbury Academy, 35 & n, 37n, 56, 58, 59, 74, 82n, 293n. *See also* Colby, James K.

Stoddard, Josephine M., 233 & n

Stores. *See* Brown, Ephraim C.; Brown & Weeks; Martin, John M.; Watts, Isaac

Strobridge, Elisabeth Clark (Mrs. Lafayette Strobridge), 56 & n, 57, 63, 119 & n, 235 & n

Strobridge, Lafayette, 56n, 119n, 185 & n

Strong, William (Wm.), 135

Stuart, Seth W., 219 & n, 220

Sugar. *See* Maple sugar

Survey and surveying, 50, 106n, 120, 121, 122, 124, 131, 143, 165, 170, 194, 196, 212, 218, 325n

Sutton, Vt., 169

Tabor, Daphne, 72

Tailoress, 253, 266

Taisey, John, 213

Taplin, Dr. N. P., 315 & n, 317, 319, 328 & n

Tavern, 39n, 46, *47*, 134n, 140, 166, 167, 176, 232; Elkins Tavern, 57; Evans Tavern, 82; Tavern House, 194 & n; Wheeler Tavern, 134n

Tavernier, Jules, 361

Taylor, Daniel (CWR's cousin), 347, 369

Taylor, Elizabeth. *See* Jesseph, Elizabeth Taylor

Taylor, Phoebe Walbridge (CWR's aunt), 368

Taylor, President Zachary, 65, 102n, 140 & n

Teachers: boarding (boarded) around, 10, 35 & n; boarding at Watts farm, 250, 265; examination and certification, 10, 52, 56, 79, 80 & n, 119, 173, 199, 201; no Vermont law against married women teaching, 51; salary, 35, 180n, 238 & n, 268, 269, 310n, 313; Teacher's Institute, 115 & n; women teachers, 48, 51, 67n, 119, 180n, 183, 184 & n, 238 & n, 282, 310n, 313, 325. *See also* Peacham Academy; San Francisco, public schools; San Francisco, Teachers Monthly Convention; Walbridge, Clarissa

Telegraph, 314, 335

Telescope, 64, 118

Temperance, 12, 33 & n, 96, 108, 126, 142, 188, 330 & n; Temperance Hotel, 132 & n; Temperance meeting, 33, 41, 103, 106, 108, 186, 190, 197, 330. *See also* Maine Law; Peacham Temperance Society

Tennent, Thomas, 325 & n

Tennessee (Pacific steamship), 191n

Thanksgiving, 85–86, 87, 88, 165, 174, 175, 242 & n, 340, 341; Alfred's drawing of, 85–86

Thayer, Rev. William Withington, 103 & n, 147

Titus, Lyman, 211

"TomTit," 90 & n

Toothache, 110; bad teeth, 84; teeth filled, 114, 190; tooth pulled, 82, 105

Topsham, Vt., 35, 72, 159n

Torrey, Professor Joseph, 98 & n

Town's Series of Reading Books, 150, 168n, 172, 175, 176, 178n

Training Day (June), 133 & n

Tuite, Annie Margaret, 359

Underwood, Caroline, 278, 366

Underwood, Narcissa Rix (ASR's cousin), 278, 366

Underwood, Nathan, 366

Underwood, Walter, 278, 366

Union store. *See* New England Protective Union

University of Vermont, 9, 24, 30n, 34n, 37, 47, 69n, 91n, 98, 111n, 112 n, 142n, 184, 293n, 309, 317n

Vaccination, smallpox, 293 & n
Vance, Reuben, 189
Vance, Robert H., 354, 356
Varney, Elizabeth (Mrs. Robert Varney), 222 & n, 299 & n, 300, 302, 315 & n, 328, 343, 346, 349, 351, 352
Varney, Henry, 222n, 301, 302
Varney, Robert, 108, 222n, 329, 343, 351 & n
Varnum, Betsey Clark (Mrs. Charles Varnum), 187 & n
Varnum, Charles, 187n, 234 & n, 235
Varnum, Harvey, 223, 326 & n, 327, 328, 329 & n, 372
Varnum, Mark, 326 & n, 327, 329 & n
Varnum, Simon, 158; son died, 158–59
Vendue (land sale), 197 & n
Venor, Francis, 187
Vermont Domestic Missionary Society, 103n
Vermont Reports (laws), 163

Walbridge, Clarissa (Clara) (CWR's sister), 12, 30n, *312*, 367; birthday, 111; clothes, 230, 231, 241, 266, 267, 339, 342, 350; conflict with Chastina, 241, 311, 327 & n; courting in Peacham, 206 & n, 282, 283 & n, 285 & n; courting in San Francisco, 309, 314, 317, 319, 324, 343n; decided to go to California, 12, 283 & n, 293; died, 360; living in New York state, 39, 46, 53, 63, 68, 71, 75n, 227 & n, 238n, 282n; living in Peacham, 64, 74, 80, 81, 82, 84, 88, 101, 108, 110, 111, 112, 113, 115, 116, 118, 119, 120, 155, 160, 164, 169, 170, 175, 185, 186, 187, 192, 193, 197, 198, 199, 204, 206, 222 & n, 228, 229, 230, 231, 232, 234, 235 & n, 236, 237, 238 & n, 239, 240, 241, 242, 243, 249, 250, 254, 261, 262, 263, 264, 266, 267, 282, 285, 286, 287, 288, 290, 292, 293; living in San Francisco, 283n, 304, 309, 311, 312, 314, 317, 318, 319, 324, 326, 327 & n, 328, 332, 337, 338, 339, 341, 342, 344, 345, 346, 350, 353, 357, 359, 360; married, 358, 359; student at Peacham Academy, 109, 110 & n, 111, 112, 113, 115, 116 & n, 118; teaching in Cabot, Vt., 238 & n, 242, 243, 249; teaching in Hardwick, Vt., 254, 257, 267, 270n, 276, 282; teaching in Littleton, N.H., 116n, 120, 133, 137 & n, 138, 143, 238n; teaching in Peacham, 238n; teaching in San Francisco, 312, 313, 326, 327, 328, 329, 330, 331 & n, 334 & n, 337, 338, 339, 344, 345, 346, 348, 349; train trip to Vermont (1871), 359, 360; trip to California (1853), 296, 298, 299, 300, 301 & n, 302, 303. *See also* Bonnet(s); Rix, Edward A.; Rix, Julian Walbridge; Rogers, Russell K.; Teachers
Walbridge, Daniel A. (CWR's father), 28, 29, 101n, 367
Walbridge, D. Augustus (Guck) (CWR's brother), 30n, 62, 147, 161, 194, 195n, 196, 202, 208, 218, 221, 249, 252, 253, 258, 270n, 272, 273, 285, 287, 337, 343, 348, 350, 352, 359, 368
Walbridge, Dustan S. (Dustin) (Dust) (CWR's brother), 24, 30n, 38, 85, 91, 101, 108, 111, 113, 116, 119, 120, 159, 166, 167n, 175, 202, 208, 214, 217, 218 & n, 221, 222 & n, 223, 368, 372; Civil War soldier, 360; died, 360; living in California, 234, 272, 273, 276, 277, 307, 313, 314; living in San Francisco, 316 & n, 317 & n, 318, 319, 332 & n, 337, 339, 343, 345, 348, 349; returns to Vermont, 358, 359 & n, 360; wages earned as wheelwright, 314, 349
Walbridge, Elizabeth, 113, 369
Walbridge, Ira, 211, 368
Walbridge, James M., 192 & n, 210 & n
Walbridge, Martha. *See* Gregory, Martha Walbridge
Walbridge, Oliver (CWR's grandfather), 211, 241 & n, 367
Walbridge, Sarah. *See* Way, Sarah Walbridge

Walden, Vt., 191, 193
Walker, Mrs. Henry, 286
Waller, Royal Hiram, 331n
Warburton, William. *See* Bristle Bill
Warner, Helen T., 120
Washing blankets, 231 & n. *See also* Clothes stick; Clothes whirl; Quilt; Soap
Watermelon, 63, 330
Water yoke, 323
Waterford, Vt., 169, 248, 259
Watts, Alice (CWR's half sister), 44, 64, 102, 115, 138, 196, 197, 236, 264, 270n, 325, 339, 360, 368
Watts, Alvah (CWR's cousin), 30 & n, 33n, 53, 61, 69, 72, 108 & n, 115, 156, 166, 192, 193, 199 & n, 200, 231, 232, 239, 369; principal of Phillips Academy, Danville, 82 & n, 84, 89, 113, 132, 142. *See also* Mental illness
Watts, Charles (CWR's stepbrother), 62, 74, 102, 221, 231 & n, 245, 248, 250, 252, 256, 270n, 279, 287, 292, 350, 368
Watts, Ella Lucy (Elly, Eleanor) (CWR's half sister), 64, 102, 213, 265, 270n, 325, 352, 360, 368; birthday, 254
Watts, Isaac (CWR's cousin) (merchant), 33 & n, 69, 82 & n, 84, 88, 97, 100 & n, 159n, 176 & n, 177, 197, 253n, 284n, 324, 369. *See also* New England Protective Union
Watts, Isaac N. (CWR's half brother), 74–75, 120, 138, 147, 270n, 285, 360, 368
Watts, Jane Bailey, 129n, 209n
Watts, John (CWR's cousin), 129 & n, 211, 221, 369
Watts, Lambert (CWR's cousin), 208, 210, 246 & n, 369
Watts, Lyman (CWR's stepfather), 24, 30 & n, 44, 53, 55 & n, 75n, 84, 92n, 97, 105, 132, 136, 137, 139, 147, 157, 172, 175, 177, 179, 190, 196, 203, 204, 207, 211, 212, 218 & n, 220 & n, 232, 239, 242, 243, 246, 249, 251, 252, 257, 260, 263, 264, 270 & n, 284, 287, 288, 298, 359, 360, 367
Watts, Lyman S. (CWR's stepbrother), 56 & n, 58, 80, 101, 113, 131, 147, 187, 204, 230, 232, 233, 235, 244, 245, 246, 249, 251, 254, 257, 258, 266, 270 & n, 272, 274 & n, 367
Watts, Martha J. (Mrs. Isaac Watts), 82, 253 & n, 264, 265; died, 284 & n
Watts, Roxana Brown Walbridge (Mrs. Lyman Watts) (CWR's mother), 9, 24, 29 & n, 30, 33n, 39, 54, 63, 64, 65, 69, 75n, 84, 110, 120, 124, 125, 128, 155, 196n, 201, 204, 218, 222n, 226, 227, 230, 231, 234, 240, 246, 247, 248, 249, 250, 252, 255, 256, 258, 259n, 260, 263, 264, 265, 267, 271n, 272, 273, 274, 275, 277, 281, 282n, 283 & n, 284, 285, 286, 289, 290, 292, 293n, 296 & n, 298, 309, 316n, 348, 357, 359, 367, 368, 369; birthday, 264; died, 360; letters to San Francisco, 317, 332, 339, 347, 357, 358; visited Rixes at Peacham Corner, 64, 67, 71, 76, 103, 120, 132, 137, 154, 160, 163, 170, 172, 179, 185, 186, 187, 190, 191, 196, 205, 206, 213, 215, 221 & n, 245; visited Ways at Hardwick, Vt., 203, 270; went to Cabot, Vt., 84, 274 & n, 284, 287 & n; went to Canada, 273
Watts, Sarah Bailey Sampson (Mrs. Thomas Watts), 129 & n, 209n, 215, 255, 368
Watts, Thomas (CWR's uncle), 97, 108 & n, 129 & n, 209n, 368
Way, Edgar Stephen, 252 & n, 368
Way, John S., 39, 52, 53, 67, 68 & n, *68*, 69, 71, 74, 75, 81 & n, 82, 88, 94, 95, 101, 111, 124, 136, 143, 188n, 219n, 367; leaves for California, 102 & n; letters from California, 99 & n, 111, 126–27, 132, 143 & n; living in Hardwick, Vt., 187, 190 & n, 191, 193, 195, 196, 197, 200, 204, 206, 207, 208 & n, 210, 211, 212, 228, 233, 240, 246 & n, 249, 253, 254, 257, 258, 261,

Way, John S. (*continued*)
270n, 283n, 284, 285, 290 & n, 291; living in Minnesota, 310 & n, 317, 323, 339, 346, 348, 352; returned from California, 11, 149, 150, 156, 157, 161, 163, 164, 166, 168, 172, 173, 175, 176 & n, 177 & n, 179, 192n

Way, John S., Sr., 170n, 173

Way, Lyman, 156

Way, Martha (Sis) (CWR's niece), 238n, 239, 291, 368

Way, Nate, 194

Way, Sarah Walbridge (Sally) (Mrs. John S. Way) (CWR's sister), 12, 24, 35, 30n, 37, 38, 39, 52, 57, 58, 62, 66, 67, 68, 68n, 69, 71, 74, 75 & n, 81, 82, 88, 101, 104, 124, 184, 367; baby boy (Edgar), 252 & n, 257, 270n; baby girl (Martha), 12, 124, 129; letters from husband in California, 99 & n, 111, 126n, 127n, 143; living in Hardwick, Vt., 190 & n, 193, 200, 204, 207, 208, 209, 210, 211, 228, 238 & n, 239, 240, 249, 257, 270n, 283n, 284, 285, 290, 291; living in Minnesota, 310 & n, 317, 360; living in Peacham recovering from birth of Martha, 130, 131, 132, 134, 136, 138, 139, 140; return of husband from California, 149, 156, 157, 164, 167, 173, 175, 177, 185; wedding, 52, 67, 70

Way, Sidney (Si), 115, 191–92

Webster, Rev. A., 176, 180

Webster, Daniel, 112 & n, 291 & n

Webster, Professor John White, 113 & n, 114 & n, 139 & n, 157–58

Wedding, 9, 24, 38& n, 39, 52, 70, 144, 202, 336, 347, 351, 362n. *See also* Clothing, wedding

Weeks, Benjamin F., 101 & n

Weeks, Hiel B., 205 & n

Weeks, Mary Jane C. Goodenough (Mrs. Benjamin F. Weeks), 57 & n, 79 & n, 92, 101 & n, 105, 109, 268

Wheeler, Alexander A., 56 & n, 65, 80

Wheeler, Catherine Blanchard (Mrs. Alexander A. Wheeler), 56 & n; 63

Wheeler, Dorcas (Mrs. Judah D. Wheeler), 56 & n, 103n

Wheeler, Eugene, 117 & n

Wheeler, Jerome, 117n

Wheeler, Judah D. (Jude), 56 & n, 103n

Wheeler, Rhoda Skeele (Mrs. William Wheeler), 117 & n

Wheeler, S. D., 71 & n

Wheeler, Sarah, 103 & n

Wheelock, Vt., 34 & n, 169

Whist, 334

White, Asa, 174

White, Mary W., 106n, 147n, 161 & n, 167, 200

White House Hotel, 100 & n

Whittle, Bill, 310n

Williams, Governor Charles Kilborn, 202 & n

Wilmot Proviso, 70 & n, 104 & n

Wilson, John, 331n

Wine, 96, 345, 347

Wolcott, Vt., 9, 28, 30, 48, 74, 75 & n, 108, 111, 117, 211, 291; Women's work for wages in San Francisco, 12; boarders, 210, 310, 312, 314 & n, 315 & n, 316, 323, 325, 326, 327, 328, 345; covering buttons for church cushions, 326; ironing, 326, 330, 332, 334, 340, 344, 353; sewing, 318, 325, 327, 328, 329, 330, 331, 332, 336, 352, 353; sewing pew pillows, 214; washing, 316, 329, 332. *See also* Walbridge, Clarissa

Women traveling alone, 227, 279, 281, 282n, 296 & n, 297

Woodward, Royal, 190, 193

Worcester, Rev. Leonard, 125, 161n

Wright, A. J., 105

Yellow fever, 296 & n, 303, 337; Panama fever, 302